MUSIC AND COPYRIGHT: THE CASE OF DELIUS AND HIS PUBLISHERS

Music and Copyright: The Case of Delius and his Publishers

ROBERT MONTGOMERY and ROBERT THRELFALL

Routledge
Taylor & Francis Group
LONDON AND NEW YORK

In association with the Delius Trust

First published 2007 by Ashgate Publishing

2 Park Square, Milton Park, Abingdon, Oxon OX14 4RN
711 Third Avenue, New York, NY 10017, USA

Routledge is an imprint of the Taylor & Francis Group, an informa business

First issued in paperback 2017

British Library Cataloguing in Publication Data
Delius, Frederick, 1862–1934
Music and copyright : the case of Delius and his publishers
1. Delius, Frederick, 1862–1934 – Correspondence 2. Delius, Frederick, 1862–1934 – Relations with music publishers
3. Music publishing – Great Britain – Correspondence
4. Music publishing – Great Britain – History – Sources
5. Copyright – Great Britain – History – Sources
I. Title II. Montgomery, Robert III. Threlfall, Robert
780.9'2

Library of Congress Cataloging-in-Publication Data
Montgomery, Robert.
Music and copyright : the case of Delius and his publishers/
Robert Montgomery and Robert Threlfall.
p. cm.
ISBN 978–0–7546–5846–7 (alk. paper)
1. Delius, Frederick, 1862–1934–Correspondence. 2. Composers–England–Correspondence.
3. Music publishers–Correspondence. 4. Copyright–Music–Great Britain–History.
I. Threlfall, Robert. II. Title.

ML410.D35M66 2007
780.92–dc22
[B]

2006029958

ISBN 978-0-7546-5846-7 (hbk)
ISBN 978-1-138-27603-1 (pbk)

Contents

Preface

This book is a business history of Delius's relationship with his publishers and the commercial environment in which he strove to make his way.

Delius was born in 1862, 24 years before the signing in 1886 of the Berne Convention, the international convention for the protection of literary and artistic works of which Great Britain was a founder member. During his lifetime came the birth of the record industry, the development of exercise of the performing right, the introduction of the mechanical right, the coming of films and broadcasting. During the currency of the copyrights since his death, further great economic opportunities have opened up for a successful composer.

It is ironic that copyright in the works of the three great twentieth-century British classical composers who died in 1934, Elgar, Delius and Holst, published in their lifetime, which originally expired on 31 December 1984 and was revived on 1 November 1995, has brought income to their estates and publishers of which the composers would not have dreamed.

Particularly important are the changes to copyright protection and opportunities to exploit copyright music that came about both during Delius's lifetime and after, while his works were still protected by copyright. Besides chronicling Delius's dealings with his publishers and the Performing Right Society through the letters, this book also covers the period after his death when the Delius Trust as the legal representative of his estate took over responsibility for administering the copyrights and promoting his music.

The singular position of the Delius Trust – the first composer trust to be formed in the UK – in setting a style and standard for many subsequent similar institutions, enables a much more comprehensive overview of Delius's traffic with the business of publication to be presented. Although the files of the Delius Trust Archive contain all Delius's known correspondence with his publishers, there are some gaps. Apart from the early exchange of letters with William Augener, the records of Delius's dealings with that company in the 1920s do not appear to have survived. His correspondence with Boosey & Hawkes during the 1930s was almost certainly destroyed in London during the Second World War; that with F.E.C.Leuckart of Leipzig, and the files of the GDT, (Genossenschaft Deutscher Tonsetzer), met a similar fate. On the other hand, the important files concerning Harmonie Verlag of Berlin, Tischer & Jagenberg of Cologne and, above all, Universal Edition of Vienna, if not absolutely complete, are sufficient to make suitable choice for the present purpose a matter of careful and difficult selection.

It goes without saying that all the correspondence with these firms is in German. It is almost certain that all these German texts were prepared by Jelka Delius from drafts made by Frederick, doubtless supplemented by verbal instructions as his abilities became increasingly limited from the mid-1920s. Given that she was so ill at the end, it does seem surprising that she was able to give so much time and thought to publishing problems.

Over the years, different hands have prepared the various translations now found in the Trust's Archive. We have carefully scrutinised all letters chosen for inclusion in the present volume and compared them with the originals where necessary. Any ambiguous or misleading renderings of technical phrases have been amended where necessary, in order to give as clear a meaning as possible to the subject under discussion. This applies particularly to the Harmonie correspondence, first translated many years ago. The Universal correspondence, in many ways the most interesting, was acquired by courtesy of the Company more recently and was transcribed by the indefatigable Evelin Gerhardi; translation, commenced by Daniel Bird, was completed by Robert Hahn. (It should be mentioned that all the Delius side of the business correspondence was always in longhand.) The whole body of all the Trust's letter holding, its copying, transcription and translation has for many years been under the watchful eye and control of its Archivist, Dr Lionel Carley, whose personal interest in the present project has also been most welcome.

Equally important in building a picture of Delius's publishing affairs has been the Delius file in the invaluable Performing Right Society Archive. PRS, to which Jelka Delius wrote in English, has kept copies of both sides of the correspondence which it has gladly made available.

The accessibility of the correspondence to the editors does not of course address the issue of copyright. The letters, being unpublished as at July 1989, are protected by copyright in the EC until the end of 2039. The editors have done their best to obtain permission to include those in the book and crave the indulgence of any copyright owners they have failed to contact. Most of the letters were written some 75 years ago. We are grateful to Lady Beecham for allowing us to reproduce Sir Thomas's letter to Delius dated 22 May 1915, to Boosey & Hawkes Music Publishers Ltd, Universal Edition, Stainer & Bell (on behalf of Augener), Oxford University Press, F.E.C. Leuckart and Breitkopf & Härtel.

We have been unable to trace Harmonie, and the solicitor, Bridgman & Co. GDT has been absorbed by GEMA.

Thanks are due to the Delius Trust for their support and in particular to Marjorie Dickinson, the Secretary to the Trust. Margaret Montgomery was very patient over the many hours it took to research and assemble the book. We are very grateful to our Commissioning Editor, Heidi May, and to Adam Richardson, our Desk Editor at Ashgate. Many thanks also to Anthea Lockley for her proof reading.

In the main body of this book, where the selection of letters which we have chosen tell their own story, we have not considered it necessary to follow strict bibliographical principles in certain respects. Thus, the address headings and signings-off are not copied to the levels of exactitude rightly demanded by Lionel Carley's *Delius: A Life in Letters*, since it is here the contents of the letters included which are of most interest and importance. Footnotes have been added to elucidate the meaning at times; to clarify reference to a particular work; or to cross-reference to other letters relating to the same point. For reasons of space we have decided, (though with some regret, for they are germane to our study) to exclude most of the letters relating to publishing matters that have already appeared in Lionel Carley's two volumes. Notes at the appropriate point cross-reference to them, giving the letter number.

What emerges from the correspondence is a unique history of how a leading twentieth-century composer earned his living from composition in the changing environment of the world of music.

Ashgate gratefully acknowledges the generous contribution of the Delius Trust in publishing this book.

List of Abbreviations

AKM	Wiener Autorengesellschaft. Austrian performing right organisation.
AMMRE	Anstalt für mechanisch-musikalische Rechte GmbH (Institute for mechanical musical rights), founded in Germany in 1909 for the exploitation of the so-called mechanical reproduction rights for phonograph records. It became part of GEMA.
ASCAP	American Society of Composers Authors and Publishers.
AUME	Austro-Mechana. Gesellschaft zur Wahrnehmung mechanisch-musikalischer Urheberrechte GmbH. Austrian mechanical rights organisation.
GDT	Genossenschaft Deutscher Tonsetzer (GDT). Founded 1903 with Richard Strauss as its first president. A German performing right organisation open only to composers. Delius was a member. In 1922 it merged with GEMA.
GEMA	Genossenschaft für Verwertung musikalischer Aufführungsrechte (GEMA), founded in 1915. German performing right organisation. It controlled AMMRE and in 1922 merged with and subsumed GDT. Title now is: Gesellschaft für musikalische Aufführungs-und-mechanische Vervielfältigungs-rechte.
M-CL	Mechanical-Copyright Licenses Co. Formed in England in 1910 to administer the new mechanical right. Merged with MCPS in 1924. Delius was a member, his membership later transferred to MCPS.
MCPS	Mechanical Copyright Protection Society Ltd. Formed in 1924.
MECOLICO	An abbreviation of Mechanical-Copyright Licenses Co. The word continued to be printed on stamps affixed to records to show that royalties had been paid, for many years.
PRS	Performing Right Society of Great Britain. Founded 1914. Delius became a member in 1920, resigning from GDT.
SACEM	La Société des Auteurs, Compositeurs et Editeurs de Musique. The French performing right society. Founded 1851.

List of Appendices

A List of Delius's Publishers

A.B. Campbell (Jacksonville, Fla.), 1885–1892
Augener, 1890
Augener, 1892 (reverted to FD in 1895; to Concorde 1899)
Miscellaneous songs published:

L. Grus (Paris), 1896
L'Aube (Paris), 7/1896
The Dome (London), 6/1899

Concorde Concert Control, 1899 (to Breitkopf, 1907) (Also Stanley Lucas, Weber, Pitt & Hatzfeld)
(Selbstverlag) Lévy-Lulx (Paris), 1905–1906
Harmonie Verlag, Berlin, 1906 (Later – in 1921 – to Universal)
Breitkopf & Härtel, London, 1907 (to Tischer & Jagenberg, 1910)
F.E.C. Leuckart, Leipzig, 1909 (later controlled through Universal)
Tischer & Jagenberg, Cologne, 1910 (later – 1930 – to OUP)
Silver, Burdett, 1913–1916
Universal (Vienna), 1913 (later to Boosey & Hawkes)
Forsyth Bros (Manchester), 1916
Augener, 1919
Winthrop Rogers, 1919 (to Hawkes, 1925)
Music and Letters, 1/1920 (later to Universal)
Anglo-French Music Publishers, 1923 (later to OUP)
Hawkes & Son, 1924 (to Boosey, 1930)
Oxford University Press, 1924–1930
Curwen (for Universal, London), 1925
Boosey & Hawkes, 1930

Chapter One

The Business Background

To put the commercial environment that existed when Delius began to publish in context, a brief survey of what went before is necessary. Delius started to publish soon after the Berne Convention, a copyright union which encompassed most European countries, had been signed in 1886. The opportunities that Berne and its accompanying legislation brought changed the relationship between publisher and composer. They required administrative procedures to be developed, and some of the problems Delius encountered were due to the fact that they were in their infancy.

The cornerstone of publishing is copyright, the exclusive right given by law to composer and publisher to exploit a copyright work, or license others to do so. The first European Copyright Act was the British Act of 1709, which gave protection to 'books and other writings'. It was not until 1778 when Johann Christian Bach successfully sued Longman and Lukey, his publishers, for breach of contract, that the High Court held that music could be protected by copyright.

There are two essential differences between books and music. First, a tune can cross from one country to another without translation. Second, whereas books are sold to be read, music, although it may be printed, has to be performed to come alive. Copyright law had addressed both these aspects by the end of the eighteenth century. The Johann Christian Bach decision was important not just because it appeared to settle the issue that music in Britain could be protected by copyright, but also because Bach was a foreigner. Music publishers often obtained their raw material from abroad and were anxious to establish that, for instance, a British publisher could have a copyright in Britain in the name of a foreign composer. In those countries that had passed copyright laws, such as France and Britain, the concept soon began to take shape that copyright could be claimed in the country where a work was first published, irrespective of the nationality of the composer. So, if a work by a foreign composer was published for the first time in your country, copyright could be claimed. In that case what was there to prevent a work being published on the same day in more than one country, with copyright being claimed in both countries? This became known as simultaneous publication. Beethoven wrote to his English publisher about it. Chopin altered notes in editions to be published in a specific country.

Although the British courts appeared to accept the proposition, every now and then a publisher would dispute another's claim to copyright in a work by a foreigner. Eventually in 1855 the House of Lords ruled in Jeffreys *v* Boosey, 'the La Sonnambula case', that a foreigner publishing a work in Britain for the first time could claim copyright, but only if he was resident here at the time of publication. This was the situation that obtained until Britain signed the Berne Convention in 1886.

The issue of a public performance right was addressed in revolutionary France in 1794, when edicts were passed enabling first French dramatic authors and then composers to license, and therefore benefit financially from, the public performance of their works.

These issues, cross border copyright and the licensing of performing rights, were the two most important aspects of music copyright to be developed in the nineteenth century. The watershed of nearly 200 years of developing copyright legislation was the Berne Convention, for the protection of Literary and Artistic Works, signed in 1886, and the national legislation that was then enacted by the contracting parties. Thenceforth there was an international legislative framework under which composers and music publishers could defend their rights. The first nine signatories included France, Germany, Great Britain, Italy and Spain, together with their colonies.

Berne, which built on the network of nineteenth-century bi-lateral copyright agreements, stipulated minimum requirements of protection, which were to be included in national legislation. Notable as far as music was concerned was the composer's right to control public performances of his works and that a composer's works should be protected during his lifetime and for a minimum period after death. Works first published in a Convention country were to be protected, without formalities, in the other signatory countries as though they were by nationals, with one exception. Works should not receive a longer period of protection in another Convention country than they received in their own. The nationality of a work was decided by the place of publication and not the nationality of the author. The signatory countries each undertook to pass national legislation incorporating the terms of Berne. This in turn provided a framework within which national copyright societies could operate. These copyright societies were collectives, organisations to which their members, whether composers or publishers, assigned their public performance and sometimes mechanical rights, rights that a society could better defend and exploit than individuals. From then on the relationship between composer and publisher changed.

Berne provided a springboard from which the music publishing business could develop, to the benefit of composer and publisher. No longer was the publisher the sole source of royalties. The performing right societies paid any fees due direct to publisher or composer. The correspondence between Delius and the two performing right societies of which he was, at different times, a member, is therefore as important as that with his publishers in trying to see the whole picture. Fortunately both sides of his correspondence with the British Performing Right Society (PRS) survive. At the beginning of the twentieth century came the establishment of the mechanical right, the right of a composer or publisher to license the making of a reproduction using mechanical means. Then came broadcasting and later films. The publisher was no longer the main instigator of exposing a work. That often lay with record company or broadcaster.

So how easy was it at the end of the nineteenth century for a composer of serious music to obtain performances of his works, or exposure in the developing media of records and films? What were the likely rewards? Why should a commercial music publisher wish to publish music by Delius? The Delius contracts are a good guide.

The Publishing Contract

Unlike the book publisher, who normally prints under licence from the author, the nineteenth-century music publisher usually bought the copyright outright. Towards the end of the century publishers began to pay royalties, often after a specific number of sales of the printed copy. The right of public representation was not always covered, as it was seldom exercised. However, in Great Britain, from 1842, when the public performance right in non-dramatic music was introduced, until the 1911 Act, there were two distinct rights that had to be registered separately at Stationers' Hall and which could belong to different owners. For a résumé of the new definition of rights under the 1911 Act see Chapter three. A selection of Delius's publishing contracts are printed in the appendix.

As one jurist wrote in the middle of the nineteenth century, the music publisher always bought his pig in a poke. However, all the Delius works taken by Harmonie, with the exception of the complete *A Mass of Life*, had been performed by the time Harmonie agreed to publish them, thus reducing the company's risk. The Delius Trust has the contracts. As with most nineteenth-century music publishing contracts for serious works, the composer warranted that the work was original, and the publisher obtained the right to make adaptations and transcriptions, including altering the keys. In the Harmonie contracts, profits were to be split 50/50 after recovery of expenses (not defined), accounting was once a year, and Delius reserved the performing right, as he would have to do under his membership of the German Genossenschaft Deutscher Tonsetzer (GDT), which he joined in 1904. The GDT was formed in 1903 at the instigation of Richard Strauss; membership was reserved to high art composers, and publishers were excluded. There seems no doubt that Delius received performing fees through GDT up to 1914, certainly covering Germany and Austria and Great Britain, although we do not know how much he received. The GDT's records were destroyed in the Second World War. All music publishers try to bind the composer to give to the publisher the benefit of any new rights that may be introduced, but in the case of the new mechanical right, copyright laws were specific that in the case of works published before the introduction of the new right, unless specifically dealt with, it belonged to the composer and not the publisher. Germany introduced legislation dealing with mechanical reproduction in 1910 and Great Britain in 1911_

The income sources from which Delius could have benefited were:

- Sales of printed music
- Hire fees
- Performing Right income
- Broadcasting income
- Mechanical right income
- Film fees
- Grand Rights fees.

To take these categories one by one:

Sales of printed music

By the time Delius began to be published, buyouts of publishing rights were giving way to royalties on sales and hire fees, sometimes with a recoupable advance from the publisher.

Under the Harmonie contracts Delius participated in 50 per cent of profits, the basis not defined, which must have contributed to the problems with Harmonie later. When Universal took over the Harmonie works, as well as publishing on its own account, Delius received a royalty of 20 per cent or 25 per cent of the retail price, often trying for 33 per cent, but never achieving it. The Leuckart contracts were buyouts of the reproduction right.

Delius was aware of the problems of delay and currency loss by his publisher consolidating international sales in Germany before the calculation of his share and, as will be seen, he negotiated to receive his British print royalties direct from Universal's British agent. His insistence on a high royalty (these days ten per cent of retail would be normal) was one reason why his publisher had to rack up the retail prices of his music, to ensure that they covered their costs. Delius was constantly worried about the high prices charged for his works which he thought could discourage sales.

Hire fees

Not all publishing contracts of the time covered the distribution of hire fees, which were only relevant to large-scale works. In general Elgar's contracts with Novello did not entitle him to hire fees, perhaps because Novello paid for the material, but from the correspondence it can be seen that major Delius works were hired out and that he received a share of hire fees. Before performing rights were administered by a copyright society, the publisher had the opportunity to combine hire and performance fee and negotiate with the hirer. The flexibility this gave to negotiations was the reason that some publishers preferred initially to stay out of PRS, until forced in, in order to receive broadcasting fees.

Apart from the Harmonie contracts under which he received 50 per cent of 'profits', Delius's share of royalties from copies 'hired or otherwise exploited' were usually 20 per cent of fees received. Hire fees feature regularly in the correspondence and we can get a good idea of how much was charged. Harmonie seem often to have lent rather than hired material, in order to encourage performances of an unknown composer. In 1904, Breitkopf & Härtel, London, which had material for some unpublished works, recommended a hire fee of 1 guinea. *Life's Dance* rates 1 gn in 1908. In 1914 Delius interceded with Universal on behalf of Percy Grainger, who was required to pay a hire fee for the Piano Concerto of £5, which Delius thought should be £2 10s 0d if performances were to be encouraged.

The 1921 correspondence shows an increase in fees. Universal charged £20 for hire of the material (presumably the complete material) of the Requiem for its first performance and proposed £6 for subsequent ones. Delius agreed, but in 1926 thought £5 for the Requiem too little. Orchestral works in 1921 rated £4–6. In 1922 a rank and file orchestral player earned £1 1s 0d a concert.

In London the Goodwin & Tabb library hire out Delius works in Great Britain and in 1922 draw Delius's ire by selling sets of performing material for *On Hearing the First Cuckoo in Spring* for £8. Delius would rather it had been hired for £2. He may have been right, as there are references to pirate performances of the piece, which must have been from purchased sets. From the Tischer & Jagenberg contract it appears that *Life's Dance* was also on sale, as the final tranche of the payments was triggered by the sale of the fortieth set of material. In 1925 Delius insists that fees for *A Mass of Life* are too high and complains that Universal are, quite rightly, charging a separate hire fee per performance. From a paper in the Trust archives it appears that hire fees were lower in the difficult 1930s, the BBC paying £1-1s-0d for most works.

A recurring topic is the difficulty of persuading Beecham to pay hire fees. He sometimes argues that Delius had given him works or material that he has been told he may use without fee. In 1931 Jelka Delius strenuously denied that Delius had ever connived at such a practice, which would have injured Universal's interests. But publishers are wary of Beecham, charge a deposit and insist that the material he has bought is for his personal use only.

The exclusion from PRS control in the UK of choral & orchestral works lasting more than 20 minutes brought more difficulties, clearly set out in Dr Kalmus's letter dated 11 January 1934. *Appalachia* moved between PRS and Universal control, (the final chorus didn't really make it a choral work). When controlled by PRS, the Hallé orchestra paid PRS a performing fee of five gns and Universal a hire fee of three gns. Once back in Universal's hand, the Hallé objected to a composite fee of eight gns.

Performing Right income

The performing right, the right of an author to authorise or forbid a performance of both his dramatic and non-dramatic musical works, was first introduced in France in 1794. Composers of stage works could then, and do now, license performances of them directly. The performing right in non-dramatic works can really only be administered collectively. SACEM (La Societé des Auteurs, Compositeurs et Editeurs de Musique), formed in 1851, ploughing a furrow that other societies would follow, took the performing rights from its composer and publisher members and exercised them on its members' behalf, so avoiding arguments between composer and performer. It took rights from its members not only for France but also for those countries with which France had a copyright treaty. By 1870 SACEM was operating in Britain (which had had a bilateral copyright agreement with France since 1851) and in 1881 it formed the International, Musical, Dramatic and Literary Association in Britain to represent it exclusively there. In the PRS files there are several affidavits, including one signed in 1872 by César Franck, empowering SACEM to take action on behalf of its composer members in Britain.

The early international attempts by SACEM were important in encouraging other European countries to form their own copyright societies. The Italian society was formed in 1883, the Austrian in 1897, the Spanish in 1899. The German composers formed GDT (Genossenschaft Deutscher Tonsetzer) in 1903, with Richard Strauss as the first President. Delius was an early member. Publishers were not admitted.

GDT held that the performing right was an author's right (Urheberrecht), as opposed to a publisher's right (Verlagerrecht).

The activities of GDT are frequently referred to in the correspondence. Contracts and letters show that Delius assigned his performing rights to GDT, as he was bound to do under his membership agreement. Although publishers were excluded from membership, they were granted 25 per cent of fees distributed and there are indications in the letters that British publishers were in some cases acting as GDT's agents. Without a network of employees or agents throughout the territories for which GDT administered performing rights, it would not have been able to operate efficiently.

It was the activities of SACEM and GDT in Britain that eventually persuaded the British music publishers that they should exercise their performing rights, leading to the formation in 1914 of the Performing Right Society (PRS).

The performing right in non-dramatic music had been introduced into British legislation in 1842 and in dramatic works in 1833. But although it had been exercised for stage works, and although there was an attempt by Harry Wall, who in 1875 set up the 'Copyright and Performing Right Protection Office', a private organisation, to exercise the right in relation to non-dramatic music on behalf of his clients, the British publishers were generally against the idea.

One should never forget that classical music is a small part of the music publishing business. In the UK the major publishers were against performing fees until the early twentieth century. They often paid performers to sing their songs to promote sales of the printed copy and felt that charging a performing fee would jeopardise sales. It was not until the decline in printed music sales early in the twentieth century and the coming of broadcasting that they were persuaded.

The early Delius correspondence is tantalisingly brief on the subject of performing rights, although one can see from Breitkopf & Härtel's letter to Delius dated 7 March 1908 and the 23 June 1913 letter from GDT that it was advising him on the Leuckart contracts.

There are several references in 1908 to a dispute between GDT and the proprietors of the Queen's Hall about performing fees for *Sea Drift* and the proposed performance of *A Mass of Life* to be conducted by Beecham in June 1909. GDT had apparently suggested fees that were unacceptable. Matters must have been resolved, but we don't know on what basis. Letters from Harmonie show that the publishers were worried that the performance would not take place, but Delius's reply shows that he appreciated what GDT were trying to do. These were early days in the struggle to establish performing fees and the threat of cancellation if any fees were charged was common.

Two sheets of paper in Jelka's handwriting from this period throw some light on the level of fees paid as well as showing that GDT was operating in London. For the performance of the second half of *A Mass of Life* in Munich in 1908 she writes that Delius received, in English money, £1-16s-0d; two performances in 1909, in London and Elberfeld rated 8/- each; three performances of *Sea Drift* in 1908 brought 5/- each: the Piano Concerto about the same.

Between 1910 and 1913, by which time Delius had signed a publishing contract with Universal and Universal was negotiating to take over the works originally published by Harmonie, there is no reference to performing rights in the surviving correspondence.

In 1913 things changed. Delius wrote to Universal querying performing fees received for performances in Vienna licensed by the Wiener Autorengesellschaft (AKM). He complains that whereas he has in the past received Mk 144 and Mk 166 from GDT for two performances of *A Mass of Life* in Berlin (say £7.50 per performance at Mk 20 to a £), he had only received Mk 17.44 for what appears to have been two performances of the Mass plus *Brigg Fair* in Austria. Universal eventually confirmed that fees in Austria were low. There is no evidence from the correspondence as to the level of fees charged by GDT in Great Britain for Delius works, but letters in 1908 from Edgar Speyer, who headed the Queen's Hall syndicate, to Richard Strauss, the President of GDT, which were copied to Delius, give an indication. Speyer was prepared to pay Mk 1,500 (say £75) to cover performing fees in all works controlled by GDT for the 1908 season and in addition 21 gns for the rights to play part of *Salome*.

From 1914 to 1920 there is no mention of performing fees. When he eventually resigned from GDT in 1920 and joined PRS, Delius said that he had received no money from GDT since 1914. As a British subject, many of whose works had been published in an enemy country, he was subject to the provisions of the 1916 Trading with the Enemy Act, and the Controller of Enemy Property administered any royalties due from Germany. Philip Heseltine, when proposing a performance of *A Village Romeo and Juliet* in 1916 wrote that a licence would be needed from the Board of Trade. The dispute with Harmonie, which exercised Delius before the war started, was still going on in 1920 and he had to be careful to pass the settlement through the proper channels.

Delius called at PRS on 18 November 1919, giving his address as a London hotel. He told PRS he was a member of 'the German Society' and said that he had been told that PRS had collected fees for performances of his works. His application was accepted and his membership certificate was sent to him on 5 February 1920, together with a request for a list of his works.

The PRS archives contain the complete correspondence between Delius and the PRS from 1919 to Jelka's death in 1935 and beyond. It is a fascinating history of the difficulties experienced by the nascent PRS in dealing with an international composer. Delius was irritable with PRS's apparent inability to account for fees on all his performances; PRS for its part patiently answered his questions and did its best.

Easy as it is to accept Delius's criticisms, it is important to see both sides. PRS was established in 1914. Even though the existence of the performing right was a fact of copyright law, it was not universally welcomed either by those using copyright music or publishing it. PRS had to fight, often in the courts, to establish its right to license and collect. It was hampered by not having a complete mandate from publishers and composers, and by the wartime environment. The PRS rule, forced upon it by its publisher members, that it should not control choral & orchestral works lasting more than 20 minutes is a case in point, frequently referred to in the later correspondence. (The ampersand is used here to show that this term refers to works for chorus accompanied by orchestra.) In 1921 35 publishers belonged to the Music Publishers' Association of which only 16 were members of PRS. Besides licensing performances and collecting the fees, PRS had to develop a means of distributing the fees collected. The first distribution, of £11,000 was made in 1917 to 297 members.

Developing a distribution system was difficult. Before moving to what is now generally accepted, that music used in a certain sphere of activity would be given points according to length etc., and the points divided into the available money, composers were allocated to a class, dependent on their publisher's view of their popularity and importance. In 1918, Haydn Wood and Hermann Lohr (*The Little Grey Home in the West*) were in Class one, Ivor Novello and Coleridge Taylor, Class two, Grainger in four. Delius was in Class eight in 1920 but was promoted to six in 1921, and five in 1922. Standard sums per class member seem to have been distributed. Those in Class one received £100, Class two £75. Delius's early payments were £45 in 1921, £70 in 1922 and £52 in 1923. PRS rules were amended in 1927 and from then on the distribution of fees was on the basis of programmes or performance returns. Fees were split two-thirds to the composer and one-third to the publisher. Unlike mechanical rights, which composers sometimes withheld from their publishers, it was generally accepted that publisher and composer shared performance fees. GDT for its part distributed at least some of its fees on the basis of programme returns before 1913, as can be seen from Delius's letters to Universal in April 1913 about poor financial returns from performances of *A Mass of Life*, and his letter to PRS dated 28 June 1928.

In its early days, PRS could only hope to know what was being performed if it had the help of publisher and composer members and was much hampered by not having all publishers and composers as members. Delius, for instance, was a member from 1920, but Universal, his main publisher, which did not assign performing rights to its UK agents, would not have been represented in the UK until there was a reciprocal agreement with AKM, the Austrian Society, in 1926. It is clear from the correspondence and margin notes that PRS went out of its way to collect for Delius in England, even to the extent of collecting on choral & orchestral works lasting longer than 20 minutes, which were not within PRS control. Several of his most important works came into this category. Delius did not always show his gratitude.

There was also the problem of correctly identifying titles of Delius works when performances or broadcasts were declared to PRS. Even today, making accurate returns to PRS is not uppermost in the minds of users of copyright works. PRS consulted Augener in 1931 over the titles of songs that they were unsure about and were told that some songs had been printed with 'fancy titles, which ought not to be used'. The song *Eastern Fantasia* was probably *In the Seraglio Garden*. The BBC declared *To the Queen of my heart* which had been registered with PRS as *To my Heart's Queen*. To this date confusions arise over titles, notably in differentiating between the opera *Irmelin*, the song *Irmelin* and the *Irmelin* Prelude, which is not the prelude to the opera.

Having received his certificate of membership, and PRS having established that he had resigned from GDT, he was asked formally to assign the performing right in all his works to PRS. By the assignment, Delius assigned

> all the right of performance in all parts of the world of each and every song with the words thereof or musical work not being a musical play the right of performance of which now belongs to or shall hereafter be acquired by or be or become vested in the assignor during the continuance of the Assignor's membership of the Society.

Although musical plays in their entirety were not within PRS control, 'separate numbers fragments or arrangements of melodies or selections' were.

The prime mover in getting him to join PRS was Charles Volkert, a PRS Director and the Managing Director of Schott & Co. who had apparently told Delius that PRS had already collected money for his works. He was surprised by the small amount he received initially. In July 1923 he wrote to PRS to confirm that he had resigned from GDT, saying that he was now entirely dependent on PRS for the collection of fees in England and abroad. 'Not only have I received nothing from GDT since the beginning of the war, but also what was due to me from the last years before the war amounting to some £75, have not been paid.'

In 1926 he berated PRS not only for not having a contract with the European societies, but also with expecting him to tell PRS the details of performances. It was surely up to PRS to find out. PRS replied in measured tones. One needs to have sympathy for both sides. Nowadays copyright societies have reciprocal copyright agreements with societies in other countries under which each protects the other's repertoire and are generally able to track down performances. In the 1920s, with an incomplete mandate from the composers and publishers, and especially with Delius's publishers not being represented, this would have been more difficult and help would have been needed.

Not belonging to PRS gave some flexibility to publishers of works that had to be hired, to negotiate composite hire and performing fees, as Augener's letter to Delius dated 4 August 1926 demonstrates.

Nothing daunted, Delius returned to the attack in June 1927, to be told that though fees in respect of performances in Germany and Austria had been received, they had yet to be distributed. Copyright fees in respect of foreign performances take time to be repatriated and distributed. He tried writing direct to AKM, but they forwarded his letter to PRS for reply. At that time a composer could only belong to one performing right society.

When in 1926 PRS did make an agreement with GDT, it would only accept fees due up to August 1914. Presumably any fees charged in Austria and Germany during the war for the performance of Delius works would have gone to the publishers. If any of his publishers collected his share, there is no record of its being sent to him, which is not to say that it was not.

It is likely that with the possible exception of those from performances in France, SACEM having a pre-war agreement with PRS, Continental European fees would have been lost to him until the exercise of the 1926 reciprocal agreements that PRS concluded with GEMA (Gesellschaft für Musikalische Aufführungs und Mechanische Vervielfältigungsrechte), GDT and AKM. In the UK, until the 1926 agreements, neither Universal nor Tischer & Jagenberg had any society link with PRS, or had a UK agent empowered to license performances. As we can see from the PRS internal notes on Delius's letter to PRS dated 23 October 1931, once PRS started to distribute fees against programme returns, Delius would have received the full fee rather than the two-thirds composer share on works where the publisher was not a member.

Once the 1926 agreements came into operation, PRS picked up the fee and sent the publisher's share on works published by Tischer & Jagenberg and Universal, (including those published by Leuckart) to AKM, in the same way that AKM would have sent the composer's share on performances in their territory, to PRS on behalf of Delius. Irrespective of any reservation expressed by a composer, once a work was published, both composer and publisher, both being members of a copyright society, received their respective shares. In the case of Delius, the Universal Edition publishing contracts specifically entitled the publisher to receive his share.

The rule, which did not apply elsewhere in Europe, that PRS did not control choral & orchestral works lasting longer than 20 minutes, caused problems. It came into force in 1927, although PRS seems to have collected on such Delius works and paid the full fee to him prior to PRS having a contractual link with Universal. When PRS sprang it on Jelka in 1931, she was justifiably irritated, especially when PRS got it wrong and changed its mind as to which Delius works were outside PRS control. These were: *Sea Drift*, *A Mass of Life*, *Requiem*, *Songs of Sunset* and from time to time *Appalachia*. Around 1930 Universal assigned performing rights in non-PRS controlled works to Cranz, its London agent. The result for Delius was that Cranz would then license, collect the fees, and then deduct its commission. But did Cranz send the Delius share back to Universal in Vienna, involving Delius in delays, two commissions and two currency conversions, or was he paid his share in England? No wonder he was so insistent that Curwen as the British publisher of the *Five Piano Pieces* paid him in sterling in England on English sales.

Some of these issues were transient. Nowadays almost all publishers and composers are members of copyright societies. From 1953 PRS controlled broadcasts of choral works lasting longer than 20 minutes, paying a supplementary fee, a bonus for length. From 1972 PRS controlled other uses of such works. The various aspects of the flow, or lack of it, of performing fees is demonstrated below.

Type of Work	**Pre 1914**	**1914–1920**	**1921–1926**	**1927–1930**	**1931—**
PRS controlled works		Formed 1914	FD joined in 1920. Neither Universal nor its UK agent had any link to PRS, which paid by composer class.	PRS paid based on performance information. Agreements with GDT/AKM/GEMA from 1927 meant that publisher shares went to the appropriate society. FD received his share of performance fees.	As before

Type of work	Pre 1914	1914–1920	1921–1926	1927–1930	1931—
Control in Great Britain of Ch. & Orch. works lasting more than 20 minutes				PRS probably collected on the works in the UK and sent the full fee to FD.	Cranz as Universal's agent licensed and collected fees on the works, until Universal Ltd formed in 1936.
Control of all Delius works in Continental Europe	FD joined GDT in 1904 and received fees.	No fees received PRS. No agreements between PRS and European societies. Did publishers receive fees?	FD resigned in 1920 and joined PRS. No agreements between PRS and European societies. Did publishers receive fees?	Agreements between PRS and GDT/AKM/ GEMA begin to operate. FD would receive his share through PRS	Agreements between PRS and GDT/AKM/ GEMA begin to operate. FD would receive his share through PRS

Delius's PRS income dipped in 1927–1928: £89 in 1926, £50 in 1927, £33 in 1928. Thereafter it rose, reaching £210 in 1933, but it must be remembered that the performance fees on the choral & orchestral works outside PRS control would have been in addition. The main reason for the reduction in fees received was an increase in the number of PRS members, persuaded to join by the collapse of the sheet music market and the introduction of broadcasting fees following the PRS agreement with the BBC. Until the fees could be re-negotiated upwards to reflect the increased repertoire, more members had to share the same pot.

Broadcasting income

The initial licences granted by PRS were flat fees per station, per year, not related to the amount of music used. The repertoire was the PRS small rights repertoire and did not include grand rights. As the PRS indicated in their reply to a circular from GDT in 1927, each work was given a points value, which was multiplied by the number of reported performances to give a total number of points for the work. When all reported works had been so dealt with, the resultant total was divided into the amount of money available for distribution.

In 1928 PRS changed its approach. Following the success of the non-PRS publishers in negotiating a scale of fees per broadcast, which yielded higher returns than those from the PRS/BBC ‘blanket agreement’, those publishers joined PRS and a new itemised contract was negotiated with the BBC. Jelka Delius found it difficult to work out what she thought Delius was entitled to and the detailed letter of 19 July 1928 from John Woodhouse, the PRS Controller, which set out the fees paid, gave a very measured response to her questions. At that time, apart from choral & orchestral works lasting more than 20 minutes, fees were distributed according to the length of broadcast, which had the effect of rewarding long works more than shorter.

As far as Delius works outside PRS control are concerned, we know that the BBC paid £5 per broadcast of the complete *Hassan*, (it was broadcast over two evenings) but we have no record of what was paid for the broadcast of *A Village Romeo and Juliet* in 1932. Jelka’s disappointment at the fees received for the 1929 Festival was partly due to the fact that when a performance was broadcast, only a performing fee for the live concert was paid. Nowadays the broadcast of a live performance would rate two fees.

Mechanical Right income

Whereas there was a gap of some 70 years between the legislation introducing the small performing right and its exercise, the ‘mechanical right’, the right of a composer to authorise or forbid the recording of his music by mechanical means, was introduced in response to the development of the recorded or mechanically reproduced music industry.

The original Berne text of 1886 did not mention the mechanical right, but support for the new right was in the 1908 text. By that time the record industry was becoming established and throughout Europe composers, publishers and collecting societies were pursuing the right to be able to license recordings made by the new industry.

Court decisions in Italy and Belgium were in favour of composers. French law was fettered by a clause similar to Clause three of the Protocol of Berne, which stated, ‘it is understood that the manufacture and sale of instruments serving to reproduce mechanically musical airs in which copyright subsists shall not be considered as constituting infringement of musical copyright’. French courts held that permission to reproduce a musical air did not cover the words. The USA introduced legislation dealing with mechanical reproduction in 1909: Germany in 1908. In this Law of Publishing it states, regarding the rules governing publishing contracts, that ‘where the publisher takes rights and distributes in print form the author retains the right of mechanical reproduction unless specifically agreed’.

The UK Copyright Act of 1911 which introduced the mechanical right into the UK took the same approach. The publisher could not claim a share of mechanical rights in works assigned before 1 July 1912, the date that the Act came into operation, unless mechanical rights were specifically covered in the assignment. Publishers later tried to negotiate in order to gain a share, but were not always successful. Delius kept 100 per cent of the mechanicals on both his pre- and post-1912 works controlled by Universal Edition, against constant pleas from Universal, until he relented in 1930 and granted a 20 per cent share for certain central European territories, excluding the UK. The Leuckart works were not included in the dispensation, as one can see from the extraordinary court action in 1931 by Universal in Vienna to try to obtain a share of mechanicals in the UK on *Brigg Fair*. This issue was never raised in the case of performing rights, where the usual share of fees was two-thirds to the composer and one-third to the publisher. Publisher contracts signed after 1912 normally assign the mechanical right to the publisher in exchange for a 50/50 split of royalties. Although Delius resisted giving mechanicals to Universal until 1930, even in the 1921 agreement covering the Harmonie works, (app. 13), he conceded them to Tischer & Jagenberg in 1912 and to his various British publishers. See the contracts with Augener for the violin concerto in 1919, (app. 10) and the Hawkes 1924 contract for violin sonata no. 2 (app. 14). It was not until 1942 that the Delius Trust agreed to allow Boosey & Hawkes Ltd, who then believed, as owners of Universal Ltd, that they were the owners of the Delius copyrights, a 50 per cent share of mechanicals on the Universal Delius works.

Delius was well aware of the need to protect his rights and his insistence in 1913 on reserving his mechanical rights in the six works published by Leuckart proved far-sighted. This is dealt with later.

No Delius recordings were made before 1914, although GDT, to whom by contract he had to cede his mechanical rights, would have been able to handle mechanical right issues concerning recordings made or sold in Germany before the war. In 1923 Delius joined the Mechanical-Copyright Licenses Co. Ltd. in London. Founded in 1910, in time for the introduction of the mechanical right into UK law, it merged with The Mechanical Copyright Protection Society (MCPS) in 1924. The sums he received as royalties were small, but the details of how mechanical rights were administered in the early twentieth century warrant an explanation.

The best starting point is the report of the UK 1909 *Committee on the law of copyright.* It was set up by the President of the Board of Trade to study the 1908 text of the Berne Convention and recommend to the British government what changes to UK copyright law were necessary to enable Britain to sign that text. Its report was the foundation of the 1911 Copyright Act, an Act that cleaned up anomalies that had crept into copyright legislation over the previous 200 years and, as far as composers and publishers were concerned, introduced, among other changes (which will be dealt with later) the following. The term of copyright, which under the 1842 Act had been 42 years from publication of a specific work or seven years after death of the composer, whichever was the longer, was replaced by all works by a composer published in his life-time remaining in copyright until 50 years after his death. An assignment of 'copyright' made by a composer before 1 July 1912, when the 1911 Act came into operation, was deemed an assignment of 'copyright' as defined by the Act and did not include the performing right unless the assignment covered the right. Lastly the Act granted to composers the right to authorise the reproduction of their musical works using a mechanical contrivance.

As Copyright legislation has expanded, so has government mechanism to prevent copyright owners abusing their monopoly rights. Article 13 of the 1908 Berne text stated that:

> The authors of musical works shall have the exclusive right of authorizing the adaptation of those works to instruments which can produce them mechanically and the public performance of the said works by means of these instruments,

but it also allowed local reservations.

The 1909 UK Committee recommended that composers should have protection against the adaptation of their musical works to instruments which could reproduce them mechanically, but several witnesses advocated a 'compulsory licence', a principle already adopted in the USA where the mechanical right had already been established in the 1909 Copyright Act.

In their evidence to the 1909 Committee the record companies said they feared that any one manufacturer might obtain a monopoly of one composer's or perhaps one publisher's works. The record business had begun with no obligation to pay royalties, and the genuine concerns of the record companies had to be respected. Strangely enough the committee was not worried that record companies might sign up performers exclusively, something which soon became common. Unsurprisingly the publishing interests went for an unfettered right.

The Committee respected the two conflicting views, but although the Bill as originally drafted gave the composer an unrestricted right to control mechanical reproduction, what became s. 19 of the 1911 Act was inserted at the committee stage, giving the record industry what it wanted. A statutory royalty of five per cent of the 'ordinary selling price of the contrivance' was imposed. The Regulations covered how the royalty was to be divided if there was more than one copyright owner, and there was a minimum royalty per work of ½d.

The 1928 Record Royalty Review Committee summed up the situation succinctly on p. 607 of its report.

> …The Copyright Act 1911, as passed, contained a clause (s19) the effect of which is to compel a composer of music, if he has granted a licence to one person to reproduce his work mechanically, to grant to any other person a licence to produce the same work in like manner upon payment of a statutory royalty.

The 1911 Act divided musical works into those published before and after the Act came into force.

The effect of this was that on the first recording of a copyright work, the composer had the right to license or refuse to license a recording and to charge whatever royalty he liked. For subsequent recordings a refusal was not an option. As long as the record company complied with the Regulations, telling the copyright owner that it intended to issue a recording of the work and to pay the royalties, the so-called 'compulsory licence' applied.

The regulations are tortuous. As the distinguished lawyer Skone James wrote in the sixth edition of *Copinger on Copyright*, the standard textbook, 'the draftsman has certainly not used clear and unambiguous language to effect [his] probable intention'. The provisions as to the payment of royalties had to deal with recordings made before the introduction of the mechanical right.

i) In the case of musical works published before 1 July 1912, record companies were exempt until 1 July 1913 from paying royalties on recordings of such copyright musical works made before 1 July 1910, and even then they only paid 2½ per cent, half the statutory rate, on that and subsequent recordings of the work.

ii) In the case of musical works published after 1 July 1910 but recorded before 1 July 1912, only 2½ per cent was payable, from 1 July 1912, on all subsequent recordings of those works.

iii) In the case of musical works published after commencement, (1 July 1912), royalties were due on sales from commencement at 2½ per cent until 1 July 1914, when the rate doubled to five per cent.

The effect on Delius can be demonstrated, quite hypothetically, as follows:

Had *Paris*, first published 1909, been recorded prior to 1 July 1912, Delius would have received no royalties on the records sold until 1 July 1913, and then only at a rate of 2½ per cent. On recordings made after 1913 it would still have rated only a half royalty. This half royalty on future recordings of the work continued following the 1928 Record Royalty enquiry, when the basic royalty was increased to 6¼ per cent, and that for pre-1 July 1912 works to 3⅛ per cent.

Delius works published after 1 July 1912 would have qualified for the full five per cent when recorded. We don't know whether the record companies operated the reduction for pre-1912 works, although they probably did, as the letter from Delius to Universal dated 21 December 1923 shows. The discrimination ended with the 1956 Copyright Act, which removed the distinction. We have no Delius royalty statements from that period.

As to the payment of royalties, the Regulations specified the sticking on to the record of pre-paid adhesive stamps to show that the royalty had been paid, unless the parties could agree to some other system. The adhesive stamps were issued on behalf of the copyright owners in the music by Mechanical-Copyright Licenses Ltd., and bore the imprint Mecolico. Very soon stamps gave way to agreements with the major record companies under which the record companies were authorised to print a facsimile of the Mecolico stamp on their labels, in return for them agreeing to pay mechanical royalties.

Commercial recordings of 29 Delius works were made during his lifetime and heard by him. Sales would have been small and we have no record of mechanical royalties received. The first two were acoustic recordings made by Eugene Goossens for HMV of *On Hearing the First Cuckoo* and *Brigg Fair*. Goossens was a champion of modern music, who gave the first concert performance in England of *The Rite of Spring* in 1921, and put on several concerts of music by twentieth-century British composers. The first recording of *Paris* was made by Beecham in 1934, but, held up in French customs, did not arrive in time for Delius to hear it before he died.

The 29 known recordings with their conductors are:

On Hearing the First Cuckoo	Eugene Goossens 1924
	Thomas Beecham 1927
	Geoffrey Toye 1928
Summer Night on the River	Beecham 1928
	Toye 1929
Brigg Fair	Goossens 1923
	Beecham 1928–29
	Toye 1928
In a Summer Garden	Toye 1928
A Song Before Sunrise	Barbirolli 1929
The Walk to the Paradise Garden	Beecham 1927
	Toye 1929
Sea Drift	Anthony Bernard, with Roy Henderson 1929
Hassan, (incidental music – 9 items)	Percy Fletcher 1923
Dance Rhapsody No.1	Henry Wood 1923
Caprice & Elegy	Eric Fenby with Beatrice Harrison 1930
Serenade from Hassan	Beatrice and Margaret Harrison 1929
	Lionel Tertis 1929
Violin Sonata No.1	May Harrison and Arnold Bax 1929
Violin Sonata No.2	Albert Sammons and Evlyn Howard-Jones 1924
	Lionel Tertis and George Reeves arr. for viola 1929
Cello Sonata	Beatrice Harrison and Harold Craxton 1926
Piano Pieces, Preludes and Dance for Harpsichord	Evlyn Howard-Jones 1929
Songs	
Cradle Song, The Nightingale, Twilight Fancies	Dora Labbette and Thomas Beecham 1929
To Daffodils	Muriel Brunskill 1925
Venevil, Twilight Fancies.	Leila Megane 1926

Film fees

The use of music in connection with cinematograph films was not subject to the compulsory licence that covered music on records for retail sale. Before the coming of the talkies, music was provided by live musicians. In 1929 the Music Publishers Association made an agreement with the Western Electric Co. Ltd to allow records of music belonging to MPA members to be played in British cinemas on payment of

1½d per seat capacity of the cinemas concerned. When music was specially recorded onto the soundtrack of the film, a synchronisation payment was normally paid for the right to record, with performing fees to be collected later as well. One can see from the enquiries from Mentor Films in 1934, when the company was exploring the possibility of making a film of the Keller novella of *A Village Romeo and Juliet*, using some of the Delius music, rather than a film of the opera itself, that Mentor was not prepared to pay a synchronisation fee.

Grand Rights fees

Grand Rights, (grands droits), are stage performing rights, as opposed to Small Performing Rights, (petits droits), rights in non-stage music. Small performing rights are normally handled by performing right societies. Grand Rights, the rights in operas, ballets etc., are handled direct by the music publisher. Publishers aim nowadays for a royalty of ten per cent of the gross box office, to be shared between composer, librettist and publisher. Although there is no evidence of the level of royalties paid for Delius operatic performances in his lifetime, it was probably ten per cent, as with Richard Strauss. The Harmonie contract for *A Village Romeo and Juliet* gave Delius 90 per cent of fees received, and the 1921 contract with Universal, 85 per cent of the fees received for performances in Germany or in German theatres in Austria, with 80 per cent for all other performances. The *Fennimore and Gerda* contract gave Delius 90 per cent and 80 per cent. As Delius wrote the libretti for *A Village Romeo and Juliet* and *Fennimore and Gerda*, there was no share for him to pass on. There is also no evidence of any payment to Keary on performances of *Koanga*.

Royalties on the sale or hire of performing material in connection with stage performances were covered by the publishing contracts.

US Copyright in Delius's Lifetime

The first US Copyright Act, based on the British 1709 Act was passed in 1790. Delius's first work published, *Zum Carnival*, could not have been registered in his name, as Delius was neither a US citizen, nor 'residing there'. Hence the registration is in the name of the dedicatee. The first International US Copyright Act, the Chace Act of 1891, included a provision for reciprocal agreements with other countries. Such arrangements were made with the UK in 1891 and Germany in 1892. It should be remembered that the USA was not a signatory to the Berne Convention, and that any reciprocal arrangements referred to works by nationals of the countries concerned. Reciprocity under Berne was on the basis of the country of first publication.

Under the US Copyright Act of 1909, the term of copyright was set at 28 years from publication, with the right of renewal for a further 28 years. For evidence of early registration of Delius works by Harmonie, Leuckart and Universal see later.

Financial

No royalty statements have survived from Delius's lifetime, and it is only through the correspondence possible to get a feel of the sums involved. It is strange that Delius, who had a keen financial sense, signed the Harmonie contracts on the basis of a split of profits, which inevitably led to disputes, but perhaps that was all that was on offer. We have glimpses of the sort of fees charged by both Harmonie and Universal, but we don't know how the term 'profit' was interpreted by Harmonie: was it per work? And given that Harmonie only started printing in 1906, could origination and printing costs have been recovered by 1911? Notwithstanding this uncertainty, it is clear that Harmonie were paying money to Delius, and that he thought it was not enough.

Although it is not possible to construct a complete schedule of publishing royalties earned by the composer during his lifetime, we do have a record of PRS fees received from 1920, and total Trust income received from the time of the setting up of the Delius Trust in 1936 to date. Any such list must be treated with caution, but nevertheless the figures give a good indication of the level of earnings. Delius works published in his lifetime were protected by copyright throughout Europe until December 1984, 50 years after the end of the year of his death. There was then a gap until, on 1 November 1995, rights in these works were revived throughout the EC, under European Directive 93/98 on the Duration of Copyright, for the balance of 70 years after his death: that is, to 31 December 2004. Meanwhile, while the works fell into the public domain in Europe in January 1985, they were protected in Japan for a further 3,794 days. Works written by citizens of the Allied countries received an extension over the 50-year Japanese copyright period, representing the period between the declaration of war on 8 December 1941, following Pearl Harbour and the Peace Treaty signed on 28 April 1952. Some works were also protected in the USA after 1984.

Royalties on sales of printed music can never have been of great economic significance to Delius or many other twentieth-century classical composers. It was the coming of fees from public performance and broadcasting and from commercial gramophone records that was important. These new sources of royalties transformed the lives of many successful classical composers. Although there are many references in the body of the correspondence to payments from publishers and collecting societies, they are not enough to enable any useful annual figures to be produced until 1920, when Delius joined the PRS. Neither the records of GDT, which paid fees to Delius before 1914, nor those of Universal Edition have survived. In compiling tables there is also the problem of interpreting the figures that survive: are they, for instance for calendar or tax years?

The sources of the historical fee information are a sheet from the handwritten PRS royalties ledger, a single sheet headed 'Statement of Royalties Received by the Trust', of unknown provenance covering 1936, the first year when PRS distributed fees to the newly formed Trust, up to 1962, and occasional information in the early Trust files or correspondence. From then on there are, with some gaps, annual Trust reports, which after a few years give a breakdown of the source of the income. Interpreting these has been difficult. Up to 1979, when the Musicians Benevolent Fund became the co-Trustee, figures were compiled by tax year. After 1979 they are by calendar year. The change is not material, as PRS did not make distributions during January to April. From 1979, we have all the annual reports.

How did Delius do compared to other British composers? During their lifetime, the PRS fees earned by Elgar and Delius seem to have been roughly the same. In 1931 Delius received £241 against £221 for Elgar. In the calendar year 1935 Elgar received £1,153 to Delius's £899 for the 1936 tax year. However, as Novello did not join PRS until 1936, performing fees on Novello works are not indicated. Cyril Ehrlich, in his history of the Performing Right Society, *Harmonious Alliance,* published in 1989, produces a chart of PRS fees to which we have added the Delius figures.

	Bridge	**Delius**	**Holst**	**Ketèlby**
1927	126	89	31	468
1930	168	241	119	1,630
1935	295	899	407	2,733
1940	605	967	648	3,493
1945	476	187	897	2,577
1950	956	1,986	1,704	2,906
1955	781	5,515	6,546	3,641
1960	569	3,153	4,563	3,168
1965	865	5,757	8,616	5,221
1970	1,482	7,844	13,027	5,269
1975	3,218	16,290	31,590	7,470
1980	17,220	24,845	58,080	12,061
1985	18,582	47,297	134,935	21,079

In considering the above figures it should be remembered that in the case of Bridge, most of the PRS income would have come from his share of performances of Britten's *Variations on a Theme of Frank Bridge*, and in the case of Holst, from *The Planets.* There would have been other sources of income for Delius that we cannot estimate. Mechanical income, of which we have no record up to 1948, and thereafter only intermittent figures up to 1980, would have been much lower than PRS fees. Grand Rights fees and royalties on printed music would have come through the publishers.

There are occasional insights worth noting, such as this schedule from the early Delius Trust files. Figures are in pounds.

Tax Year	**PRS**	**MCPS**	**Augener**	**OUP**	**B&H**	**Total**
1948/49	2,905	206	49	105	367	3,632
1949/50	2,986	238	34	155	635	4,047
1950/51	3,767	291	24	132	296	4,510
1951/52	3,895	371	36	145	428	4,875
1952/53	3,343	239	41	97	313	4,033
1953/54	3,539	208	70	71	334	4,222

Delius also had investments spread around the world of which we know very little. Eric Fenby wrote that he was, as behoves a Yorkshireman, very close about his personal circumstances. Stephen Lloyd, in his biography of Balfour Gardiner records Gardiner as noting in 1923 that as a result of the war, Delius was in financial straits and that the Deliuses might have had to sell the house in Grez. He bought the house 'for a large sum', FF 70,000, documents being drawn up to allow Frederick and Jelka to live in the house rent free until the second death. Medical expenses would have been high, and Delius's letters give the impression of someone who liked to travel well. It is interesting to note that in 1934, when Delius's PRS fees alone were £311, it has been estimated that a clerical worker earned £193 a year, a teacher £480, and a solicitor £1,238.

A schedule of earnings and a selection of publishing contracts are given in the Appendices.

Chapter Two

Delius and his Publishers: A Historical Summary to 1934

As is not unusual when studying a composer's publishing history, Delius's first chapter recites a long list of more-or-less fruitless enquiries and their associated refusals. Few young composers indeed have been as fortunate as, for example, Sergei Rachmaninoff, whose ops. 0, 1 and 2 were purchased within months of their completion by a publisher who subsequently remained loyal to his protégé for the rest of the former's life. Even fewer, perhaps, shared the fate of Delius – unusual for so great a composer in that only by his forty-fifth year was he first to see any of his major scores in print, though by then he could look back on a decade of public performance, and the accumulation of over twelve hundred pages of operatic full score. The opening paragraphs of the present study, then, must be devoted to the years preceding that breakthrough, by examining the history of those sadly-few publications which punctuated Delius's continuous early efforts to sell his wares.

The earliest of Delius's compositions to appear during his lifetime was the polka for piano solo *Zum Carnival*. According to Beecham, who presumably had the information from Delius himself, since no other source has been uncovered, this 'was published at the beginning of 1885 in Jacksonville' [Fla.] (by A.B. Campbell). Only two copies of this piece are known for certain to have survived the disastrous fire in that city in 1901; one is in the Haydon Burns Library of Jacksonville, the other in the Library of Congress, Washington DC. Both these copies clearly claim copyright in the name of the dedicatee, Delius's friend William Jahn, and both are dated 1892. As the first international US Copyright Act dates from 1891, this could explain a re-publication at a later date (by which time Delius was far away) without disproving the truth of Beecham's statement which logically dates the first issue from a time when Delius was still in America.

The first of Delius's works to be published in England consists of an album of *5 Lieder (aus dem Norwegischen)*, dedicated to Frau Nina Grieg and issued by Augener & Co in London in 1890. These songs had been composed in 1888 and the MS was immediately sent to Grieg, whose reaction was enthusiastic. On Grieg's visit to London earlier that year to play his Piano Concerto he stayed with George Augener, the British agent for his Leipzig publishers C.F. Peters, and probably introduced Delius to Augener; the subsequent publication of the songs by the latter was no doubt a result. (With Grieg on this visit was also Max Abraham, head of the Peters firm, but if he and Delius were introduced by Grieg, the outcome was less fruitful, as will be seen in due course.) No contract or correspondence appears to have survived to document the terms of the 1890 Augener transaction, although the publishing contract would no doubt have followed the form of that for the

1892 Augener publications which followed. The indifferent English translation and failure to interline words after the first verse inevitably rendered this original edition somewhat less than 'user-friendly'; however, two years later Delius wrote to Augener offering two further sets of songs.

Augener duly issued these *3 songs, the words by Shelley* in 1892, closely followed by a set of *7 Lieder (aus dem Norwegischen)*, the latter dedicated to Nina Grieg; but whereas the 1890 album remains in their (successor's) catalogue to the present day, the later publishing history of the two 1892 books is the most tortuous to be found amongst any of Delius's works. Five letters, each signed by William Augener, document their withdrawal by Delius from that company.

Meanwhile Max Abraham makes a fleeting appearance in the saga. Evidently influenced by Grieg to examine some of Delius's works, his letter of 2 February 1891 firmly rejects the appearance of songs until 'you have made a name for yourself with other works'.[1] Two years later Delius sent him a major chamber work, the three-movement Sonata in B for violin and piano, a work stated by Grieg to be 'full of talent, in particular (that) the adagio is wonderful'. Grieg had suggested some rewriting (possibly some enharmonic simplification, in view of the many sharps involved) to ease the problem of reading, and Abraham seized on this as an excuse for a further rejection of Delius's work, complaining that the form was 'too free, the key is changed too frequently and the first and last movements are so difficult to play that reasonably large sales for the work are unthinkable'.

A little later, Christian Sinding, who had been a fellow-student of Delius at Leipzig reported to Delius (16 April 1893) that Grieg's 'words have been quite misconstrued, and it was his wish that the sonata should be printed'. He really was pretty angry with Dr Abraham, whom Sinding summed up as a 'sly old fox'. Abraham's quick change of feet in Delius's case was not reflected in his treatment of Sinding, the output of whose 'song and piano piece factory' was immediately issued by his firm with an indiscriminate abandon only equalled by subsequent almost total neglect.

For the rest of the nineteenth century, despite Delius's increasing industry as a composer of works on the larger scale and the welcome commencement from 1897 onwards of fairly regular public performance, publications continued to be mainly confined to isolated songs. In July 1896 a *Mélodie de F. Delius sur des vers de Paul Verlaine* 'Le ciel est, par-dessus le toit' was published in Paris in *L'Aube*, 1e Année, no. 4. (The last 11 bars in this issue differ completely from its later republication.) The same year a set of '*5 chansons, musique de Fritz Delius*' was issued by L. Grus fils in Paris. This collection included two of the Seven Songs (*7 Lieder aus dem Norwegischen*) withdrawn from Augener in 1895, one transposed to a lower key; one of the Shelley songs (also transposed down); a song to Emmanuel Geibel's words 'O schneller mein Ross' written in 1888, and another Verlaine song 'Il pleure dans mon coeur'. Finally, in June 1899, another of the Seven Songs appeared in *The Dome*, vol. 3, 'reproduced by arrangement'. By then, however, a major step (as far as performance was concerned) had been taken when Delius arranged for a lengthy

---

1 Lionel Carley, *Delius, A Life in Letters*, Scolar Press, (Aldershot) 1983, vol. 1, letter no. 73.

concert programme, which surveyed his major compositions to date, to be given at St. James's Hall, London, on 30 May 1899.

Perhaps understandably, Delius's discouragement at his publishing problems comes to the surface during this period: 'my money matters are just as bad as ever, nay! even worse. I cannot sell a song; it seems ridiculous when one comes to think of it but I cannot make a fiver' (Delius to Jutta Bell, 15 July 1896).

In December the same year he wrote to the same correspondent: 'I have written five songs to J.P. Jacobsen's poems – I think they are good. However, I cannot find a publisher who will pay me and I am not going to publish anything more gratis even if I die of starvation.' (The last sentence is a probable reference to the terms of Grus's – and indeed, Augener's – publications.) As a result of his contact with the Concorde Concert Control, who had organised his orchestral concert, the ten songs withdrawn from Augener in 1895 were now re-issued by Concorde, who advertised them in a flier containing selected reviews of the orchestral concert ('1000 of these are going out'). Mention is also found in the correspondence of these copies being handled 'on a royalty' by Stanley Lucas, Weber, Pitt & Hatzfeld (Delius to Jutta Bell 16 June 1899) and, after their being wound up, by Hatzfeld on his own (undated letter from George Clutsam to Delius). Meanwhile Delius approached the Danish publisher Wilhelm Hansen (who had already rejected the incidental music to *Folkeraadet*) 'and mentioned my songs but he did not seem anxious to publish them. Said he had so many things in hand etc'. (Delius to Jelka Rosen, 11 August 1899). He proposed not to visit Schott's 'as I have just had my hair cut very short – it was so hot…I have nichts geniales – in my appearance' (ibid). Meanwhile, Aibl Verlag had refused his work as that of a composer 'new in Germany'. Three years later, a renewed approach to both Hansen and Aibl was equally fruitless; so too were offers to Forberg, Kahnt, Kistner, Lauterbach & Kuhn and Siegel made during 1903–1904.

The year 1905, then, reveals the extraordinary position of a composer of a whole range of major works, choral and orchestral, most of which had won generally acclaimed performance, and of no less than five operas, one of which had recently been staged (using MS material), but whose total published output consisted of less than a couple of dozen songs. This was now to change. Despite Delius's failure to win the Sonzogno prize in 1903 with his one-act melodrama *Margot la Rouge*, steps were subsequently taken to have the vocal score of this work (which was prepared by no less than Maurice Ravel) issued in a lithographed author's edition (propriété des Auteurs; Autogr. Lévy-Lulx, Imp. Crevel Frès., Paris). Fritz Cassirer, who had conducted the performances at Elberfeld of the opera *Koanga* in 1904, was planning to set up a new opera house in Berlin, and was equally determined to include *A Village Romeo and Juliet* in his opening season. Although the Komische Oper did open in November 1905 and performances of Delius's score were originally planned for March 1906, the event did not in fact materialise until February 1907. It may well be, however, that these plans encouraged Delius to arrange, in anticipation, private publication in Paris of a similar vocal score of *A Village Romeo and Juliet* to follow that already issued for *Margot la Rouge.* When this was duly carried out, Jelka's German translation was included in the text (and her liaison with the printers on difference in French and German usages ensured accuracy in the finished result).

Meanwhile, Delius had completed his chef d'oeuvre *A Mass of Life* (for the choice from Nietzsche's *Zarathustra* poems, Fritz Cassirer's assistance was accepted) and the slightly-earlier *Sea Drift* had received its world premiere at the Tonkünstlerfest of the Allgemeine Deutsche Musikverein at Essen in May 1906. Here at last it seemed clear that the composer would no longer be denied a position of significance, and an approach was made to him in early 1906 by Alexander Jadassohn, head of the recently set up publishing house of Harmonie Verlag, Berlin, with a view to commencing preparation and issue of Delius's most recent major scores forthwith. Contracts were duly signed as follows:

20 February 1906	*Appalachia*; *Sea Drift*
27 March 1906	*Five Songs*
11 March 1907	*A Village Romeo and Juliet*
8 April 1907	*A Mass of Life*
17 June 1907	*Piano Concerto*

These contracts granted publishing rights to Harmonie for the world for the life of copyright. Delius for his part, as a member of GDT, reserved his performing rights, as he was bound to do under his membership agreement. Delius was to receive 50 per cent of profits, undefined as to how calculated and when paid.

The full scores of all these works were printed by lithography from hand-copied originals; vocal and piano scores, however, were conventionally engraved.

All the Harmonie contracts, as indeed all the others Delius signed with German publishers (though not those with their English counterparts) contained the clause: 'The original manuscript remains with the publishers as their property.'

Transfer of a work between publishers at a subsequent date apparently does not necessarily include transfer of the manuscript; hence it is perhaps not surprising that the final manuscripts used as *Stichvorlagen* for the above group of works, with one significant exception, are at present untraced – if indeed they still survive. The exception is *A Mass of Life*, of which Delius's two-volume manuscript (formerly in the possession of Sir Thomas Beecham) is now in the British Library; a copyist's copy remains in the archive of Universal Edition (London).

Despite the dates on the above contracts, *A Village Romeo and Juliet* did not appear in printed form from Harmonie until 1910. (Both for the Berlin premiere in 1907 and even for Beecham's London staging in 1910, the privately-printed earlier vocal score had to be used by the performers.) Three slightly earlier-composed unaccompanied choruses also appeared in 1910, possibly delayed owing to the need to include a piano part for rehearsal purposes, as stressed to Harmonie by their English agents, Breitkopf & Härtel. The latter firm, meanwhile, had taken over the *7 Songs from the Norwegian* and the *Three Shelley Songs* after the failure of their earlier publishers. Increasing friction in his dealings with Harmonie may explain Delius's hope in 1907 that Breitkopf & Härtel might publish his latest, purely orchestral, work: *Brigg Fair*. From the evidence of Breitkopf & Härtel's letter dated 5 February 1908, in which Breitkopf declined to take *Brigg Fair* because Harmonie had first refusal there was probably a clause under which Harmonie had first refusal on future works.

By 1909 another publisher was involved in Delius's musical affairs – F.E.C. Leuckart of Leipzig. Contracts were drafted with this house to cover the following works:

Songs of Sunset

Brigg Fair

In a Summer Garden

Dance Rhapsody No. 1

Paris

The Song of the High Hills

The first score to be published was that of the orchestral work *Paris*, which appeared in 1909 in lithograph form similar to those already issued by Harmonie. Maybe the masters had already been prepared by Harmonie. All the remaining works were conventionally engraved and appeared during 1910–1911 except the last item, which followed a little later. As regards the history of the final manuscripts used as *Stichvorlagen* for the works in question, again it seems that their survival is in most cases unlikely, since some of Leuckart's archive is known to have been destroyed during the Second World War.

Again, however, Beecham had the original (and a copy) of *Brigg Fair*; though in this case its history since 1952 and present whereabouts remain undetermined. However, manuscripts of slightly earlier versions of most of the other Leuckart works still survive and are now in the British Library.

Next, contact was established in 1910 between Delius and Dr Gerhard Tischer, of the recently established firm of Tischer & Jagenberg based in Cologne. Contracts were signed for a number of song publications; the *7 Norwegian* and *3 Shelley Songs* were now re-engraved and so appeared in a definitive form (though the new English translations, at first sometimes laughably faulty, were subsequently improved) and the two Verlaine settings which had appeared separately in Paris in 1896 were joined by a specially-written third. All these occupied T & J's edition numbers 10–22 inclusive, and whilst they were being prepared, T & J continued to issue the earlier ten songs using the remaining original sheets but within their own newly-designed wrappers. It was Delius's wish – not necessarily carried out by his German publishers – that the original words should appear above the translations, and his correspondence with Dr Tischer goes into considerable detail over some of the proposed versions for which he insisted on Jelka's being substituted. He allowed the Verlaine songs to appear with a German translation but refused that settings of this poet (or of Nietzsche) should appear in English. Tischer wisely added the parenthesis '(where available)' to the clause defining the ownership of the manuscripts; except for those of the Shelley songs, which remain to this day unlocated, all the remainder have by now reached the British Library, though not all by the same route. In 1912 T & J issued a major orchestral score, (purchased outright for a lump sum) the final and definitive version of *Life's Dance* (which was engraved by Breitkopf & Härtel) and, two years later, the two most famous of Delius's orchestral works – *On hearing the first Cuckoo in Spring* and *Summer Night on the River.* Whereas the manuscript of *Life's Dance* returned to the composer, for some reason that of the two short pieces used by the engraver has never come to light and its present location and indeed survival remains in question. T & J's contract of 9 December 1913 not only covered the two short orchestra pieces but also another five new songs, though it was 1915 before these appeared, and by then the First World War had broken out.

Meanwhile a minor publishing transaction led Delius to sell (for £10) *Two Songs for Children* to the American publisher Silver, Burdett & Co. in 1913, for exclusive American use in their educational *Progressive Music Series*, whilst retaining to himself all other rights. (In the event, only one of the songs appeared in the series in question, in 1916.)

Also in 1913 begins the association with Universal-Edition of Vienna which lasted for the remainder of Delius's life. Universal became his principal publisher, and his correspondence with Emil Hertzka and Alfred Kalmus is voluminous and detailed; fortunately it survives almost complete. Performances, rights, availability of copies for sale, quality of copied parts or of printed issues, selling prices or hire fees, royalties, translations, publicity material, arrangements, textual details; these are some of the subjects covered, often at considerable length and with considerable animation. The first work to be discussed was the opera *Fennimore and Gerda*, performance of which was originally planned to take place in Cologne in 1914. Because of the outbreak of the war that year it was delayed until 1919 (the unique manuscript full score surviving in the meanwhile…). However, Universal had already published *An Arabesque* in 1913–14 (though it was 1920 before the full score appeared).

Before tracing the later stages of Delius's association with Universal it may be as well to record other publishing ventures resulting from the War. In May 1915 Beecham purchased four works from Delius, who was suffering financially from the fact that his principal publishers were now enemy aliens, and arranged for their publication in England. The Violin Sonata (completed in 1914) and the piano score of the early *Légende* were issued by Forsyth Bros. in 1916–17; three songs appeared from Winthrop Rogers in 1919 and the orchestral *North Country Sketches* of 1913–14 from Augener in 1921–23. Subsequently Winthrop Rogers also issued the Cello Sonata in 1919 and the two part songs *To be sung of a summer night on the water* in 1920. Augener later published the series of major scores composed during those years: Violin Concerto (1916) in 1919–21, Double Concerto (1915–16) in 1920–22, *A Song before Sunrise* (1918) in 1922 as well as the String Quartet of 1916–17, *Dance Rhapsody* no. 2 (1916) and *Eventyr* (1917) in 1921–23. On the dismemberment of Augener in the 1960s, most of the Delius manuscripts were rescued for the Delius

Trust through the prompt action of Ernest Chapman; those outstanding – *Dance Rhapsody No. 2* and the String Quartet – ultimately joined their companions, first in the Trust's archive and subsequently in the British Library.

Immediately after the cessation of hostilities in 1918, plans to stage *Fennimore and Gerda* were resuscitated, now in Frankfurt where it appeared in late 1919; material was prepared and revised by Universal though the printed full score did not appear until 1926. The *Requiem*, begun in 1914, was published in 1920 and the recently written Cello Concerto in 1922. Also, after long preparation, the run of successful performances of *Hassan* with Delius's incidental music commenced in 1923, first at Darmstadt, then in London; piano scores were issued accordingly in 1923 and 1924. (The manuscripts of all the Universal works were deposited in the British Library by Dr Kalmus in 1964, – except for the *Hassan* material, which however reached there ultimately, though by comparatively devious routes.)

Meanwhile two major regroupings had taken place in 1921. By the first of these, under discussion since 1913, all those of Delius's works originally published by Harmonie were finally transferred to the Universal catalogue under new contracts between that firm and the composer. Also, an arrangement was made whereby his works in the Leuckart catalogue were subsequently controlled under licence by Universal. In a further move, Universal issued their own newly engraved editions of the works assigned to Winthrop Rogers. Universal's London agents in 1925 were Curwen, to be followed a few years later by Cranz.

With the waning of Delius's physical powers in the 1920s a number of inevitably smaller projects were carried out, with the increasing assistance of Jelka. A harpsichord *Dance*, first issued in the opening number of *Music & Letters* in January 1920, subsequently appeared from Universal: so did an album of *Five Piano Pieces* a few years later. *Three Preludes* for piano were published by the Anglo-French Music Co. in 1923; Universal re-engraved them for their own edition for European circulation. In 1924 Oxford University Press's newly set up Music Department issued the *Two Songs for Children* and another more recently finished unaccompanied chorus in their Choral Song Series. Lastly, also in 1924, the second Violin Sonata was published by Hawkes & Son, to be followed by a (compositional) silence until the arrival in 1928 of Eric Fenby in an endeavour, ultimately unexpectedly successful, to assist Delius in the completion of those scores perforce left unfinished by his total incapacity of the previous years.

In 1931 all those works previously published by Tischer & Jagenberg were transferred to Oxford University Press, with whom Delius accordingly signed new contracts. The same year Hawkes & Son amalgamated with Boosey & Co, and had already taken over Winthrop Rogers in 1925. It was under the Winthrop Rogers imprint, however, that Boosey & Hawkes published that last flowering of the 'Fenby works', beginning in 1931 (*A Song of Summer*, *Irmelin Prelud*e, *Fantastic Dance*, *Songs of Farewell*, Violin Sonata no. 3, *Caprice* and *Elegy*, *Cynara*, *A Late Lark* and *Idyll*). The manuscripts of all these were passed to the Trust's Archive in 1976, except for the works originally published by Winthrop Rogers which are thought to have been destroyed during the Second World War. All the others are now in the British Library.

With the agreements between Boosey & Hawkes and Universal, for B & H to acquire Universal's rights in their Delius works, negotiations for which started in 1937 and were only completed in the 1950s, the return of Delius's music to his native land, which started with the Oxford University Press agreement of 1931, was effectively completed – though the works originally sold to Leuckart remained in the Universal catalogue. So the position was established on the basis of which all the works were handled by their current publishers, or their assignees, when the Collected Edition was finally launched.

Chapter Three

The Management of Delius's Publishing Affairs, 1934–2004

Delius's Will

Delius died at the house in Grez-sur-Loing on 10 June 1934, after more than a decade of gradual physical decline.

On 31 August 1918, in Paris, the Deliuses had drawn up wills, which were witnessed by their friends Henry and Marie Clews; the executors were to be Henry Balfour Gardiner, Percy Grainger and Philip Heseltine. 'In the event of their simultaneous deaths, everything. . . was to be channelled into the foundation of a trust to help young English composers...'[1] However, on 27 September 1922, back in Grez, Delius made another and simpler will, by which he left everything to his wife Jelka.[2] This was clear and unambiguous – provided only that Delius predeceased his wife.

The uncertainty surrounding this contingency came to an acute climax during 1934. Jelka Delius had cancer and despite her stubborn determination to carry on during what seemed likely to be her husband's final decline, she was forced to enter hospital for a major operation in May that year. A flurry of letters etc. given in Carley, vol. 2 records the confusion that this caused, and Delius's letter to Balfour Gardiner on 19 May asked him to be the executor of a revised will drafted that day, in the event of Delius now outliving his wife. In such an event this draft would have entrusted Eric Fenby with books, printed scores and manuscripts, whilst a concert scheme featuring Delius's own works and those of deserving young British composers was to be handled by Sir Thomas Beecham. Gardiner and Fenby hurried to Delius's bedside, where he reaffirmed these wishes, which they duly noted down.

In the event however, Jelka returned home in time to be with her husband throughout his last hours – but as his final wishes had not been put into legal form before his death, all his possessions passed to his wife in accordance with the will of 1922. In fact she made sufficient recovery to be able to take a decisive part in the affairs of her husband's estate before the inevitable final course of her disease set in. She died on 28 May 1935, a mere two days after her husband's reburial at Limpsfield in Surrey.

1 Carley/2/194.
2 Carley/2/250.

The Setting-up of the Delius Trust

Soon after Delius's death, confronted with the need to ensure appropriate settlement of his musical estate, Jelka turned to Beecham. Two long and remarkable letters to him dated 2 and 17 September 1934, never previously published but given here complete, reveal her frank comments on the persons concerned. It was unfortunate that, in her efforts to assert her authority to make provision for what she and Beecham saw as the way forward, rejecting Delius's instructions to Balfour Gardiner and Eric Fenby, she caused hurt to two friends who had supported and indeed housed her and her husband. Beecham's advice, in view of her short expectation of life was that a trust be set up on her death in order to handle the performance, re-publication and recording of Delius's musical legacy; in his opinion the proposed concert scheme was already covered by the Patron's Fund of the Royal College of Music. Thus the first such official body dedicated to the exploitation of a single composer's works was born and in 1936 the (Madame Jelka) Delius Trust came into being under the terms of her Will dated 27 May 1935.

In those days, before the setting up of the Charity Commission, a trust would be deemed charitable only in retrospect. Until 1945, when the Inland Revenue relented and agreed that the Trust was charitable under s. 37 of the Income Tax Act 1918, income tax was paid on all Trust income. However there was still uncertainty in the Trustees' minds as to the long-term position of the Trust. Under the terms of Jelka's will, once it appeared that the intentions behind the setting up of the Trust had been fulfilled, it should be wound up, the residue going to her brother; there might be a claim. This uncertainty was also apparent to Boosey & Hawkes. Not only was Boosey & Hawkes's ownership of the Delius works it had purchased from Universal being queried by Alfred Kalmus of Universal, but also the company was being asked to commit funds to the printing of Delius's music which it might not recover. To regularise matters the Trust went to the High Court to ask for a declaration of the Trust's charitable status. In an important judgment in the High Court, Chancery Division, on 12 March 1957, Mr. Justice Roxburgh ruled that this Trust, set up as it was by Jelka Delius's will towards the advancement of the musical works of her late husband, was in fact a valid charitable trust – no less valid, in the judge's words, because the name involved was Delius and not Beethoven. In all fairness it should be said that surviving correspondence shows that the Rosen family never had any intention of trying to upset the Trust, a point made clear in the High Court by Counsel representing them. A further hearing before Mr. Justice Wilberforce on 8 June 1964 set up a Scheme for the regulation and management of the Trust, assisted by a panel of advisers, consequent on the death (in 1961) of Sir Thomas Beecham, who had been the sole surviving adviser. (Valuable advice was given during their terms of office by Sir Thomas Armstrong, senior adviser 1961 to 1994, and Major Norman K. Millar, adviser and later co-Trustee from 1961 to 1991.) The Trust Deed was further varied on 25 October 1991 and 1 April 1997 in order to broaden the Trust's objectives; the latter revision also permits the promotion, under certain circumstances, of the work of young composers, thus reflecting what Delius had himself originally envisaged. Eric Fenby was never invited to become either a

Trustee or an Adviser, although he carried out valuable work on behalf of the Trust and continued to promote the composer's works.

The Complete Edition

One of the three main terms of the Trust deed of 1935 specified the 'publication and issue of a uniform edition of the whole body of the works of my late husband... under the editorship of Sir Thomas Beecham'. The lengthy history of this project, which was begun in the 1950s but only completed in 1993, (with some supplements appearing into 1999) has been described in Robert Threlfall's *Editorial Report on the Collected Edition* (Delius Trust/Boosey & Hawkes, 1990).

Sir Thomas Beecham's Declaration of 1947 concerning certain works

A minute dated 31 March 1947 of a meeting of Trust officers refers to certain works by Delius which Sir Thomas Beecham then stated had been given to him by the composer for his 'sole use and as [his] property' in 1929. It was agreed that he should make a formal declaration to this effect, in case the Trust be confronted with any counterclaims to ownership and this he did on 29 July 1949. The works were:

Florida

Summer Evening

Sleigh Ride

Autumn (unidentified)

Over the hills and far away

Folkeraadet

Marche Caprice

The Magic Fountain

Spring Morning

Scherzo

In 1955 a separate agreement was reached between Sir Thomas and the Trust whereby Sir Thomas gave up 50 per cent of his interest in *The Magic Fountain* for a 50 per cent interest in the opera *Irmelin*, which he had conducted in Oxford. Some of the works were later published by Sir Thomas; others remained unpublished at his death. The manuscripts not already in the Trust's Archive passed to it in 1982 as part of an agreement with the Beecham Trust, together with a vast amount of other Delius manuscript material which was also in Sir Thomas's hands at the time of his death, but was not involved in the 1947 Declaration.

The transaction recorded in Beecham's 1947 Declaration was unusual. There was no formal assignment of copyright by Delius and as a member of the PRS he could not have assigned his performing right. Correspondence in the PRS archives shows that publishers with which Beecham published the works entered into correspondence with PRS to see if it would accept that one of their composer members had given away some of his copyrights. Much against its rules, PRS reluctantly agreed to pay the composer's share of royalties on the works to someone other than the composer or his estate. Nevertheless it must be stressed that the Trust had accepted the Declaration.

This was not the only such transaction between Delius and Beecham. In 1915, because of Delius's financial problems during the war, as a British composer whose works had chiefly been published in Germany, the copyrights therefore being impounded in Britain under the Trading with the Enemy Acts, an agreement was drawn up between the two whereby Beecham bought and published four of Delius's then recent works, the copyright to revert to the composer once the expenses of publication were paid off.

This was an honourable transaction. The copyrights duly reverted to Delius but although some payments were made under the agreement, it is not clear whether Beecham, who ran into financial problems, was able to make them all.

The review of Delius's publishing affairs necessitated by the 1995 copyright revival led to a re-assessment of the terms of the 1947 Declaration. Unsure as to where royalties on the works in the 1947 declaration should be paid, the Delius Trust took legal advice. In order to tidy matters up, the Trust then successfully claimed that under s. 5 (2) of the 1911 Copyright Act, the works in question having been assigned to Beecham during the composer's lifetime, they would revert to his estate 25 years after his death. A settlement was made with Lady Beecham and the Beecham Trust under which the Delius Trust also acquired the Beecham interest in his arrangements of Delius works. All the works concerned remained with their original publishers. A further explanation of Reversionary Rights is given later in this section.

The Delius Trust Music Manuscript Archive

All such material as was in the Archive at the time was described by Rachel Lowe in her *Catalogue of the Music Archive of the Delius Trust*, published by the Trust in 1974. The receipt of the extensive Beecham Accession in 1982 and various minor acquisitions were similarly documented in Robert Threlfall's *Frederick Delius: A Supplementary Catalogue* (part 2), likewise published in 1986. After an extensive programme of microfilming was completed, the primary Music Manuscript Archive, that is that portion in Delius's own hand or in certain cases in that of his wife or Eric

Fenby, was transferred to the British Library in 1995, thus realising Jelka Delius's wish that it should go to 'Museums or libraries where people could see them'.[3]

Sets of the spools of microfilm were simultaneously lodged with the Royal Academy of Music and the University of York to facilitate study by scholars.

The Ownership of Universal Edition

Following Jelka's death, the management of her interest in the Delius copyrights passed in due course to the Delius Trust and was soon complicated by the political situation in Austria. The most valuable works had been assigned to Universal in Vienna, which also administered, as part owners, the six Leuckart works.

Up to 1939, Boosey & Hawkes, having superseded Cranz as Universal's agent in the UK, represented the Universal Delius works for Great Britain, the Empire and the Americas. Control of copyrights in the USA required more positive action than in the countries of the Berne Convention, of which the USA was not one. Under the US Copyright Act of 1909, the term of copyright was set at 28 years from publication, which had to be registered with the Library of Congress, with the right of renewal for a further 28 years. The Harmonie and Leuckart works had been registered in the USA before the 1914–18 war, there being copyright treaties between the USA and both the UK and Germany under which each country protected the copyright in works by nationals of the other country. Universal had also registered its works in the USA. From 1936, Boosey & Hawkes registered renewals in its own name, its ownership being formalised by assignments of rights dated June 1939 and June 1940. But some of the early renewals had been assigned by Universal Vienna to its associate New York company, with the possibility of the royalties being sent back to Vienna. When the Trust found out about this in 1940, it appealed to the Foreign Office for support for its contention that it was wrong for the earnings of a British composer in the USA to be used to the advantage of Germany. In a measured reply, the Under Secretary of State replied to the effect that whereas it was not possible for the UK government to intervene with the US government, it seemed possible the Trust might be able to claim that the assignment to Universal was not wide enough to cover 'broadcasting and analogous rights', giving good ground for legal action there. The Trust had some success in this although at the price of considerable post-war problems with the British Controller of Enemy Property in relation to the ultimate repatriation of the royalties. After the death of Emil Hertzka in 1930, Frau Hertzka had a controlling majority of shares in Universal Vienna. The company had financial problems and discussions were opened in 1937 regarding the possibility of Boosey & Hawkes Ltd. buying into Universal Vienna. These were abandoned when, after the *Anschluss*, the Ministry of Propaganda appointed a State Commissar to whom Frau Hertzka was forced to sell her shares.

However, in 1936, Universal Vienna had formed Universal Ltd., managed by Frau Hertzka's nephew Alfred Kalmus, and transferred to it certain rights for the territory of the British Empire and the Americas. Negotiations between Universal

3 See her letter to Beecham dated 2 September 1934.

Vienna and Boosey & Hawkes Ltd. were later resumed on the possible purchase by Boosey & Hawkes Ltd. of all the shares in Universal Ltd. together with Universal's rights in the works of five composers. These were, rights for the British Empire and the Americas in works of Bartok, Delius and Kodaly, and worldwide rights in works of two 'non-Aryan' composers, Mahler and Weinberger.

The agreement for Boosey & Hawkes Ltd. to purchase Universal Ltd. together with the other rights, was confirmed by the new German owners on 17 August 1939 and ratified in London by the Boosey & Hawkes Ltd. Board on 3 September 1939, too late for the consideration to reach Vienna.

Boosey & Hawkes Ltd. believed that it owned the rights in the Delius Universal works for the territory of the British Empire and the Americas, although, as far as the six Delius works published by Leuckart are concerned, Universal is described in the contract only as an agent for Leuckart. In 1938 Universal Vienna raised with the Trust the matter of mechanical rights, long an irritation to them. Delius had eventually agreed in 1930 to give Universal a 20 per cent share of mechanicals in certain Central European territories and now the Trust agreed to Universal or their agent having a 20 per cent share of mechanicals for the other territories. Alfred Kalmus tried for 30 per cent without success, but in February 1942 the Trust agreed to Boosey & Hawkes retaining 50 per cent of mechanicals in their territory, that being the normal publishers' share at that time.

Although complete royalty records have not survived, the Delius Trust files contain a royalty statement from Universal Vienna covering the payment due of 1065 Austrian Schillings for the period August 1945 to July 1946. When the war was over, as can be seen in Dr Roth's letter to Philip Emanuel, the Trust's lawyer, dated 19 May 1950, (App 22) Frau Hertzka and Alfred Kalmus eventually managed to regain control of Universal and right the wrongs of the forced sale; Boosey & Hawkes's ownership of worldwide rights in the Universal works was confirmed by contract dated 1952. However, as can be seen from Dr Roth's letter, while ownership was in doubt, the Trust was in limbo, unable to persuade Boosey to spend money printing Delius works. As far as one can tell, both PRS and MCPS continued to pay royalties to Boosey & Hawkes during this time.

Ownership of the Term of Copyright under the 1911 Act

Those involved in the management of musical copyrights have constantly to reconcile the original grant of rights with changes in law and practice, which have taken place since the original assignment.

Although the major works were published in Germany, by 1920 Delius had resigned from GDT and joined PRS; and in the 1930s Universal Vienna, which had become by far his most important publisher, transferred its rights in Delius works to Universal Ltd, and thence to Boosey &Hawkes Ltd.

The most practical course will therefore be to consider Delius's rights primarily in relation to the UK 1911 Copyright Act and subsequent legislation.

The 1911 Act

The 1911 Act was passed following the 1909 Copyright Committee that was set up to consider what changes were necessary to UK copyright law to enable the UK to sign the 1906 text of the Berne Convention.

The three most important composer rights to be addressed were copyright, (the reproduction right), the performing right, and the mechanical right. Of these the mechanical right was a new right (for details of which see the earlier section), which under the 1911 Act did not belong to the owner of an assignment made before the Act was passed unless specifically mentioned.

The reproduction and performing rights, as defined in the 1842 Copyright Act, had to be registered separately at Stationers' Hall and could belong to different owners. In defining the scheme of the Act we can do no better than quote from *Joynson Hicks on UK Copyright Law*, published in 1989, by David Lester & Paul Mitchell.

> The Act provided that where any person was immediately before the commencement of the 1911 Act entitled to a particular right as regards any copyright work or to any interest in such a right, he was from the commencement of the Act entitled to a substituted right under the 1911 Act or to the same interest in such a substituted right.

Similar legislation was passed in other Berne Convention countries, but with regard to Delius, his new post-1 July 1912 publishing contracts with Universal (covering the Harmonie and Universal works) and the 1913 Leuckart contract clarified the rights ceded in the new terms. Both publishers had reproduction rights; Delius reserved his performing and mechanical rights in pre- and post-1911 works, although Leuckart later contested this. (See later in this section.)

Term One of the main provisions that UK legislation had to address under Berne was the introduction of a period of years' protection from the death of the author. Under the 1842 Act copyright lasted work by work until the longer of 42 years from publication or 7 years after the death of the composer. Under the 1911 Act the term became from the first of public performance or publication until 50 years after the death of the composer. Under the 1956 Act the term was further defined as being until 50 years after the end of the calendar year in which the composer died.

Under s. 24 of the 1911 Act a publisher of a work assigned to him for life of copyright before 1 July 1912, the commencement date of the 1911 Act, could require a new assignment to convert the original term into the new one, with a proviso. The proviso was that under s. 24 (a) he could not assume ownership of any rights not covered by the original assignment. Any such negotiation was not relevant to Delius and his publishers as post-1912 contracts clarified the situation.

In the case of works assigned during the composer's lifetime, after the commencement date of 1 July 1912, s. 5, the so-called Reversionary Rights clause was relevant. That clause stated that where the composer was the first owner of the copyright, as Delius was, then with certain exceptions that do not apply to Delius works, no grant of any interest in the copyright of a work made by the composer, other than by will, could vest rights in an assignee beyond 25 years from the composer's death. The balance of the 50-year term devolved upon the composer's estate, which could decide whether to retain them, re-assign them to the old publisher, or indeed assign them to a new publisher. Without going into too much detail, works that did not revert included works written as part of a collective work, defined as a newspaper, encyclopedia or a work written in distinct parts by different authors. No post-1912 Delius works came within the provisos which might have prevented a Delius work reverting.

The proviso in s. 5(2) of the 1911 Act was not repeated in the 1956 Copyright Act, although its effect was preserved for assignments made between 1 July 1912 and 1 June 1957, the commencement date of the 1956 Act. Reversion can still be, and sometimes is, claimed today on works that qualify. (See Delius and Leuckart later.)

Reversionary Rights were not an issue until the 1970s and up to 1956 do not rate many lines in Copinger, the standard copyright textbook, as, even if the works did revert, the original publisher could, under s. 3 of the 1911 Act continue to print on payment of a royalty. It was not until the 1970s, when an American lawyer raised the issue with a number of estates, that many publishers realised that they had omitted to secure the reversion. When an estate claimed reversion, it only applied to the UK and those former British Empire territories, mainly Australia, New Zealand, Canada and South Africa, that had incorporated the 1911 Copyright Act into their legislation, albeit not in a uniform manner. Even so, it did present the opportunity to re-group a composer's works together and remove them from a publisher found to be wanting. The Delius Trust's Reversionary Rights Agreement with Boosey & Hawkes Ltd., giving that publisher a continuation of its existing rights for the remaining 25 years, was signed in 1972, 38 years after the composer's death.

In December 1984, UK copyright in Delius works published during his lifetime came to an end, although that was not the end of the story. Up to the commencement of the 1988 Copyright Act in July 1989, works first exploited posthumously were protected for 50 years from the date of first public exploitation or publication in the UK and similarly in other Berne Convention countries, effectively extending the period of copyright.

In Europe some countries gave extended protection to their nationals to cover war years, from which all EU/EEA nationals would now benefit. In the case of France, works in existence at 1 January 1948 and published prior to 31 December 1920 received an extra 14 years and 274 days. Works published between 1 January 1921 and 1 January 1948 received an additional eight years and 122 days. The totals are cumulative, so most Delius works will qualify for the full 14 years and 274 days. Those published or first performed in France before 31 December 1920 will be protected until 1 October 2018 and those published or first performed after 1 January 1921 until 1 May 2012. Belgium gave an additional ten years for works published before 1924: Italy an additional eight years, to 1 May 2012, rescinded in 1996 when Italy introduced a period of 70 years after death and grudgingly re-instituted in 2004. The eight years is the period between the United Kingdom declaring war on Italy on 3 September 1939 and the peace Treaty signed on 27 November 1947.

In Spain, Delius works are protected until 31 December 2014, 80 years after his death, as that was the period in operation when the works were written. After Spain joined the EU on 1 January 1986, the copyright term became life plus 70 years. The USA position is explained later.

In Japan, under the Peace Treaty with the Allied Powers, copyright in works by nationals of the Allied Powers received an additional period of protection in Japan equal to the time between Pearl Harbour and the Treaty. Delius works were therefore protected in Japan until 22 May 1995.

So, after 1984, for varying numbers of years, most Delius works fell into the public domain throughout the European Community, until revived there for the balance of 70 years from the end of the year of the composer's death by the implementation of EC Directive 93/98 on the Duration of Copyright, a move that could not have been anticipated in 1984.

The Harmonisation of the Duration of Copyright in the EC

The pressure to harmonise the term of copyright through the EC came from the record industry. A recording, as opposed to any copyright musical works on a recording, is usually protected by copyright for a period after publication of the record. The period of protection for recordings varied throughout the EC, so that recordings that had become public domain in one member state were often marketed across the EC, undercutting sales of the same recording in territories where it was still protected. Under the EC Directive, authors' rights would last until the expiry of 70 years after death; related rights such as the copyright in recordings would last for 50 years from publication. The main criterion for a work acquiring the life plus 70-year term was that it was protected in at least one member state on 1 July 1995.

By the early 1990s, with the exception of some posthumously published works, all published Delius works were in the public domain throughout the EC and would have remained so had it not been for the Phil Collins case.

The Phil Collins Case and how Delius copyrights came to be revived

In 1983, a concert given by the singer Phil Collins in California had been illegally recorded and the subsequent bootleg records put on sale in Germany, where in due course Phil Collins sued. Had Phil Collins been a German national he would have succeeded, as German law protected its citizens no matter where the performance took place; however the German Court held that as a UK citizen suing in Germany he had no such protection. The case was referred to the European Court of Justice,[4] which held that under the Treaty of Rome Phil Collins was being unfairly discriminated against on grounds of nationality. To show that such discrimination was not unique, the defendants raised the issue of term of protection under the Berne Convention. Under Berne, works first published in a Convention country are protected, without formalities, in the other signatory countries as though they are by their nationals, with one exception. Works do not receive a longer period of protection in another Convention country than they receive in their own. Thus, before European

4 *Phil Collins* v *IMTRAT Handels-GmbH(1993)* 3 CMLR 773 (ECJ); [1994] FSR 166.

harmonisation a work by Richard Strauss published in Germany would receive life + 70 years protection in Germany, but only life + 50 years in the United Kingdom. A work by Delius published in the UK would receive life + 50 years protection in both countries. The European Court of Justice declared this to be discriminatory.

As a result Germany amended its law, to grant nationals of all EC countries the same period of protection in Germany as German composers received. And so it happened that as Delius works came within the criteria laid down in the Directive as being protected in at least one member country on 1 July 1995, the copyrights were revived for the balance of the 70-year period in those EC countries where they had fallen into the public domain 50 years after Delius's death. The basis of the revival was that the owner of the copyright when the works had originally gone out of copyright would own the revival period.

Special provisions were made for acts done while the works were in the public domain, but the revival of copyright necessitated a thorough review by the Trust of its publishing arrangements. New contracts were negotiated with all the publishers involved. Inevitably the review threw up anomalies, in particular in relation to the Leuckart works and the Beecham Declaration.

Leuckart

As can be seen in the letters, the publication of the six Leuckart works was originally covered by separate contracts, under which Delius reserved mechanical and performing rights, as he was bound to as a member of GDT, and was entitled to 50 per cent of profits. In 1913 the separate contracts were consolidated into one, in which Delius sold his publishing rights outright, but by dint of manual crossings out, continued to reserve mechanical and performing rights. In 1921 Leuckart sold 50 per cent of its interest in the six works to Universal, which thereafter administered them. When in 1930 Delius granted Universal a 20 per cent share in mechanicals from Germany, Austria, Czechoslovakia and Switzerland, he specified 'my UE works'. Having at that time only the separate contracts for the six works, the Trust maintained a claim for 100 per cent of mechanicals in the Leuckart works from MCPS, although in 1953 Philip Emanuel wrote to MCPS confirming that when in 1942 the Trust had granted a 50 per cent interest in Delius mechanicals to Boosey & Hawkes, the Leuckart works had been included, as the Trust believed it was the owner of the Leuckart mechanicals.

That is how matters remained until in 1975 Leuckart produced the 1913 contract, which it interpreted as an outright sale of mechanical rights, and put in a claim through GEMA. The Trust took the opposing view, maintaining that the deletions in the 1913 contract had reserved the mechanical rights to Delius. Matters were unresolved when the works went out of copyright at the end of 1984.

When the Delius copyrights were revived in Germany, Leuckart pressed its case again. By this time however the Trust was better prepared and was able to show, with the aid of the original 1913 contract, Jelka Delius's handwritten notes, and, most importantly a postcard in the Grainger Museum in Australia, that Delius had specifically told Jelka to delete his ceding of mechanical rights from the 1913 contract before she signed it.

Apart from this issue, there had been little evidence of contact with Leuckart since it had sold half its rights to Universal, so the Trust took the opportunity to claim Reversionary Rights in the six works, keeping 87.5 per cent of UK mechanicals and settling for a 50 per cent share in the EC outside the UK.

Works remaining in copyright after December 2004

These come into three categories, works remaining in copyright in the USA and Spain; posthumously published works and war year extensions granted in France, Italy and Belgium. War year extensions have already been covered. One ought also to mention for good measure that the copyright period in Mexico is 100 years after death.

Works published in the USA

The term of copyright is complicated by the US decision in 1976 to move from two periods of 28 years from registration of first publication to a pma period. Before the 1978 Copyright Act, copyright in the US ran from registration of first publication, not first performance. The move from the old system to protection lasting until 70 years pma necessitated a number of extensions to works copyrighted under the old rules. Working back from 1976, the situation can be summarised as follows:

Delius works published during his lifetime, not later than 31 December 1905 received 28+28=56 years from registration.

Works published during his lifetime, but after 1 January 1906 and before 31 December 1922 received 28+28 years plus an additional 19-year extension, making 75 years from the date of registration.

> So, *In a Summer Garden*, published and registered in 1911, was protected until 31 December 1986.

Delius works published during the composer's lifetime between 1 January 1923 and 1 January 1978, when the 1978 US Copyright Act took effect, received a further extension of 20 years under the 1998 so-called Sonny Bono legislation, taking their total period of protection to 95 years from the date of registration.

> So, *Songs of Farewell*, published and registered in 1931, will be protected in the US until 31 December 2026.

Works written during the lifetime of a composer on or after 1 January 1978 are protected until 70 years after the composer's death.

Posthumously Exploited Works

The effect of the provisions in the copyright acts relating to posthumous publication is to ensure a minimum period of protection after publication or first performance.

Works by Delius received protection for life + 50 Years under the 1911, 1956 and 1988 Copyright Acts, increased throughout the EC to life + 70 years in 1996, as a result of the Phil Collins case.

But works by Delius first published or first performed posthumously between I January 1935 and 1 August 1989 were further protected for 50 years in the UK from the earliest of publication or first performance, extending the period of protection.

> *Sleigh Ride*, first performed in 1946, received additional protection to December1996. At that point, but for the EC Directive it would have gone out.

The UK 1988 Copyright Act contained an important provision in para. 12(4) of Schedule 1, which was not amended by the 1995 Regulations that brought in the 70-year term. Under that paragraph, '...musical works of which the author has died', unexploited at the end of 1989, ceased to have indefinite protection, but instead received 50 years in the UK from the end of 1989, whether exploited or not, that is, to 31 December 2039.

> The *Negro Songs*, first published in 2004 will be protected in the EC until December 2039.

In the USA a similar provision to that referred to above was introduced in the US 1978 Copyright Act. Posthumous works unpublished as at 1 January 1978 receive 50 years from 1978, whenever they are published.

The situation has been further complicated by the revival of Delius copyrights under the EC Copyright Directive, and the move to life + 70 years. After Germany amended its copyright law in 1993, following the European Court of Justice decision in the Phil Collins case, all works of EU origin qualified for protection in Germany until 70 years from the end of the year in which the composer died, including posthumously exploited works. Thus the three movements of *Florida*, first performed posthumously in 1937, initially protected in Berne countries until the end of December 1987, would have been revived in Germany in 1993, and after 1 July 1995 revived throughout the EC until 31 December 2004.

Neither the EC Directive on harmonisation nor the UK legislation introducing the Directive increased the minimum period of 50 years protection for posthumously exploited works. In the case of Delius works posthumously exploited before 31 December 1954, the 50-year posthumous period is co-terminus with the end of the life + 70 years period, whereas those first posthumously exploited between 1 January 1956 and 1 July 1989 received 50 years protection, to beyond 31 December 2004. As explained above, works unexploited at the end of 1989, ceased to have indefinite protection, but instead received 50 years in the UK from the end of 1989, whether exploited or not, that is, to 31 December 2039.

1892–1899

Delius's early attempts to find a publisher are dealt with in detail in the Historical Survey. The only surviving publishing correspondence for these years is with Augener, which in 1890 published his *5 Lieder (aus dem Norwegischen).* Then in 1892, it bought outright from Delius rights in *3 songs, the words by Shelley*, and *7 Lieder (aus dem Norwegischen).* Only the contract for the 1892 publications has survived, (See Appendix 1) but it is probably the same wording as that used in 1890.

As can be seen from the letters, Augener soon regretted its purchase… 'songs are a dead failure with us'. By the time that Delius bought back the plates, stock and rights in the *7 Lieder (aus dem Norwegischen)* and the *3 songs, the words by Shelley*, only 142 of the Shelley songs had been sold and 270 of the *7 Lieder (aus dem Norwegischen).*

No 1

Delius to Augener

16 January 1892
Paris

Dear Mr Augener,

I send to you by the same post 3 songs to words by Shelley which it is my intention to publish and which no doubt will be more suitable than the first ones.[1] Should you not be able to use them I beg you to keep them until I call myself at your office for them, as I am coming, in a month or 10 days, over to London for a short stay. The terms I leave entirely in your hands hoping you will do the best for me you can. I intend to publish shortly several other works which I will show you when in London, should it interest you.

I think the best manner to publish the 3 songs, should they suit you, would be in the ordinary song form and singly.

Please give my kind regards to all your family and allow me to wish you also a happy new year. I spent a pleasant summer with the Griegs on Troldhaugen and later one of my overtures[2] was also performed in Christiania in the Musikforening. Grieg and Sinding were present. With kind regards.
I remain,

Sincerely Yours,

---

1 *5 Songs from the Norwegian* which Augener published in 1890, and which Augener kept.

2 *Paa Vidderne* (On the Mountains).

No 2

Augener to Delius

4 December 1894
London

Dear Mr Delius,

I am sorry I could not write sooner with reference to your songs, but I have been rather busy since my return. I have gone thoroughly into the matter and give you enclosed the price at which we are ready to deliver over to you the plates and the copyright, including that of the English words.[3] The copies we still have in stock must of course remain our property, so that we can execute any orders that come through the works being advertised in our catalogues, etc. We should be glad to receive your decision soon, so that we know whether to keep them in the reprints of our catalogues, or not.[4]

I was fortunate on the way home, and had a splendid crossing, after the rough weather in Paris.

With Kind Regards,
Yours faithfully,
W. Augener

5 Songs, no 8829A	
English Translation	£2-12-6d
13 engraving plates @ 4/6d	2-18-6d
Engr. title page	1-10 0d
	£7-1-0d

———

7 songs, no 8829B	
English Translation	3-0-0d
28 plates & engraving @ 4/6	6-6-0d
	£9-6-0d

———

3 songs, no 8824, (Shelley)	
18 plates & engraving @ 4/-	3-12-0d
Engraving title page	1-8-6d
	£5-0-6d

———

3 By Grist.

4 Augener kept the five songs. *7 Lieder (aus dem Norwegischen)* and the *Three Shelley songs* were returned to FD. He did not withdraw the five 1890 songs 8829A from Augener. They remain in the catalogue to the present day.

ꕥ

No 3

Augener to Delius

19 November 1896
London

Dear Mr Delius,[5]

In answer to your letter of the 15th inst. we have still the following stock of your songs:[6]

170 copies	3 Songs (No. 8824)
270 ¨	7 ¨ (No. 8829B)

which you can have at the rate stated in my former letter. I am not in a position to make you a new offer for them; songs are a dead failure with us. I will endeavour to hear your Légende in January.

Augener

ꕥ

No 4

Augener to Delius

13 December 1898
London

Dear Mr Delius,

We have looked into the stock of your songs and find that the return made on the 8th is quite correct, and the one made in 1896 must therefore have been wrong. We have of

8824 – 158 copies
8829B – 230 copies

and they were printed in 1892, 300 of the former, and 500 of the latter. Since that year no impressions have been taken.
Yours faithfully,

---

5 Augener had kept stock to fulfil orders, but was now prepared to sell it. There is no record that FD bought the copies.

6 *7 Lieder (aus dem Norwegischen)* and the *3 songs, the words by Shelley*. When Tischer & Jagenberg took them over, they complained that Augener still had copies in their window.

1900–1909

1900–1906

There is a gap in the surviving publisher letters between the last of the Augener letters of 1898 and the emergence of Harmonie in 1906. Although up to 1906 he had no publisher, except Augener for some songs, Delius was beginning to have works performed from manuscript material. Paris and the Mitternachts Lied (the final movement of *A Mass of Life* without the final section) were performed through his own efforts.

Paris, written in 1899 and first publicly performed in 1901, had had three performances by 1903, and 12 by the time Leuckart published it in 1909.

In 1904, Delius became a member of the Genossenschaft Deutscher Tonsetzer (GDT), the German Performing Right Society founded in 1903, of which Richard Strauss was the first President. Although there is no mention in the few letters of these years of Delius receiving hire or performing fees for the manuscript works, he certainly told PRS that he had received fees from GDT before 1914. He changed his name from Fritz to Frederick on marriage to Jelka in 1903.

In 1906, Harmonie Verlag, a recently formed publisher, which he had visited in 1901, approached Delius. Little is known about the firm and it doesn't appear in Grove. On 20 February 1906 Delius signed contracts for *Appalachia* and *Sea Drift* with Harmonie.

But why should a music publisher be interested in Delius? The sources of income from the exploitation of the copyrights were few. Apart from sales of printed music, probably not great, there were performing and hire fees. Publishers could not belong to GDT, although they did receive a 25 per cent share of any fees distributed. The publishers charged hire fees. All the works taken by Harmonie, with the exception of the complete *A Mass of Life* had been performed, thus reducing Harmonie's risk. The Harmonie contract gave Delius 50 per cent of the profits, but this seems to be qualified in Harmonie's letter dated 8 June 1906. In that letter Harmonie indicate that the 50 per cent after costs only applies to the production of printed music and that royalties will be paid. But on what? Delius would have received performing fees from GDT, but what share did he receive of hire fees? It seems strange that Delius, who had such a shrewd financial brain, would have signed such a vague contract, but he may have been in no position to bargain.

An immediate problem for Harmonie was the production of accurate and readable performing material for *Appalachia* and *Sea Drift*, the first two works that they took from Delius. Oscar Fried, who conducted the performance of *Appalachia* with the Berlin Philharmonic on 5 February 1906, had summoned Delius in early January.

> Come to Berlin at once! The orchestral parts of Appalachia really are in an incredible state! I have not enough time to put it in order…No time signature! No dynamic markings – or very deficient ones. Whether flute or piccolo is not clear! With the two bassoons one

never knows whether tenor or bass clef. The material must be put right before the first orchestral rehearsal, otherwise I cannot perform it…'

Delius must have commissioned the orchestral material referred to above before Harmonie was involved, but Harmonie seem to have got on with the job. By early May 1906 the production of full score and piano score of *Sea Drift* was well under way, and the orchestral material of *Appalachia*, presumably corrected by Delius for the Berlin performance in February 1906, was with the engraver.

In the event the full scores of both, which must have taken months to produce were not available until November 1906, when Harmonie sent them to the following possible conductors: Mottl, Richter, Wood, Suter, Mengelberg, Hutschenruijter, Dupuis and Busoni.

No 5

Harmonie to Delius

1 January 1906
Berlin

Herrn Fr. Delius,

Herr Cassirer, the conductor of the orchestra of the 'Komische Oper' here, tells us that some of your works, in particular 'A Village Romeo & Juliet', are shortly to be performed here.[1]

We take the liberty of bringing our publishing house to your notice and of asking you to consider our publishing and distributing your works.

In commending our services to you, we shall be pleased to give you any further information,

Yours faithfully,
Harmonie

---

1 1907 in Berlin.

No 6

Harmonie to Delius

8 June 1906
Berlin

Dear Sir,
Many thanks for your letter. Herr Cassirer, the conductor, has already told us a lot about your symphonic works and we are not averse to possibly pursuing this matter further.

Our company decided to abandon the previous publishing practice, under which the author only received one single fee[2] even when his work was a great success, whilst the publisher sometimes made a fortune out of it. We have made it a rule – and all our authors are very satisfied with it – that, as long as the work's copyright lasts, the author and his heirs receive a share of all the takings, which include not only royalties on performances but sales of musical scores and publications. Also working on this basis, we naturally have to limit our risk as much as possible, and in this case the author is a co-publisher. Author and publisher are co-partners, for whilst the former makes his intellectual contribution the latter assumes the risks of production and sale. The takings are equally shared after expenses have been covered, but this fifty-fifty sharing only applies to publications and the sale of musical scores. The author will naturally, as usual, receive the larger share of royalties and takings at performances while the music publisher, when he assumes no risk will merely receive his usual percentage.

We hope you will be agreeable to our proposals, as most authors are.

Yours faithfully,

1907

1907 was the beginning of Delius's success. There are reports of eight performances of the Harmonie works; two of *Appalachia*, four of the piano concerto, one of *Sea Drift*, and the performances at the Komische Oper in Berlin of *A Village Romeo and Juliet*.

Other performances were planned. Delius was busy cajoling Harmonie regarding performing material. *Sea Drift* needed new choral material for the first English performance in 1908. A two-piano arrangement of the piano concerto was sent to Hertz, and a piano reduction of *Appalachia* to Henry Wood. The vocal score of

2 A lump sum. A buyout.

A Mass of Life was in preparation but although it had been printed, its English translation was unsatisfactory.

By August a row was in progress over mistakes in the score and parts of the piano concerto. What had gone wrong? We only have Harmonie's letters for that particular episode. Delius appears to have approved Röder's manuscript full score.[3] Szántó had then made alterations to the solo piano part, and in so doing had altered the lengths of some bars, necessitating changing all the orchestral parts. Had Delius altered the manuscript after approving it? Either way, the parts were ready for the English performance in October.

In December Delius writes that Breitkopf have offered Mk 300 for *Brigg Fair*. 'It isn't much, but I think it will do to get Breitkopf's as publishers' he wrote to Granville Bantock in December. *Brigg Fair* was first performed in January 1908 in Liverpool, conducted by Bantock, but not published until 1910 and then by Leuckart.

Meanwhile Harmonie, who must have heard that Breitkopf were considering publishing *Brigg Fair*, write to Delius in December 1907 claiming the right of pre-emption. As Delius writes to Bantock on 2 January 1908, he had discovered that Harmonie had a clause in their publishing contract requiring him to submit all of his works to them first, a not unreasonable clause from the publisher's point of view. Should any other publisher make an offer, Harmonie had 14 days to match it.

Harmonie had appointed Breitkopf & Härtel as their agent in London, and in February 1908 Breitkopf in London wrote to Delius withdrawing their offer to publish *Brigg Fair*, as Harmonie had first refusal. The work was performed four times in England in 1908, a lot, but not again until 1910, the year it was published by Leuckart. In the interim, Delius had avoided giving the work to Harmonie and contracted for what would be six works with Leuckart.

No 7

Harmonie to Delius

6 May 1907
Berlin

Dear Sir,

Thank you very much for your letter of the 3rd inst. In accordance with your wishes we sent Mr Henry J. Wood a piano arrangement of your 'Appalachia'. We are sending you ten copies of the arrangement by the same post. As soon as you need more, will you please write to us? Our printer says that if especial care is taken when the scores are written, the manuscript can be better and more clearly reproduced. The choral parts of Sea Drift, which were at the time very hastily written, will naturally have to be completely re-written and then the words will show up much better and far more clearly. As soon as we have got the copyist to produce enough copies of

3 Röder was the leading music engraver in Leipzig.

the arrangement by Herr Rumpel we will send the score and the piano arrangement of 'A Village Romeo and Juliet'. We have not yet got Otto Singer to produce the piano arrangement of 'A Mass of Life', as he wrote to us that it would appreciably diminish the work he had to do if he received two scores to make the arrangements from. He would then not have to copy all the choruses but could just stick them together and set the piano part underneath.

We regard the fee which Herr A. Kalisch wants for translating as extremely high and advise looking for another translator.[4] We have a very good English translator available, in the person of Mr John Bernhoff, and think he would certainly not ask anything like the fee of Mk 800 which Herr Kalisch wants. Will you please write to us again about this?[5]

We envisage the production for the Mass as follows: We will have the English translation made from the original score and entered on it and we will then have the handwritten reproduction[6] printed, from which Herr Otto Singer can make the piano arrangement.

There is nothing further to mention today.

Yours faithfully

No 8

Harmonie to Delius

6 June 1907
Berlin

Dear Sir,

We acknowledge the receipt of your letter, for which you have our best thanks, and also wish to inform you that, in accordance with your wishes, we have sent Hertz,[7] the conductor, the piano arrangement and the libretto of your opera.[8] We

---

4 For *A Mass of Life*.

5 Alfred Kalisch (1863–1933) was FD's choice. He was an English writer and critic, who later translated several Richard Strauss operas into English. Harmonie went with Bernhoff and it is his, not very satisfactory, translation of *A Mass of Life* that appears in the 1907 Harmonie edition. The German translations of both *Sea Drift* and *A Village Romeo and Juliet* were by Jelka Delius.

6 All the Delius full scores published by Harmonie were lithographed from a manuscript copy specially written on transfer paper. The English translation of *A Mass of Life* was added to a copyist's score, now in the archives of Universal Edition London.

7 Alfred Hertz (1872–1942), German born, conducted at Elberfeld from 1895 to 1899 and was a supporter of Delius's music. He conducted the 1899 London concert, but not the performance of *A Village Romeo and Juliet* in 1907.

8 By 1907 there was a privately printed v/s of *A Village Romeo and Juliet*, printed in Paris with German text only. Both *Sea Drift* and *A Village Romeo and Juliet* were set in

will send Herr Singer the piano concerto as soon as C.G. Röder's printing office, to which we sent the score for a quotation, lets us have it back.[9]

We are also in favour of a full score being written[10] for the first performance in future. We have already written to Mr John Bernhoff about translating 'A Mass of Life'. We have asked for a draft translation of the text and will let you know about it at once.

We have already informed you that Messrs Breitkopf and Härtel of London have acquired the sale and distribution rights of your works for England and the Colonies. The one exception is your opera, which we wish to distribute in England, as well as elsewhere, for the time being.

Yours faithfully.

No 9

Harmonie to Delius

21 Aug 1907
Berlin

Dear Sir,

We are very surprised by your letter of the 16th inst. At your request Röder corrected the orchestral parts exactly according to the score.[11]

The changes are unfortunately not as insignificant as you assume.[12] After the corrections were made, all the parts were immediately printed and those intended for Mr Wood sent off as quickly as possible. What altogether amounts to a thousand parts will now, of course, have to be corrected by hand.[13] We had the score altered in accordance with the corrected piano arrangement. It is not possible to print a fresh proof, as the score is handwritten. We have either to print the whole edition or postpone the printing altogether until after the first performance.[14]

We disagree with you about the changes in the piano arrangement, as we do not see why Signor Szántó could not have made the changes before now. If we now have the arrangement printed, who can give us a guarantee that Signor Szántó will

---

English. Jelka translated both into German.

9 Otto Singer arranged the orchestral part of the piano concerto for the second piano.

10 The score would have been handwritten onto transfer paper in order to be lithographed.

11 This refers to the piano concerto.

12 FD had made various re-touchings to his score, which didn't fit in with Harmonie's production schedule.

13 There could well have been 20 sets of parts, each containing about 40 instrumental parts, and each instrumental part consisting of several pages: A formidable task for those days.

14 The first performance of the final, one-movement version, was given by Szántó, Wood conducting, on 22 October 1907 in the Queen's Hall.

not find other changes which he wishes to make? Moreover we unfortunately cannot now put the score at your disposal, as it is already at the printer's. We must disclaim all responsibility for this, as we had already informed you exactly how production took place and dealt with the matter in exact accordance with your instructions. Would you like us to send a new score to Mr Wood, after getting Röder to correct it afresh? We have already sent the piano arrangement of 'Sea Drift' to Herr Cassirer, the conductor, and are very surprised that he says he has not received it. Today we are for the second time sending a copy to the address given.

Yours faithfully.

No 10

Harmonie to Delius

30 August 1907
Berlin

Dear Sir,
We acknowledge the receipt of the letter which you were good enough to send to us, dated the 23rd inst., and now write to explain the following to you.

When, in accordance with your wishes, you were sent the parts for correction, you returned them with the remark that you found Röder's corrections excellent and that you therefore wanted the printers only to have these.[15] You also wrote to Röder to the same effect. You should have written back to tell us explicitly that you wanted to have the parts back again after printing. We could not possibly so infer from the letters you sent to Röder and to us. The changes made by Signor Szántó, in our view, certainly concern the parts. One bar has been completely omitted, so that it will have to be omitted in all the parts. One bar has been extended from a 3/4 time to a 4/4 time (at the moment we are no longer sure which bar and which time, as we no longer have any manuscript here). This will now, it appears to us, have to be changed in all the instrumental parts. We did not promise you to have the score engraved. We specifically emphasised that engraving costs appreciably more and helps in no way whatever to get the work distributed. This is particularly the case because Röder's handwriting, if he is able to get on with it quietly, is very presentable and satisfactory from every point of view. At the moment the score has not yet been printed but is being worked on, which means that the music copyists are writing on transfer paper, so that they cannot do without the score. We again emphasise that we believed

[15] This refers to the piano concerto. Before the first performance in England on 22 October 1907 by Theodore Szántó, conducted by Henry Wood, the solo part was extensively re-written by Szántó. See Robert Threlfall, *A Catalogue of the Compositions of Frederick Delius*, Delius Trust 1977, pp. 164–67 and Robert Threlfall, *Frederick Delius, A Supplementary Catalogue*, Delius Trust 1986, p. 94.

we were exactly carrying out your instructions and acting in your interest and we certainly took the greatest pains to satisfy you. The expenses which the corrections to the piano arrangement have involved us in alone amount to Mk 36 and this amount will not cover insertions in the parts, as the copies have already been printed. We naturally dislike such pointless expense, even if it only amounts to a hundred Marks, particularly when, as here, it could be avoided by deciding in time what the final form of a score is to be. What is more we think that the score which was sent to Mr Wood, after, at your request, being corrected by Röder, must be almost perfect. In any event, the printers say that the full score completely corresponds with the parts, so that the only possibility is that there were mistakes in the manuscript, which would then naturally appear in the parts.

As you will remember, you have often changed your plans and we have, in every case, fallen in with your wishes. For example, you first intended to have the piano arrangement printed after the first performance but have now said you agree to its appearing beforehand. The same is true of the corrections of the score, which we let Röder do first, so as to make things easier for you, as you would then merely have had quickly to revise what he had done. You preferred to trust completely in the reliability of the printer and here again we followed your wishes.
We think this explains everything.

Yours faithfully

No. 11

Breitkopf & Härtel London to Delius

14 November 1907
London.

Dear Mr Delius,
I have much pleasure in informing you that I have taken over the Songs from Messrs Maynard[16] and there are approximately 1980 copies, for which I have sent him a cheque value £3-18-6d, which works out at about ½d per copy.

I am at once having fresh covers done with the name of our firm, and am also having the copies cut, so that in their new form they will be practically a new edition.

On all copies sold I propose that we should pay you 4d per copy with the usual allowance of 7/6,[17] and I shall be glad to receive your confirmation of this arrangement at your earliest convenience.
Thanking you in anticipation, and waiting your reply.

---

16 Maynard was the representative of Concorde Concert Control to which the *7 Norwegian songs* went between Augener and Breitkopf & Härtel.

17 7 copies sold count as 6, effectively a discount. Breitkopf is just selling off Concorde's stock.

ഇരുഇരു

No 12

Breitkopf & Härtel London to Delius

28 November 1907
London

Dear Mr Delius,

We have pleasure in informing you that your songs are now ready and we are sending a set to you by this post. At the same time we give below particulars of the stock taken over by us from Messrs Maynard, and we trust everything is now quite in order.

Yours faithfully,

German Songs No.	1	198 copies
	2	215
	3	187
	4	206
	5	213
	6	208
	7	213
English Songs No.	1	186
	2	200
	3	174
	Total Copies	2000
Sent to press (44 sets)		440
To Professionals (53 sets)		530
	In stock	1030 copies

Yours faithfully

ຣ໑ຌຣ໑ຌ

No. 13

Breitkopf & Härtel London to Delius

11 December 1907
London

Dear Mr Delius,

I have to tender my apologies to you for the delay in replying to you concerning 'Brigg Fair' but I have had a rather long correspondence with the Leipzig house on the subject. I have now the pleasure of informing you that they have expressed their satisfaction at having the opportunity of entering into business relations with yourself, and they are willing to produce the 'Brigg Fair', having decided, if their terms are acceptable to you, to engrave the Score and to print the Parts in autography. For the copyright they propose paying to you the sum of Mk 300.

If the work meets with the success it fully deserves, which I personally have great hopes of its doing, they state that they will be very pleased indeed to have the opportunity of taking up other of your works.

I am aware that the terms offered are perhaps not exceptional, but speaking for myself it would give me the greatest pleasure if you could see your way to accept them as it is, at least, a beginning and will, without doubt, lead to greater things.

I send you forms of agreement and receipt for your perusal and hope that I may hear from you on the subject at an early date.

I may tell you that in order to save any possible delay, the copying of the parts is being actively proceeded with.

Yours sincerely

ຣ໑ຌຣ໑ຌ

No 14

Harmonie to Delius

31 December 1907
Berlin

Dear Sir,

What is understood in Germany by right of pre-emption is that a publisher who possesses this right is entitled, within a period of fourteen days, to accept any contract which another publisher has offered the composer. We therefore respectfully request you to let us see the form of contract proposed by the publishing house concerned.

We will then let you know as soon as possible whether or not we intend acquiring the work in question on the same terms.[18]

Yours faithfully,

1908

In little more than a year, Delius had made his mark on the British music scene. In 1908 there were 21 known performances, 16 in Britain. He was busy attending performances and pursuing Harmonie, with whom relations were becoming strained. In March he received a curt note demanding Mk 1.15 for sending music to London, which surely could have been recovered in general accounting. In April, they bristled over pre-emption but dropped their claim as part of the legal settlement in December 1909, by which time they were losing interest in Delius. They certainly took no more Delius works.

Breitkopf & Härtel, who had offered to publish *Brigg Fair*, backed off in the face of Harmonie's claim to pre-emptive rights, the right of first refusal of future Delius works, but were soon Harmonie's London agent, and in contact with Delius regarding their handling of hire material, especially unpublished works. They suggested a hire fee of from one to two gns, on which Breitkopf would take 25 per cent. Note that Breitkopf write that anyone performing 'would have to arrange with us concerning the performances, that is both for the hiring of the material and for the performing fee of the GDT'. Without a national network GDT would have needed the publishers, even though they were not allowed to be members. Beecham, frequently a source of irritation to publishers, maintained that he was entitled to use material given him by Delius without fee. Although this might have applied to hire fees for unpublished works, as Delius indicated,[19] free use could not have been granted by him for published ones.

A letter from Harmonie to Delius, dated 6 March 1908, indicates that GDT refused to license a performance of *A Mass of Life* at the Queen's Hall until the fee had been settled. The first London performance of *A Mass of Life* was on 7 June 1909, but perhaps a planned performance for 1908 came to nothing.

Brigg Fair was eventually published by Leuckart in 1910, the full score being engraved rather than produced by lithography. One of Delius's most frequently

---

[18] Two of the contracts with Harmonie – those of 20 February 1906 for *Appalachia* and *Sea Drift* and of 8 April 1907 for *A Mass of Life* – included an added clause: 'I leave to Harmonie the option to purchase future compositions.' In each case, the clause has been deleted, with no indication of when or by whom. FD consulted a Berlin lawyer in 1908, as a result of which Harmonie may have dropped their claim. The issue festered on until at least April 1908. There is no record of how FD came into contact with Leuckart, but by 1908 relations with Harmonie were becoming strained and we know that he was seeking another publisher.

[19] Br & H to FD 29 December 1908.

performed works, it had seven known pre-publication performances, 12 by 1912 and 22 by 1917. Heseltine's contention that there were 36 performances in Germany in 1910 does not appear to be correct.

Running through the year is correspondence with John Lane, Ernest Dowson's publisher, regarding the use of Dowson's words in *Songs of Sunset.*

Delius met John Lane in Paris and later wrote to offer two gns a song. Lane refused and sent a contract asking for 15 per cent of performance fees, (the songs only to be performed as a cycle) and control over performances, which would not have been possible. Delius seems to have settled at two gns a song.

A letter from Bridgman, a firm of solicitors, covers the interesting point of whether Delius could translate the Dowson songs into German without permission. Under the 1886 International Copyright Act an author had ten years from publication to produce a translation. Outside that time it could be done without permission.

The issue of Szántó's alterations to the solo part and the orchestration of the Piano Concerto continued to annoy Delius. He accepted Szántó's suggestions regarding the solo part, but, as he wrote to Jelka in December 1908, as far as the orchestration was concerned, he had only asked Szántó to indicate where the orchestra was too loud. With the help of Hermann von Glenck, a young Zurich born conductor and composer, the concerto had been partially re-scored for Szántó's performances. In his letter dated 28 September 1908 to Szántó in which he criticises the alterations,[20] Delius shows the depth of his knowledge of orchestration.

Delius continued to press Harmonie over the lack of availability of his music in England and the need for a proper catalogue and price list.

No 15

Harmonie to Delius

25 January 1908

Dear Mr Delius,

In reply to your communication of the 22nd inst, for which you have our best thanks, we have the honour to inform you that we some time ago gave C.G. Röder, the printer, a draft of the title page of the 'Mass', with instructions to send it to you for your expert opinion and to agree the matter with you direct. This, in fact, took place and we assumed that this arrangement accorded with your wishes. The note 'vocal score with German words by Otto Singer' could not mean that the German words were by Otto Singer, but that the vocal score with the words (i.e. not just the two hand piano arrangement) was by Otto Singer. Any misunderstanding of this is completely impossible, as directly above this, on the same page, appears the statement: Words from 'Thus spake Zarathustra' by Friedrich Nietzsche, selected and arranged by Fritz Cassirer. You may rest assured that any misunderstanding is

[20] Carley/1/292.

completely impossible and that no one will suppose the German words to be by Otto Singer.

The price of Mk 16 – netto, 8/- net is correct. As is customary, we charge special prices for England and we do so for practical reasons. It was at the special request of Messrs Breitkopf and Härtel of London that we started doing so at the time of 'Sea Drift'. If you are familiar with English conditions, you will, for example, know that, although Verdi's 'Othello' with the English words costs 20L[ira] (16 marks) its price in England is only 8/-. We could quote you many similar examples.

We can easily correct the mistake of the two title pages by printing this page afresh and then substituting it for the old one.

We look forward to receiving the song for the mixed choir a capella* and the names and addresses of those to whom we are first to send the vocal score of the 'Mass'.

In accordance with your wishes, we have to-day already sent Professor Schillings the piano arrangement,[21] with the request to let us have the corrected proof-sheet back.

Yours faithfully,

* Received to day. We will decide about it as soon as possible.

No 16

Breitkopf & Härtel London to Delius

5 February 1908
London

Dear Mr Delius,

In reference to your 'Brigg Fair', we have just received from our Leipzig house a communication to the effect that they find themselves unable to take advantage of your very kind offer as regards the publication of the work. Firstly, in view of the fact that Harmonie have the first refusal and our people, after due consideration, have come to the conclusion that acceptance of the work might possibly lead to some friction between themselves and the above named firm, which they naturally wish to avoid, and secondly, our Leipzig people have concluded arrangements whereby the copyright of all the musical publications of Harmonie be transferred to us for Great Britain, and our firm will also take over the sale of these same publications for Berlin and district, Belgium, and America.

This being the case we shall have control of your compositions published by Harmonie and be in a position to introduce them as advantageously as if they were issued by ourselves.

---

21 Of *Sea Drift*?

We trust that we have explained the position quite clearly, and beg to remain, Dear Sir,

Yours faithfully,

༄༅

No 17

Harmonie to GDT

15 February 1908
Berlin

Dear Sir,

We beg to acknowledge the receipt of your communication of the 14th inst. It is unfortunately clear to us that the fears entertained by our Herr Fliegel[22] cannot, after all, be immediately dismissed as groundless. In any event we definitely refuse to forbid an orchestra, which wishes to perform one of our pieces, from doing so until this dispute is settled, because of a dispute between you and the orchestra.

At the moment it is of the greatest importance to us to produce Delius's work, 'A Mass of Life', as soon as possible. We therefore respectfully request you to let us have a definite answer as soon as possible to our last letter regarding the performing fee. Moreover the dispute with the Queen's Hall Orchestra is clearly a matter which does not, in this case, concern us from the business point of view. With due care, you will be able to collect your fee when the contract has been agreed, so that you, the composer and we are in any event covered. We await an answer by return of post.

Yours faithfully,

No 18

Harmonie to Delius

6 March 1908
Berlin

Dear Mr Delius,

It is a matter of the greatest regret to us that we can get no further with the GDT about your granting the performing right of your 'Mass of Life' to the Queen's Hall

22 Herr Fliegel signed the Harmonie letters.

Orchestra in London.[23] We beg you to do everything in your power to ensure that this performance takes place. For your information we are sending you another letter from the Society, dated February 28th. Please let us have it back.
Enclosure

Yours faithfully,

ཤཁཤཁ

No 19

Breitkopf & Härtel London to Delius

7 March 1908
London

Dear Mr Delius,

Many thanks for both your letters which, owing to my being absent from business, I regret I have not been able to reply to earlier.

As regards Bradford, the proposed performance of 'Brigg Fair', which was down for the 6th March was at the last moment abandoned, the Hallé Concert Orchestra writing me to this effect on the 25th ult. and the reason for this I am, of course not able to tell you.

Yes, I heard 'Paris' and was immensely pleased, and am looking forward with considerable pleasure to the London performance of 'Brigg Fair'. – I have not arranged anything about the Beecham performances of your works, in fact, – I never had in my hands the orchestral material of 'Paris'.[24] I was under the impression that everything was settled between your good self and Beecham so did not interfere.

Shall I arrange about the performances of whatever works of yours which are in M.S., and take the entire charge of your interests? If so, it would be just as well if we could come to a perfect under-standing, and if you would instruct Beecham or anyone else who might be in possession of any of your works to let us have the orchestral scores and parts, and also tell them that they have to arrange with us concerning the performances i.e. both for the hiring of the material and for the performing fee of the Genossenschaft. Up to the present I only have charge of your 'Dance of Life'[25] and 'Brigg Fair'.[26] One score of the former is in the hands of the Secretary of the London Symphony Orchestra, who hope to give a performance of it again shortly, and the original of the latter is in Beecham's hands.

---

[23] FD replied on 8 March that when next in London he would discuss the matter with the Director of the Queen's Hall Orchestra. The first incomplete performance of *A Mass of Life* was in Munich on 4 June 1908. The first complete performance was by Beecham, conducting The Beecham Symphony Orchestra, on 7 June 1909 in the Queen's Hall.

[24] Still in MS in 1908?

[25] *Life's Dance* was engraved by Breitkopf, but published by Tischer & Jagenberg.

[26] A copy of the manuscript of *Brigg Fair* was made. The original manuscript and a copy remained in Sir Thomas Beecham's hands until the 1950s, but the present whereabouts of either are unknown.

By the way, don't you think it advisable to have a copy made of the Score of 'Brigg Fair'?

I will see about the orchestral parts of 'Appalachia' and then make such corrections as you desire, but it would save a great deal of trouble and time if I could get the parts which were used by Cassirer. Where are they?

I would propose, if it is agreeable to you, that we should charge for the hire of the orchestral material of your works, i.e. such works which are in M.S. and not published yet, a nominal, hiring fee, from £1-0-0d to £2-2-0d for one performance, such amounts to be credited to your account less a commission of 25 per cent to us for working expenses.

I think that you will agree that this is quite a fair offer, and shall be glad if you will kindly confirm the same.

Hoping to see you shortly in London, and trusting that you are quite well.
I am, with very kind regards,

Yours sincerely,

No 20

Breitkopf & Härtel London to Delius

11 March 1908
London

Dear Mr Delius,

Yours of the 10th inst. to hand. I am glad to learn that my proposal meets your views and I am arranging matters here accordingly.

Mr Beecham has the material of 'Paris' and the 'Norwegian Suite'[27] in his possession and I shall be glad if you will kindly instruct him to send these in to me in order that the firm may take charge of them.

As regards 'Brigg Fair', and any other of your works, I will see in future that arrangements be made with the Genossenschaft – 'Paris' was performed a little while back without any arrangements being made. Do you think it advisable for me to write to Berlin on the subject, or would you prefer to let the matter rest as it is?[28]

Re the Genossenschaft. I may tell you, in confidence, in case you should not have heard already, that there is some trouble in the air between them and certain parties in London, but I hope that this will be satisfactorily cleared up at an early date.
Trusting you are well, and with kind regards.

Yours sincerely

27 Incidental music to Heiberg's *Folkeraadet*, performed in Oslo in 1897. Beecham retained the original material, which is now with the Delius Trust.

28 This seems to indicate that UK publisher subsidiaries of German firms were acting on behalf of GDT.

ꕥꕥ

No 21

Harmonie to Delius

20 March 1908
Berlin

An inspection of our accounts shows an amount owing to us by you of

Mk 1.15

For sending music to Herr Kalisch in London on your instructions. We now respectfully but earnestly request you to send us this amount immediately. If we do not receive it within eight days[29] we shall start proceedings for its recovery and we request you, if you wish to avoid further steps, to pay this amount.

ꕥꕥ

No 22

Delius to Harmonie

10 April 1908
Grez-sur-Loing

Dear Sir,

Some time ago I sent you two songs for Male Voice Choir and Mixed Choir.[30] Since then I have written a third, and a firm here is offering me, for each of them, 10 guineas, in other words, Mk 210.

I am asking you now to let me know by return whether you wish to acquire the three songs from me on the same terms, that is: Mk 630?

I call your attention to the fact that my legal adviser has informed me that it is not necessary for me to show you the contract in writing.

I have been offered the sum by word of mouth, but the written contact will not, of course, be drawn up until I have accepted.

Please send your answer by return to Grez-sur-Loing.

Yours faithfully

---

[29] An indication of bad blood?

[30] The two songs were: *On Craig Ddu* and the *Wanderer's Song*. The third was *Midsummer Song*.

No 23

Harmonie to Delius

15 April 1908
Berlin

Dear Sir,

The third of the choral songs which you offer us is so far completely unknown to us. Moreover we must unfortunately warn you that you appear to be insufficiently informed by your legal representatives as to the manner in which a right of pre-emption is exercised. The information with which we have been supplied gives us no idea what sort of contract it is. The publisher in question seems to wish to acquire all the rights in the pieces in question without giving you any share or royalty whatever. We must again request you to send us the draft contract, which the firm in question submits to you, for our inspection and we will then let you know whether or not we are prepared to be a party to it.

Yours faithfully,

No 24

Bridgman & Co. to Delius

16 April 1908
4, College Hill,
Cannon Street,
London, E.C.

Dear Mr Delius,

I am sorry that I had not the opportunity of having a word with you on Tuesday evening.[31] I have been considering your difficulty with regard to the publication of your songs, the words of which are written by Ernest Dowson.

[31] We have no record as to the final agreement. The Dowson poems were published in 1896. Dowson died in 1900. Under the then Copyright legislation, they would have been protected until the longer of 42 years after publication or seven years after death, remaining protected until December 1938. The 1911 Copyright Act allowed for the old term to be converted into until 50 years after the death of the author. The copyright indexes of the Delius Trust date from after 1938 and contain no mention of continuing payments to Dowson's estate.

Bridgman is correct with regard to translations. The 'Additional Act of Paris' (1896) of Berne conferred upon authors first publishing in any of the countries of the Union, or their

I am afraid that with regard to the publication of the words in English, there is but one conclusion to which I can come, and that is that Ernest Dowson's publishers can restrain you from so publishing the words. Once you had arranged with them for the publication, I do not think that they could in any way interfere with the performances of the song, but I understand that they make it a condition of allowing you to publish the words in English at all. With regard to the German translation of the words, the position is different and rather more complicated. Translations of original works were dealt with by the Convention of Berne and the International Copyright Act of 1886.

I am inclined to think that, provided the songs in question were first published more than 10 years ago, and that no authorised translation into German has hitherto been published, you might safely publish the songs with the German words.

The remarks as to translation apply to any other country represented at the Convention of Berne.

Would not the best way be to instruct your Publishers to interview the Publishers of Dowson's poems, and try and come to some reasonable arrangement?

I should be happy to see them myself for you, but I do not think the matter is one in which you should incur any unnecessary expense.

Believe me,

Yours faithfully,
Paget J.M. Bowman

No 25

Delius to Harmonie

19 April 1908
Grez-sur-Loing

Dear Sir,

I am sending you today for inspection the third choral song, which is as yet unknown to you, and ask you to let me know your decision at once. For this song I am asking a fee of 10gns, (Mk 210), payable once only and I renounce all other percentage rights.[32]

Yours faithfully,

---

representatives, the exclusive right of making or authorising, in other countries of the Union, translations of their works during the whole duration of the right in the original work, but the exclusive right of translation ceased when the author had not, within ten years of the first publication of the work within the Union, published a translation for which protection was claimed. The Dowson poems had been published in 1896 and had not been translated. Delius was free to translate them into German.

[32] The third song was *Midsummer Song*. Harmonie eventually published all three songs against a lump sum, a buyout, in 1910.

ഌൽഌൽ

No 26

Breitkopf & Härtel London to Delius

4 May 1908
London

Dear Sir,[33]

In accordance with your instructions, we beg to advise you that we have this day handed over to Messrs Novello[34] & Co Ltd the Score and Parts of your 'Brigg Fair'. We venture to remind you that up to the present nothing has been arranged in respect to the charges for copying the work, and we therefore enclose invoice amounting to £7-7-1d presuming that this will be for your account;[35] should you possibly have arranged for this item to be charged to Messrs Novello kindly let us know.[36]

Thanking you in anticipation,
We are, Dear Sir,

Yours faithfully,

ഌൽഌൽ

No 27

Breitkopf and Härtel London to Delius

7 May1908
London

Dear Mr Delius,

I am in receipt of your letter of the 7th inst, for which I thank you, and I hope you will pardon me for thinking that the misapprehension in regard to the account must

---

33 Probably this manuscript material was used for the performances of *Brigg Fair* in Birmingham on 19 February, and by Bantock in January.

34 Novello were the English agent for Leuckart.

35 FD complained about the cost of 4d per page. On 11 May Breitkopf wrote reducing it to 3d.

36 The invoice attached to this letter states:

To copying Orchestral Parts of *Brigg Fair*			
= 417 pages at 4d per page, incl. paper.	6	19	-
64 Paper Covers, including Binding, 1d each		5	4
Cloth Binding to Full Score		2	9

	£7	7	1d

64 separate parts, given 32 for wind etc., would probably have meant a small string section of 4:4:3:3:2

be on your side, as we have had many hundreds of works copied in this country and the very lowest we have been able to get them done for has been at the rate of 4d per page, including paper.

I note that you mention the figure of 2½d per page, and if you know anyone here who does good work at this rate I should be very glad if you could let me know the address of the party or parties, as this is very cheap indeed.

In the case of 'Brigg Fair', I may tell you that the price charged to us was 3d per page and 1d was added in order to recoup the firm somewhat for the trouble and expense incurred in regard to the work, and you will no doubt agree with me in thinking that after taking everything into consideration this is a very small margin indeed.

Under the circumstances I venture to hope that you will see your way clear to accept the account as it stands.

In reference to the three bells[37] which we had done specially for 'Brigg Fair' I have approached Messrs Novello with a view to their taking these off our hands, and if you could use your influence with them on this point I should feel very much obliged indeed.

Trusting you are well and with kind regards.
I am,

Yours sincerely,

No 28

Harmonie to Delius

20 May 1908
Berlin

Dear Sir,

With further reference to your letter of the 9th inst. we respectfully inform you that we unfortunately cannot use the material of the 'Midnight Song',[38] which has been sent. Röder was already working on the parts so that he was unable to give effect to the instruction not to incorporate this number. We must therefore decline to agree to the credit item towards the cost of producing the complete material,

---

[37] There are 3 bells in *Brigg Fair*. Bb C & D. on the bottom of the treble stave. The lowest note on a set of tubular bells is normally middle C, so the Bb would not have easily been available. It seems that a special set was made. The early version of *In a Summer Garden*, the next work that he wrote, used the same 3 bells, omitted from the final version.

[38] *Midnight Song* is the last movement of *A Mass of Life*. The full score of the Mass was first printed before the first performance and contains a large number of errors. Harmonie later issued four pages of errata but never published a corrected score.

The orchestral parts for the *Midnight Song* were prepared for the 1899 concert. FD had written a score and had copyist's parts made and wanted to save money.

amounting to Mk 60, and we place the complete material at your disposal. As Röder will already have informed you, the strings were sent to Herr Ludwig Hess in Munich on the 18th.

You will also have been told that the rest of the material has been sent. We much regret that reaching a settlement about your great works always involves complications and expense. You always want to have the complete material printed after the first performance. The provisional material is an unnecessary expense, it has to be produced in the shortest possible time, which involves higher rates of pay and it causes inconvenience to all concerned. It is a matter of regret to us that these expenses naturally further postpone the time when a profit accrues.

Yours faithfully,

No 29

Harmonie to Delius

1 September 1908
Berlin

Dear Sir,

As most conductors, societies and solo players who have performed your works, published by us, have so far refused to pay any fee for the hire of the material, we suggest fixing a low selling price for the score, orchestral parts, extra strings and choral parts, so as to enable every society to get the complete material cheaply. Large institutes and societies, at any rate, would do well out of such an arrangement, as the amount charged for the material would be less than such bodies are capable of paying. Yet we are of opinion that the main advantage of this is that it would cause your works to be really frequently performed.
We hope you will agree with our suggestion.

Yours faithfully
We propose the following: [in Mk]

	Score	Set of Orch Pts	Extra Str.	Chorus pts Each
Piano Concerto	15	25	2	n/a
Sea Drift	20	30	3	1.00
Appalachia	20	30	3	0.50
Mass of Life pt 1	25	50	5	1.50
Mass of Life pt 2	30	50	5	1.50

ꕥ

No 30

Delius to Harmonie

8 September 1908
Grez-sur-Loing

Dear Sir,

I have just received your letter of 1st September containing the price-list of my works. I cannot judge these prices from a business standpoint. It seems to me however that as the first part of the 'Mass' is considerably shorter than the second, that it should be reckoned at Mk 25.[39] I always find it more practical and better to have fixed definite prices, as you propose.

I repeat once more that before new editions of the orchestral scores of 'Sea Drift', 'Appalachia' and the Piano Concerto are printed, a few small printing errors must be corrected.

When the time comes I will do it myself.

Yours faithfully

ꕥ

No 31

Harmonie to Delius

14 September 1908
Berlin

Dear Sir,

We have taken note of your communication of the 8th inst., for which we thank you very much. We would nevertheless prefer not to reduce the price of the score of the first part of the 'Mass' to Mk 25 but rather to increase that of the second part proportionately. The score of the first part of the 'Mass' is at least twice the size of that of the piano concerto, of 'Sea Drift', and of 'Appalachia'. The price you suggest would therefore bear no relation to these.[40]

---

39 It is in the 1 September letter from Harmonie.

40 The following prices appear on the back page of the v/s of *A Village Romeo and Juliet.*
Sea Drift Mk 25
Appalachia Mk 40
Piano Concerto Mk 25
Mass of Life Pt 1 Mk 40
Mass of Life Pt 2 Mk 60

We should also like to inform you that the Philharmonic Choir in Vienna is thinking about the Mass and we are hoping to arrange a performance. Perhaps you would be so good as to write to the Genossenschaft that you will be as accommodating as possible as regards the conditions under which this choir can obtain the performing rights.

Yours faithfully

No 32

Harmonie to Delius

28 October 1908
Berlin

Dear Sir,

We have received your letter of the 24th inst., for which you have our best thanks. In accordance with your instructions, we sent Mr William Ritter a piano arrangement of your work. We also sent the full score of the piano concerto back to Mr Henry J. Wood.

We absolutely refuse to accept your criticisms about the reprint of the piano score of 'Sea Drift'. Some time ago you explicitly made changes in the piano score, which we got Herr Otto Singer to deal with in part. We thought this was the last of the corrections. Moreover the reprint was required so suddenly that we no longer had time to send you the proof sheets again. We once and for all respectfully request you in future to deal with matters as follows.

Directly you find a mistake in one of the works, please inform us of it by return of post. We shall then immediately have the mistake removed from the plate,[41] so that, in the event of a reprint, the old mistake cannot possibly re-appear. This method is advisable, if only because mistakes are usually again forgotten if the works concerned are gone through, one after the other, shortly before reprinting takes place. We also refer you to the correspondence which we have already exchanged. Indeed we cannot understand how you can again and again be so dissatisfied, though we cannot complain that you have not given us friendly encouragement. We nevertheless assure you that we are as keen as ever on dealing with your works and as interested in them as we always have been

Yours faithfully,

[41] None of the Harmonie orchestral scores were engraved: only the two-piano version of the piano concerto, the 5 Songs and the various vocal scores.

ꩠꩡꩠꩡ

No 33

Delius to Harmonie

22 November 1908
Grez-sur-Loing

Dear Sir,

I have received the two copies of the 2nd part of the Mass and thank you very much for them. I have just heard from England that my Mass cannot be rehearsed there without choral parts in the English 'Tonic Sol-fa' as is customary in England.[42] You will remember that you also had this done for Sea Drift and I beg you to apply to the same person at once and have it effected immediately, as the performance planned for London will be impossible otherwise.[43] So it is of the greatest importance that it should be done at once. I have already had a telegram about it – Furthermore will you please send Fräulein Olga von Welden, Rothebühl Strasse 91, Stuttgart, a copy of my 5 songs, which she wishes to sing there at her concert.

Why do you not send me the piano scores of A Village Romeo & Juliet, which I have already asked for twice? Please do this at once, as I am leaving at the end of the week.

Yours faithfully,

ꩠꩡꩠꩡ

No 34

Delius to Jelka Delius

1 December 1908[44]

Dearest,

You must write to Harmonie at once and say I never asked Szántó to make these alterations but only to indicate the places where the orchestration was too loud, that I shall not pay any part of the expenses incurred, and that none of Rumpel's alterations[45]

---

42 *A Mass of Life* was not published with Tonic Sol-fa until 1932, but copies must have been made in 1909. See Delius to Harmonie, 15 Jan 1909.

43 The rehearsals were for the June 1909 performance at the Queen's Hall conducted by Beecham, with the Beecham Symphony Orchestra and the North Staffordshire Choral Society.

44 Letter dated 'December 1908'. Assume 1st December.

45 Alterations to the text. See FD to Harmonie 26 December 1908. Rumpel was an in-house composer employed by Harmonie. He wrote the piano part to the Three Unaccompanied Part Songs and may have worked on the v/s of *A Village Romeo and Juliet.* Harmonie appear to be trying to charge FD for making the Szanto alterations with which FD did not agree.

must be printed (R & J), as I want to make them myself. Ask them why they did not inform me beforehand etc. Nearly all the notices on 'Sea Drift' are excellent.

෴

No 35

Breitkopf and Härtel London to Delius

24 December 1908
London,

Dear Sir,

We beg to acknowledge and thank you for your favour to hand and have taken note to let Dr Cowen have the material of 'Brigg Fair' for the performances in Glasgow and Edinburgh.

We propose to charge £1-1-0d for each performance for the use of the material, which we trust will be correct; our reason for mentioning this being that in a recent letter to us Mr Thomas Beecham writes as follows:-

'I was informed by the composer some weeks ago that I could have the use of any parts and scores of his works free of charge – i.e. works over which he had full control.'[46]

We shall be very glad to receive your reply on this point at your convenience. Wishing you the Compliments of the Season.

Yours faithfully,

෴

No 36

Delius to Harmonie

26 Dec 1908
Grez-sur-Loing

Dear Sir,

I have received the piano score of the opera, but I asked for 2 copies, so please send me the other one; please call in again all the copies which have been prepared and send them to me here, so that I can at least make the music legible and correct the text. The copy which you sent me is hardly legible with the best will in the world: music and text crossed out everywhere and written in beside, instead of being erased and pasted over. Who copied the music? It is illegible and looks as though it had been done by a complete novice. Apart from that, it had Rumpel's text, against

[46] Certainly if the works were not published, FD could ostensibly allow free use, without a hire fee, but as a member of GDT, they would have charged a performing fee.

which I protested from the start and which does not agree with the libretto at all. Did you submit copies of the libretto too? Do you think, then, that a theatre manager or a conductor would go to the trouble of deciphering such hieroglyphics as these?

Since I received the piano score I have been busy correcting the music and pasting over the text, so that only one version is visible, and that the right one; but for that I need the copies of the libretto too, so that I can also enter the corrections in those. Please send me half a dozen at once. I must send this copy, as soon as it is ready, to Herr Schillings, General Musical Director in Stuttgart, so I need a copy of the libretto by return; I cannot submit the score without it. I shall send a further copy to Mottl, the general Musical Director. I need a third copy for London, and would have taken it with me if you had sent it to me on time. Please send to me all the piano scores which have been prepared. I shall correct them one after another and submit them to theatres I know.

Have you now found the missing half of the vocal score[47] I prepared for printing? I have here only the first half, which you sent me in England. At that time you promised to have the missing parts from scene 4 to the end done again from the score, which was also ready for printing…has this been done? If so, then please send me that too, as I have no model for correcting the 2nd half and have to enter text and declamation from memory, which prolongs still more a task which is already unpleasant enough.

So, firstly, libretto by return and if possible the 2nd half of the missing piano score.

Yours faithfully

No 37

Breitkopf and Härtel London to Delius

29 December 1908
London

Dear Sir,

We are in receipt of your letter of the 27th inst. concerning the 'Dance of Life' and we think the best and most businesslike course will be to make a definite charge of £1-1-0d for each performance.

As regards the fee payable to the Genossenschaft, it will, of course, be necessary for Dr Cowen or the Secretary of the Scottish Orchestra to apply direct.

We note your instructions re supplying your M.S. Parts to Mr Beecham free of charge but to bring them back here when finished with – under these conditions we, of course, can hardly accept any responsibility.

Thanking you for your kind wishes which we heartily reciprocate.

---

[47] Schmitt's MS vocal score was in 2 volumes; the second volume contained scenes 5–6.

We are, Dear Sir,[48]

Yours faithfully,

ഇരുഇരു

1909

Delius is still concerned about high prices and hire charges for his music in England and somewhat paranoid about Breitkopf & Härtel, Harmonie's British agent. Are they doing a good job, or are they promoting their own composers rather than those for whom they are only an agent? He cites Beecham in evidence of Breitkopf's unhelpful attitude in London, but publishers have to run their businesses and Beecham expects to have music for nothing, as Delius had in fact suggested he could. In Germany Harmonie seems to be prepared to lend performing material free to help establish Delius as a composer. It is not clear whether all performing material is on sale or only for hire, and Harmonie keep changing their minds as to whether they should advertise fixed selling prices.

Preparations are in hand for the first British performance of *A Mass of Life* on 7 June at the Queen's Hall, with Beecham conducting his own orchestra and the North Staffordshire Choral Society, for whom Tonic Sol-fa parts are needed. Tonic Sol-fa was used by most choral societies and Beecham advised using Curwen to produce the material. John Curwen, since becoming involved in the 1840s, had spent his life promoting this method of getting choirs to sing without understanding the staves. The Tonic Sol-fa edition of the *Mass* was obviously produced for the 1909 performance but not published until 1932.

William Wallace produced a singable English translation of the *Mass*, far better than that by Bernhoff which Harmonie had commissioned and printed in the score. Harmonie grudgingly gave permission for it to be printed in the programme, something they could not prevent, Nietzsche being out of copyright, but they only licensed the translation to be used for the one performance. The correspondence, complete with examples of the arcane English translation is printed in Sir Thomas Beecham's Life of Delius.

There is no reference to the performance in the publisher's correspondence, and Delius is soon deep into correspondence with G.R. Sinclair, the organist of Hereford Cathedral over his appearance at the Three Choirs in 1909 to conduct the first performance of the *1st Dance Rhapsody*. 'I ought to tell you that we do not pay any fees to composers' wrote Sinclair in April.

At the end of the year Harmonie takes Delius to court in Berlin over Mk 2000, about £100, something of a pyrrhic victory for them, as of the £100 that Delius sends them in December, 90 per cent is due back to him, but for what? Delius is entitled to 90 per cent of grand right fees. Could this be late payment for the Berlin performances of

---

48 The letter of 27 December has not survived. We can presume that FD agreed to a £1-1s-0d hire fee and that Beecham could use his manuscript parts of unpublished works without paying a hire fee for the material.

A Village Romeo and Juliet or, less likely, an advance payment for the Covent Garden performances to come in February 1910? Harmonie makes a new contract as part of the settlement, which makes no reference to pre-emption, but relations are not good between composer and publisher. Harmonie took no further Delius works.

In December 1909 the Committee appointed by the British Board of Trade to examine the law of copyright in the United Kingdom reported to the government, their report leading to the 1911 Copyright Act.

No 38

Delius to Harmonie

4 January 1909
Grez-sur-Loing

Dear Sir,

I am returning to you today the score of my Piano Concerto. I have undertaken a few alterations, which I have entered in red ink. I have erased some things. All the parts must therefore be collated [with the score] when you prepare them. The material for Herr Szántó's version cannot be used – please have completely new parts prepared, as my alterations are by no means as extensive as Szántó's and frequently consist only of dynamic markings.

I wrote today to professor Schmidt-Lindner of Munich, who is playing the concerto this month under Mottl, to ask <u>when</u> the concert takes place. If there should still be time, I would ask you to have a score and parts prepared for him too. The parts for Herr Szántó[49] must of course be done <u>at once.</u> I have just seen that the Munich performance will take place either on the 8th January or the 26th February. In the former case, therefore, it is already too late, and in the latter Herr Schmidt-Lindner can use the material you are now preparing for Herr Szántó, in other words both use the score prepared by me.

Please get the parts done by a professional musician who is really reliable. The Szántó version may in no circumstances be used again and I ask you to withdraw the parts.[50] The new impression of the score may only be made after Mottl's performance.

In my last letter I forgot to mention especially that the half of the vocal score of the opera which you wish to reprint must also have the English text with the music, as with the full score.

Yours faithfully,

---

[49] Presumably to allow Szántó to play his revised piano part with FD's amended orchestral parts. Szántó's amended orchestral parts no longer exist.

[50] FD allowed two performances by Szántó with his (Szántó's) amended orchestration. Copying was laborious. String parts were engraved, as several copies were needed. Wind/brass parts were by hand.

ꕥꕥ

No 39

Delius to Harmonie

15 January 1909
Grez-sur-Loing

Dear Sir,

Please send me now the score of the Piano Concerto as corrected by me, together with the parts prepared from it, so that I can correct all the proofs before printing.[51]

I hope you have started on the Tonic Sol-fa in accordance with my last letter; otherwise it will be too late for the London performance.[52] Please hurry its execution as much as you can.

Yours faithfully,

ꕥꕥ

No 40

Delius to Harmonie

This is a translation of two almost illegible carbon copies of letters dated 1st April 1909. Parts of each draft have been cancelled by Delius. They are in italics. What was the final letter? It must have been sent, as Breitkopf replied on 6 April, the letter having been forwarded from Harmonie, answering the questions regarding Beecham, Sea Drift *and* A Mass of Life.

1 April 1909
Dear Sir,

2nd Draft

Mr Beecham, who is performing my 'Mass' on the 7th June, has just written to tell me that Breitkopf & Härtel in London do not want to sell him a score of the work. They are just prepared to loan him one, saying that he must not make any notes on it

[51] FD had only returned the marked up score, from which new parts would have to be made, on 4 January. Schmidt-Lindner was playing the concerto on 8 January, so there was no time to prepare new material for that. Asking for new material within a fortnight was unreasonable.

[52] For the Queen's Hall performance of *A Mass of Life* on 7 June 1909. The Tonic Sol-Fa parts must have been produced then, but were not published until 1932. In his letter of 28 January 1909, Beecham re-iterated the need for a Tonic Sol-Fa version of the Mass for English choirs. From his letter one can gather that most music printers could produce a version, but that Curwen was the best source.

etc., but must hand it back clean and new. You know yourself that it is impossible for a conductor to rehearse such a work without notes, underlinings, etc.
The corrections to the piano part [of my concerto] are in Mr Szántó's copy. The orchestral score with my corrections I have here. I will send you both as soon as I have seen Mr Szántó, who is now in Paris. These two copies must be used for the new impression.

Pugno will not play it again this season and I hope the new edition will be ready by the autumn.

I repeat, without the sale of my scores my music cannot become widely known.

Yours faithfully.

Dear Sir,
Mr Beecham, who is performing my 'Mass' on the 7th June, has just written to tell me that Breitkopf and Härtel will not sell him a score of it. They will only hand it over on loan and he does not want that, as he wants to write on it his own notes, expression marks. Etc… Naturally he wishes to keep these and use them again for any other performances later.

What does it mean, people not being able to buy my scores in England? Surely you fixed the price of them yourself. It is absolutely opposed to our interests – you should try to sell as many scores as possible.

Beecham will not be able to perform the 'Mass' unless he gets a score immediately. Please instruct Breitkopf & Härtel at once to send Mr Beecham a score of it without delay. I urgently advise you, unless you wish to make performances of my works in England impossible, to make the charges for parts moderate. Please also inform me what Mr Beecham paid Breitkopf and Härtel for the material for 'Sea Drift', because he has complained about the high price.[53]

I thank you for sending the piano concerto to Pugno.

No 41

Breitkopf and Härtel London to Delius

6 April 1909
London

Dear Sir,

In accordance with a request which we have received from the 'Harmonie' Co. we beg to advise you that after some long troublesome correspondence a sum of £5-5-0d was paid for the Manchester performance of 'Sea Drift'.[54]

---

[53] £5 5s 0d. See next letter.

[54] Hire fee for material.

Respecting 'Mass of Life', we should like to explain that we have also had considerable correspondence with Mr Beecham and his agent extending so far back as December 16th 1908, but up to the present no arrangement has been made with us in regard to the performance.[55] We have written to Harmonie asking them whether they will be willing to sell the full score outright for the forthcoming performance and as soon as we get their reply we shall arrange accordingly.[56]

We would take this opportunity of stating that we do all that we possibly can, both in your interest and our own, and we trust that you will understand that it is not our desire to raise difficulties of any kind but we naturally like to have matters arranged on a satisfactory and businesslike basis.

We beg to remain, Dear Sir,

Yours faithfully,

No 42

Delius to Harmonie

15 April 1909

Dear Sir,
I have just received a letter from Beecham protesting against Breitkopf and Härtel's methods. I quote the following from it:-
'My main complaint is the following. I paid Breitkopf & Härtel five guineas for the material of 'Sea Drift' for Manchester and five guineas for London. In addition I paid them five guineas as a guarantee that I would return the material in a week.

It was returned one day over the week, where-upon Br & H refused to refund the five guineas I had paid them as a guarantee but I have now heard – about two days ago – that Br. & H are willing to deduct the five guineas from what I will have to pay for the 'Mass'. They are asking for £20 from me for the use of the material for the 'Mass', and, moreover, a further £25 to be deposited with them as a guarantee of its return. They want another five guineas from me for the score, if I buy it, and in addition I must promise not to use it for public performances'.

You will see from this what difficulties Br. & H are putting in the way of performances of my works in England.[57] You will see, to your own loss, that not many conductors will accept such conditions. It is probable because of these prices that Wood, the conductor, who also wanted to perform the work 'cried off'.

55 Beecham had not agreed a hire fee for the 7 June performance.

56 Printed in 1907. There would have been copies for sale.

57 One can sympathise with both sides. Manuscript or lithographed scores and parts were expensive to produce, and Beecham seems to have been a bit cavalier with music supplied by publishers, as well as believing that he could perform FD's music without payment for the use of the material. If orchestral works such as *Brigg Fair* were being hired for about £1, £5 for *Sea Drift*, where chorus material was needed is not necessarily out of place.

I think I must tell you honestly that it seems to me to be completely opposed to your interests for you to have as your representative in London a publishing firm like Br. & H, which takes such colossal pains to sell its own works. It is obvious, therefore, that they should put the greatest possible difficulties in the way of their business competitors. I ask you therefore to set definite, fixed [selling] prices for my works (as other publishing firms do) so that overcharging of this sort is absolutely impossible. Br & H flood the whole of England with price-lists of their publications. I frequently get letters from England asking where my music can be found and what are the prices of my scores. I enclose a Br. & H catalogue for 1909 in which I will mention, for instance, Bleyle, [published by] Kistner Press. You will see how prices and everything else are given exactly. You will see at the same time that my works, with the exception of the piano-arrangement of 'Sea Drift', are not mentioned here at all. Both Bleyle[58] and I have German publishers for whom Br.& H are agents.

The only difference is that Bleyle is completely unknown in London whilst I am in the forefront of public interest. I am therefore, the most dangerous competitor to Br. & H. So print at once for Germany and England price-lists of my works which you have published: the piano concerto, 'Appalachia', 'Sea Drift', the 'Mass', and songs, with the exact prices for score, orchestral parts, choral parts, extra parts and piano arrangements. Have Br. & H put them in their catalogue as soon as possible. Of course, neither the score of the 'Mass' nor any other of my scores must cost more in England than in Germany. Please tell me your purchase price for the large score of Parts 1 and 2 of the 'Mass', secondly, for the orchestral parts, thirdly for the choral parts? Please let me have an answer at once. As things stand at the moment, we run the risk of seeing Delius performances in England completely paralysed, and I should warn you of it. You know what a practical people the English are – they do everything in a straightforward, businesslike way and do not venture into matters as doubtful-looking as this.

I am surprised that you, as businessmen, do not grasp better an opportunity as good as my music offers. For instance, two big concert promoters have written to me to ask where my works can be obtained in England. At least the concert associations should receive catalogues of them. Not to mention the songs, which would of course be sold throughout England, if people saw announcements of them.

I must confess that five guineas for the hire of 'Sea Drift' is far too much. Br. & H would not ask for, nor get, that for a work published by themselves; not by a long way. For the hire of the material of the 'Mass' £20 is far too much.

The matter of the guarantee money mentioned in Beecham's letter is also completely inadmissible in dealing with a top-flight London orchestral undertaking.

I have several reasons, which I do not wish to mention more fully here, why I do not wish to entrust my works blindly to Br. & H.

It would be better in the future to look around for another agent. If you wish, I could make enquiries to this end when I go to London in June for the performance of the 'Mass'.

---

[58] Karl Bleyle (1880–19?) His date of death is not in Grove. Kistner was a long established music publisher in Leipzig and much larger than Harmonie.

But in any case, price-lists and announcements at once – because the new programmes are made this summer.

As far as I remember, you wrote me at the time that the score of the 'Mass' was to be: Part 1, Mk 25, part 2, Mk 30 or 35. That is not 5 guineas (Mk 105) by a long way.

Yours faithfully

No 43

Harmonie to Delius

19 April 1909
Berlin

Dear Sir,

We received your registered letter of the 15th inst. And beg to inform you as follows: We have not so far had the slightest cause to complain about our London agents, Messrs. Breitkopf & Härtel, but we will nevertheless, in future, keep a check on what they are doing, in particular as suggested.

Messrs Breitkopf & Härtel have undertaken to incorporate the works which our publishing house is dealing with in one complete catalogue, and to send them out in the form of a prospectus. We will write to them fully today.

We must obviously as a rule rely on Messrs Breitkopf & Härtel, as we cannot know the circumstances prevailing there to the extent that they do. We feel that the prices they have fixed for 'Sea Drift' and 'Mass of Life' are in no way excessive. However we are informed that Mr Beecham's reputation in London is not of the best, particularly in business matters, and that one must be careful when dealing with him.

We obviously cannot appoint other agents, as we have made a five year contract with Messrs Breitkopf & Härtel.

We do not want to lay down absolutely fixed prices for the 'Mass of Life' or any other great concert works. It would be most unfair if a small society had to pay the same for orchestral material as an institute. The Berlin Philharmonic Orchestra can naturally pay much more than the Blüthner Orchestra here. You will admit that we could easily give you a great many other examples of comparisons. Small institutions and societies will only start playing your works after they have been made famous by well-known first class orchestras.

You know that we in Berlin have never received a fee for material from Fried.[59] Professor Schmidt-Lindner and Herr Szántó are others who have frequently received the necessary material for the piano concerto from us, free of charge, and we should never have the slightest objection, except under special circumstances, to delivering

[59] One wonders why Harmonie was not charging hire fees in Germany and Austria. GDT were probably collecting performing fees.

the material for the 'Mass of Life' free of charge. As you write to us that you are in fashion in England, it would surely be a mistaken principle to let Mr Beecham alone have the material free.

We will tell our agents to deal with Mr Beecham and possibly reduce the price for him. If Messrs Breitkopf & Härtel feel they must have security, we shall have to agree to this precaution temporarily. But we cannot believe that they want to offend Mr Beecham, as this would be injurious to them.

As soon as we hear from Breitkopf & Härtel we will let you know.

Yours faithfully,

No 44

Harmonie to Delius

26 April 1909
Berlin

Dear Mr Delius,

We are very much obliged to you for your detailed letter of the 23rd inst., but we are convinced that you take too gloomy a view of things as regards Breitkopf & Härtel. We cannot believe that a firm with its reputation would deliberately compete against publications for which it has accepted the agency.

We do not at the moment wish to set fixed prices for the sale of orchestral material and scores in shops.[60]

You yourself admit that one cannot charge a large orchestra the same amount as a small one and yet we can hardly reduce the prices in every single case. It is when your works are established and orchestras need to acquire them that we can charge fixed prices for scores and orchestral parts. At the moment it would merely limit their distribution without achieving any advantage, for, as you know, we have, in most cases, distributed the material free.

You must really trust our having enough business experience not to act against your own interest.

If some prospective purchasers received our catalogue and it showed fixed prices (eg. for the Mass) they might be put off by the amount asked and, without further ado, give up all idea of sending in for the score and piano score.

England is, of course, a special case. As regards it, particularly so far as concerns Beecham, we must rely on the advice of our agent, who has explicitly assured us that he has acted completely in our interest. We have already again written to

---

60 It appears that orchestral material *was* on sale, making it more difficult to track public performances but that Harmonie were lending material in Germany, without charge, to help establish Delius.

Messrs Breitkopf & Härtel, asking them to be as accommodating to Mr Beecham as prudence allows.

We hope you now agree we what we have done.

With best wishes,

Yours faithfully

No 45

Harmonie to Delius

1 May 1909
Berlin

Dear Sir,

Thank you for your detailed letter. We enclose Mr William Wallace's letter which we are returning to you.[61]

We are willing to consider laying down fixed prices for all your orchestral works. Before we make proposals to you, we respectfully request you for your views on this and to let us know what you consider the appropriate price for each work. We will immediately inform you whether we can agree to these prices or feel they ought to be varied.

We have no objection to the 'Mass of Life' being performed in Mr Wallace's translation. We again state, however, that Mr Wallace is not entitled, in connection with your work, to have this text printed or let any publisher have it in any manner whatsoever.[62]

Under the German law of copyright, once we have acquired the compilation of the German text of your 'Mass of Life', we become the sole persons entitled to

[61] William Wallace, (1860–1940) qualified as a doctor before deciding to concentrate on music, as composer and writer. He had some success as a composer but his apparently acerbic manner caused problems. He was secretary of the Royal Philharmonic Society for two years.

[62] Harmonie were within their rights in limiting the use of Wallace's translation. Copinger 1904 puts the situation thus, on p 72.

'By the international Copyright Act, 1886, where a work being a book or dramatic piece is first produced in a foreign country to which an order in council under the International Copyright Act applies, the author or publisher as the case may be, shall, unless otherwise directed by the order, have the same right of preventing the production in and importation into the United Kingdom of any translation not authorized by him of the said work as he has of preventing the production and importation of the original work. Provided that if after the expiration of ten years or any other term prescribed by the order next after the end of the year in which the work, …was first produced, an authorized translation in the English language of such work… has not been produced, the said right to prevent the production in and importation into the United Kingdom of an unauthorized translation of such work shall cease'.

publish it. You will admit that it would be impossible for us to give you the licence requested. But it would be equally impossible for us again to pay so as to acquire this translation as well.

We exceptionally allow Mr Beecham to print the text for his present performances in London, but with a notice saying sole publisher: Harmonie, literary and artistic publishing house, Berlin; London publishers, Breitkopf & Härtel.

As soon we receive your definite decision as to the prices to be fixed, we shall print and dispatch a special catalogue of your works.

We are pleased to inform you that your 'Mass of Life' has been accepted to be performed in Elberfeld in the middle of December of this year.[63] We offered the material at a cheap price and will let you have further details soon.

Yours faithfully

No 46

Delius to Thomas Beecham

3 May 1909
Grez-sur-Loing

Dear Beecham,

I have just revised my copy of the full score of the 'Mass' & found a few mistakes which I have marked with a cross in the margin – I send you my full score as it will no doubt save you a considerable amount of trouble simply to copy them off into your copy – if you have been able to get one at a reasonable price – Dr Haym of Elberfeld informs me that he is also giving the 'Mass' in Autumn & and is coming over for the London performance & hopes he may attend the rehearsals – Wallace's translation is ripping & reads like an English poem – When shall I turn up? I employ a Bass Oboe which is a 'Heckelphone' & played by an Oboe or English Horn player,[64] to be had in Germany from Heckel the inventor & instrument maker – Can be hired – If you have a Sarrusophone instead of the Double Bassoon all the better – Let me know what B & H charged you for the 'Mass' as I want to compare it with their German terms – No more of my things will be edited by Harmonie, who have only the Piano Concerto, 'Appalachia', 'Sea Drift' & the 'Mass'. All my other works will be edited by a better editor & easier to get at – My lawsuit, I hope, will be ended within the next few months – 'Paris' which was free, is edited by Leuckart – Leipzig.

---

[63] Conducted by Haym on 11 December 1909.

[64] FD is wrong. The heckelphone and bass oboe are different instruments. The heckelphone is far more powerful, and inappropriate for *A Mass of Life* or any other of the six works for which FD scored the bass oboe. Although some of the manuscripts are marked heckelphone, the printed scores say bass oboe.

Will you be able to come over here before the Mass? How is the Choir getting along – In the Piano Score there are also a few mistakes – 112, in the 2nd half of the bar ought to be G & not A – [65] At the end of the 2nd Dance Song – 97 – The chorus at the ending is missing – but it is correct in the full score – Also 4 bars after 89 there is a change in the 1st Sopranos which is also correct in the full score – The Bass Oboe or Heckelphone is simply a long instrument –

With love to you all
Yrs ever
Frederick Delius

I shall bring my Dowson[66] with me to show you.

ꕥꕥ

No 47

Delius to Harmonie

9 July 1909
Grez-sur-Loing

Dear Sir,

I very much regret I am unable to accept the statement of accounts up to 1st July 1909 which has been presented to me, as I know of a number of performances of my works for which no record at all for the supplying of musical material appears in the statement.

As soon as I have received your signed contract and Mk 600 I will send you the three choral songs and at the same time a sample to show what is usual for such pieces in England. Each song must be separate and may not cost more than 3d.

Yours faithfully,

---

65 Page 112, 1st altos and 2nd tenors.

66 *Songs of Sunset*.

ဢဢ

No 48

Harmonie to Delius

17 December 1909
Berlin

Dear Sir,

With reference to the publishing contract between us, we write to you to confirm that we have today agreed as follows:[67]

1. Annual statements of account shall show which works have been published in the year in question and the size of each edition.
2. Directly we arrange to publish a new edition of a work, it shall be our duty to give you prior notice thereof and to enable you to make changes thereto.
3. When we enter into contracts for the performance of your opera 'A Village Romeo and Juliet', we shall arrange for the fee for the performance to be kept separate from the fee for the hire of the material, unless you agree to the fee being otherwise determined.
4. We undertake to have the score, the piano reduction and the orchestral and choral parts of the opera 'A Village Romeo and Juliet' produced (as regards the piano reduction, this means that it shall be engraved) as soon as the arrangement of the piano reduction shall have been approved by you, and the score and the choral and orchestral parts written. Production of the choral and orchestral parts shall, however, not take place until the original parts, which are now to be sent to London, have come back from there.[68]
5. We have, in accordance with your wishes, again credited you with the sum of Mk 900 (900 marks) for advertisements in the Harmonie Almanac, with which we had debited you.
6. We shall credit you with the amount you advanced for the production of the performing material of the opera 'A Village Romeo and Juliet'.[69]

Please be good enough to inform us that you agree to the above terms.

Yours faithfully,

---

[67] A letter dated 18 December 1909 from Magnus & Ruer, Berlin solicitors, indicates that they had represented FD, who had been sued by Harmonie for Mk 2000. From Harmonie's letter to FD dated 5 January 1910, FD appears to have had to pay the Mk 2000, but then took 90 per cent in grand right fees. The 17 December agreement from Harmonie was part of the settlement.

[68] This probably means that although the piano reduction of *A Village Romeo and Juliet* would be engraved, all other material would be hand written, and where necessary copies produced by lithography.

[69] FD always maintained that he paid for the production of the performing material of *A Village Romeo and Juliet* for the 1907 Berlin performances and was never recompensed by Harmonie.

1910–1919

1910

At the beginning of an eventful year Delius was in London for the two performances of *A Village Romeo and Juliet* at Covent Garden in February, conducted by Sir Thomas Beecham, and much exercised in getting performing material from Harmonie. He found many mistakes in the proofs of the vocal score, and the material was late getting to London. Singers used the Paris edition of the vocal score, with handwritten English words; the orchestral material was that prepared for Delius for the 1907 Berlin performances and Beecham had to conduct the performances from a handwritten score.

Then in February had come 'the case of the missing copyist', so bizarre as to be almost certainly true. One of Harmonie's team of copyists disappeared with 17 pages of the full score, and couldn't be found. The missing pages had to be re-constructed from the parts. Delius was furious, and not placated by Harmonie's long letter of explanation.[1]

A Village Romeo and Juliet had two performances in the middle of a run of seven of Richard Strauss's *Elektra*, which was receiving its London premiere, and Beecham even managed to slip in one performance of Ethyl Smyth's *The Wreckers*. Given the late arrival of the performing material for *A Village Romeo and Juliet* and the difficulties of *Elektra*, notwithstanding that '(it) came to London from Berlin – with singers scenery and stage managers – a finished work', it is not surprising that the *Village Romeo* was not a success. As Delius wrote to Heseltine in 1916, 'the attempt to mount the Village Romeo with English singers, Chorus & stage manager was a miserable failure – inefficiency and inexperience bursting out from every crack – the only good point was the splendid English orchestra & Beecham conducting'. Delius felt that whereas in Berlin the staging had been good, the opera spoilt by indifferent orchestral playing, the opposite was true in London. The 1916 correspondence between Delius and Heseltine, when Heseltine was keen to mount the opera in turn shows his true feelings about the performances.

The next performances were in London in 1920 and Wiesbaden in 1927. There are no references in the 1910 correspondence as to what Delius thought about the opera's reception, and he left London soon after.

By June, already in contact with Leuckart, Delius was also negotiating with Tischer & Jagenberg, from whom he asked an advance of Mk 500 and 50 per cent of the profits for some songs. No more Delius works were published by Harmonie apart from the vocal score of *A Village Romeo and Juliet*. By the end of 1910, Leuckart had quickly published *Brigg Fair*, Dance Rhapsody No. 1 and *Paris*. T & J had published some songs and been offered *Life's Dance*. The extant letters to Leuckart

---

1 Carley/2/332.

show none of the problems that Delius had had with Harmonie over the accuracy of the material.

Delius's reputation was growing, with help from Beecham, who conducted six Delius performances during the year, two of *A Village Romeo and Juliet*, one each of the piano concerto and *Paris* and two of *Brigg Fair*. In addition *Brigg Fair* received its first US and first Russian performances.

A comment in a letter to Jelka dated 18 June refers to money being received from GDT for performances.

ꕥ

No 49

Harmonie to Delius

5 January 1910
Berlin

Dear Mr Delius,

We duly received both your letter of December 24th of last year, for which we thank you, and thereafter, from London, the remittance referred to for £100.[2] You are, as agreed, entitled, by way of settlement, to the proportionate amount of this for performing rights.* In accordance with your instructions, we have to day paid this amount into your account with Messrs. Arons Bros, 34 Mauerstrasse.
Please take note of this,

Yours faithfully,

Harmonie.

[Handwritten PS]. The agreement with Beecham is perfect.
*Mk 1,400 Less 10 per cent. A total of Mk 1,260

---

2 This letter is difficult to understand. The mathematics does not add up. £100 is some 2,000 marks. Delius was entitled to 90 per cent of grand right fees. Could this be either grand right fees for the 1907 performances of *A Village Romeo and Juliet*, or advance payment for the Covent Garden performances? Whatever the answer, Harmonie seem to be taking an administration fee of ten per cent off FD's fee, as well as their own per cent.

ꕥ

No 50

Harmonie to Delius

13 January 1910
Berlin

Dear Mr Delius,

With further reference to your last communication, we must respectfully inform you that our attempts to obtain the producer's libretto, pictures of the décor etc. from Gregor[3] have been in vain. He says he regards any producer's libretto which he himself produced as his own literary property, particularly when he has put on works which were in manuscript, and that he is only prepared to hand such librettos over in return for a fee. He will anyway be tomorrow sending us a specification of the scenery still available and which might be available for sale.

He will then let us know the minimum he would charge for the use of his producer's libretto. We have moreover received the only existing photographs of the four scenes, except for the one of the small house with the garden and the one of the last night in the old house, and are today sending them to Beecham. The remaining solo material has been in Beecham's hands for a long time, as have the piano scores which were sent him.[4] There was no time to write the English text in, but we sent him a definitive copy containing it and asked him to have the text written in in England. This ought to be easy with more people available particularly when one thinks that it is much more difficult to get the English text copied here in Germany than in England.

Eighty choral parts were sent to Beecham from Leipzig on the 12th inst. The score will be ready in five or six days' time at the latest. Owing to the need for speed this will be carefully corrected here. The orchestral material is completely ready and will be sent to Beecham tomorrow or the day after. As Beecham has still given us no details as to the size of his orchestra he may have to have some string parts copied in England. However, Lindemann's piano arrangement is far more difficult than could have been anticipated. A great deal of thought and reflection are often necessary in order to render the complicated harmonic polyphony correctly. You will immediately appreciate this and be the best judge of it. It will consequently for the present be impossible to send you proof sheets. We shall have our work cut out even to produce the number of provisional piano scores (and then without covers, etc.) needed for the London production. Lastly Lindemann is undoubtedly a good musician, who will leave no error which could affect the performance. Above all Beecham already has the score. We should of course be most willing to send you proof sheets in London before the piano arrangements are delivered were it not, as we have already said, that this would be far too late. As soon as the first proof sheets of the arrangement are ready you will be receiving copies of them. Please let us have

---

3 Gregor directed the 1907 performances in Berlin.

4 Harmonie's vocal score had not yet been published. Beecham's London singers used the Paris printed edition, with a German text, and the English written in.

your criticisms of them by return of post so that the arrangement can be published even before the London production begins.

We should also like you to know that one of our leading artists has supplied us with what we regard as a most attractive design for the cover, inner title and book design. We shall let you have at least a proof of this cover picture before a definitive print of it is made. You can then decide whether to accept it or have a simple drawn cover. As we say, we consider Herr Telemann's design to be outstanding.[5]

You may rest assured that we shall do all in our power to make this matter a success. Should, however, any small delays or minor details cause Mr Beecham to become insulting or make complaints, we respectfully request you to investigate the matter carefully before doing anything else, as we are most anxious not to get on bad terms with him again.

We enclose a copy of the communication which we are today sending to Beecham, together with a copy of a list of the scenery which it might be possible to sell.[6]

Yours faithfully

enclosures

No 51

Harmonie to Delius

21 January 1910

Dear Mr Delius,
Thank you very much for your letter of the 18th inst., enclosing the proof corrections to the choral parts,[7] which we have just received. These contain indeed a few really stupid mistakes, for which the proofreader is not so much to blame as are the copyist and engravers. You should however realise that the latter would probably not have got your corrections completely right if they had only read through them once. At the same time you must remember that these choral parts only had to be printed with the greatest possible haste because it would have taken far, far longer to make a hundred separate copies. This is quite apart from between eighty and a hundred copies then having to be checked for printing mistakes. And the greatest burden would have been correcting the English text so many times.

---

5 The coloured lithographed cover, including Telemann's indeed outstanding design with the poppy field in Scene 3, is only to be found on Harmonie's vocal score of *A Village Romeo and Juliet.*

The earliest ('provisional') copies – see letter from Harmonie to FD dated 31 January 1910 – have this cover but no title page.

6 This has not survived.

7 For *A Village Romeo and Juliet.*

Unfortunately we have no English copyist here and you will have to admit that the mistakes are of such a kind that they would immediately be spotted by English choristers. We are therefore of the opinion that they would not to the slightest extent delay production or even rehearsals. We are pleased to have been able to send Beecham the choral parts in such good time.

We are getting a competent Englishman to go through the piano score, which will, we hope, contain no such mistakes. Before definitely publishing the piano score, we shall once again be sending you proof sheets, which we ask you to deal with at once.

Yours faithfully,

Enclosed: one proof sheet from the proof sheets of Appalachia to be dealt with please.

ꙮ

No 52

Harmonie to Delius

31 January 1910
Berlin

Dear Mr Delius,

Mr Beecham will have received the first four scenes (thirty copies of each) of the new piano score by today. We are sending the fifth scene off today and the sixth will follow at the latest on Tuesday, if not Monday.

You will be receiving the proof sheets for the libretto direct from the Berlin music printing works and we respectfully request you always to return them to the printing works as soon as possible. In the meantime you will be receiving a complete piano score. Please do not correct this, however, as Herr Lindemann is correcting one and then letting you have it, so that you can also add your corrections to his.

The manuscript orchestral material which was sent was the Komische Oper's correct version. It is, unfortunately, impossible to get the producer's libretto out of Gregor.

We have provisionally had one hundred copies [of the piano score] printed, but do not think we shall be able to sell so many. There would, however, have been no point in printing fewer, as the cost would have been the same. Thirty copies would have cost just as much and ruined the plates.

We received the corrections for 'Appalachia' and the manuscript for corrigenda for the 'Mass of Life'. We sent the latter straight to the printer.

With our respects,
Yours faithfully,

PS We offered to make Novello & Co of London our agents for England, but heard today that they declined our offer.

ꙮ

No 53

Harmonie to Delius

10 February 1910
Berlin

Dear Mr Delius,

We cannot understand your still not having received the piano score and proofs of the libretto. Postal communications with France must be beyond belief. We are anyhow sending you, by the quickest available means, a few more piano scores and the original score, together with the first proof sheets of the libretto and five author's copies of your a capella choral songs. The score is naturally not bound, partly because the sheets have to be kept separately so that they can be written on and also because Herr Lindemann was never able to dispense with more than part of the manuscript at a time. (In 3 parcels by book post.)

We cannot understand the muddle in England. We sent the Komische Oper's provisional material[8] a very long time ago and received not a single complaint from Mr Beecham or Mr Quinlan.[9] We are equally unable to understand the bars said to be missing in the copy of the score and in Lindemann's piano score. Lindemann told me that you had personally informed him that everything which was crossed out in red pencil was cancelled and to be ignored. Lindemann and I thereupon went though the piano score once again and verified that he had meticulously observed this instruction. In most of the places where you have crossed things out the matter is beyond doubt, as you have yourself written in red pencil 'this half bar is not valid' and drawn a red arrow as far as the entry. In other cases you have made similar notes. The copy which has been made exactly corresponds to the piano score itself. I can only imagine that Mr Beecham, who received the individual scenes of the score one after another, must have got them out of order when sorting them.

As regards the sixth scene, may I respectfully inform you that thirty copies of this were sent to Mr Beecham by parcel post, via Ostend, as long ago as Friday, the 4th inst. and that the score was dispatched by book post on Monday. Beecham now has 30 complete copies of the piano score. We think there can be no doubt that this is enough in any event. If you need more, so as to make it easier for the rehearsals and to deal with understudies, they will of course be available to you.

---

8 Presumably provisional material because it had been used in Berlin but not published. To be sorting out parts ten days before the performance, in the days before faxes, was running things fine.

9 Beecham's Agent.

We now unfortunately have some very disagreeable news for you. A normally very conscientious and reliable music copyist was given some sheets of the original score to copy. They were the beginning of the second scene from page 49 to 65, i.e. seventeen pages. Since then he has disappeared and all newspaper appeals, police investigations, etc. have failed to find him. We have, therefore, with every possible care, had the pages of the score reconstructed one by one from the parts and have already sent a copy of this to Beecham. We are adding the second copy to your original score.

However, unfortunately, the seven last bars of the parts were crossed out, but have been left in in Lindemann's piano score. As a result, the man who was reconstructing the score from the parts did not, in his haste, include these seven bars. We have already sent Mr Beecham two correct score sheets for these seven bars, with words and vocal part, and asked him to have the score corrected from the parts (which for seven bars would be very little trouble) and to send us a copy. Yet despite our entreaties, which have been most courteously addressed, we have had no answer from him.

May we therefore most respectfully ask you to be good enough to take the trouble of ensuring that these seven bars in the parts are written in on both the score pages which have been sent and already distributed. Would you also be good enough to let us have one of these at once and add the other to the original score. The name of the musician who lost the score sheets is Emil Haffke. We will, if you wish, send you a full account of all the appeals we have made and all the investigations we have carried out.

Yours faithfully

No 54

Harmonie to Delius

11 February 1910
Berlin

Dear Mr Delius,

The Vienna Philharmonic Choir is prepared to perform your 'Mass of Life' but requires the sole performing right until March 1911. As neither the Wiener Autorengesellschaft[10] nor we are capable of granting this request we are being asked to undertake to let no one else have the performing material 'till then.

The Society is prepared – and indeed says it is only able – to pay the perfectly ludicrously small sum of Mk 150, from which, moreover,10 per cent commission would be deducted for our agent in Vienna. May we respectfully ask you to let us know immediately whether we should agree to this or not and what conditions you think we should lay down.

10 Wiener Autorengesellschaft. Harmonie was probably a member, as publishers were not members of GDT, although granted 25 per cent of distributions.

'Appalachia' has been well received in Hamburg, where the conductor was John Julia Scheffler. The critics are not exuberant but they speak well of it.

Yours faithfully

No 55

Harmonie to Delius

16 February 1910
Berlin

Dear Mr Delius,

We received your last two letters and much regret that you are being so impatient. We have, in any event, done everything that it was possible for us to do and are in no way morally responsible for the loss of the pages of your score. We did not report their loss to you earlier, firstly because you could not have made use of them in Grez and secondly because we were hoping, as indeed we are still hoping, to get them back.

We told Herr Lindemann how pleased you were with his work.[11] We are also gratified to know that our Herr Fliegel has been proved right in his opinion that Herr Lindemann was just the man for this job. We agree with everything you say.

We instructed the printers to send you the proof sheets direct. If, despite their repeated written promises and confirmations, they did not let you have them, there was nothing more we could do. As there was obviously not enough time to get you to check the remainder of the proof sheets, we got an Englishman here to do this.

The printers tell us that another fifty piano scores and a larger number of librettos will be ready for dispatch tomorrow evening. We have already told Breitkopf & Härtel that you want them to let the newspapers have critics' copies both of the piano score and of the libretto. We respectfully request you to get in touch with Breitkopf & Härtel immediately. Another possibility would be to get the dispatch seen to by Mr Quinlan, who wrote to us today and whom we should be glad if you would give instructions to. We leave the decision to you, in any event.

We are, moreover, tomorrow sending you, in accordance with Herr Lindemann's instructions, the complete proof sheets of the piano score. Please make your changes on these.

We in due course took the list of dramatis personae from the score and prepared it from this.

Yours faithfully,

---

[11] Lindemann made the piano score for Harmonie; the earlier Paris edition incorporated Florent Schmitt's piano arrangement.

ꕥ

No 56

Breitkopf & Härtel London to Delius

4 March 1910
London

Dear Sir,

We beg to advise you that the stock of your 'Abendstimmung'[12] is getting low, and under the circumstances we would ask whether you have the plates of this in your possession or whether you would like us to have fresh plates engraved at your expense for the purpose of printing a new edition, which we would be pleased to keep on sale on the usual terms.

Thanking you in anticipation of an early reply.

Yours faithfully

ꕥ

No 57

Harmonie to Delius

12 March 1910
Grez-sur-Loing

Dear Mr Delius,

In reply to your letter of the 10th inst., for which we thank you, may we respectfully inform you that we have been in touch with Herr Oscar Fried, who has no objection to our granting Herr Schreker and the Vienna Philharmonic Choir the sole performing rights of your Mass until the autumn of 1911. We have therefore written to this effect to the Philharmonic Choir's business manager, Dr Robert Löwi, and its conductor, Herr Schreker. We have unfortunately still not received back the reviews relating to the Hamburg performance of Appalachia. We yet again beg you to let us have them.

---

[12] *Abendstimmung* is no. 3 of the *7 Norwegian songs*, published by Augener in 1892 and subsequently bought back by FD in 1898. This was probably what would now be known in the record industry as a 'pressing and distribution deal' whereby FD owned the plates (which he had bought back from Augener) and Breitkopf printed at FD's expense and took a commission on sales.

FD wrote to Breitkopf in reply to this letter inviting them to take over publication, which in a letter to him dated 8 March 1910 the company declined.

We received the corrected libretto[13] and sent it straight back to the printers. We respectfully ask you to let us know whether you object to the edition as a whole or whether we should withdraw the order from the printers unless they at their own expense let us have a new edition gratis. We hear that Beecham has, absolutely without authority and completely off his own bat, had an English libretto printed. We have already written to him asking for a statement of his receipts and expenses, and have as yet not even received a reply. Perhaps you can now get Mr Beecham to deal with this letter.*

We will inform you further as to the expenses estimated to have been occasioned by the loss of the score but the facts may have to be established first.

Yours faithfully,

*PS Reply just received.

PS I have had a talk with Professor Schillings in Stuttgart and Herr Polanski, the conductor of the court orchestra in Munich. Both gave me personal assurances that Romeo & Juliet would be put on at the Court Theatre next season.

No 58

Harmonie to Delius

24 May 1910
Grez-sur-Loing

Dear Mr Delius,

Despite our reminder Beecham has still not sent the original score of 'A Village Romeo & Juliet'. Would you be so good as to write to him yourself?[14]

Herr Carl Schuricht, the conductor of the 'Rühl'schen' and of the Conservatorium Choir in Frankfurt am Main is thinking about producing your Sea Drift and we are negotiating about the material. He wants as much of a concession as possible and hopes to get the material cheaply (Mk 50).

Please let us know if you have any special wishes.

Yours faithfully

---

13 This presumably refers to the German libretto of *A Village Romeo and Juliet*. Harmonie didn't produce an English one, hence Beecham's actions referred to in the same paragraph.

14 This was the manuscript, from which Beecham had conducted at Covent Garden. FD duly did as he was asked on 2 June 1910. 'Do be a good chap and send it off at once, or I shall have trouble. They seem to think I don't want to send it and will sue me for it, as it belongs to them by contract. As it is going to be given in Germany this winter, and they want to get all the material ready and cannot print the score without my original manuscript. I have had enough worry and trouble with this work already and don't want any more.'

ꕥꕥ

No 59

Delius to Tischer & Jagenberg

15 June 1910 (assumed date)
From Wasserheilanstalt,
Mammern
Untersee, – Bodensee
Schweiz

Dear Herr Doctor,

I have just received your letter of the 4th inst – I do not understand why there should be a limit to my share of the royalties – After all, it is only just that I, the composer, as well as my heirs should have a share in the profits – All my contracts have the conditions which I proposed to you – All my large choral & orchestral works published by Harmonie as well as those published by F.E.C. Leuckart.

All I sold outright were 3 small choral songs to Harmonie for Mk 600. Since I believe in the future of my music, I have always preferred the conditions that I have proposed to you, instead of settling for one large once-for-all payment.[15]

And just now my music is beginning to make headway – There cannot be many more copies at Breitkopf's in London – You can of course ask for precise information & at the same time inform Breitkopf's that you are now going to publish these songs.[16] You could also withdraw the remainder as soon as the new edition is ready – In one song I have a small alteration to make Venevil I would however like to read the proofs of all of them – I am staying here for another 8–10 days & then I return to Grez Would you accept Breitkopf & Härtel as agents in London? If you agree please send the Mk 500 to Gebr Arons, 34 Mauer Str Berlin, for my account – With kind regards

Yours sincerely

---

[15] FD wants royalties rather than a buyout.

[16] T & J were to publish all the songs originally published by Augener except the earliest *5 Songs from the Norwegian*. FD doesn't mention the low sales of the *7 Norwegian Songs*!

ꕥ

No 60

Delius to Tischer &Jagenberg

13 July 1910
Grez-sur-Loing

Dear Doctor,

I have received the contract form[17] and will send it back to you in a few days.

What have you arranged with Breitkopf & Härtel about the 450 (circa) copies of the songs which are still available?[18]

The English translations of the songs are so bad that I do not wish to have them published again. In England, German and French songs are never really sung except in the original version. If however you insist on the songs being translated you must have a completely new translation prepared. I can recommend to you in this respect Mr William Wallace. 11 Ladbroke Road, Notting Hill, London.

For the Verlaine songs, too, I would prefer a French text or a really artistic translation. Possibly there are in existence some translations by Stefan George and it remains to be seen whether these texts would sound well to music. The French songs must in no case be translated into English too for they become obscure in three languages. Please point out to me in the proofs in due course the mistakes in declamation in the German version, so that I can put them right.

With best wishes,

---

[17] FD is falling out with Harmonie and enters into correspondence with Tischer & Jagenberg in June 1910. There is no mention of the firm either in Grove or in Krummel and Sadie. On 23 June he writes to Jelka from Mammern 'Send me the letter to Tischer here and I will copy it off and send it – enclosed is what I want to write – I will offer him the 7 German songs and the 4 new ones for Mk 1500 or the 7 German for Mk 1,000'. Then he had second thoughts in case he annoyed Sander of Leuckart (postcard to Jelka 24 June). Tischer refused his proposal, and FD countered on 7 July with Mk 500 and 50 per cent of net profits, presumably for the songs. From FD's letter to Tischer dated 24 July 1910 it seems that Tischer only paid Mk 300 advance.

[18] On 24 August 1910 FD wrote to T & J to say that he had heard that although he, FD, had bought back copyright and plates of the *7 Norwegian songs* and the *3 Shelley songs* from Augener in 1895, Augener still had them on sale. They were remainder copies that Augener had not sold.

On 8 September FD wrote with more details. There were originally 300 of the *Shelley songs* and 500 of the *7 Norwegian songs* printed. Augener had retained the remaining copies, when FD had bought back the copyright, offering 4d for every copy sold. He suggested that T & J offered the same price to clear out the stock. For a start T & J re-issued the Breitkopf/Augener sheets in their own new covers.

ꕥ

A letter discussing the niceties of the German translation of 'Shelley's beautiful words' may be found in Carley vol. 2 letter 346.

ꕥ

No 61

Delius to Tischer & Jagenberg

11 December 1910
from
Dr med. Lahmann's Sanatorium
Weisser Hirsch
bei Dresden

Dear Herr Doktor,

I have been ill again & have therefore not been able to attend to any of my publishing matters at all until now. Now that I am feeling better again I would like to come to a decision with regard to the publication of my choral work 'Songs of Sunset'.

As you have expressed the wish to publish one of my larger works I should like herewith to offer you this one. Indeed I am also in negotiation with Leuckart; but as I have still to take a fairly long period of convalescence in the South, I cannot this time accept the former terms (50 per cent) & require a once for all fee of Mk 5000.[19]

Please let me know whether you are interested – However I cannot definitely promise my assent as yet as Leuckart has not yet replied to me.[20]

I am staying here until the end of the month. I look forward your prompt reply and remain with best wishes to you both and to Herr Jagenberg

Yours

---

19 Say £250.

20 *Songs of Sunset* was in fact published by Leuckart. Tischer later published *Life's Dance*, the only large work FD had available at the time.

ꟷ

No 62

Breitkopf & Härtel to Delius

28 December 1910
London to FD at
Dr med. Lahmann's Sanatorium,
Weisser Hirsch
bei Dresden.

Dear Mr Delius,

I am in receipt of yours of the 23rd inst, for which many thanks, and am extremely sorry to learn of your indisposition, from which I trust you will soon be completely recovered.

Regarding your question as to the songs, I would explain that what we are offering is the original stock of copies which we had from you, plus those copies which were recalled from Messrs Augener & Co., it being necessary to dispose of these first, but you may rely upon me to do all that is possible to get them cleared without delay when, of course, they will be sold in the new form.

Respecting the price of 'Paris', it is unfortunately the general practice in this country to allow 25 per cent discount from the list prices, hence the reason for the 40/-. You are, of course, aware that Messrs Leuckart allow no discount whatever in Germany from their price of 30/-.

Trusting that I have succeeded in making myself clear on this point, and wishing you the Compliments of the Season and a speedy recovery.
I am,

Yours sincerely,

1911

Delius was ill at the beginning of the year, and had to cancel visits to hear performances in Vienna and Berlin. The two performances of *A Mass of Life* in Vienna feature in the 1913 correspondence with Hertzka of Universal regarding the low performing fees paid in Austria, even though, according to Jelka Delius, both performances were sold out.

There are 18 recorded performances of Delius works including seven of *Brigg Fair*, one being in Chicago, and two of *A Mass of Life*. In England Beecham conducted eight performances.

Delius queried his Harmonie royalty statement, going into great detail over missed performances, for which he considered he had not received print or hire royalties. It certainly seems that Harmonie were at fault, but, given that Harmonie had undertaken to share profits with Delius, it is not clear how profits were calculated. Given that Harmonie only started to print performing material in 1906, it would surely be unlikely that the costs had been recovered by 1911. Unfortunately we do not know enough about the way Harmonie accounted.

The first performance of *Songs of Sunset* took place on 11 June at the Queen's Hall, with the Dowson text for which Delius had negotiated with John Lane in 1908. It was published by Leuckart, on the basis of a 50/50 split of publishing profits, against which Leuckart paid an advance of Mk 1,000. Performing and mechanical rights were reserved by Delius. Subsequently the publishing contract was replaced in 1913 by a comprehensive one covering all the Leuckart works. This was essentially a buyout by Leuckart, but as can be seen elsewhere in this volume, the terms were disputed in the 1990s, following the copyright revival. Unlike Harmonie, Sander, the Managing Director of Leuckart, realised that English choirs disliked singing from single line copies, a recurring theme in the correspondence. Delius completed the manuscript of *An Arabesque*, finished *Fennimore and Gerda* and began the *Song of the High Hills*.

At the beginning of 1911 Beecham dropped his plans to stage *A Village Romeo and Juliet* at Covent Garden that Autumn. There was talk of a production at Elberfeld that came to nothing. Delius dedicated *Fennimore and Gerda* to Beecham, who had reservations about the work and never performed it.

In England the 1911 Copyright Act was passed, coming into operation in July 1912, introducing, among other things, a copyright period of 50 years after death, covering all works exploited in a composer's lifetime, rather than that of 42 years after publication or seven years after death, whichever was longer, per work, established in the 1842 Copyright Act. Of more immediate interest, it introduced the mechanical right, enabling composers to benefit from the newly established gramophone industry, and paved the way for the founding of the British Performing Right Society in 1914.

No 63

Leuckart to Delius

23 February 1911
Grez-sur-Loing

Dear Mr Delius,

On my return the day before yesterday from St Moritz I received your last letter and hasten to bring to a definite settlement the question of your Songs of Sunset.

You will find the contract form for these herewith, which I ask you to return to me furnished with your signature, while I shall send the payment on account of Mk 1000 due to you direct to Mr Gebr. Arons in Berlin, according to your wishes.

Production of the work has been begun and indeed the score, string and choral parts are in print and the wind parts in manuscript. Do you have any written out parts so that we can save costs by eliminating these from the material needed?

Also I must ask for an immediate delivery of the piano score, which is indeed necessary for the previously mentioned performance in England, for I know this much, that the English and American societies sing mostly from vocal scores and not from single line choral parts.

Will you confirm the dedication to the Elberfeld Choral Society, as you have already dedicated your 'Paris' to Dr Hans Haym?

In itself I have nothing against this dedication, but it would be more practical if by dedication of the work to another big society you should interest new circles in your activities.

Finally I ask you to send immediately your corrections to 'Summer Garden' and in anticipation of further news, I am, with best wishes,

Yours etc. Wishing you best success and for your cure.

Martin Sander
Nb. Deleted from contract in manuscript.[21]

1. Particularly with all existing ...to...cinema presentation.
2. Relevant additions, abbreviations and alterations to undertake...
3. Deciding date of publication
4. I renounce the right...themes...to...incorporate
5. In the case where the performing right reverts...to...transfer to publisher.
6. Claiming purposes

No 64

Delius to Harmonie

11 November 1911
Grez-sur-Loing

Dear Sir,
I have just received your settlement and should like to inform you that it appears to me to be quite wrong in several points. I shall go through the various works in order referring also to the earlier settlements for 1908, 1909 and 1910, since after all I was initially justified in hoping that the missing points would eventually come to be dealt with.
1. Appalachia

[21] The contract, showing FD's deletions, to which Leuckart had presumably agreed, can be seen at Appendix 3.

The following performances known to me have taken place. Cassirer London, Beecham London, Hanley Basle, Stuttgart Prague Hamburg and London 16/6/1911. This last will probably not yet have been included. Hamburg is included in the calculation, but for the other 6 performances there only appears

Choir parts Mk 103.65

Orchestral parts Mk 164.97

You have sold 6 scores as you inform me, 2 of these to Stuttgart, 1 to Heilbronn, 1 to Munich, 1 to Frankfurt/Main and 1 to Novello London. There are then 2 missing for London for neither Cassirer nor Beecham got theirs from Novello. Furthermore 1 for Prague, 1 for Basle and 1 for Hamburg, that is 5 in addition to your calculation. What does this mean? Furthermore in the settlement Mk 100 for the parts supplied by you are missing. (see the previous remarks).

2. Seadrift

Here there is missing all the orchestral material for Sheffield-Wood and all the orchestral and choral material for Beecham-Hanley, Manchester, London and material for Mason-Choir March 1911 London.[22] For the material for each performance Beecham paid a hire fee of Mk 100. For Basle, Frankfurt and Elberfeld performing material has been included in the calculation. However you allow on the whole for only 2 scores although at the very least 6 must have been sold. Basle, Wood, Beecham, Frankfurt, Elberfeld and London.

3. Mass of Life

Any account for Beecham's performance of the Mass of Life 7/6/1909 is lacking. Please compare this with my last year's complaints. In your reply you refer me to the copy of the account of Breitkopf and Härtel which is generally difficult for laymen to understand but from which it is at least clear that in March and June 1909 scores and orchestral material were used.

You yourself tell me by letter that Professor Haym has paid Mk 423 for the material of the Mass. In your settlement however I find only Mk 302.20. Why? Furthermore the score bought by Haym Elberfeld has still not been included. How can it be that this is not included in your books? In reply to your question Haym informed you that he bought it and paid Mk 100 for it. It is really not permissible simply to omit to enter such a transaction in the books. What is supposed to happen if you don't even keep account of the sales of my works?

4) Why does the production of 1000 choir parts cost Mk 719.30? That's quite impossible. – On the 24/1/1911 you charge Mk 50.7 for 400 new covers for the vocal score. I checked personally in Elberfeld that the vocal scores had no new covers at all, but that Mk 16.00 was simply scored through and Mk 8.00 written instead. Please explain. I also learned that they had great difficulties in Elberfeld in obtaining at all a sufficient number of vocal scores. Finally they obtained only 25. What is the meaning of this? Is the first edition exhausted? I repeat that if you are making a new edition I must at all costs go through the vocal score to make corrections.

5. Piano concerto

In all your settlements you include for this work only one score and one material. However the following performances have taken place with material which was paid

[22] The Edward Mason Choir.

for: London Wood, Munich Mottl, Munich 1910, London Beecham 1910. That makes 4. Furthermore at reduced prices or gratis Berlin Fried, Leipzig Halle Budapest. In the settlement there is no mention at all of these although I have already repeatedly asked you from what material Beecham played. You know that I forbade you to supply any version except the latest.

6. Romeo und Julia auf dem Dorfe

Here I wish you to explain why music has been copied [at a cost of] Mk 592. It's quite out of the question that one of my scores, 200 pages in all, should cost Mk 592 to copy. I also refuse to pay for the reconstitution of the parts of the score that you have lost and request you to remove this item and also the item of Mk 10.15 for advertising and a telegram in order to obtain lost parts of the score. It would really be more appropriate if I were to charge you for my repeated telegrams from London about the delay in sending the material and the libretto which never appeared.

I emphasise again that all these complaints refer to the net result of the 4 settlements. In addition I draw your attention to the fact that many of the missing amounts, for instance for the material of Seadrift and Appalachia are included in Breitkopf and Hartel's account and are missing only in yours. If I do not now receive a fully corrected settlement I shall lay the whole matter in qualified hands.

Respectfully,

ꙮ

1912

Nineteen Delius performances are known, including three of *In a Summer Garden* in the USA.

Delius was much occupied with trying to reach a final settlement with Harmonie, to whom no further works were given and becoming irritated that Jadassohn was obviously avoiding him. The full story only emerged in the 1919 correspondence with Hertzka, by which time any monetary settlement between a UK citizen and Germany was the concern of the Public Trustee, as Custodian of Enemy Property under the Trading with the Enemy (Copyright) Act of 1916.

In April he went to meet Jadassohn, who avoided him, but he must by that time have been in contact with Universal Edition, as he wrote to Szántó on 8 August 1912 to say 'UE have taken over all my works published by Harmonie'. This statement was somewhat previous as it took UE some time to make an agreement with Harmonie.

Only two publisher letters survive from 1912, from Delius to T & J, regarding the contract for *Life's Dance* and Delius's willingness to sell the copyright in the works outright, as he was short of cash. Such a sale would not have included performing and mechanical income. There is also a letter from Henry Wood, telling Delius that he had persuaded the Birmingham Festival to put on *Sea Drift* that November. Birmingham had an orchestra of 100 and a chorus of 300. What did Delius think about balance? Was the chorus too big? For Sheffield in 1908 he had had an orchestra of 60 and a chorus of 280. Delius replied, but we do not have his comments.

No 65

Delius to Tischer & Jagenberg

20 March 1912
Ebereschenallee 7
Westend – Berlin

Dear Herr Doktor,

In reply to your kind letter I sent you both my scores by registered post today & ask you to acknowledge receipt by postcard at once.

I would really very much like to have my works published by you, but as I said, I must have a good fee now, as my works are, after all, now being played everywhere.

I therefore require a sole payment of Mk 5,000 for the 'Dance of Life' & 4,000 for the Arabeske. If you want to have the 5 songs too, then Mk 1,000 for these.

I consider the 'Dance of Life' really to be my best orchestral work. I have had it in my file for some years now, as the ending did not quite satisfy me; but at last I have found what I was looking for & it is now a fully mature work.

Please let me know your decision as soon as possible, for I have taken no other steps as yet.

With best wishes from both of us to all of you

Yours

No 66

Delius to Tischer & Jagenberg

28 June 1912
Grez-sur-Loing

Dear Doctor,

I received your letter yesterday. Before I decided anything at all in the matter of the songs, I would like very much to hear how much you would offer me as an outright payment. You know that I believe in my music and so in principle always suggest keeping a share in it, but I would consider an advantageous payment offer from you.

In my view, it is not a bad beginning that the songs have already brought in Mk 420 for the avalanche must always start rolling as a small snowball.

Now for other questions:[23]

The performing right 'means' for me a not insignificant source of income, as a member of GDT. If GDT were to be disbanded, it would lie in my power to transfer my works to another Composers' Society in order to obtain the proceeds of the performing right, – so says my lawyer. I had not in mind the right of preventing performances of the work. I am not concerned with that. It is in your own interests to put a spoke in the wheel of unsatisfactory concert promoters.

With best wishes from my household to yours.

Yours

1913

Delius was now an international figure, feted at concerts, lunching at 10 Downing Street, and very confident about his music.

He attended six of the 15 known performances of his works. *A Mass of Life* was performed twice in Munich and once in London. There were two performances of the Piano Concerto and *In a Summer Garden*: performances of *Brigg Fair*, *The Walk to the Paradise Garden*, *Appalachia*, and the first performances of *On Hearing the First Cuckoo* and *Summer Night on the River*: *Lebenstanz* was performed in the USA. A disappointment was that the performing material for *An Arabesque* was not ready. The hoped for premiere in Vienna did not take place, and plans for a performance in 1914 were overtaken by the start of the war. It was not performed until 1920.

Delius is trying to shake free of Harmonie, from whom he can get no satisfactory royalty statements and answers to his questions. He is in negotiation with Universal, who he hopes will buy out Harmonie, but he is hedging his bets. He is also in negotiation with Leuckart, (of which more below) and Tischer & Jagenberg, to whom he assigns publishing rights in *On Hearing the First Cuckoo* and *Summer Night on the River* among other works.

As a member of GDT, a composer only organisation, he is able to take good advice from the Society on the wording of various proposed contracts. Their letter dated 23 June 1913 is the only one to survive and it is interesting to compare their advice with the final wording of the contracts. GDT only accepted serious composers. Composers not acceptable to GDT, such as Lehár, joined the Austrian Society, the Wiener Autorengesellschaft, (AKM) which did accept publishers. It was AKM which would have collected the performing fees for the Vienna performances of *A Mass of Life*, on behalf of GDT, about which Delius complained. AKM apparently paid less per performance than GDT.

In his dealings with Universal, the fiasco over the late availability and questionable accuracy of *A Village Romeo and Juliet* material provided by Harmonie for the 1910

[23] Does this refer to Lebenstanz? GDT did not accept publishers as members, so if FD is referring to Lebenstanz he has a point. T & J would want a share of performing fees. It is usual, in publisher contracts to specify that if a performing right society returned the rights to the composer, the composer would cede them to the publisher.

Covent Garden performances still irritated, but he was now pursuing Universal over the premiere of *Fennimore and Gerda* and laying down conditions regarding the production. He tried to drive a hard bargain over fees and royalties from Universal. He insisted on 90 per cent of grand right fees, tried unsuccessfully for a royalty of 25 per cent of the retail price on printed music. Universal agreed to pay a 20 per cent royalty on sheet music sales and the proceeds of hiring out the material, with 15 per cent on any other uses. Delius for his part did not grant Universal a share of mechanical fees.

For the first time Emil Hertzka, (1869–1932) comes into the correspondence. Hertzka had become Managing Director of Universal in 1907 and remained so until his death in 1932. It is difficult to avoid thinking that Hertzka, who actively sought out the best composers in Europe, soon found that Delius was not going to make money for Universal, especially after Delius became incapacitated. The Hertzka who appears in the Delius correspondence, whom Delius seldom met, and who was rarely able to get to a Delius performance, including the 1929 Festival, is not the same as the Hertzka described by Hans Heinsheimer, who ran the Universal opera department under him. That was a person constantly on the move, turning up at performances and encouraging his composers. He frequently seemed at the last minute unable to get to a Delius performance, and when he did show interest, it was when there was a chance of one of Delius's works becoming popular. *The Walk to the Paradise Garden* and the music for *Hassan* are two examples, as the letters show.

No 67

Delius to Harmonie

2 February 1913
Grez-sur-Loing

Dear Sir,

With reference to the agreement to be concluded between you and Universal Edition AG, I agree that in the case of the complete transfer of ownership of my works published by you to Universal Edition, I waive all material and other claims against you.

Moreover, I also waive any entitlement to any share of the amount paid by Universal Edition to you for the transfer of the works.

Yours faithfully,

No 68

Delius to Universal

9 February 1913
Grez-sur-Loing

Dear Herr Doktor,

I thank you for your kind letter & the interest that you show in my work.

After your last letter it would please me greatly to think that all my works were in your hands. However, what you propose for my musical drama I cannot accept.[24] On the one hand the other publisher is pressing for a decision & on the other hand I cannot make a publisher's acceptance of my work contingent on an immediate public success. Not a single one of my works has enjoyed an immediate success. My music drama A Village Romeo & Juliet still awaits its true premiere; until now it has only been played under the most unfavourable circumstances and I still maintain that it will become a repertory piece.

In Berlin, merely because of stage conditions, the entire hay-barge scene, and thus the entire ending, was left out. The orchestra was thoroughly 4th rate and in no state even to attempt to play the music. In London the orchestra was splendid, but thanks to the incredible dawdling on the part of Harmonie, the singers only received their parts a fortnight before the premiere, so that they were quite ridiculous on the stage, since they did not even know their notes and acting was out of the question.

You will probably have heard that in Berlin in 1902 my orchestral work 'Paris' was given a mute reception[25] & described by the critics as Unmusik, whilst last March 1912 it was given in Berlin to thunderous applause and success, & received glittering notices.

In order to bring about a good production of a stage work, printed material must be available; vocal scores must be available so that not only the whole stage ensemble but also the critics, press & public be provided with them long enough before the premiere, that they may orient themselves.

You should also not forget that, quite apart from immediate success or non-success, musicians & music lovers from the broadest circles buy the vocal scores of my works, even from abroad.

I consider this stage work the most complete that I have yet written and it should only appear under the most favourable conditions. The piece is now entitled 'Fennimore and Gerda' (2 episodes from the life of Niels Lyhne). The additional 3 Gerda scenes[26] have rendered it considerably more effective from a scenic standpoint.

With kind regards I am,
Yours always sincerely

---

[24] This probably refers to the point also raised by GDT in their advice dated 23 June 1913, when they pointed out that under UE's proposal, UE could withdraw from *Fennimore and Gerda* within three weeks of the first performance if it wished to.

[25] Conducted by Busoni.

[26] Later reduced to 2.

ꕥ

No 69

Delius to Universal

17 February 1913
Grez-sur-Loing

Dear Herr Doktor,

I have just received your letter of the 14th and wish to propose the following conditions in response:

I demand a fee per performance of 90 per cent [of publisher's receipts] for Germany and Austria & 80 per cent for abroad. As a royalty I require 20 per cent of the price on all the material sold or otherwise used. On the other hand I do not require an advance, which reduces your risk considerably: The vocal score must be produced immediately & the editing undertaken by yourselves, with the addition of the two new scenes, of course.[27]

There are now only two scenes, as I have combined the final two. The work has benefited greatly from this ending.

I hope that we can conclude the matter on this basis & it would please me greatly if you could also acquire the works I have published with Leuckart.[28]

It is of great importance for my continued undisturbed creativity that I should be in the hands of a reliable publisher & that I am relieved from the constant unpleasantness which I have had hitherto. I will not hide the fact from you that it is for this reason I am turning down a considerable cash advance that has been offered to me from another quarter.

With kind regards

Yours sincerely,

ꕥ

No 70

Delius to Universal

1 March 1913
Grez-sur-Loing

Dear Herr Doktor,

---

[27] This refers to the addition of the 2 *Gerda* scenes to *Fennimore*.

[28] In 1921 Universal bought 50 per cent of Leuckart's interest in the 6 Delius works published by Leuckart.

I have just arrived back from London where I attended a performance of my Mass.[29] Sadly the production was a little rushed; Mr Beecham found it impossible to dredge up 2 copies of the Mass of Life in the whole of London. Of course he had counted on finding them available at Breitkopf & Härtel, as they used to be. A Village Romeo & Juliet is likewise nowhere to be found any longer – Several people have complained to me about it. Each copy had to be ordered individually from Vienna & it took several weeks before they received it. In Munich they had the Mass in only one shop and not a single one of my other works in the place. These would also have had to have been ordered individually from Vienna; this was of course of no use to people who had come from afar for the performance & it simply stood in the way of sales. I should have thought that there should be a stock of my works in all the great centres, that is of the utmost importance, especially in London, the centre of the whole of England.

Is it not possible for you to place A Village Romeo and Juliet in a good theatre? The work is still basically awaiting its premiere. Only Vienna would be out of the question because of Gregor who has so mutilated it once already, by among other things omitting the whole of the ending, that he has done me great harm. Frankfurt is very much inclined to give it but preferred to go for a premiere with 'Fennimore & Gerda'. However, I believe that were one to negotiate skilfully with Frankfurt, it would be achievable. Bodansky-Mannheim was also inclined. Munich might also be considered. The Intendant, Baron Frankenstein, is extraordinarily interested in the work. I do ask that you make energetic efforts on behalf of the work.

I now plan to publish my 'Arabesque' for baritone solo, mixed chorus and orchestra and 6 songs. Are you interested in these?

With best wishes,

Yours

No 71

Delius to Universal

10 April 1913
Grez-sur-Loing

Dear Herr Doktor,

I am sending you a registered packet containing my 'Arabesque' and 5 songs; in each case they are the only copies in existence. The loss of the 'Arabesque' would be irreplaceable for me.

I request 25 per cent of the retail price and Mk 1,000 down payment, with which you hopefully are in agreement. The songs[30] must each appear individually and not

[29] Beecham at Covent Garden on 10 March.

[30] Presumably the *5 Songs* later published by T & J?

as a collected volume & the original text must be on the top line, with the translation beneath. If you wish to have the as yet untranslated songs translated, I recommend to you Dr Heinrich Simon of Frankfurt a/M. He translates excellently and understands my music very well.

Perhaps you are attending the Jena Tonkünstlerfest on 4–8th June where, as I hear, my orchestral piece 'In a Summer Garden' is to be performed. I would be very pleased to meet you there.

As far as Romeo and Juliet is concerned, I cannot understand this situation. You are announcing the work – which is an absurdity if you do not hold the title to it. What I told you about the vocal scores for the 'Mass' in London came from Beecham himself. Another friend told me that he tried to buy a copy of the vocal score of Romeo and Juliet in London & that he received it only after 5 weeks. I truly hope that you will investigate the matter properly. It is completely unclear to me what is going on there. Of course it did colossal harm to our common interests to have an agent who behaves in this way.

With best wishes,

Yours,

This of course in confidence – I wish to have no unpleasantness with Herr Kling.

No 72

Delius to Universal

25 April 1913
Grez-sur-Loing

Dear Herr Doktor,

I have received your letter and the songs – many thanks!

As far as the Arabesque is concerned, I will gladly give it you for publication under the following conditions:

An advance of <u>Mk 1,000</u> and <u>15 per cent</u> of the retail price as you propose.[31]

I hope that will be all right with you. I am <u>very</u> pleased that you have taken Breitkopf & H. as the sole agents for London. Furthermore. I ask you to inform me with whom I am now dealing regarding my opera, Harmonie or Drei-Masken Verlag. Harmonie have owed me a settlement for years. It is my keenest wish to negotiate with these people and bring the matter to an end. There is also an entr'acte in Romeo & Juliet which is frequently played in concerts, especially in England.[32] Could this

---

[31] FD asked for 25 per cent of retail in his letter dated 10 April 1913.

[32] This entr'acte was first entitled *The Walk to the Paradise Garden* in print in the vocal score published by Universal in 1922, but there is some evidence that Beecham used the title earlier in his concert programmes.

not be published on its own as an orchestral piece. I am asked so often about it, yet only the full score of the whole work exists.

What is the position concerning the new edition of my Piano Concerto?
With best wishes

Yours

ꙮ

No 73

Delius to Universal

29 April 1913
Grez-sur-Loing

Dear Herr Doktor,

In my statement for this year from the Genossenschaft Deutscher Tonsetzer is an entry which seems to me to be quite erroneous. In it the sum of Mk 17.44 has accrued to me from the Wiener Autorengesellschaft. This small sum can only, in my view, be related to a performance of Brigg Fair which took place in December 1910, while the fee for 2 performances of my Mass of Life on 17 & 18th February 1911 in Vienna still remains unpaid. When I raised the matter with the Genossenschaft in Berlin, I received the reply that the Mk 17.44 represent the fees for 2 perfs of the Mass and Brigg Fair, and that the Wiener Autorengesellschaft pays precisely these modest royalties for serious music. Since, in Berlin, I receive Mk 144-166 for two performances of the Mass, this appears to me to be barely credible. You as a publisher will know approximately how high a fee is paid in Vienna for a work that fills an evening, & I would be very grateful to you for this information. It seems all the more amazing since I have come across various pieces in the press concerning the Wiener Gesellschaft's dazzling results. Thus there must be some mistake in Berlin which I would like to clear up.[33]

With my thanks in advance,

Yours sincerely

---

[33] Mk 20 = £1. Austria apparently paid much less than Germany. Mk 150= approx £7 10s 0d. AKM paid about 40d.

ꕥ

No 74

Delius to Universal

5 May 1913
Grez-sur-Loing

Dear Herr Doktor,

I have just received your letter of 2.5. Good – to accommodate you I will accept your proposals, although you will remember that at the time I should have had 20 per cent of the retail price of each copy sold of libretto, vocal score etc. For this reason I hope you will accommodate me with the Arabesque, as I have already refused one down payment of Mk 1,000 & therefore cannot accept your proposed Mk 600, & besides I need the money.

To return to 'Fennimore and Gerda', hopefully you will shortly reach a formal agreement with the Kölner Theater. My conditions are as follows:

1. Performance to be held between 15th October & 15th December this year, with at least 5 (five) performances guaranteed.[34]
2. All sets to be produced new according to drawings prepared in Denmark, which I shall provide myself. 8 different sets are required for the 11 scenes in the work, of which 2 represent rooms, the others landscape views which are, however, quite simple and dispense with large scale stage construction because for the most part, they consist of large painted views. I absolutely will not have my work produced with the usual horrendous and tasteless decoration which does not suit my music at all.
3. My wishes for the production must be respected absolutely.
4. A full complement of first-rate talent must be engaged, the more so because Thomas Beecham intends to engage the entire cast of the premiere for performances next season (June) in London & possibly Paris.

If Cologne does not wish to fulfil these conditions, or cause any difficulties, the performance will pass to Frankfurt, who are very keen to have the premiere.

In the matter of royalties I trust to your judgement. I also hope to hear your reply concerning the Genossenschaft performance royalties, as I would dearly like to resolve the matter. It pleases me greatly that you have confidence in my work, as you assured me in your last letter. Just now I am taking paths that are quite different to those taken by others. When you have heard 'Fennimore & Gerda' you will immediately understand my point of view.

Yours very sincerely,

---

[34] The 1914 performances did not come off. The premiere was at Frankfurt on 21 October 1919.

No 75

Delius to Universal

6 May 1913
Grez-sur-Loing

Dear Herr Doktor,

I have just dispatched the full score, vocal score & text of Fennimore and Gerda to you.

In my letter of yesterday I did not deal with everything which I have already put in writing concerning the 37 pages of the score to be added to the vocal score. Since Lindemann's fee is quite generous, you will be able to see to it that he adds these 2 scenes without additional cost.[35]

However, you must insist that he does it immediately, he is a great dawdler. You can have him start right away on the Fennimore material & the vocal scores, so that Cologne can have the material as quickly as possible. Some time ago I reached agreement with Herr Brecher, who told me that my publisher should now make contact with him.

Thank you very much for kindly providing information about the Autorengesellschaft. Those Mk 17 for two performances of the Mass & Brigg Fair are just miserable; I should never have thought it poss. What's the point of belonging to a Genossenschaft?

With kind regards

Yours

No 76

Delius to Universal

13 May 1913
Grez-sur-Loing

Dear Herr Doktor,

I have just received your letter with the two contracts, which I shall return in a few days. You have made a slight error in regard to 'Fennimore and Gerda', namely 15 per cent instead of 20 per cent for the stage material. I do ask you above all to have the material for the singers prepared as quickly as possible, so they may have time to work themselves into their roles. And to have the end of the vocal score of

[35] This refers to the addition to *Fennimore* of the 2 *Gerda* scenes.

'Gerda' completed. Of course the deadline of 15 December may be extended a little if necessary.

I must thank you very much for your comments concerning the Wiener Autorengesellschaft. However, there is a misunderstanding which I would ask you to clear up with the Wiener Gesellschaft, or else there could be unpleasantness. The Mass brought in Mk 144 and 166 for each of 2 performances, making Mk 72 and 83 per performance. The Gesellschaft's comments on the Berliner Genossenschaft's mode of calculation is thus inaccurate. Besides, the Mass was also given twice in Vienna, the 2nd occasion being a popular concert. Please also inform the Wiener Autoren Gesellschaft that in this way I have received Mk 17 for 2 performances of Brigg Fair and 2 performances of the Mass, and that for this reason it is not worth the trouble of belonging to an Autorengesellschaft for so little reward.
With best wishes

Yours

ᘓᘒᘓᘒ

No 77

Delius to Universal

9 June 1913
Grez-sur-Loing

Dear Herr Doktor,

I have just returned from Germany & have consulted in Cologne with Brecher & the director Reymond. So the performance in Cologne is definitively agreed;[36] however, because the Cologne Opera is already rather heavily booked with new works, the premiere would for preference take place in autumn 1914, if in the coming season the date is too late in spring.

However, Brecher demands most strongly that the material be faultlessly prepared and told me that the material that you supplied for Korngold was so bad that even after 4 reading rehearsals it was impossible to eliminate all the errors. And of course, in comparison with my work, that was child's play. I must therefore insist that the entire orchestral material be printed, that is to say, from engraved strings & manuscript wind.

I shall return both contracts in a few days' time. There were a number of passages where amendments must be made.

In Jena, my work 'In a Summer Garden' enjoyed a resounding success.

Once again, then: faultless orchestral material is the first condition for a good production.

With best wishes

---

36 *Fennimore and Gerda.*

No 78

GDT to Delius

23 June 1913
Berlin

Dear Mr Delius,

I return to you attached the three publisher's drafts you sent to me and the supplementary agreement in respect of 'Fennimore & Gerda' and make the following comments.

1. Leuckart Contract

I have deleted everything from the draft which you should have deleted out of regard for your obligations to the Society. For the rest you can therefore sign this publishing contract – but I should like to bring to your attention one point which needs elucidation. You write that you will receive as payment for this contract Mk 16,000, payable in four instalments of Mk 4,000 and you mention that you have already received Mk 1,200 in advance so that you had altogether a fee of Mk 17,200. If the Mk 1,200 in question were in fact paid to you as an advance, Leuckart could, if this is not expressly made clear, subsequently establish a claim that this advance should of course be deducted from the collective fee of Mk 16,000, which alone is mentioned in the contract form. It will therefore be necessary for you to mention in your accompanying letter that Mk 16,000 are due to you according to the contract in addition to the Mk 1,200 already received by you, so that this sum should not therefore be deducted from the amount of Mk 16,000.

2. Arabesque Contract[37]

To the heading 'cession of copyright with the sole exception of the performing rights' you must for greater clarity add, at the same place I have marked with a cross, 'and mechanical rights'. In the same way, at the place I have marked four lines later after 'sole exception of the performing rights', you must add 'and mechanical rights'. Finally you must insert 'or otherwise exploited' at the place marked by me with a double cross in the fifth line from the end; otherwise it could in fact happen that the 15 per cent would only be paid to you on copies sold and that in numerous cases, the Universal-Edition would be only hiring out the material in which case you would have no claim. One cannot be too prudent.

3. Form of Contract for 'Fennimore and Gerda'

Here also 'and mechanical rights' must be inserted after the two lines of the heading, and in the same way four lines later as in the contract form for 'Eine Arabesque'.

Had the contract appeared without my cuts you would only have reserved the concert performing rights so that the Universal Edition, according to the substance of the contract, would have gained the stage performing rights and not simply that

[37] These suggestions were incorporated in the 25 June contract with UE.

stage performing licence. In respect of stage performances you would in that way have been able to make no protest nor have any voice in the various productions. I recommend you therefore to take the standpoint that the stage production rights, according to the substance of the contract, remain reserved to you and that you only give the publishers the licence to perform so that they are dependent on your decision in all doubtful cases. If you accept this proposition, you can otherwise sign the form of agreement and must make the respective alterations by separate agreement.

4. Separate Agreement for 'Fennimore and Gerda'

For the same reasons as in the 'Arabesque' contract, you must also make this correction in the paragraph marked by me with an 'a': '20 per cent on every stage copy bought and paid for or otherwise exploited' and later; '15 per cent...sold or otherwise exploited' sheet music and text editions. I recommend you to strike out altogether the paragraph immediately following. For according to it the publisher could do the greatest damage by cutting up the whole opera into little bits, putting them in various albums and paying you one settlement of Mk 100 instead of the 15 per cent under paragraph a). The Universal Edition operates in fact to a very large extent with such albums. In paragraph c) you must mention that the publisher does not obtain the performing rights himself but is only licensed by you for stage exploitations, something like the following '...from the publisher's receipts, I receive, while licensing you to exploit my work on the stage, from the performing rights...'. In the same sentence I should put the cost of a foreign translator onto the publisher, who already gets 20 per cent for stage exploitation abroad. It must therefore run: 'My share is to amount to 80 per cent from all other theatres, for which the cost of a foreign translator's share is to be borne by you'. In paragraph d) it must run: 'Accounting for concert performing fees will be according to the conditions of the GDT'.

For the rest you may definitely sign but I would not like to omit to draw your attention to the fact that for you it is a very hard condition that you should allow the publisher the possibility of withdrawing from the contract within three weeks of the first performance, and without giving any reasons, while you, if you wished to exploit the work further, would under the circumstances have to recompense your later publisher for the huge sums laid out by Universal Edition.

Frankly the Universal Edition will not undertake the slightest preliminary risk, but this will all be borne by you. I should find it fairer if you at least shared the risk, so that in the case of a withdrawal from the contract by the Universal Edition, you would only have to compensate them for half of the expenses still not met. If you share my view, you should insert at the point marked E) by me 'up to half'.

With Best Wishes,

Dr Kopf

ꟷ

No 79

Delius to Universal

25 June 1913
Grez-sur-Loing

Dear Herr Direktor,

I am returning the two contracts concerning the Arabesque & Fennimore & Gerda. I think all is in order. Tomorrow I shall send the power of attorney to you & the registered letter to Harmonie.

I would ask you kindly to pay the Mk 1,000 for the Arabesque into the Commerz u. Disconto-Bank, Berlin, Charlottenstr 47.[38]

We were very sorry not to be able to take our leave of you after the concert. I also truly regret that you heard such a miserable performance of Appalachia.[39] Beecham seems out of his depth with a 2nd rate foreign orchestra. I would never have thought it. But of course he has hardly any experience of other orchestras.
With kind regards from us both

Yours

No 80

Delius to Universal

27 June 1913
Grez-sur-Loing

Dear Herr Direktor,

I enclose the power of attorney; I have simultaneously sent a registered letter to Harmonie. On the 5th July I travel to Norway from Antwerp. My wife is to follow at the end of July or the beginning of August & we intend to take a wonderful tour through the western fjords & to Lofoten – this is the most beautiful part of all Norway. If you and your wife wish to accompany us on this tour we would be happy indeed. It will be by boat for some of the way.

Concerning the passage that deals with the album,[40] which I have struck through – it is invalid because fragments of this work cannot appear in this way. Even so, any

---

38 Advance as in contract.

39 An apparently unsuccessful (to FD) performance by Beecham and the Colonne orchestra, in the Paris Châtelet Theatre and a rare appearance by Hertzka at the performance.

40 *Fennimore and Gerda* Contract.

one of your successors could issue the opera in incomprehensible fragments, which I wish to avoid.[41]

With kind regards from us both, also to your wife, whom we hope to meet soon. I am as always yours

Frederick Delius

I shall send you all the documents concerning the settlements with Harmonie & the outstanding items.

ꕤꕤ

No 81

Harmonie to Delius

10 July 1913
Grez-sur-Loing

Dear Sir,

May we make reference to your letter of the 27th ult.[42]

Since your lawyers and, in the spring of last year, at your instigation, an auditor, dealt with the affair and came to what was, for all practical purposes, a negative result, the matter is closed from our point of view.[43] Despite this we will gladly strike an agreement with you and credit you with amounts reflecting the value of the individual works,[44] but we must ask that your proposals are made more accommodating to us than those you have recently made.

Yours faithfully,

ꕤꕤ

No 82

Delius to Jelka Delius

10 July 1913
Hotel Westminster
Kristiania

---

41 See the GDT letter dated 23 June 1913. Again FD has followed their advice.

42 FD had sent a power of attorney to UE the same day.

43 FD continued to believe that he had been short changed by Harmonie, the more so because Jadassohn had declined to meet him.

44 This point was covered in the UE/Harmonie agreement.

Dearest – Enclosed both Contracts which please send on – On Leuckart's other one write like I have done at the top – *Sowie des Rechtes für Mechanische Musick Instrumente* – Just for forms sake – It is pouring here. I leave for the station presently. I have signed both Contracts – you might ask Leuckart to send one back signed by him – Hertzka's letter sounds very nice – In haste & with love Fred.

Please ask Sander to send me a copy of the full scores: 2 of Paris: 2 of Dance Rhapsody – 2 of Summer Garden, 2 Brigg Fair 2 of Songs of Sunset – Say that I always received 5 copies from other Editors & I have only received from him 1 of Paris, 3 of Dance Rhapsody 2 of Summer garden, 2 of Brigg fair & 3 of Songs of Sunset – Tell Hertzka that I am under contract with the Genossenschaft for Mechanische Musikinstrumente – & that we hope still to see him in Norway in August –

Don't forget to cross out as I have done – 'mit Ausnahme des Passus der Mechanische Musick Instrumente, der in Fortfall kommt-

Perhaps it was stupid of me to alter this & if you think so then leave the one you send to Sander just like it is.[45] If you think there is no Kniff behind it. If you write '*Sowie des Rechtes für Mechanische Musick Instrumente*' then you must cross out the end of No 3: about the Passus etc.

No 83

Jelka Delius to Universal

13 July1913
Grez-sur-Loing

Dear Herr Direktor,

I sent the contract on to my husband & have just received it back with his signature.[46] Concerning the 'mechanical rights', my husband asks me to tell you that, as you correctly suspected, he is forced to this restriction by his agreement with the Genossenschaft. It is such a pity that it should be so.

At the same time that the power of attorney was given to you we asked Harmonie to send all further settlements to you. In spite of this we received today the enclosed letter. Since it follows from this letter that Harmonie are wary of you & would gladly reach a settlement, I am sending you today all the documents concerning the dispute, amongst which is a list sent to Harmonie in January 1913 detailing sums which my

[45] These alterations are for the Leuckart contract dated 10 July 1913, which was the subject of a dispute between Leuckart and the Delius Trust in 1996. This contract consolidated the separate agreements made for each work. In the main body of the contract FD, as is shown above, while ceding the copyrights in the works, reserved the performing and mechanical rights. In the second part he took a lump sum for the publishing rights. Later Leuckart claimed, without success, that FD had sold his performing and mechanical rights, which he had not.

[46] We have none of the enclosures. The contract would probably be for *Fennimore and Gerda*.

husband still claims. This sum could possibly be reduced a little in order to settle the matter.

Please first read my document dated Nov. 1911, then the accounts, etc. in the order in which I have arranged them. It will be difficult to plot a course through them!

I have kept back certain pieces of evidence from Breitkopf & Härtel, Dr Haym, Suter etc. & some earlier documents, so as not to demand too much of you. We do hope that the two of you can come to Norway. I leave on the 30th inst. from Rotterdam for Bergen, where I am to meet my husband. Do try to come too!

At the moment I am busy with my Fennimore & Gerda sketches.
Please convey my greetings to your dear wife

Jelka Delius

Enclosed contract & letter from Harmonie

No 84

Jelka Delius to Universal

20 July 1913
Grez-sur-Loing

Dear Herr Direktor

I received your letter of the 16th inst. yesterday. I am afraid I cannot send you the contracts because these are locked in a special briefcase, the key to which is in the possession of my husband. The terms of the contract are however, extremely simple:

Harmonie see to the publishing of the works & make all the necessary outlay. Only when the outlay has been covered by income do Harmonie & my husband share the profits, so in other words Delius receives 50 per cent of the income once expenses have been covered. Each work is accounted for individually. All restrictions re Mechanical reproduction rights are the same as in your contracts with my husband. The court case with Harmonie which my husband won concerned a clause in one of the contracts in which Harmonie wanted to secure an option to purchase all later works by Delius.[47] So that clause is completely invalid. Seadrift was the first work to be published by Harmonie & as you see, its costs are already covered. My husband however has, of course, yet to receive his share of the surplus.

Besides these works, Harmonie still owns several of my husband's English part songs which they acquired for an outright payment and on which my husband therefore has no claim.

---

[47] This was the December 1909 case.

I hope that it is now possible, after all, for you to pursue this matter. I thought that these contractual terms were already known to you!

What a shame that you are not coming to Norway! From his letters my husband sounds really hale and hearty.
With kind regards

Yours sincerely

No 85

Delius to Universal

1 September 1913
Grez-sur-Loing

Dear Herr Direktor,

I send my warmest thanks for your good news and am glad that everything is proceeding so well. However, I would greatly prefer it if the engraving of the score were to be made before the premiere, so that it could be conducted from an engraved proof, & I could also have a copy so as to be able to check carefully whether and which alterations are necessary before the final printing is made. Leuckart & Tischer always do this – for there is never much to be altered, merely some fine detail in the orchestration which I am unable to hear clearly without a score in my hand.

One other thing: The work is entitled An Arabesque (not: 'Arabesque'). Dedicated to Halfdan Jebe.

Is the orchestral material also fully corrected? As soon as the score of the Arabesque is engraved I will myself correct the first proof here.

As far as Harmonie is concerned I will of course do everything to support you – of course my demands must be covered in advance by a cash settlement.
With kind regards from us both

Yours

No 86

Delius to Universal

1 October 1913
Grez-sur-Loing

Dear Herr Direktor,

Many thanks for your letter of the 24th. I am only considering songs for the Tonkünstler-Verein concert – the 5 songs which you have taken over from Harmonie and the 3 Verlaine Songs which Tischer has published & an Indian Lovesong (Shelley) also published by Tischer. D'Albert has said nothing to me of chamber music – and neither have I written any.

Sadly, the premiere of the 2 Small Pieces for Orchestra at the Gewandhaus cannot be postponed, so I cannot attend. If the premiere of the Arabesque is to take place on the 26th November in Vienna, the preparation of the material is very urgent, in order to rehearse the choral & baritone parts immediately. I therefore urgently request that you send me the first proof without delay. The work is difficult & cannot be rehearsed overnight. Who is to sing the baritone part? The singer must have time to get a little used to it, & a rushed premiere of my music would serve no purpose whatsoever. The baritone must be a singer of the finest sensibility and truly musical, in the Felix v. Kraus vein. Who would you have on your list for the songs? You have not written to me at all about Cologne and how things stand there with Fennimore? I should also be pleased to know what you have arranged about the settlement which is due to me from Harmonie. You will also have received my statement for this year from Harmonie. Last year I was also owed money. It would of course please me greatly if you would take the affair in hand once and for all.
With kind regards

Yours

No 87

Delius to Jelka Delius

27 October 1913
Hotel Residenz
Ludwig Domansky
Vienna

Dearest – Your letter arrived yesterday Of course it is a horrible nuisance to have come so far for no concert, but it has not been for nothing – I have come at last to an arrangement with Hertzka after a fearful pitched battle – This is the result – I am to draw a line thro Harmonie's old account – Hertzka pays Jadassohn Mk 15,000 for his share in my music (It would have been much more but for advantages that Hertzka had given Jadassohn). From the moment the Contract is signed I receive 25 per cent of the Ladenpreis of everything sold with the exception of the 'Messe' when I receive 20 per cent for piano scores & 25 per cent for the rest. I consider I have made a good business – as I should anyhow never have got a cent from Harmonie &

my profits begin now at once[48] – He engraves the Piano Concerto[49] quite new – edits separately the R & J. entracte – edits also the scores of 'Seraillets Have'[50] etc – in fact goes in entirely for my music. The other composers who are on percentage profits only get 10 per cent. It took all my eloquence to prove to him that he was doing a good stroke of business – He has of course, now, to settle it with Harmonie. Instead of the Concert we had a box at the Opera for Die Königin von Saba – Goldmark. Gregor gave us a box – The music has really good things in it – but only when 'das Jüdische hervortritt'[51] – otherwise it is Wagner & Meyerbeer – I have made the acquaintance of Loewe & of d'Albert – Loewe has the Tonkünstler orchestra & is giving 'Lebenstanz' next season. He has also the Orchestra in Munich & gave 'Brigg Fair'. They are all very nice to me here & it was worthwhile coming. The food is very good every way. As yet I have seen A Variety Theatre & the Opera – But there is very little 'Eleganz' & I see very few pretty women – Of course they may be seen perhaps more on the Prater, but I have not been there yet – I am now correcting the parts of the 'Arabeske'[52] – As we hope Nedbal will lend us his Orchestra next Tuesday for 20 minutes during one of his rehearsals so that I may get an idea of the whole – with chorus & solo.

On Monday next before the other concert there is also a rehearsal of the chorus & Solo – Cyril Scott is playing his quintet on the same evening – I shall probably leave on Wednesday morning, pass the night at Munchen (Wolfs Hotel is very good & only Mk 3 a room) leave on Thursday morning for Paris – Schrecker I am certain is a jew – altho' he talks all the time against jews – He looks rather like Fried but fatter – He is a mixture of Busoni & Fried if you can imagine that – but nice & his wife is the prettiest woman I have yet seen in Vienna not a jewess[53] – They thought the 'Arabeske' 'wonderfully translated'.

In order to clinch the affair with Hertzka – I promised him that should I publish the Sonata & the Requiem – He should have them on the same terms as the others, – 25 per cent. Now dearest, adieu. I am off to the Universal to correct. Write soon. How Norsk of Ranghild – Hun angre.[54]

lots of kisses & love

Fred

---

48 See later for an argument between FD and UE as to whether FD received a royalty on stock taken over from Harmonie, or only on new printings.

49 UE did in fact issue a new edition of the 2-piano version of the Piano Concerto, but not of the orchestral score. The Entr'acte only followed, in a piano arrangement, about 20 years later and the orchestral scores of the songs not at all.

50 Danish for *In the Seraglio Garden.*

51 'when the Jews stand aside'.

52 Reading between the lines, it seems that the promised rehearsal did not come off due to the very bad orchestral parts, or if it did, it was delayed until early December. It seems probable that the first performance was on 28 May 1920, in Newport. One of FD's first letters to UE after the war, in 1918, takes up the state of the score and parts, now ready for publication, as if the war had never happened.

53 A hint of anti Semitism?

54 She's sorry.

ꕥ

No 88

Delius to Universal

27 November 1913
Vienna

Dear Direktor,

In order to offer you the opportunity to take over in their entirety all my works published by Harmonie, I declare myself prepared to forego all legal entitlements, of a material or any other nature, which are due to me with respect to Harmonie, through which action the opportunity will arise for the proposed new agreement between us concerning the works in question to come into force.

If, however, Harmonie does not find itself prepared to transfer the works in question to you in their entirety I shall, through my lawyer and without further delay, energetically press those claims to the entitlements due to me in various ways.
Yours faithfully

ꕥ

No 89

Delius to Harmonie

2 December 1913
Vienna
attn. Mr Alexander Jadassohn

Dear Sir,

With reference to the agreement to be concluded between you and Universal Edition AG, I declare that in the case of complete transfer of ownership of my works issued by your publishing company to the U.E. I waive all the material and other claims against you to which I am entitled once and for all.

I also agree not to receive any share of the amount paid by Universal Edition to you for transferring the works.

Yours sincerely,

No 90

Delius to Universal

11 December 1913
Grez-sur-Loing

Dear Herr Direktor,

I am sending to you today the corrected parts & the printed corrected score of my Arabesque. I am keeping the manuscript here until I have corrected 1.) the vocal score, which I have not yet received, & 2ndly) the woodwind, which I must go through once again.

When all my corrections are done I should also like to read one last proof of the score, as there were an incredible number of mistakes in it. Of course, nothing may be printed finally until I have heard a performance.

I should like to restate here that never in my life have I seen such sloppily unprofessional execution of orchestral parts,[55] I even note that before I received them they had been corrected again, but please cast your eye over the horns, celeste etc. & see what I have had to correct in pencil. I shall be unable to undertake so much work in future and if the opera parts are similar, I must with regret return them uncorrected. The copyist has so little knowledge of the conventions that he writes for the 2nd horn what is written for the 1st, & has the 4th horn also playing what the 3rd should be playing.

With parts like these the concert simply could not have gone ahead. Because of the masses of corrections they are now quite unreadable. My dear Direktor, I hope that I need not return to this subject.

I hope you have received Margot-la-Rouge and that you have finally reached agreement with Harmonie.

With best wishes from us both, to you and your wife

Yours

No 91

Delius to Universal

26 December 1913
Grez-sur-Loing

Dear Herr Direktor,

[55] This is why the November rehearsal was cancelled.

Enclosed please find 2 agreements for the works published by Harmonie & the 2 new works.

My lawyer has made a few small amendments to them and wishes me to sign them only in this form. I think you will find this all right, for the amendments are not vital.

Above all, however, my adviser expressly asks that I do not sign the letter of notice to Harmonie before the agreement between you and Harmonie has been concluded and you, that is to say Universal-Edition, have delivered to me both agreements with your signature.

In the songs, I have struck out 'also with orchestra' because only 3 of them are orchestrated and I should like to have all 5 together published for orchestra by you.

Please be so kind as to have both contracts copied out & returned to me in duplicate, with one copy of each bearing your signature.

I still await the 2nd proof of the orchestral score of the Arabesque & the vocal score of same.

I am currently correcting the copy & original of the vocal score of Fennimore. Please only send me already corrected material, which saves a terrible amount of work for which I really have no time whatsoever. The copy is very clearly and well written but a great many sharps and flats etc. are omitted.[56]

The orchestral parts of Fennimore and Gerda must be fully corrected before they are sent to me. I see from the choral parts that you entitle Fennimore 'opera'. The word 'opera' is inappropriate, here is the correct title:

Fennimore and Gerda

Two Episodes from Jens Peter Jacobsen's Niels Lyhne

in Eleven Pictures

Set to music
by
Frederick Delius

We both thank you sincerely for your kind wishes & reciprocate the same to you and your dear wife. Please also send my kind regards to Dr Kalmus!

Yours

[56] FD must have wondered if he was going to have the same problems with UE of accurate performing material as he had had with Harmonie.

1914

Thirty-two known performances were logged. There were possible future performances of *Fennimore and Gerda* and *A Village Romeo and Juliet* which were to come to nothing. There was also the intriguing suggestion that Nijinsky might dance to the *Dance Rhapsody* No.1. Had he done so, would this have pointed Delius in a new direction?

The publishing correspondence is concerned with errors in the performing material and Delius trying to pin Hertzka down as to exactly what Universal had agreed with Harmonie over the stock that Universal had bought, although the formal agreement was not concluded until after the war. Delius painstakingly pointed out the mistakes in the parts for *Fennimore and Gerda* and *An Arabesque.*

For a non-orchestral player, Delius was surprisingly solicitous in insisting on clear writing, and decent cues, although he was probably more concerned that bad parts would inhibit the performances. One oddity was that although he wrote to Universal pointing out the need for cues in the bass oboe part, he never spotted that in writing for it at pitch, using bass and C clefs, rather than in the treble clef, an octave above the pitch required, he was making life unnecessarily difficult for the player, something not corrected until the 1990s.

War started in August. The Deliuses left Grez-sur-Loing in September, and by November were in England. A letter from Delius to Norman O'Neill shows a rare glimpse of Delius showing interest in anything other than his music. By 1919 when correspondence with Universal resumes, it was another world.

The performance of *A Mass of Life* in February 1914 in Wiesbaden was the last of which we have a record until 1925.

No 92

Delius to Universal

12 January 1914
Grez-sur-Loing

Dear Herr Direktor,

I am very sorry that the matter has not been settled. Moreover I do not understand your letter. Either you had made an agreement with Jadassohn or you had not. My returning the agreements a little sooner or later could change absolutely nothing because after all you had my agreement. Very well! I ask you to let me have a definite answer, either yes or no, as soon as possible. If nothing comes of the matter I shall take legal action against Herr Jadassohn.

The vocal score (copy) of Fennimore which you sent me is incomplete because all red notes have been left out. If you have sent a similar one to Brecher he will not be able to do a thing with it. Please send him the original vocal score and a corrected copy of the score.
With kind regards

Yours

ꕥ

No 93

Delius to Universal

16 January 1914
Grez-sur-Loing

Dear Herr Direktor,

I have just received your ltr dated the 13th[57] & make haste to reply.

I have made no alteration whatsoever to the contract discussed in Vienna, because when you spoke to me of the Mk 2, 233.23 paid by you I understood that it concerned material you have taken & and already sold, but not the entire remaining stock. I should be receiving my 25 per cent for each copy sold from 1 January 1914.

The second point re retail price I would gladly delete since it is really of no special significance to me.

What you say about my extraordinary care & my lack of trust surprises me coming from a head as level as yours. You must know yourself that it is of the greatest importance for our later good collaboration that we both supervise business arrangements quite clearly & down to the smallest detail before we embark upon them. The fact that I have made that a rule since my previous bad experiences is something we discussed in Paris, & and you yourself recommended I do nothing before having consulted my adviser.

If I had not the fullest trust in you, I would certainly not have placed my settlement with Harmonie in your hands. Besides one cannot base contracts on trust. You could disappear tomorrow and a second Jadassohn take over at the head of Universal-Edition.

Believe me, you have my fullest confidence.
With best wishes

Yours

Frederick Delius

---

[57] We do not have the Universal/Harmonie agreement, or that between FD and Universal covering the purchase by Universal of the Harmonie stock and rights. Nevertheless the thrust of its terms is clear from FD's complaint.

PS I am today returning some of the parts of the Arabesque; however because I have no score here I can only look through them à peu près. Those passages marked in the margin must be compared with the full score.

ꧻꧻ

No 94

Delius to Universal

22 January 1914
Grez-sur-Loing

Dear Herr Direktor,

I have received your letters (17th & 20th January)[58] & frankly admit that I really do not understand you. Your replies are really too vague for me. Please kindly answer me the following questions.

1. Is the Mk 2,233.33 you paid, for the entire stock of material that is still in Harmonie's hands? Or for what and for how many copies did you pay?
2. If you intended not to pay me 25 per cent on these copies in your stock, on what did you want to pay 25 per cent per copy sold as of 1 January 1914? Because you told me expressly that I would receive my percentage from 1 Jan. 1914 onwards.[59]

I have altered absolutely nothing in the contract, but merely introduced clarity; if, however, you believe that I have changed something, please explain to me in clear words.

Why has a deterioration suddenly taken place for you?

If our relations, as we both wish, are to remain on pleasant terms I must not remain unclear about these matters.

Kind regards
Yours
PS For both my new works I wish to retain the utmost freedom.

---

58 We don't have these letters.

59 A good business-like point. Had the stock remained with Harmonie, FD would have been entitled under the terms of his contract to 50 per cent of profits when costs had been recovered. It seems reasonable that under the new agreement, once Universal had bought the stock, they should pay a royalty on all sales from the date of purchase.

ஐ௸ஐ௸

No 95

Delius to Universal

28 January 1914
Grez-sur-Loing

Dear Herr Direktor,

You still have not answered my main questions, above all: Of which copies am I actually supposed to receive my 25 per cent from 1st Jan 1914 under these conditions?

You told me expressly as one of the main advantages of our agreement that in this way, from 1 Jan. 1914 I should receive 25 per cent of each copy sold. Of which copies then?

If I am to renounce all my demands on Harmonie & for some considerable period am to receive absolutely nothing instead of my 50 per cent [of profits], then I truly I do not know where the advantage lies for me.

Moreover you write to me that you have taken over a 'large stock' from Harmonie. From your books you must know how many copies you have taken over for Mk 2,233.[60] Also I do not understand what further claim you have against Harmonie for copies which you have bought.

You must admit yourself that your explanations are very vague. Just 2 questions can clear the whole matter up, namely how much stock you have taken over, & how much is still with Harmonie.

Please answer me these questions.

Would you suggest to Weingartner that he performs the two small pieces for orchestra which are published by Tischer & Jagenberg,

On hearing the first Cuckoo in Spring
And Summer night on the River

They are both quite new; apart from Nikisch in Leipzig, no one in Germany has played them yet.

Kind regards

Yours

ஐ௸ஐ௸

No 96

Delius to Universal

31 March 1914
Grez-sur-Loing

60 £110.

Dear Herr Direktor,

I am just looking through the orchestra parts of Fennimore; & I see that sadly they are terribly bad and illegibly, shoddily, written. It must certainly be the same copyist who did the Arabesque & I protest against this. This is how he writes e.g.

Who could read that on the player's stand?

What is that supposed to mean? Is it meant to be 4/4?

he writes fortissimo thus

You see, just like in the Arabesque, now and again [in divisi passages] he has suddenly written both halves of the violins on the same stave so that the effect is quite wrong by virtue of having all the violins playing what should be played by only half of them. – Also the lines are written so close together that notes far above the stave (vielgestrichen) can no longer be understood at all. You should take a look at Leuckart's parts alongside these. He engages first-class copyists – there is hardly a single mistake in them. I am still on the first violins but I tell you, if the parts are as bad as these I shall return them to you with the request that they be prepared by a first class copyist.

With reference to the Arabesque, I shall take the necessary steps where the translation is concerned.

With kind regards,
Frederick Delius

4 April

So as to do you no injustice, I did not send the letter until I had seen further parts. Well, you have told me yourself that you would not shrink from any expense to come up with faultless material. – And then you send me such parts. A good performance depends on good material. There are not many errors in the notes, but the notes are unreadable & untidy & squashed up as though someone was trying to save paper. In addition, cues are missing throughout the horn parts. Why should some poor horn player count over 100 bars & then have no cue? In the 3rd flute the cues are completely absent up until the closing scenes. In the bass-oboe there are no cues whatsoever. Again and again, the divisi strings are written incorrectly; from all this I see that your copyist is not versed in the conventions in these respects. Before[61] printing, the whole of the material must be redone afresh. – In the strings there are

---

[61] Although FD had insisted on engraved string parts and lithographed (from manuscript) wind in his letter of 9 June 1913, it is clear that his demands had been ignored.

always a couple of well written copies & the rest then bad & hasty, as if he wanted to be finished as quickly as possible. I am really quite angry about these parts. As early as last year Brecher warned me about your material; but it seems that everything I say fails to bear fruit.

The result will be bad rehearsals & all round dismay. I have only just started and the horns & the bass-oboe & 3rd flute must be completely redone. Where should it be done? Brecher is sure to have a good copyist, so it could be done in Cologne. How is it that your reader has not seen the faults? You cannot expect me to do such a job & this is the last material of this kind that I shall correct.[62]

I hope you have corrected those small errors in the Arabesque vocal score which I told you about. Please send me a few copies; I have also had requests from England about the performance & am in contact with a translator. I shall write to you shortly about the fee for same.

With kind regards

No 97

Delius to Universal

20 April 1914
Grez-sur-Loing

Dear Herr Direktor,

In reply to your last letter I would like to say that you are still in error. I did not personally do corrections to the Arabesque at all, it was the editor of the vocal score. You did indeed send me a copy for perusal, from which I would be able to see whether it was a usable vocal score and I took the opportunity to indicate a number of mistakes, but naturally believed that, as usual, the editor would do the final proofreading. If he has done so, then he has done it badly indeed, but not I. When I have completed correcting – I always write 'ready to print' on it. Please note this for future works; print nothing before I have written 'ready to print' on it.

Am sending today all the strings and the harp, 1st flute 2nd & 3rd flute, 1st oboe & bass oboe & triangle.[63] In all the latter the notes are corrected & correct, but many cues are missing. In the bass oboe there are none at all & it must therefore be redone, as must the 3rd flute. Whether you are able to insert cues legibly in the others I cannot judge. Otherwise they must be done yet again from scratch by a truly competent copyist.

The celli are all completely corrected & well written. The double basses on the other hand are dreadful; the 1st copy is corrected; but because the division of the instruments is completely and utterly wrong, I have not corrected the extra parts.

---

62 FD followed up with a postcard on 7 April having discovered more errors.

63 These comments refer to *Fennimore and Gerda.*

In the same way, the violins & violas, which are likewise continuously wrongly divided, must be re-corrected according to the 1st copy of same which I corrected. I request that all those passages corrected with coloured pencil should be done from scratch both in the first copy & where the divisi is wrong. It will otherwise be impenetrable. Also those pages which are so squashed up like e.g. page 8 in the 1st violins page 33 1st violins, also page 5, in the 2nd violins p. 2, must be replaced. I advise and request you to have the violas re-done because nothing can be done with the incorrect divisi & the notes are so illegible. You will receive the full score & the rest of the material from England.

With these corrections I have really done my utmost & worked myself into the ground, in a way I shall never do again.[64] I now ask you as a matter of urgency to do your part to bring the material to a fully usable & properly corrected state, because I shall not correct it again. I do not wish the rehearsals to serve the purpose of improving the material, instead of assisting the expression of my music.

At the same time I am sending you today the text ready to print.

I also advise you to buy the piano concerto urgently in accordance with your proposal; we would then enter into our terms discussed in Vienna (25 per cent for me).

Please also a line to let me know whether you have received the settlement from Harmonie?

With best wishes

No 98

Delius to Universal

9 May 1914
Grez-sur-Loing

Dear Herr Direktor,,

Today I am sending the corrected choral parts of the Mass back to you. I request that you compare these parts again very carefully with the new vocal score,[65] because in the 2nd Tanzlied alone I have discovered two further glaring errors; e.g. at the end the 2 bars are missing again, the other passage is 3 missing notes which I have written in in pencil. Those passages you indicated as questionable I have corrected properly – however I have not made comparisons.

There remains one passage which Schuricht altered and which I would like to retain. I therefore ask that you insert the correction in all vocal scores & full scores: Namely p. 78 of the new vocal score in the 2nd bar solo soprano, 1st soprano & 1st tenor should sing the G instead of C, thus:

---

64 Having lost the first performance of *An Arabesque* because of unplayable parts, FD was desperate to have a usable set for *Fennimore and Gerda*.

65 Presumably a reprint.

I have corrected it in the parts.
Besides this, page 112 of the new vocal score is an error. Page 112, bar 1, chorus 1 [must] read

And similarly in the same passage Chorus II tenor. In the parts this is already corrected but please put it in the vocal scores and full scores.

In addition, I ask you to send the whole of the material concerning Harmonie that we sent you earlier to Herr. Justizrat Heinitz, Hardenbergstr 1a Berlin-Charlottenburg, and to advise me here at the same time whether Harmonie have given you an answer within the time period set by you.

Yours most sincerely

No 99

Delius to Universal

19 June 1914
Grez-sur-Loing

Dear Sir,

I discover from my lawyer that he has not yet received the material from you concerning Harmonie. Moreover because he is very sceptical about the outcome of the settlement from Harmonie I would ask you to send him the material sent to you last summer in its entirety. Address Herr. Justizrat Heinitz,[66] Hardenbergstr 1a Berlin-Charlottenburg.

I have spent Frs 10.50 for receipt & dispatch of the packet for ‘Fennimore’, which does not include the packets of scores & parts from England; I shall inform you of this sum in a few days from London & ask you to credit me with the Frs 10.50 provisionally.[67]

Besides this, I ask you once again not to hand out advance copies of my works without my prior agreement. E.g. Beecham is giving a Delius concert in London at the beginning of July in which he wants to present the Arabesque. Instead I must now wait until Wood,[68] God knows when, gives it in the English provinces, because

66 Died in the war.

67 This relates to FD to Universal (20 April 1914), which refers to receiving parts from England.

68 Universal had offered the first performance of *An Arabesque* to Wood without telling FD. In fact Wood withdrew, although the card from Universal on 1 August telling FD this never arrived.

he has no choir in London, whilst Beecham has the entire cast of the Russian Opera at his disposal.

Yours most sincerely,

ഇന്ദഇന്ദ

1915–1918

The War Years

The Deliuses left Grez in September 1914, becoming tangled up in the traffic chaos caused by the German advance to the Marne, and went to England at Beecham's invitation. Initially involved in attending performances of his works, Delius was soon at work composing, as though nothing had happened.

His last surviving letter to Hertzka at Universal until after the war, dated May 1915, was written as though there were no barriers to musical life as before. It is full of the usual complaints about the non-availability of his music in London and the USA, where performances were taking off. If war had not broken out, Delius's American reputation would have been different.

In May 1915, Beecham, to help the Delius finances, entered into an agreement with Delius to buy the copyright of four pieces for £900,at the rate of £300 per year, and publish them, on the basis that the copyrights would be returned when the purchase price had been recouped, which as far as we know was what happened, although in 1918 Beecham was unable to honour the payments. This was a generous act by Beecham to help alleviate Delius's financial position. The £900 would have been very welcome. The works he took were no money spinners and were not immediately published. The *Légende* was published by Forsyth in 1916 and the Violin Sonata no.1 by the same firm in 1917. *North Country Sketches*, first performed by Beecham in 1915, was not published until 1923 although there may well have been manuscript score and parts available.

Irrespective of the difficulties of obtaining performances and fees for them, whether in England or on the Continent, on the outbreak of war, the United Kingdom copyright in works published in Germany or Austria before the outbreak of war was vested in the Public Trustee under the Trading with the Enemy Acts. That this happened to Delius can be inferred from Heseltine's letter to him of 11 October 1916, when, referring to the possibility of a production of *A Village Romeo and Juliet*, Heseltine writes 'the question of performing fees can be arranged with the Board of Trade here'.

There was still a lot of interest in Delius's music. There were 30 recorded performances in 1915, of which 20 were conducted in England by Beecham and several were in the USA, where Grainger was promoting his music.

Then performances dropped off: five in 1916, seven in 1917, nine in 1918: after which activity declined still more until 1923 when there was a marked increase.

In late 1915 the Deliuses returned to Grez for the duration of the war and in 1916 Delius was at work on the Requiem, – ' I don't think I have ever done better than this', he wrote to Heseltine. Beecham disagreed. 'The *Requiem*', wrote Beecham in his biography of Delius had 'excited less interest than any of his other large-scale compositions'. He felt that its invention was not on the same level as in previous works and, more important, it was a strange psychological miscalculation by Delius: – a non-Christian Requiem, dedicated in 1914 'to the memory of all young artists fallen in the war'.

Delius's fall from the position of pre-eminence that he seemed to have achieved by 1914 is perceptibly noted by Beecham. 'It would really seem that his sequestered life at Grez over the preceding period of seven years had not only increased his attitude of isolation and independence, but had bred in him a spirit of growing indifference towards the ways of thought and action to be found in the majority of those around him'.

There were to be no further works on the scale of the *Requiem*. He turned his attention to instrumental compositions, and, needing money, sought English publishers, certainly until he could re-establish himself with Universal.

The war over, Delius wrote to Hertzka in December 1918, picking up the correspondence as though nothing had happened in the meantime, full of ideas and eager to sort out his financial affairs.

He returned to London with seven manuscript works, including the *Poem of Life and Love*, *A Song before Sunrise*, *An Arabesque*, the Cello Sonata and the Double Concerto, which he was keen to place.

No 100

Thomas Beecham to Delius

22 May 1915
8a, Hobart Pl. S.W.
London.

My dear Delius,

I write to confirm the arrangement proposed in my letter to you of April 29th last and since accepted by you which I here set out again – That I buy from you

The Sonata for Violin and Piano (£300)

The Légende for Violin and Orchestre – (£150)

The North Country Sketches – (£250)

Three Songs (£200).

The total amount payable to you will be therefore £900 to be disbursed by me over a period of three years in equal payments of £300 per annum – After the expenses of publication are cleared off, I will hand over to you the copyright of the above works to be your own property.

You can accept this letter as binding upon me and as the equivalent of a written contract – If you write me formally an acceptance of this, the matter will be in order.

Yours

Thomas Beecham

PS Having already paid you £50 (per letter of the 29th last) on account of this agreement, the remaining sum due to you is £850.

There are no further publisher letters until after the war

No 101

Delius to Universal

1 December 1918
London

Dear Herr Hertzka,

At last the war has come to an end and it is now possible – thank God – to resume our relations. Above all I would like to hear how you have fared during this long time?

I am now sending you the final proof of the score & parts of the 'Arabesque' and the excellent English translation, so that the work can now be published.

How do things stand with 'Fennimore & Gerda'? I hear that Brecher is now in Frankfurt.

I have many enquiries from America; just like here my music has not been obtainable over there for a long time now. It is of the greatest importance to have a good agency in both countries. For London I recommend Augener rather than Chester. As Augener has published a violin concerto and a double concerto of mine he will be far more interested in getting things circulated than Kling.[69] There is to be a centenary festival in America for Walt Whitman (poet of Sea Drift). The Boston Publishing Company wants to publish an American edition of Sea Drift. What is the position with Harmonie now? In this matter we must arrive at a final arrangement. As you know I have not yet got a single penny for all these works: Appalachia, Sea

[69] Not strictly true. The Violin Concerto MS is dated 1916. It was first performed by Albert Sammons on 30 January 1919, and it was published in 1921 by Augener. The Double Concerto MS is dated 1915. It was first performed on 21 February 1920 and published by Augener in 1922. Both works were assigned to Augener in 1919.

Drift, Mass of Life, Piano Concerto, A Village Romeo & Juliet, 5 Songs. Also there must be no delay in bringing out a new edition of the piano concerto. Everybody wants to play it and no material is to be had.

Trusting to have good news from you soon.

With kind regards,

ꙮ

1919

The year began with high hopes. The Deliuses were still in London, where Delius had four first performances: The cello sonata, the violin concerto, *Eventyr* and the revised 4-movement version of the 1916 string quartet. All four works, which had been composed during the war, were well received and Delius felt confident of his future. There were plans for a visit to the USA to see Grainger.

Fennimore and Gerda had its first performance on 21 October in Frankfurt. Beecham had plans to revive *A Village Romeo and Juliet* in the autumn of 1919, but Delius, remembering the problems over material for the 1910 performance postponed it until the following year.

Universal had still not concluded an agreement with Harmonie and Delius was short of money. He met the Public Trustee in London without having any funds released. He was sure that Harmonie had made profits from his music, which should be split 50/50, but he couldn't prove anything. Harmonie was prepared to offer him something to settle the dispute and Delius told the Public Trustee that Harmonie owed him Mk 14,000. At the end of the year a deal was done between Universal and Harmonie, and Delius undertook to abandon his action against Harmonie if a satisfactory agreement could be reached.

As he told Hertzka, he had sold works to British publishers to raise money, but he was able to offer the *Requiem*, *Dance Rhapsody No.2* and the *Poem of Life and Love* to Universal against an advance.

No 102

Delius to Universal

10 August 1919
Fosheim Saeter
Norway

Dear Herr Direktor,

Your letter of 31st July finally reached my hands yesterday evening, after your telegram arrived at lunchtime. It baffles me why the letter was not sent on to Norway since the address Bergen, Poste restante was written on the back. I wrote immediately to Zeiss and Brügmann[70] – unfortunately without knowing the latter's address. I addressed it to the newspaper Politiken, which once published an interview with him about the opera.

Hopefully you have only made a small run of vocal scores,[71] so that any errors can be corrected later on the plates. You can imagine the pleasure with which I look forward to this premiere. We are all ready to travel from here direct to Frankfurt and only hope that this will be permitted without further difficulties for us; for this reason I have asked Geh. Zeiss to send me a ltr stating reasons for the necessity of my journey. Whether Brügmann receives our message before his leaving for Germany is, of course, open to doubt. We have my wife's sketches for the sets here & only await details about whether to send them or bring them.[72]

As far as Harmonie is concerned, the power of attorney which I gave you before the war naturally remains valid. At the moment I can do nothing else, because my financial matters in Germany are now fully in the hands of the English 'Public Trustee', to whom I had to declare my assets and outstanding sums owing to me in Germany during the war. I gave the Public Trustee Mk l4, 000[73] as the sum owed to me by Harmonie. Since Harmonie has been publishing my works, 1906, I have not received a pfennig, I even paid Mk 1,100 for the material for A Village Romeo & Juliet to be prepared and Harmonie then took over this material without refunding me the costs and lent it to Beecham for his opera performance. My lawyer was in the process of bringing an action against Harmonie for fraud when the war broke out and I have not yet made contact with him again.

If, however, you can reach a settlement with Harmonie which is satisfactory for me I would drop my action, so as to be rid of this unpleasantness once for all. Harmonie must pay of course & transfer its interests to you. I personally wish to have nothing to do with Harmonie, and the contract which we discussed in Vienna once should be valid in future.

---

70 Dramaturg at Frankfurt?

71 The 'provisional printing' of *Fennimore and Gerda.*

72 *Fennimore and Gerda* was first performed on 21 October 1919 at Frankfurt a/ M.

73 Mk 14,000 at the 1919 exchange rate was £62. The Mk 1,100 FD paid for the *Village Romeo* material in 1906 was worth £55.

Please do not complete the final printing of the Arabesque – full score, before I have heard the work myself in Vienna. I replied to a letter from Prof Schneider of Vienna (Musikblätter des Anbruch) a few days ago and am looking forward to the impending performances of the Arabesque, Mass of Life & Appalachia.[74]

Please, Herr Direktor, do everything in your power to clear up the affair with Harmonie so that we can finally be free of this unreal firm.
With best wishes from us both

Cordially yours

We have not received your letter & telegram to Grez.
A postcard, attached to the letter reads:
From now on please address correspondence to
Poste restante
Kristiania

We have heard from Dr Zeiss that the premiere[75] is set for the 18th Oct & intend to travel to Frankf. between the 15th & 20th.
With best wishes
Yours

No 103

Delius to Universal

14 August 1919
Fosheim Saeter
Røn, Valdres
Norwegen

Dear Herr Director,

We have just arrived here in Norway & are staying for the time being at this address. Yesterday I received 2 vocal scores of Fennimore & Gerda via London. I was very pleased about this & hope Lindemann has corrected it well throughout, because my handwritten copy is heaving with mistakes. You can imagine how excited I am about further news, because I only heard about the impending premiere in Frankfurt in the Danish papers. Please write to me here as soon as possible. I have not received a letter from you yet.

Sir Thomas Beecham wants to give A Village Romeo & Juliet in November & of course he needs all the material.[76] I therefore request that you make contact with him as soon as possible. Write to him adr Sir Thomas Beecham Bart, Covent Garden

---

74 None of these performances seem to have taken place.

75 *Fennimore and Gerda*

76 This did not take place.

Opera House, London. Before leaving I promised Beecham that you would write to him & naturally I am counting on you yourself to arrange all practical matters with him. Please also send him the vocal score of Fennimore & Gerda; he is very interested in this work & it is expected that he will give it in the next spring season in London; thereafter he [intends] to go to the New York Metrop. Op. with his entire troupe & give it there as well. The prospects are thus very good.

The Arabesque has already been sent on its way to you from London & only requires the last correction. I wrote all the rest to you in an earlier letter which you have hopefully received in the meantime & replied to. Yesterday I heard from Tischer that you are well – I am truly happy about that – after all these dreadful years of war.

Tischer wrote that he would be interested to know which of my works would be reprinted in the Entente countries. Nothing has been reprinted, but everything has long since sold out.

Hoping for news soon
Kind regards

Yours

No 104

Delius to Universal

18 November 1919
Hotel Tour Eiffel
1 Percy Str.
Oxford Str.

Dear Herr Direktor,

Many thanks for your kind letter, which arrived before our departure.

I have postponed the performance of Romeo & J., which was to take place on the 26th. The material that Beecham is using is the old one prepared by me, because no one here really knew who to go to. However the vocal scores are entirely missing.[77] Could you not send a very large consignment of same here immediately?

It is partly for this reason that I am postponing the performance – though only for a few days. I hope that you have been able to travel to Berlin at last & that you have settled the whole business with Harmonie. Just now it would be colossally important. Because I am telegraphing you at the same time as this, I hope that the vocal scores are already on their way. I am constantly receiving letters about the piano concerto & the songs, etc. Just now this must all be here, where the interest thanks to the opera is so lively. I have had a long discussion in very friendly terms with Volkert (Schott-Augener) & we have finally agreed to hand over the Requiem to you, because there are so many more opportunities for performances of it in Germany & Austria. With

[77] The material should have been returned to Harmonie after the 1910 performances.

the choir situation here it is far too difficult. However the Requiem will be done here in London in early March & conducted by Coates. I have therefore, because, as you know, I must have money, transferred the Ballad for Orchestra[78] & my String Quartet to Volkert.
The works which you will get are therefore[79]

1. The Requiem
2. A poem of Life and Love
3. North Country Sketches
4. The Second Dance Rhapsody

However I am counting on you giving me at least Mk 12,500 for the Requiem, the other works at Mk 5,000 each as agreed. I have made a sacrifice, to secure you the Requiem, because I am convinced that it is a work which will gain the greatest significance in Germany.

I have not received any critiques of Fennimore, and have read the one by P. Bekker. I am of course <u>very</u> keen to hear what is going to happen with Stockholm & Copenhagen? If it were possible to photographically reduce the set drawings I would like to have them here & also for America.

I have not yet received my vocal score of Fennimore & also Ph. Heseltine, who is to translate the work & also wants to publish a long article about it in a music paper – has not had a vocal score; his address is

35 Warrington Crescent
Maida Vale
London.

With kind regards from us both
Yours

PS I hope it is clear to you that I am making a Mk 20,000 sacrifice by giving you the 3 orchestral works for an advance of Mk 5,000 each!!!!!
[ps in FD's handwriting]

No 105

Delius to Universal

6 December 1919
Grez-sur-Loing

[78] *Eventyr.*

[79] In fact, *North Country Sketches* and the Second Dance Rhapsody went to Augener and not UE. Also, *North Country Sketches* was one of the works sold to Beecham, for which FD had received money, although Beecham did not publish it until 1923.

Dear Herr Direktor,

Yesterday I received your ltr of 1st December and immediately telegraphed you: 'Accepte', because I want to be done with Harmonie once and for all despite everything. When I travelled to Munich in 1912 to talk with Jadassohn, he went to Berlin, in spite of a previously agreed rendezvous. I then wrote to him and protested & he gave me another rendezvous a fortnight later in Munich with my official accountant. I arrived there from Venice. The accountant and I were at his office at 10 in the morning, but Jadassohn was absent again & there was a bookkeeper there who had not a clue about anything. It then transpired that he kept no book at all on my work – there were just a few cards there, (the so-cld. card-system) they were quite incomplete & unsatisfactory, so that most questions could not be [answered] at all. My accountant explained to me that I was probably dealing with a swindler & advised me to pursue a legal course. At that point I turned to Counselor Franz Heinitz [in] Berlin, who took the matter in hand.

The 1912 account was… so wrong, that we then prepared the Munich Revision. In the case of several of my works, he had already made a 2nd edition and probably more. E.g. the Sheffield Festival did 'Seadrift' in 1909 & alone took 400 vocal scores. Print runs of only 1000 & then a further 200 appeared on the account & only a few were said to have been sold!!! Everything was like this. E.G. I personally paid 1,100 marks for the material for R. & Juliet for performances in London and Berlin, and Jadassohn then took payment for the use of it for the London performance.

Heinitz never received replies to his letters to Harmonie, and just as the action for fraud was about to be brought, the war broke out. You know how Jadassohn – an eel – he always knew how to string the affair out.

I still possess all the correspondence of course, that is to say I believe so, and could produce it again. I hope he will now really send the account & [I would] ask you to forward same to me immediately. If Jadassohn talks about a coupleof hundred Marks then that is just grotesque, since he owes me Mk 1,100 for the R. & J. material alone. Jadassohn's get-out, that I regarded the Mk 12,000 expenses as my investment is just laughable. Since Counselor Heinitz, who had all the material, has died in the meantime it would prob. be complicated to throw light upon all these details once again from the start &, as I said, if Jadassohn's account is <u>in any way acceptable</u> I would sooner wipe the slate clean.

To reiterate, the claim that after the investigation with the bookkeeper, I did not press most energetically and send official letters of protest through Heinitz this claim is entirely false.

But in spite of everything I give you my consent. Act as swiftly as possible. My wife is in the process of preparing the title page for the vocal score.

Please send me the corrections of the Fennimore score with the amendments & also of the vocal score after all the same small amendments have been made in the latter.
With kind regards from my wife and me,
Cordially,

Yours

No 106

Delius to Universal

30 December 1919
Grez-sur-Loing

Dear Herr Direktor,

I have just received your letter of the 18th Dec. and am sending att. the signed paper. I am making this sacrifice, as I told you, because I have so much faith in your publishing house and your enterprising spirit. However I hope fervently that you will manage the repayment by Harmonie of at least the 1,100 marks which I paid in cash for the R. & Juliet material.

As far as the new works are concerned, I must draw your attention to the contract which we discussed in Frankfurt, which may only be interpreted as a draft, not as a finalised agreement. Broadly speaking it is roughly valid, but with some amendments, namely I need English money, although I have received a £200 advance from Augener's,[80] it will not last until I get my money back, that is why the contract must read as I told you from the very beginning in Frankfurt:

£50 advance for Poem of Life and Love
Mk 5,000 advance Dance Rhapsody No.2
Mk 10,000 advance Requiem

Unfortunately I cannot give you the songs for orchestra which we discussed because I see, having looked at them again, that 3 of them have appeared in Tischer & Jag. as songs with piano & one of them is with Harmonie Verlag – 5 songs.

You can pay £50 immediately and £50[81] in 3 months, the rest within 6 months – or, if you would much rather, 9 months.

The situation is also, am I right, that I receive 25 per cent [of the] gross [retail price] of those quantities of Harmonie works that are in stock.

For some weeks, Heseltine has been busy working on the translation of Fennimore from my copy. He would like to leave his fee, & also those for the vocal score and translation of the Requiem with you. He intends to go to Vienna, where he will then use the money up.[82] Please come to an arrangement with Mr Heseltine himself. He is truly an excellent translator & does splendid vocal scores. He has also transcribed North Country Sketches for 4 hand piano; he also translated the Arabesque & did the piano score of my violin concerto. The English text must be in the new edition of 'Fennimore' of course. I shall receive it in a few days and will send it on to you straightway.

---

80 For *North Country Sketches*?

81 At the 1919 exchange rate of Mk 227 to the £, the total advance would only be some £66.

82 See FD to Heseltine 27 Oct 1919. FD writes that Hertzka had offered a fee of 2,000 kronen to Heseltine for the English translation and FD advised Heseltine to leave the money in Vienna rather than converting to sterling.

I wish to emphasise once more that not only in the case of Harmonie but also in our new contract as it stands here, I am making a great sacrifice because I can get £100–150 advance for an orchestral work at any time in London. However, I should like, if at all possible, to concentrate my works with one large good enterprising publisher.

On 21 Febr. my Double Concerto (violin & cello) is being premiered in London by the Harrison strs with Wood & on the 26th Feb. my Song of the High Hills (orchestral & choral work premiere) Coates cond., I shall be in London for it. I am pleased that you have sent the vocal scores to Augener & find the price very appropriate.

With kind regards and New Year wishes

Yours

1920–1929

1920

The year was full of money worries. Delius reneged on his promise of four works to Universal, assigning *North Country Sketches* and the *2nd Dance Rhapsody* to Augener against a £250 advance. That meant that only the *Poem of Life and Love*, (not quite finished) and the *Requiem* were still available. Hertzka was not very pleased, but in October Delius, having discovered that Augener was having problems getting the new works engraved quickly, wrote to Hertzka suggesting that he took *North Country Sketches*, the 2nd Dance Rhapsody, *Eventyr* and *A Song before Sunrise* back from Augener and gave them to Universal, who would have to pick up the £400 advance already given by Augener to Delius. Nothing happened. Universal signed a publishing agreement for the *Requiem* in October but declined to accept Delius's terms. Against the Mk 10,000 advance requested they paid Mk 5,000; for printed music sales they paid a 20 per cent royalty, but on the proceeds of hiring material Hertzka would only offer 25 per cent rather than the 50 per cent asked for. This was quite reasonable. Delius had not contributed to the cost of the production of the performing material.

Delius and Universal were still trying to settle the Harmonie business. *A Village Romeo and Juliet* received three performances at Covent Garden in March and April. There were first performances of the Double Concerto and the *Song of the High Hills*. Perhaps more exciting was an approach in July from Basil Dean in London, commissioning Delius to write incidental music for a production of James Elroy Flecker's play *Hassan*.

He was elected a member of the Performing Right Society in February 1920 and by 1922 had resigned from GDT, from which he said he had received no fees since 1914. As there were no reciprocal agreements between PRS and the Austrian and German copyright societies until 1926, it is unlikely that he received any performing fees from performances in those countries until at least 1927, unless Universal paid him. As members of AKM, Universal presumably did receive fees, but there is no record of them being passed on to Delius or of his asking for them.

Negotiations with the Public Trustee continued, Delius being careful to abide by the rules. A sum of money paid him in settlement by Harmonie was returned because it did not go through the proper channels. As inflation took off in Germany, the exchange rate worsened. The dollar rate fell from 6.6 marks to the dollar in 1918 to 100 in 1920. For the pound sterling it fell from 20.78 in 1913 to 226 in 1919 and 404 in 1920. Universal's advance payments were worth little.

No 107

Delius to Universal

11 February 1920
Grez-sur-Loing

Dear Herr Direktor,

Because I have had no reply whatsoever to my last letter, I fear that one of your letters has been lost. I await most eagerly news of the conclusion to the Harmonie affair.

You understand my concern is to hand in my demands without delay to the Public Trustee in London so that I receive them on favourable terms.

On the 17th I travel to London and will be staying at

Norman O'Neill Esq.
4 Pembroke Villas
Kensington W

Please write to me in detail at that address. I believe my proposals concerning works to be published have arrived safely in your hands. Because when I arrive in London I urgently require at least £50 of the £100 advance. Miss… wrote to me that she sent you £75 because you wrote to her that you had to pay me in £ Sterling. So I suspect that all is in order.

Beecham begins his new season at Covent Garden on the 24th inst. & because Romeo & Juliet is on the programme, I think it will indeed be staged beg.[inning of] March.

On the 21st February my double concerto is being given in London by Wood (Harrison's) on the 26th Coates is doing my Song of the High Hills in the Philharmonic. The Requiem must be postponed of course.

You will have received the vocal score & translation. I will send you the full score from London.

Please write immediately to London – letters still go so slowly.
With best wishes from us to you

Regards yours

ꕥꕥ

No 108

Delius to Universal

12 April 1920
Grez-sur-Loing

Dear Herr Direktor,

I received your letter of the 7th April today & alas I gather from it that your negotiations with Harmonie have completely failed.

I therefore request that you return the signed power of attorney to me without delay. I will then write to Harmonie by registered post & demand an exact statement with a given date for payment. After that we can consult each other on what else we must do. Is the address of Harmonie still Georg Wilhelm Str. 17 Berlin-Halensee? U. A. w. g.[1]

I have extensive material on Harmonie here, but I sent you the fair copy etc., before the war at your request. I believe it was after my last visit to Munich (Mass of Life end of 1913). Please look it out. My wife and I both remember it well.

In the next few days I will send you some criticisms of Romeo & Juliet.

It was with such shared feeling that we both heard of the loss you suffered through the death of your father. In all the chaos of London I believe I did not mention it. With kind [regards] from both of us,

Yours

ꕥꕥ

No 109

Delius to Universal

30 April 1920
Grez-sur-Loing

Dear Herr Director,

6 weeks ago you wrote to me that in a fortnight I would have a decision on the Harmonie affair, but have not yet received anything & absolutely must now hand in my return to the Public Trustee, impossible to wait any longer. I therefore request that you advise me without fail how the affair stands.

My stay in London with my various works was <u>very</u> successful & the reception enthusiastic for the Double Concerto, Song of the High Hills & Romeo & Juliet. I stayed for the premiere on the 19th. The audience was marvellous & the performance

---

1 I.e. 'an immediate answer required'.

extraordinarily good. My wife sent you the title page of Fennimore a few days ago. She was ill, hence the delay.

Please, my dear Herr Director, write to me immediately about Harmonie, won't you?

With kind regards from us both

Yours
Frederick Delius

ꕥꕥ

No 110

Delius to Universal

15 May 1920
Grez-sur-Loing

Dear Herr Direktor,

I will gladly wait a fortnight, but any longer is impossible – because I must hand in my return to the Engl. Trustee – And you know how Jadassohn is, he always wriggles away from you – Please write to me what he is putting down as the total of his debt to me. And in any case get him to send me a statement.

All the material for possible proceedings against Harmonie is in Berlin among the effects of Counsellor Heinitz.

Have you received the vocal score of the Requiem with Heseltine's Engl. translation? Unfortunately I have not been able to reserve all the works for you – because I still have none of my money back & we have to live. As a result I have additionally had to hand over North Country Sketches & the 2nd Dance Rhapsody to Augener & have received a £250 advance for them. However, I have reserved my two main works for you: The Requiem and the 'Poem of Life and Love' As soon as I hear from you I will send you the full score of the Requiem. The first performance is to take place in the Philharmonic in London next season & for this reason the whole of the material must be prepared right away. –

I am now busy on a new choral work,[2] which I might be able to give you.

With best regards from us both

Yours
FD

P.S. I shall send the critiques of Romeo & Juliet in a few days, I am expecting them from a friend in London –

---

2 *Songs of Farewell.*

ഇരു ഇരു

No 111

Delius to Universal

20 May 1920
Grez-sur-Loing

Dear Herr Direktor,

I have just received the enclosed statement from Harmonie. I have replied that I cannot accept it & will pursue court action against Harmonie. This is the old, wholly unaltered incomplete false statement from before the war.

I now ask you to do your utmost to reach a settlement with Harmonie or else we will have to proceed against them in court & I am so completely in the right and have the proof, all the relevant material in Berlin, that I am quite certain of my case.

I received the enclosed telegr. yesterday. Is it not now possible at long last to have a stock of my work and material in London, so that performances are not rendered impossible again and again? It would be enough if a complete hire set of material of each of these works were available there. But that must be with a well-known firm – you are losing so much through this neglect. All the people are used to getting this in London & not to having to write long-windedly to Austria.

I truly hope that this time you will come to a decision with Harmonie. Do it just as quickly as you can.

With best regards from both of us

Yours

Please let me know.

ഇരു ഇരു

No 112

Delius to Universal

24 June 1920
Grez-sur-Loing

Dear Herr Direktor,

Today I am sending you the material concerning Harmonie, which I have just received from Berlin; also the letter, which I have just received from Harmonie.

Everything that Harmonie says in it is of course completely incorrect, as you can also see yourself from the material. We <u>never</u> agreed that I should provide the R. & Juliet material gratis. Moreover Harmonie always promised as a matter of course to credit me with this material. Besides all the orchestral & choir material, there were

80-90 autograph piano scores, which he sold. And besides this he pocketed Mk 700 or 800 as a hire fee from Beecham for the orchestral material.

This unfortunate stupid error, that the first letter to Harmonie was sent without the figure 2,200 filled in (which my wife did not know exactly), Harmonie bring up this error as the most important fact & do not go into all the other questions. I hope that you will write to me as soon as possible to say exactly where matters stand now. With these papers in your possession you can proceed with energy so that at last we can be rid of this firm.

Everything he says about the Munich meeting is also false. There was only one young woman who was completely disoriented & it emerged that there was no bookkeeping whatsoever concerning my works, so the off.[ice] accountant gained no insight into it.

I have not yet received the piano score of Fennimore & Gerda for correction.

Hoping that you are well and with best wishes from both of us,

Yours

No 113

Delius to Universal

21 July 1920
Grez-sur-Loing

Dear Herr Direktor,

Some time ago I wrote to you to ask you to write with the exact figure of my balance with Harmonie according to their reckoning, which you have. Also, I do not wish to claim only the cost of an action against Harmonie. Why have you come to no agreement with Harmonie? What has been the stumbling block? You send me no details, so I am unable to form a picture of the state of affairs. Hopef.[ully] you now have the full score of my Requiem which I had sent you from Augener's. Please also send me the contract so that the whole thing can quickly go into preparation.

The other work/orchestral work 'Poem of Life and Love' which I have reserved for you is not quite finished. I have some more work to do on it. You can therefore send the contract for it now or later, as you wish.

For the material (hire fee) for the Requiem you can ask the Philharm.[onic] Soc. for £20; that is what Leuckart asked for & received for the Song of the High Hills. As far as the Mk 10,000 advance for the Requiem is concerned, perhaps you could pay me Mk 5,000 on signature of the contract & 5,000 in 6 months.

It would please me greatly if you came to an agreement with Harmonie so that we could avoid these proceedings.
Kind regards

Yours

P.S.
I have just been told that the committee of the Elberfelder Concertgesellschaft has unanimously chosen my Mass of Life for performance in the coming season.[3]

ഇരുഇരു

No 114

Delius to Universal

14 August 1920
Grez-sur-Loing

Dear Herr Direktor

Have just received your letter of 7 Aug. I understand your reasons very well. For myself, the main concern in this case is that the Requiem appears quickly, because I promised it for the London performance. I therefore accept your conditions, but as an absolute Condition on my side, that vocal scores & choral material are ready & delivered by end of November the latest.[4] The soloist & the choir must rehearse it for at least 3 months.

As far as the Poem of Life and Love is concerned, I repeat that it is not quite ready yet. Of course it would be much more advantageous for me if Augener had also published this Requiem, which he was so keen to do. But he already has all the other works & he has too few engravers & it goes too slowly.

As far as Harmonie is concerned, I have asked Rösch[5] for advice. If I have to take action alone I would rather do it through the Genossenschaft. However, if, despite this you were still able to come to an agreement with Harmonie, I would forgo the advance for A Poem of Life and Love & Requiem to show you how much I would like to place all my other works with your house.

Can you not arrange for Mengelberg to do 'The Mass of Life'? Etc.

So please, inform me without delay & I hope that you will initiate the work without delay.

Kind Regards from my wife and me

Yours,

PS How are things with Fennimore? I should so like to send Beecham the vocal score with Engl. text as soon as possible.

PPS You have only sent me one score of the Arabesque & no vocal scores with Engl. text. A few copies of each please.

---

3 No record of such a performance.

4 Perhaps the first performance was planned for the spring of 1921, but it didn't take place until 23 March 1922 at the Queen's Hall conducted by Coates.

5 Director of GDT.

No 115

Delius to Universal

14th September 1920
Hotel Imatz
Hendaye
[Basses Pyrenées]

Dear Herr Director,

In the contract you forgot to cover my share of the income from the use of the orchestral and choral material. Naturally I must enjoy the same conditions with you as I do with Augener. That is to say, 20 per cent of the gross retail price + 50 per cent of the [income from other] exploitation of the material.[6]

In order to accommodate you, I have 'quasi' foregone an advance – please add this clause to the contract + send same back to me here – I am in Hendaye for a few weeks Also, I am not permitted to sign the clause 'exploitation of mechanical rights'.
Kind regards

Your devoted

No 116

Delius to Universal

11 October 1920
Grez-sur-Loing

Dear Sir

I hope that you have returned the sum of money which Harmonie Verlag Berlin handed over to you for me, as I recently asked Herr Dir Hertzka to do. Because I must make my claims on Harmonie through the English Public Trustee, I am not permitted to accept any sum personally.

I would ask that when you begin the engraving of my Requiem score (orchestra), you make it larger than the Arabesque, which is much too crammed together & unclear as a result. It must be highly readable, especially because it is for double choir & orchestra & soli. I also await the return of the contract with the minor amendments which I have made.
Yours faithfully,

---

6 The publishing contract for the *Requiem* shows that Universal only paid an advance of Mk 5,000 and against 20 per cent of gross sales but only 25 per cent of hire revenue, instead of the 50 per cent for which FD asked.

No 117

Delius to Universal

13 November 1920
Grez-sur-Loing

Dear Herr Director
Hopef[ully] this will reach you! I am pleased that you are back. Augener is having colossal difficulties getting my most recent scores engraved in England & after my repeated harassment he is now willing to transfer these scores to you if necessary[7] or to have you engrave them. This concerns

The Ballad: Eventyr
North Country Sketches
Dance Rhapsody II
Song before Sunrise.

Do approach him and discuss the matter with him.
Hopef[ully] this reaches you while still in London.
The day after tomorrow I am leaving for Frankfurt where we wish to spend the winter. Send mail to Dr Simon.
I advise you to take on these scores .In all I have received £400 advance for them.
In great haste

Your devoted

No 118

Delius to Universal

1 December 1920
Canton Hotel
Frankfurt a/M

Dear Herr Direktor,
We are now both here and my wife has brought your letter with her. I am very pleased that you met Heseltine in London. He really is a very remarkable person of great intelligence. I have already given Winthrop Rogers my consent concerning the

[7] On 1 March 1920 in a letter to Jelka, FD wrote that Augener had paid 'another' advance of £250 against royalties for the 2nd Dance Rhapsody and the *North Country Sketches*.

Songs & Cello Sonata & hope that the matter is also now in order between you.[8] As far as my move to London is concerned I admit I am thinking seriously about it. We aim to stay here until the end of February & and then travel there.

I am particularly pleased about this sole agency in London. Who is it?

Now about the contract:

I am in agreement with your amendments, so I will accept the 25 per cent but I would like to have these two works separate, because the Poem of Life and Love is not ready yet. But I will definitely give it to you once it is finished & what is more, without an advance, on the same terms as the Requiem. I have therefore crossed the poem off the contract. I enclose the signed contract.

After you had left for America I received rather peculiar letters from Jadassohn, in which he offers to come to an agreement with me about the works on some terms which I am to propose myself; to the first letter I replied that he might make clear proposals himself.

However, he did not do that & so I sent the correspondence to the Genossenschaft, asking their advice. The Genossenschaft suggests that I get out of the contract & Harmonie should then pay me a certain sum in settlement of all claims, which I should estimate.

2nd proposal

Harmonie supplies a correctly ordered settlement covering all the past, upon which the contract will be voided. Of course this all seems very problematical to me, because Harmonie will without doubt never send a proper statement &, it appears to me, want to press for a certain cash sum. However, from all this I observe that Harmonie is afraid of court proceedings on my part & would very gladly see a fitting solution. I therefore believe that now would be the time for you as a skilled businessman to make another attempt with them. I had already informed you that after the negotiations failed with you, I threatened Harmonie with court proceedings, whereupon the letters arrived.

Meanwhile I had also unearthed a letter from Jadassohn as evidence, in which he confirms his liability for Mk 1,100 for the material for A Village R. & J. The power of attorney which I gave to you as an option during your negotiations, I also nullified with Harmonie after the breakdown of same. Harmonie did not want to agree to this annulment however, what is the situation with this?

Of course I would very much like to discuss all this. Are you not travelling via Frankfurt in the near future?

With kind regards, from both of us

Cordially yours,

[8] Universal issued editions of the works for European distribution.

No 119

Jelka Delius to Universal

30 December 1920
Schaumainkai 91
Frankfurt a/M

Dear Herr Direktor,

We are now installed in a charming private flat on the Main & feel very content here & will stay several months. I am now very keen that in this time we should, if at all possible, repair all the many threads that the war broke, so that a lot of Delius music is played here. Tonight we are going to a concert where Daisy Strauss will sing many Delius songs (Verl. Tischer). A Hungarian violinist Arányi[9] wants to perform the Violin Concerto published by Augener & prob. also the Double Concerto & play at many venues (she has already played it with piano in Berlin etc; but now it will be with orchestra. Every day I see that the pers[onal]. presence of the composer is a great spur to all of this. There is great interest in the Violin Sonata & the Cello Sonata published by W. Rogers as well. I hope that you will have the Songs & the Sonata ready for Germany very soon. Schuricht has visited my husband. He would really like to give one of the bigger choral works, above all the 'Mass of Life' in Berlin & is thinking of the 'Anbruch' concert series. He said he would be more than happy to give his services as conductor for no fee, if you could arrange all the rest in this concert series of yours. How are things with it? Theodore Szanto is playing the piano concerto on 31 January in Budapest. He is in Paris & because he is then passing through Vienna he could poss. play it there too, if you could arrange something there?

The Genossenschaft believes that it can wind up my husband's contract with Harmonie without him having to pay. He would then take possession of his works again & then come to a new agreement with you. I enclose the letter from the Genossenschaft & request return of same. If there is anything standing in the way of Delius's admission to the Verband deutscher Bühnenschriftsteller[10] & Kompon. please advise immediately. Otherwise he will register himself. We now both send our warmest New Year wishes.

Yours,

---

[9] Jelly d'Arányi. (1895–1966). A British violinist of Hungarian birth. Great niece of Joachim. Born in Hungary, she settled in England in 1909. A colourful personality and fine player. There is no record of her ever playing the Delius concerti.

[10] Society of stage producers and composers?

1921

In February Universal concluded an agreement with Harmonie to acquire the copyright in their Delius works together with Harmonie's stock of Delius material for Mk 40,000. Around the same time Universal bought a 50 per cent interest in the six Delius works published by Leuckart.

We do not have a copy of the agreement between Harmonie and Universal, but that between Delius and Universal, dated 10 January has survived. An important aspect of this agreement was that Delius expected, quite rightly, that he was entitled to his 25 per cent sheet music royalty on sales or exploitation of the stock taken over from Harmonie. He was keen to establish the actual stock levels and this issue was to cause problems with Universal, which Delius believed was not paying as it should.

While in London he retrieved his manuscript performing material of *A Village Romeo and Juliet* from Goodwin & Tabb, the main London music hire library, where they were held as part of the assets of the bankrupt Beecham Opera Co.

Delius was still at work on the music for *Hassan*, the London performance of which was postponed. Publishing contracts were signed both with Reandean for the stage rights and with Universal for worldwide print rights, as well as stage rights outside Great Britain, the colonies and the USA.

In June Universal accepted the freshly written Cello Concerto and the *Piece for Harpsichord*, Delius making yet another abortive attempt to secure a print royalty of 33 per cent. It is unlikely that any publisher would have paid so high a royalty.

There were still financial pressures, although Delius found enough money to have a small chalet built for them in Norway. The Controller of Enemy Property released dividends on his American securities but there were still difficulties over publishing royalties due from Germany. The exchange rate of the mark to the pound sterling fell to 8,000 as the inflation neared its climax. There was no correspondence with the PRS during the year.

No 120

Delius to Universal

6 Feb 1921
Schaumainkai 91
Frankfurt a/M

Dear Herr Direktor,

According to the news I am receiving from London it seems that your price for the Requiem was too high for the Philharmonic Society. Please inform me what your quote for the material for this performance was hire or sale? Please make it as low as possible, so that I can arrange the performance for the autumn.[11]

For the full score I should like to ask you as a matter of urgency to choose a format that is a good deal bigger than that of the Arabeske which is printed much too close together and is thus unclear.[12] Please also prepare the score as quickly as possible, so that I can correct it and Coates can have a complete corrected proof a few months before the performance. The full score may, of course, only go for final printing after the premiere.

I do not know whether I told you that during the war, I wrote a violin sonata and published it with Forsyth Bros. Ltd, 36 Great Titchfield Str. London W. I would like to advise you to take the rights for Germany for this sonata, under similar conditions as the Winthrop Rogers pieces. It is a very effective piece. If you want to take it on I will write in person to Forsyth about it; I believe no difficulties will stand in the way of this matter.

Augener has meanwhile made contact with Schott about sales of the other works.

To return to your letter of 10th January, I would ask you urgently for the return of the power of attorney which I made out to you some time ago in order to negotiate with Harmonie. Otherwise great complications will arise, and it is for precisely this reason that I only reluctantly gave you this power of attorney. It was only conditional and you should not have put it in the hands of Harmonie, before the matter was agreed.
With kind regards

Yours

No 121

Delius to Universal

10 February 1921
Schaumainkai 91
Frankfurt a/M

Dear Herr Direktor,

I telegraphed you accept 25 per cent opera 85 per cent, and I believe that will be all right with you. The 25 per cent was after all in line with our agreement of last year. We had fixed the opera at 90 per cent; but I will let you have it at 85

---

11 The first performance was on 23 March 1923 in the Queen's Hall conducted by Albert Coates.

12 This was in fact carried out – the *Requiem* full score was larger than that of *An Arabesque*.

per cent because of your commitments with Harmonie.[13] Admittedly you must pay Mk 40,000, [but you] do have all the accessible works, records, material etc. and need only proceed now and disseminate things in America and England where there is such great demand, and where they were unavailable for so many years. I am personally making a sacrifice because I am renouncing all my claims on Harmonie and e.g. the expenses of Seadrift and the songs have long since been covered.

I attach the formal contract in these terms.[14] Of course I am extraordinarily pleased to know that these works are in your hands and finally out of Harmonie's clutches, and that you have really succeeded in reaching terms with Herr Jadassohn.

I just received your letter of the 8th February and truly regret that despite my advice, you have asked…for the [hire of the] entire Requiem material.[15] That makes Mk 7,500 and it goes without saying that the performance only failed [to come off] because of that. In future I ask you to moderate your prices for all my works; then the performances will double and triple. Leuckart has already missed 3 performances of 'Song of the High Hills' because of his excessive demands. You must consider that the concert societies in England are not subsidised, and with the colossal expensiveness of orchestras etc. they always operate at a loss. But at £20 I will bring about the performance in autumn and I would like to correct the score as soon as poss., so that I can give Coates a print for rehearsal. Attached a letter from Gatti, an Ital. critic; please do the necessary.
With kind regards, also from my wife

Yours

No 122

Delius to Universal

16 February 1921
Frankfurt a/M

Dear Herr Direktor,

In accordance with your wishes I am sending you today copy of my letter & telegram of yesterday to Harmonie.[16] I am pleased that all is now in order.

When I leave here I shall send you the full score of Seadrift complete with a few corrections. Whenever a new edition is to be prepared these minor alterations

---

[13] 'The opera' is *Fennimore and Gerda*. This should be interpreted as:- I telegraphed you that I will accept a royalty of 25 per cent of the retail price of sheet music sold and 85 per cent of the gross box office for operas and I believe that will be all right with you.

[14] The contract dated 10 January 1921 between Delius and Universal covering the Harmonie works.

[15] It appears as though UE charged Mk 7,500 for the hire of the material, but there is a gap in the letter. Sterling equivalent probably £20 at the beginning of 1921.

[16] Delius telegraphed Harmonie on 15 Feb agreeing to the UE settlement.

are to be made beforehand. On transfer of all stocks of sheet music material from Harmonie please send me the figures for each item, will you?[17]

I have received the vocal score of Fennimore & Gerda (Engl) & only regret that you have used such very poor paper[18] for the title page and that it is so unsoundly bound. The copy sent to me arrived with its back cover already completely torn. The back at least would have to be reglued & reinforced. I ask you to send me another 4 or 5 copies in London, once I am there. I will then inform you of my permanent address there.

Is the material for the Requiem ready, so that it can be available in London? Vocal score? Choral parts?
With best wishes

Yours

No 123

Delius to Universal

4 April 1921
21 Lancaster Rd
Hampstead N.W.3

Dear Herr Direktor

I heard with great pleasure that you have also made an agreement with Sander,[19] so that these works are also now in your hands.

For my part I have had a discussion with Mr Goodwin (Goodwin & Tabb) today.[20] This firm controls practically all orchestral performances in England & would like to take over all my orchestral & choral material to exploit it as hire material for concert performances. Goodwin told me that he has already spoken to you about this and in order to achieve numerous performances, these materials must not be hired too expensively. I propose the following approximate sums as practical:

Choir works of the duration of Seadrift, Songs of Sunset etc	£6-6-0d
Orchestral works like Paris, Brigg Fair etc	£3-0-0d. Or Maximum £4-0-0d

[17] This issue becomes important later.

[18] No doubt the poor paper quality was partly due to the post-war restrictions.

[19] Sander, i.e. Leuckart.

[20] Goodwin & Tabb was the major hire library so Goodwin would have known the English market conditions.

Appalachia	£5-5-0d
Piano Concerto	£4-4-0d
Requiem 1st performance	£20
further performances	£6-6-0d
Mass of Life	£10-10-0d

This firm is very good and trustworthy. Today I searched in vain for your depot in Wardour St. Please give me the exact address as soon as possible; because as soon as I have the address I will have it publicised in the press, & particularly in The Daily Telegraph music column.

Thank you very much for the vocal scores of Fennimore and Appalachia, which I will deal with immediately. Please also send me a few copies of my Requiem, because I have given mine to Coates, I also hope to receive the corrections of the full score very soon, so that Coates can have a proof promptly.

Hopefully the Piano Concerto is also in print again now of course I must correct the new edition, because there are a number of errors in it. Frederick Lamond has just asked me about it. No one can get it.

And I would like to correct a new impression of the 5 Songs which have sold out, because there are errors in it. The song 'Autumn' e.g. is not by Jacobsen but by Holstein. I have no copy here.[21]

With kind regards from both of us

Yours

No 124

Delius to Universal

30 April 1921
21 Lancaster Rd
Hampstead

Dear Herr Direktor,

I have received your letter of 18th Apr. I fully understand what you say about Goodwin and Tabb. The essential thing is, however, that your London firm has the material for my works and can supply it on hire and at reasonable prices, without having to write for it to Vienna every time – which people just do not do & which is also far too long-winded. As a result performances keep being missed and the people choose something which is available instead –

---

21 The correct attribution of this song was not made until the Boosey & Hawkes issue of 1977.

The material for A Village Romeo & Juliet is in the library of the Sir Thomas Beecham Opera Co. which is bankrupt at the moment; however I have claimed it through Goodwin & Tabb, in whose hands the library is.

Today I am sending a perfectly corrected copy of my Cello Sonata.

I have just received the correction of the Sander songs.[22] About the translation of same I have told him to come to an agreement with Heseltine.

As far as the Romeo & J. material is concerned, that which is in the Beecham stock is only handwritten, produced for me personally in fact – this is precisely what the dispute was about and I claimed the Mk 1,100 that it cost me from Harmonie. It seems that despite all promises, Harmonie never printed the material.

Also please register my membership as an extraord. member of the Deutsche Buhnengenossenschaft. Unfortunately I mislaid the address on the journey & am therefore not yet a member.

In September, a drama by Elroy Flecker, a very gifted young deceased Englishman is being staged by the Rean-Dean company, which has commissioned me to write incidental & entr'acte music. I have done this and the music is ready. It is an oriental affair from the One Thousand and One Nights. Would you be interested in publishing it? The vocal score to begin with, (Heseltine is going to prepare it), because it is normal for the vocal score to be ready for the premiere, as very good sales of it can be made. I would forgo an advance, but demand 25 per cent. Please let me know straight away because Augener would like it, but he is unfortunately so dreadfully slow. The drama is called

Hassan or

The Golden Journey to Samarkand.

It will also be translated into German – It is one of the best modern dramas, a serious piece. I have composed it for sm. orchestra, 26 solo instruments and it is to be staged with quite magnificent sets.

I am so very happy that so many of my works are now in your hands and I shall also be delivered as soon as possible of a cello concerto which is now absorbing me completely.

With kind regards from both of us

Yours

---

22 These are the Nietzschelieder.

No 125

Delius to Universal

10 May 1921
21 Lancaster Road
London NW3

Dear Herr Direktor,

Some time ago I sent you Walther Brueggmann's directing instructions for Fennimore & Gerda. It is excellently done & I would like to have it produced so that it can be delivered to theatres at the same time as the other material. Have you received it? I have also received your catalogue of my works & see with amazement and regret that you are demanding quite impossible prices – 40/- with 100 per cent surcharge[23] for a lithographed score of Appalachia, in other words over Mk 1,000 or 10,000 krone is pure madness & you will not sell a single copy. Only musicians buy these scores; the whole thing is prohibitive and you just will not cover your costs. £10 for the lithographed score of the Mass of Life is the same. Please immediately drop the 100 per cent if you do not want this music to be boycotted completely.

Several of my friends have acquired scores via friends from Germany.

I advise you to produce all these scores immediately in miniature format & sell them at 5 or 6 shillings, the Mass in 2 volumes: so that young musicians can buy them, like those of Leuckart's which have already been printed.

After full consideration I can sadly not see how I could arrange Appalachia for orchestra alone without spoiling the work.

I would like you to have a new score of Seadrift produced. The score contains many mistakes and I have also made a few significant amendments[24] which heighten the effect of the work considerably. I will send you the score. My young friend Cecil Gray will convey my greetings to you personally.

Kindest regards

23 On Austrian prices?

24 To the orchestration.

ꕥ

No 126

Delius to Universal

25 May 1921
21 Lancaster Road
London NW3

Dear Herr Direktor,

Your letter of the 19th reached me yesterday. As far as Brueggmann is concerned, I do not know if he would demand a fee, nor how much I advise you to contact him personally. Address Schauspielhaus, Frankfurt. I am very pleased that Cologne are to stage the work. Of course this time you will do the sets according to our agreement, based on my wife's sketches. Although the arrangement of the furnishings & position in the rooms may be as in Brueggmann's[25] instructions.

I am very pleased that you intend to lower the prices of the music, or that you already have & also that you have sent the miniature scores for printing.

In a few days I will have Goodwin & Tabb send you the material for 'Romeo & Juliet' which he acquired from the Beecham library.

I will send the Seadrift score with all corrections in ink & pencil to you tomorrow; I hope you will engrave it as quickly as possible, as a number of performances are coming up; among others one in Bradford in October.

With reference to 'Hassan', I wish to add a small clause to the contract, namely that all money due to me which is received in America and England will be paid to me in dollars & pounds st[erling] and not in Austrian crowns or German marks.

Enclosed is the contract – I have crossed out 'Cinematic Reproduction' because I have no use for it.

I would ask you to make haste with the Cello Sonata, because the Harrison sisters intend to tour Germany & Austria shortly. You know that the cellist Beatrice Harrison is a quite outstanding artist, who plays the work splendidly & has also made something of a stir here She will also play my Double Concerto with her sister.

PS I would be pleased if you could also acquire Tischer's things; in which case we would of course keep to my old contract conditions with Tischer.

F.D.

The vocal score of Hassan will be ready on the 4th June. I will have it sent to you straight away & please then make a copy of it immediately & as soon as it is ready, send a copy to Reandean c/o St. Martin's Theatre, West Str. London; & engrave the other copy straight away, so that in September, when the work appears here, it is on sale. Reandean must of course have one copy as quickly as possible for the rehearsals.
Kind regards from us both,
Yours

---

[25] Stage director?

No 127

Delius to Universal

4 June 1921
21 Lancaster Rd
London NW3

Dear Herr Direktor,

Enclosed I am sending you back the signed contract for Hassan.

This morning I heard from Heseltine, who has done the vocal score for Hassan, that he has also made a copy because Dean the theatre director has been waiting for it so keenly as the rehearsals will begin very soon. I will send you a copy so that engraving can be started straight away. I have already sent you a corrected copy of Seadrift and ask you to begin engraving the score as soon as possible, as it will be performed in October in Bradford at a large music festival.[26] Of course all these amendments must also be accurately entered into the orchest. & choral material. I also ask you to also have all the other autograph scores engraved first, so that the miniature scores turn out really clear & legible. There are errors in Paris, Songs of Sunset, Appalachia & especially Mass of Life. I have the scores of all of them and will send you them in corrected form, apart from the Mass of Life which is in Grez. I ask you then to send me my scores back. If you must have the Mass [corrected] before autumn, you would have to send me the 2 volumes of the score with correction sheets to Poste restante Kristiania, Norway. We are travelling there on the 17th inst. I have instructed Goodwin and Tabb to send you all the material (choir & orchestra). The Piano Concerto material is also there; but because this work is to be performed in Manchester's Hallé concerts, I feel it would be more practical to leave it here with Goodwin and Tabb.

The pianist Frederick Dawson adr: Delf View. Eyam via Sheffield, who is to play it in Manchester asked me today what the material costs to hire & I ask you to reply to him directly, or through Goodwin and Tabb. If you prefer me to leave the pia. conc. material in stock with the Continental Publ. Co, can I also do this? Mr Cyril Jenkins has sent the material for the Arabesque direct back to you in Vienna. I had already written to Dr Tischer in the meantime.

Thank you very much for the 5 Songs; I am very pleased that they came out so quickly.

Heseltine who did the vocal score for Hassan – a very significant piece of work – must receive at least £5-5-0d, and I ask you to send him this sum at his current address: Hotel Moderne Camaret Finistère France.

My Cello Concerto is now complete, and if you wish you can also send me the contract for it. I require no advance, but 25 per cent of the retail price.[27] I could also place a small piece for harpsichord (or piano) with your firm?

---

26 Possibly 26 October. Delius was present.

27 Universal agreed to only 25 per cent.

With kind regards from us both.

ജ്ഗ്ജ്ഗ്

No 128

Delius to Universal

6 June 1921
21 Lancaster Road
London NW3

Dear Herr Direktor,

With reference to the Cello Concerto, I would be very pleased to place it with your firm. But because I am being offered 4d in the shilling here & a considerable advance, I would ask you to give me at least 33 per cent for this work, without advance of course. I consider the work very good and Beatrice Harrison will play it all over Germany, Austria Holland, Scandinavia & America. H. Wood will premiere it here with B. Harrison. Of course I prefer to know that the work is in your enterprising & energetic hands.[28]

Wood is asking me for Theodor Szanto's address, because they want to engage him for the next season to play my pia. concerto here. Please send his address immediately to Sir Henry J. Wood 4 Elsworthy Road N. W. 3 Hampstead London. I have received the Piano Concerto & am pleased that it has now appeared!

With best wishes from us both

Yours

ജ്ഗ്ജ്ഗ്

No 129

Delius to Universal

10 June 1921
21 Lancaster Road
London NW3

Dear Herr Direktor,

---

[28] The Cello Concerto was published by UE in 1922. The first performance was given by Alexandre Barjansky on 31 January 1923 and Beatrice Harrison played it under Eugène Goossens in London on 3 July 1923.

Sadly the songs[29] are so completely useless. The translator placed the chief value merely on the rhyme and sacrificed rhetoric ring and meaning. One cannot approach modern songs these days like this; Dr Simon[30] had already translated a few of these songs very well and also wanted to do the rest. Would you not care to approach him?

My wife has rewritten one song and it could be used as is. Everywhere, the translator has trotted out the well known banal phrases which are empty of meaning. The original poetry by contrast is extraordinarily beautiful and fine.

I am sending you the 'Hassan' vocal score in a few days. It must be produced as quickly as possible so that it can go on sale simultaneously with the London premiere, but of course it must not be sold beforehand under any circumstances.

I received the enclosed letter from Dr Simon today. I had never spoken or written to him about any kind of fee, but I find it thoroughly understandable that he should demand a small sum for his work and the payment of it naturally falls to you. Of course it would be very advantageous if he were to launch the work in Germany.

With kind regards from us both Yours
FD

Hope you have sent the £5 to Heseltine – it was a very considerable task.

If it is not against your agreement, I should like to have the Engl. text printed in any case.

No 130

Delius to Universal

15 June 1921
London

Address until further notice Kristiania Norway Poste restante

Dear Herr Direktor,

I have just received your letter of the 10th June with the two contracts.[31] There is however, a sm[all] error: I asked 33 1/3 per cent for these two works; my stock is very much on the up here and I can get 4d in the shilling here and a significant

29 ? The Four old English Songs, of which UE's publication includes a German translation.

30 Heinrich Simon.

31 There is a contract dated 15 June covering the Cello concerto and the piece for harpsichord, in which the royalty on printed music is 25 per cent, the figure Delius asked for in his letter of 4 June. UE never conceded 33.3 per cent.

advance. Of course I prefer your able firm. I forego an advance, as I said, for you. Enclosed I return the contract amended & signed in this respect.

I am sending you the score of Paris from Norway; Appalachia on the other hand I will send only at the end of August from Grez, where my corrected copy is.

In October the Harrison sisters go on tour in Austria, Germany, Holland and Scandinavia and will play my double concerto throughout. I would recommend these two great artists most highly to you; they will of course visit you in Vienna & I would ask you to do everything to be of assistance to them. Beatrice Harrison will also play the Cello Concerto later at many venues.

Two a capella choral pieces, quite new, will be premiered here[32] on the 28th. They are published by Winthrop Rogers. They are called: To be sung (of) a Summernight on the Water. I have just attended a rehearsal & am sure that these choral pieces are extraordinarily effective and that they could be performed throughout Germany. Can you contact W. Rogers & also make a German edition of these choral works. They are wordless.[33]

So we are travelling to Norway on Friday & the address Kristiania Poste restante will find us anywhere in the mountains

With kind regards from us both

Yours

No 131

Delius to Universal

29 June 1921
P. Molmen Hotel
Lesjaskog
Gudbrandsdalen Norway

Dear Herr Direktor,

I have just received your letter of 21.6 & wish to answer your questions immediately:

1. Choral parts for London need not be prepared.
2. The Reandean Director is having a copy of the score made at the moment and as soon as it is ready I shall send you my original score which you can then publish, along with the orchestral material.
3. Reandean represents stage rights of the work for England America & the Engl. colonies, but not for central Europe; for this area they belong to the widow of the author, Mrs Elroy Flecker, who lives in Paris. My wife would very much

---

32 Given by the Oriana Madrigal Society in London on 28 June 1921.

33 This was done. UE re-issued the two choral pieces.

like to translate the drama into German if this has not been done yet, & we will write to her from here via Reandean, because I do not have her address. I will then advise you of the address and result immediately.

As far as the Cello Concerto is concerned, I shall keep my promise if in fact I accepted these conditions on 4th June, as you have written. However, I again advise you that in London I am being offered 4d in the shilling. Please therefore send me the contracts once again, amended in this respect. At the moment Beatrice Harrison is herself doing a piano score of the Cello Concerto, because of course it is very important to her to rehearse it as soon as possible with Sir H.J. Wood, who wants to premiere it in England. As soon as you are ready with it, I shall have the full score sent to you, which may be engraved straight away, in such a way that the premiere is conducted from a proof of the engraving, so that any necessary corrections can be made The same goes for the orchestra score of Hassan.

In Hassan there are several numbers which could make interesting pieces on their own, especially an oriental dance.

Please send corrected translations of the songs here – they must be thoroughly good translations.

On the'Requiem affair[34] I fully share your opinion & I was also quite amazed I shall try to arrange for him to receive some share through the Genossenschaft.

In future I shall of course leave matters of vocal scores up to you. In this case with Reandean, things were so pressing that it had to be done straight away; but now the premiere has been postponed until October – because of the English strike.

Please send all corrections here, where I shall attend to them right away.

Kind regards

Yours,

No 132

Delius to Universal

11 July 1921
P. Molmen Hotel
Lesjaskog
Gudbrandsdalen
Norway

---

[34] FD was by 1921 a member of PRS. The London premiere of the *Requiem*, published by UE in 1920, was on 23 March 1922, conducted by Coates, with the first German performance in Frankfurt on 1 May 1922. Was FD trying get GDT to recognise Simon's right to a share for his words? Caught between GDT of which he was no longer a member, and PRS, which had no representation agreeement for Germany/Austria, FD would probably not have received performing fees for the Frankfurt performance.

Dear Herr Direktor,

Have just received your ltr of the 4th inst.

In the vocal score of A Village Romeo & Juliet there are some corrections to be made, especially in the arrangements, concerning the scene change between the 5 & 6th scene during the entr'acte. It was very effective in last year's Covent Garden performances. However, I have no copy of the vocal score; therefore please either send me one or wait with the new printing until I am back in Grez-sur-Loing on the 1st September. If you now have the material used by Beecham in your possession, please see whether these points are indicated in it, as well as certain improvements to the English text which I should like to have in the new edition. If you have such a copy please send it here, so that I can look through it closely & add the scenic details to the German translation. The autograph[35] vocal scores are not useable.

I have the score of Appalachia in London, & have just written to ask for it; so I shall be able to send it to you corrected in about a fortnight.

Have you received the score of Paris from here? How do things stand with the 3 (choruses) which you have taken over from Harmonie? Have they been translated into German? If not, then it must be done!

How do things stand with the violin sonata? Have you reached terms with Forsyth? And what about Tischer? When does the Cologne Opera aim to stage Fennimore? Some news please because I should like to arrange things, including possibly my return journey accordingly. Please send all corrections here.

With best wishes from us both
Yours

No 133

Delius to Universal

18 July 1921
Molmen Lesjaskog

Dear Herr Direktor,

Have just received your letter of 13. 7. with the attached copy of the contract.

I just received the new 'Sackbut' and observe with regret that despite your promise, you have not lowered your horrendous prices for my works in England and still make a 100 per cent surcharge. For you to price the score of Appalachia at 40/- is just too much. It should cost from 20/- to 25/- shillings with no 100 per cent surcharge of course The vocal score of the Requiem should cost no more than 6/- to 8/- shillings. The Mass of Life is a full evening's music in 2 volumes & Appalachia and the Requiem should of course cost considerably less, Seadrift 20/- and the 100 per cent taken off in all cases. You must realise that it is not only against your interests

35 Ie. Those lithographed in Paris c1906.

but also against my own if my works are significantly dearer than those of other composers – They will hardly ever be performed in that case. Perhaps this is just down to a misunderstanding, which I would ask you to correct as soon as possible.

Is the score of the Requiem being engraved so that I can have a proof for Coates. If so I would be able to correct the score & parts here right away.

When is Fennimore being done in Cologne?

With kind regards,

No 134

Delius to Universal

15 Sept 1921
Grez-sur-Loing,

Dear Herr Direktor,

I am in the process of sorting out my papers here and in doing so I find that the contract for Hassan is couched in unclear terms and could lead to misunderstandings. When I offered you 'Hassan' I thought, as you will also see from my letters, that I had advised you, that of course stage performing rights for England, America and Canada contractually belonged to the Reandean Company. And I believe that should have been clearly expressed in the contract.

The right of all distribution and sales of vocal scores & orchestral scores and material for concert performances in England, Canada and America as well as performing rights for stage performances in Germany, Scandinavia & all other countries belongs to me.

I hear from Dr Simon that the drama has been translated into German and Hartung plans to perform it, for which Dr H. Simon has suggested my music.

I do not quite realise that I did not remark this omission immediately, but at the time I was so absorbed by the composition of my Cello Concerto that I did not take any notice of it.

Reandean has the performing rights for 'Hassan' the drama including my music in England, Canada & America and produces material for the performances, manuscript of course as I advised you from London.

I therefore ask you to draft the contract quite clearly in this way, so that no difficulties arise for me. Because I have a new work in my head just now I would like to be fully at ease with this point.

Today I am sending you the corrected score of the Cello Concerto. Unfortunately a young friend[36] made the copy rather badly from my pencil sketch. But – I have completely corrected this copy & please have it engraved immediately so that it

[36] C.W.Orr, whose copy was <u>not</u> completely corrected by Delius, with the result that the score published by UE contained many errors, which survived for over 50 years.

is ready for Beatrice Harrison's first performance. I advise you only to prepare the piano score after the proof of the engraving. Because so much is corrected in pencil it could be missed.

So Miss Harrison plays the Elgar concerto & mine. I fear that with the limited number of orchestral concerts the opportunity will hardly arise for her to play yet a third Cello Concerto. So I have written nothing to her on the subject. When you meet her in Vienna you could discuss the matter with her.

With kind regards from us both

Yours

PS The Hassan full score, individual pieces & vocal score may of course be sold everywhere.[37]

No 135

Delius to Universal

18 Sept 1921
Grez-sur-Loing

Dear Herr Direktor,

I have just heard from my lawyer in London who has handed to the English Public Trustee my claims on the German publisher who owed me money at the outbreak of the war. He writes that the German moderating office (at the instigation of Mr Martin Sander) is causing problems.

I do not know whether you know, that at the outbreak of war, Mr Sander[38] still owed me Mk 12,000 for the works he published.[39] This sum must of course be paid back at pre-war levels. Before that has occurred these works do not belong to him, thus he also cannot accept any payment from you for these works.

I am telling you this for your own information and I advise you for your own sake to exert some pressure on Sander.

With best wishes from us both

Yours

---

37 This is not what FD wrote to UE on 19 Nov 1921. In that postcard there were to be no copies before the London premiere.

38 Sander owned Leuckart.

39 See GDT to FD, 23 June 1913. Mk 16,000 was due for the purchase. Perhaps Sander only paid the 1913 instalment as 12,000 were still due. FD was unwilling to be paid in depreciated currency as the debt was so old.

No 136

Delius to Universal

12 December 1921
Grez-sur-Loing

Dear Herr Direktor,

Can you influence the Darmstadter Theater to postpone the premiere of Hassan until the end of February or March?[40] I am not contractually bound in Germany to wait for the London premiere. Reandean would of course rather have seen it, but would travel to Darmstadt for it anyway. It is just that the orchestral material & copy of the score that must be made cannot possibly be done by January. I am writing to Reandean today instructing him to send you the score. Of course I cannot demand that he lets you have his score & parts for the German performance. You can then have a score and parts prepared.

You will receive the corrected vocal score of Romeo & Juliet in 2 days. Quite a lot has been corrected in the English text.

I would like to ask you to omit the ugly black shaded bouquet on the inner title page.[41]

I would also be very pleased if you were to send me a few more copies of the miniature edition of Paris! It is very nice.

I will send you the Hassan vocal score proof as soon as I get it back from Heseltine.

We would so like to buy 2 real Viennese rocking chairs, woven rush and rounded bentwood. Could you have us sent a price list or best of all, an illustrated catalogue from some Vienna furniture workshop? I would be very grateful to you!

With best wishes from us both

Yours

[40] The Darmstadt premiere, delayed for financial reasons, was not until 1 June 1923 in a German translation by Ernst Freissler. The London premiere was on 20 September 1923. UE were keen to obtain the Reandean performing material, but FD felt that he couldn't ask, as Dean didn't want *Hassan* staged in Germany before London (see FD to UE 15 Jan 22).

[41] This appeared on the title page of the Harmonie vocal score.

ꕤ

1922

In 1922, correspondence with PRS begins in earnest. One of the first queries from PRS was whether Delius owned the performing right in *Appalachia*, which Delius confirmed that he did. As a member of first GDT and then the PRS he would have been required to assign the performing right to his society. GDT considered the performing right an author's rather than a publishing right. When Delius resigned from GDT he would have recovered the right which he then assigned to PRS.

It seems as though Volkert, of Schott & Co., who had persuaded Delius to join PRS, had told Delius that PRS had already collected money for him, which cannot have been correct. Until 1927, PRS had no distribution system capable of distributing fees in relation to concert programmes. Up to that time composers and publishers were allocated to a class, each class member receiving a standard fee. Jelka wrote of their precarious financial position. They may have expected royalties from *Hassan* already, and they had certainly gone ahead with their Norwegian hut and some expensive medical treatment. Delius encouraged Universal to arrange performances, but Continental performances would not have paid performance fees to Delius. GDT had no contractual link with PRS until 1927. That meant that GDT would not have paid him for performances in Continental Europe between 1914 and 1926. For British performances, as said above, PRS had no distribution system until 1927.

Although unwell Delius, managed, with help from Philip Heseltine, to correct proofs of the Cello Concerto, to be performed in February 1923 by Barjansky. There was more trouble with Leuckart, Sander apparently refusing to meet Delius's claim, through the Public Trustee, for the final tranche of the Mk 16,000 Leuckart had undertaken to pay under the 1913 agreement. However the final instalment of Mk 4,000 was dependant on Delius producing the *Lieder*, which were eventually published by Universal, so perhaps Leuckart had a point. Leuckart had paid Mk 4,000 in 1913 and it seems that the company had now paid a further Mk 8,000.

ꕤ

No 137

Delius to Universal

21 February 1922

Dear Herr Direktor,

Directly after I wrote to you last, the whole of the Requiem material arrived and I have set about correcting the parts. The strings were good; then I took on the flutes which, sadly, have been quite shoddily done. In all the woodwind there are masses of bars missing. Because I am in pain at the moment and should not strain myself at all, it is impossible for me to go through all these parts, & errors like these just cannot be corrected in this way. I am therefore sending the parts back to you & ask you to have them revised alongside the score by a fully responsible reliable editor. You know that the premiere is taking place in London in mid-March & because, with the quite horrendous orchestra charges there, the rehearsals must be limited to a minimum, it is absolutely necessary to supply entirely error-free material; Otherwise there will be a hideous performance which will fundamentally undermine the impression of the work, especially because I unfortunately cannot go to London because of my illness. Coates, who is conducting, is taking matters over only at the last minute &, gifted as he is, he is not among those who do thorough homework in advance. So it is of the greatest importance. Enclosed is a sheet with the main errors in the woodwind. So please revise all parts with the exception of the strings.

Unfortunately at the moment I cannot walk, must relax completely, therefore cannot go to Darmstadt to visit Hartung; however I shall write to him and also make contact with Hagemann here. I would be so very pleased if he performed A Village Romeo & Juliet. Because I must stay here about 3 months, I hope to be able to attend the Hassan premiere in Darmstadt, also the Frankfurt performance of the Requiem. I have already written to Pander telling him that I am here.

The English songs have not arrived yet.

I have just heard that my violin sonata is to be played next month in Vienna by a Hungarian Frau Steffi ? (the name escapes me[42]) & I hope you are hearing the same. The old Engl[ish]. songs have not arrived yet.

Enclosed with your consignment of music was a Fr[en]ch. catalogue 1914–15. For a new edition a number of amendments must be made, sheet attached.

With best wishes from us both

Yours

No 138

Delius to Tischer & Jagenberg

20 March 1922

Dear Doctor,

I have just received a letter from the English conductor Albert Coates, who is going to perform my 'Requiem' on the 21st March. I quote the following passage.

'I was going to do your "On hearing the first cuckoo in Spring" in Rome on April 5th and the Roman management were very keen on my doing it. I had however a bitter disappointment because Goodwin & Tabb inform me this morning that your publishers will not allow this material to be hired. I know that the Roman management would not be willing to buy it, just for one performance, and I therefore

---

42 Geyer.

have had, to my great regret, to substitute another work. I wish you would write to your publishers and tell them, that this is a very foolish policy of theirs'.

The letter from Goodwin and Tabb accompanies this letter and I see from it that the material costs £8 to buy. In the first place this price is far too high. £4 would be more than enough for these short pieces.

I confess however that it is quite incomprehensible to me that you will not let the material out on hire through Goodwin & Tabb, a quite excellent and completely reliable firm, for about £2 per performance. It is not the custom in England to buy material; it is always hired.[43] You miss in this way a great number of performances and harm yourself and me. Anthony Bernard also wanted to do the pieces in London and I now begin to understand why it never came to anything.

That such a work, if Goodwin & Tabb had it in hand, should be given unauthorised performances, is quite out of the question.

When do I get my account? As you see from the address, we have moved.

With best wishes to you and your dear wife,

FD[44]

No 139

The Performing Right Society to Delius

7 April 1922
London

Dear Sir,

We thank you for your letter of the 4th inst.[45] And note the Genossenschaft Deutscher Tonsetzer controls the performing right of your work 'Appalachia' for the continent, but you do not state whether you are the owner of the performing right. Will you kindly inform us on this point, and also as to the place of first publication

---

43 FD wrote to T & J on 19 December 1922 noting that the small orchestral pieces were 'being played a good deal. Of course I want you to make good my share of the sale of these performance versions in the currency of the appropriate country, as Universal Edition does'. Could these have been piano reductions?

44 It is interesting to put hire fees in context against players' fees. The Musicians Union price list for 1926 had recommended fees for orchestral rank and file players, ranging from a minimum of 12/6d a night for west End theatres, to £1 5s 0d for symphony concerts and recording sessions.

During the Hallé Orchestra's 1929–30 season, Jelly d'Arányi and Moiseiwitsch each received £52 10s 0d a concert (Ehrlich, *The Music profession in Britain since the 18th century*, pp. 205–7).

45 PRS had written to FD on 27 March asking for publication details of *Appalachia*, and confirmation that he had retained the performing right.

of the work. It is necessary that we should have information on those two points[46] in order that we may be in a position to collect fees for the performance of the work in this country. If you are not now the owner of the performing right, will you please be good enough to inform us who is the present owner.

No 140

Delius to Universal

16 April 1922
[Postcard]
Wiesbaden

Dear Herr Direktor;

This is the entr'acte between the 5th and 6th scenes[47] but I must ask you to send me a vocal score so that I can indicate precisely where it begins & how far. This intermezzo is extreme.[ely] popular in England & it would definitely be worth making a separate edition of it; for piano too; it already exists for pianola.

Please let me know as soon as you hear about Cologne & Darmstadt, so that I may make my plans. At last I am beginning to get a little, better.
With best wishes

Yours

---

[46] Delius wrote to say that he was the owner of the performing right in all his works and signed a form of assignment at the British Consulate in Paris.

[47] The Entr'acte was written for the Berlin 1907 performances and published in both the vocal and full scores of the Harmonie 1910 edition. Previously FD had written a shorter entr'acte, using the same thematic material. The expanded version, now known as *The Walk to the Paradise Garden* was written because a longer time was needed to change scenery. Perhaps a rare example of FD altering a theatre score for practical reasons?

The orchestral parts prepared for the 1907 performance show the original short entr'acte crossed out and the new one pasted in. They also show that Delius, having introduced some new material in the new entr'acte, went back over the opera inserting bars here and there which used the new material. The original parts, which were found recently in the Boosey & Hawkes Hire Library, are in the possession of the Delius Trust.

For the original version see RT Cat 36–7. The UE score of 1921 was the first to give the new title and the stage directions for the pantomime during the entr'acte.

No 141

Delius to Charles Volkert of Schott & Co.

7 May 1922
Wiesbaden

Dear Mr Volkert,[48]

many thanks for your letter. Will you kindly inform the Performing Right Society that I am resigning from the German Genossenschaft and wish to be solely a member of the British Society and beg them to collect all my fees both in England and abroad? I have already written to Berlin to this effect. I shall be very pleased to receive the fees you mentioned, and hope you will kindly always further my interests in the British Society.

I am gradually mending and I sincerely hope you are doing the same.

With kindest regards,

No 142

Delius to Universal

25 May 1922
Schwarzwald Dir. H./Kr

Dear Herr Direktor,

Heseltine has just written to tell me that he has sent the Cello Concerto to you. However, because he mentions various points that give rise to doubt, & has made a string of minor corrections, I must ask you to send me a further proof of the result after corrections have been carried out, which I will then look through again. It concerns me greatly that the work should appear without any errors. I shall do it here as soon as it is received, so that no further delay arises. Heseltine goes on to say that as he had the score for correction he took the opportunity to prepare a piano score. I advise you to have it sent to you by Heseltine urgently and to acquire it. For it is certain that he, having become so used to my scores by now, can do it better than some stranger, & definitely with the greatest care & attention. Moreover, much important time will be saved thereby. Heseltine loves the work & will also bring it to the attention of good cellists.

---

[48] Delius wrote to UE on 6 May to the same effect, giving the exchange rate as the main reason, although PRS had already pointed out that he could not belong to more than one Performing Right society.

Just recently in The Daily Telegraph I read a lengthy & most admiring article about Heseltine's piano score of my orch. work 'North Country Sketches' published by Augener. It says there: 'This piano arrangement is so exquisite that it is nearly the equal of the score (second best after the score) We have never seen work of this kind executed more thoroughly or sensitively; – this is perfection in its way'.

I am here until the end of June.

Cordially yours

No 143

Delius to Universal

20 June 1922
Wildbad Dir

Dear Herr Direktor,

By now you will surely have received the corrected Cello Concerto from Heseltine & also his piano score, so please send me a proof of the score in Norway where I shall correct it straight away.

Address Delius
Lesjaskog
Gudbrandsdalen
Norway.

We travel there on the 22nd. The chairs have not arrived yet. Did you pay carriage in Vienna? Please also send all my settlements, dollars, £ and marks, everything to Norway.

I am having the greatest unpleasantness with Leuckart; who does not want to pay the demand for fees concerning those works which you rec[ently] bought from him through the trustee. Because his contract stated that the first instalment had to be paid to me on the 1 Aug. 1914[49] through the Commerz & Disconto Bank & he has not done so, he is surely in breach of contract. He disputes the demand because he claims I did not have my domicile in England. Although we also periodically spent time in Norway and France during the war, we did have a flat in London the whole time & other sums have been paid to us via the English trustee from the German trustee. Thus his reasoning is entirely untenable I am telling you this because it will, in all probability, come to proceedings & because your purchase could also become invalid; I find it quite unbelievable that this person is disputing it at all & told you nothing about all this at the time of purchase.

Dr Heinrich Simon Frankf. a.M. Untermainkai 3 is to write a sml biography or monograph about me for Verlag Piper (Munich). It should be ready for my 60th birthday on 29 Jan 1923. The little work will contain a number of excellent portraits

[49] The 1913 contract read 1 August 1913.

by Beckmann and Munch. Dr Simon was here yesterday to discuss it all. He asks that the following works of Delius be sent for his perusal on loan straight away, and I would ask that you do this as soon as possible as he has some spare time just now. They are 5 Songs, piano scores of Paris, Appalachia, Seadrift, Songs of Sunset, Brigg Fair, In a Summer Garden, Tanz Rhapsodie, Fennimore & Gerda, Song of the High Hills, Arabeske, A Village Romeo and Juliet; and the [3?] choral songs.

The cure has done me good and I hope, with Norway to follow, to be back on my feet again.

With kind regards from us both,

PS It is intended to devote a concert to my work on my 60th birthday in Frankfurt. The works for which no piano scores exist must be sent in full score form to Dr Simon. He will return them promptly.

No 144

Delius to Universal

2 July 1922
[Postcard]
Lesjaskog. Gudbrandsdalen
Dir/K. 7/7. 22 Norwegen

Dear Herr Direktor,

At last we have arrived up here, the chairs however have not yet. Kindly please make enquiries.

Leuckart must have the plates for the song volume,[50] for it was he who sent me the proofs for corrections. I sent the latter back to him by post, and in reply to his request, recommended Heseltine as a translator, but have not heard whether he came to an agreement with him: and I doubt it. If my corrections have gone astray in the post, it goes without saying that the plates are with Leuckart. I am prepared to correct the cello conc.[erto] & piano score here, also send everything else here as soon as poss.[ible] because I have a piano here and time to do it; and would like to have everything ready as soon as poss. I heard from Dr Simon that Hassan is to be done with my music at the beg.[inning] of September in Darmstadt, and a few months later in London, prob.[ably] shortly before Christmas. Please do all in your power with Leuckart, whose behaviour is inexplicable to me. There is sufficient proof that my domicile at the time of the armistice was London & for which reason my other claims have been paid out. The claim on Tischer, which was only due after the outbreak of war, has also been paid out.

[50] Nietzschelieder.

With best wishes from us both

Yours

ഇ൜ഇ൜

No 145

Delius to Universal

14 August 1922
[Postcard]

Dear Herr Dir,

1. In the full score of the Cello Concerto please insert Moderato above tranquillo, 6 bars after 10.
2. In the 5th bar after 20, where 12/8 time begins, it must read Allegro Moderato, instead of Allegro con moto. & the same 5 bars after 200, where the same is repeated. Please do not omit this.[51] Also, the full score may not go for final printing until after the premiere. I am just correcting the score & will then send it to Heseltine for further perusal. It will prob[ably] be performed next season in London; Do you already have dates for the Cologne perf. of Romeo & Juliet?

Kind regards

ഇ൜ഇ൜

No 146

Delius to Universal

21 August 1922
Lesjaskog

Dear Herr Direktor,

I have just completed the careful correction of the Cello Concerto and sent it to you. The piano score was so very full of errors made in haste that I must ask you to send another proof of it, & enclose this one with it again, so that I may double check again accurately. I have also inserted a few dynamic markings in the cello part. I

---

[51] This has never been done; only an errata slip added to the Collected Edition volume in 1997 finally records it.

request that you insert them in the score. I am sending them on a separate sheet. Please do not forget.[52]
We are staying here only until the 7th Sept. and travel from here via Hamburg Cologne to Grez. I am just writing to Klemperer to speak to him, poss[ibly] in Cologne, where we will be for 1 day, on the 12th Sept.

I have also just looked through the libretto of R. & Juliette. Without a vocal score however, it is impossible & you will have to send it either immediately to me here, or to Grez, & it must be the one I corrected last year, in which there is also the new entr'acte scene.[53] It is completely missing from this text sent to me, & also there are no details ref.[erence] the dream of S. & V.

I repeat that I must see all proofs of new editions, to correct out the mistakes.

Please print all scores on better paper in future

With kind regards

Please send the vocal score of R. & Juliet to Grez,, where we will do it straight away.

Please insert in the Delius Cello Concerto dynamic markings for the solo cello part in the score.

First entry	F
3 after 10	p
5 after 20 at 12/8	mf
4 before 40	mf arco
5 after 40	f
7 before 60	p
3 after 60	mp
2 after 80	mf
3 before 90	f
5 after 110	p
2 after 140	cresc
3 after 140	f
1 before 190	cresc
at 190	f
4 after 190 at c#	dim
5 after 200 at 12/8	mf
3 after 210	mf
7 after 210	mp
at 290	mp, and p in the last part of bar deleted
3 after 310	> at 4/4 pp

52 This was ignored as regards the full score, but the dynamics in question were added to the piano reduction.

53 Ie. The new stage directions added during the *Walk to the Paradise Garden.*

Frederick Delius everywhere please & not Friederich.

7 after 320 in 4/4 bar first violin plays at beginning of bar, first quaver 'a' instead of 'b'.

No 147

Delius to Universal

21 Sept 1922
Grez-sur-Loing

Dear Herr Direktor,

Your settlement astonishes me greatly & I firmly believe that this is a case of a string of errors; for I can not believe that you would do me down in such a shabby and blindingly obvious manner.

1. In the settlement my percentages are calculated according to the most laughable prices and not according to the retail price with its several hundred per cent mark up.

2. Furthermore for the hire fee of the Requiem I have been charged £20 not £5,[54] in other words the 25 per cent due to me. And besides I demand that in pounds sterling as we agreed, and not converted into marks It must be calculated in the appropriate currency of the country concerned.

3. The calculation of the sales of my music abroad is completely missing, America and England for instance.

In London you calculate 10/- plus 100 per cent for 1 voc[al] score of the Requiem.

I have returned the cheque sent to me today from Zurich because I am unable to accept the settlement in its entirety.

I ask you to take control of the matter yourself, and to send me a satisfactory settlement as soon as possible.

With kind regards

No 148

Delius to Universal

11 November 1922
Grez-sur-Loing

---

[54] What does this mean? It probably means that the statement should have showed the hire fees charges as £20, of which of which 25 per cent was due to FD.

Dear Herr Direktor,

Hassan arrived today, & I corrected it straight away, but unfortunately, because of the Armistice Day observances, I cannot send it today. Attached is also the dramatis personae corrected & complete with translation – I have also translated the phrases beneath, although I understand that they have appropriate formulas for them. The vocal scores may not, of course, go on sale in England yet. The performance will prob. take place there after Christmas. It is a crying shame that I am informed of the Darmstadt premiere so late; as I wish to travel to Frankfurt in 10–14 days anyway.

I forgot to reply to you about the Nietzsche songs. The 4 must of course appear together, as Nietzsche songs; the other song must appear on its own.[55]

With kind regards

Yours

No 149

Delius to Universal

30 November 1922
Domplatz 12 I St.
Frankfurt a/M

Dear Herr Direktor,

It would please me enormously if you would come and visit me here. We have been here for some days.

I have indeed received the Cello Concerto. As you will recall, I sent you a correction sheet for the score from Norway, which I now request you make use of. I have no material here. My copy of the score along with some other sheet music is on its way here by parcel post. How do things stand with the Hassan parts? Please send the latter and the orch parts of the Cello Concerto for correction, at this address.

I see that the Grainger arrangement of the Dance Rhapsody for 2 Pianos is in the catalogue; please send me a copy of it! Also, Heseltine has not received a copy of the piano scores for 'Hassan' & Cello Concerto. Hoping to see you here soon.

Cordially yours

[55] The 'other song' – only appeared in 1981. 'Im Glück wir lachend gingen'.

No 150

Delius to Universal

18 December 1922
Domplatz 12

Dear Herr Direktor,

Today the proof of the Dance Rhapsody in Grainger's arrangement for 2 pianos arrived & it seems to me that it is quite excellently done. However, I should first like to hear it & therefore please send me another proof immediately. I will then have it played to me here. I will then send you everything back straight away; it is up to Percy Grainger to do corrections of course; you have probably sent it to him already. His address is Augustins Konzertdirektion Amsterdam or 163 Johann Verhulststr Amsterdam.

As far as the choral and orchestral material for A Village Romeo and Juliet is concerned, I must remind you that this material belongs to me personally. As you know, I had it prepared at my own expense & this cost Mk 1,100. If you must use this material, then you must of course reimburse me with that sum in gold marks. It goes without saying, but to avoid misunderstandings, I wish to mention it once again and receive your confirmation.

It will please us greatly to receive you here,

Cordially yours

No 151

Delius to Universal

26 December 1922
Frankfurt a/M

Dear Herr Direktor,

With reference to the material for Romeo & Juliet, I naturally believed that you were in the process of having all the material printed & it is absolutely imperative to do it (by the way the work has never been performed in Paris) However, I would permit you to use this material under the following conditions:

1. That you have the full score of Fennimore and Gerda engraved immediately

and print all the material for this opera,

2. ditto re: A Village Romeo & Juliet
3. That the full scores of Appalachia and Paris are also engraved as you promised me.

Please reply about the parts for the Cello Concerto and Hassan, which as far as poss. I wish to correct immediately; for which reason I need the full score & piano scores of course

With kind regards

1923

Eugene Goossens made the first commercial recording of a Delius work, *Brigg Fair*. Delius was 60, and not in good health. *Hassan* opened in Darmstadt in June and in London in September, where it ran for 281 performances. At £25 per week for London performances it would have brought Delius about £1,200 in grand right fees. In September Pathé frères Pathéphone enquired about a gramophone recording of *Hassan* and Percy Fletcher, the Musical Director of *Hassan* recorded nine items. Delius, who had kept his mechanical rights, had joined MCPS in London and they acted for him over royalties. The statutory royalty of five per cent of the ordinary retail price would have been paid. This would not have been the case in respect of Columbia's recording of the 1st Dance Rhapsody, conducted by Wood, about which Delius wrote to Universal in December. The work being originally published in 1910, only half royalties would have been payable.

At the beginning of the year there was talk of staging *A Village Romeo and Juliet* in Cologne, which came to nothing. Delius told Universal that his own set of parts could be used by Universal as long as Universal honoured its promise to have *Fennimore and Gerda* engraved.

There was acrimonious correspondence with Tischer & Jagenberg, who proposed to pay Delius his royalties for 1919–1922 in devalued currency. Delius, or more probably Jelka, had some success in forcing Tischer to pay more realistic sums, related to the exchange rate at the time the royalties were earned. He also caught out Tischer trying to charge him for expenses not in the contract and he tried some moral blackmail on Tischer to try to get him to pay the final instalment on *Lebenstanz* even though it was not due until the 40th sale of the material.

As Delius wrote to Tischer 'Naturally German paper money has gone up in proportion to the devaluation. A pair of boots which cost Mk 250 in 1921 now costs 80,000 or 100,000. Every child knows that.'

Delius tried to dissuade Universal and T & J from consolidating their foreign royalties in Germany and have them pay him in the currency of the country of origin. German inflation was rampant. The mark, valued at 4.2 to the dollar in 1914, fell to 100 in 1920, and in 1923, at the height of the inflation, before the introduction of the rentenmark in November 1923, the exchange rate was 18,000.

In London PRS signed its first agreement with the BBC allowing the BBC to broadcast the PRS repertoire.

No 152

Delius to Universal

8 January 1923
Frankfurt a/M

Dear Herr Direktor,

Yesterday I sent you back the string parts of the Cello Conc. corrected & the rest will prob. follow tomorrow. The Grainger Dance Rhapsody will also go off to you today & also, for Herr v. Klenau, a 4hand. arrangement of my orchestral suite, North Country Sketches, which I would ask you to give to him straight away. Attached are questions answered about Cello Concerto. In addition, you have a score fully corrected by me which I sent you from Norway & I would ask you urgently to compare same with the score which is to be used on 31 January & also give that to Klenau for correction.

As far as the material for Romeo & Juliet is concerned, you may use it, on condition, however, that you have the material reproduced (lithographed) after the Cologne performance & also have the Fennimore score engraved, as you have promised me in the past.[56]

So how are things with the Romeo and Juliet for the Zurich Festspiele, where there was an inquiry about the opera? I feel it very important that I should see the work with Keller's subject performed there.[57]

I have yet to see the new score of Appalachia & ask that you send me a copy. Also some of the miniature scores & some Hassan & Cello Concerto piano scores.

I hear continued complaints that no one can get hold of my works. Even in the case of orders placed with music dealers here it is always: 'Not available'. And they do not have your catalogue of my works. Would it not be quite simple for you to arrange that? There is great demand here. I would like to have some catalogues too.

Is it really impossible for you to have my Fennimore & Gerda performed at a first class venue? Would Vienna not be possible? Munich, Dresden, Leipzig, Hamburg, Darmstadt, Wiesbaden?

Kind regards

Yours

PS It is typical that you have engraved the opera by Schoenberg and not Fennimore!!!

---

56 The engraved score of *Fennimore and Gerda* appeared in 1926.

57 Keller, the author of the book was from Zurich.

ꕥ

No 153

Delius to Tischer & Jagenberg

17 January 1923

Dear Doctor,

The English Public Trustee has asked me to deliver an exact account of all the sums owing to me in Germany. Would you please let me have an exact account therefore of what you owe in respect of Life's Dance, the orchestral pieces and songs? As soon as possible please.[58]

With best wishes to you and your wife and also the Jagenbergs.

Yours,

ꕥ

No 154

Delius to Universal

25 January 1923
Frankfurt a/M

Dear Herr Direktor,

I have received the packet with the material, for which many thanks. However, I am really furious about the score of Appalachia. It is just the old autograph Harmonie score, but made quite impossible by the omission of one variation. I shall not tolerate a score of mine going out into the world with this empty space. Besides this, all the other errors are still in it. All these scores must be recalled from the trade immediately; and then the score must be engraved anew.[59] Naturally, had I imagined that you would not make a new engraving of the score, I would of course have let this variation stand and simply added a remark: This variation may be omitted at will. I repeat here, that

---

[58] FD wrote again on 11 February saying that he had not yet received the account. Leuckart had sent theirs at once. FD had sold the six works to Leuckart outright in 1913 against payment of Mk 16,000 in 4 stages. He maintained that he had only received the first 4,000. Then on 13 February he wrote to say that the German Clearing House disputed his account with T & J on the grounds that he was a French citizen. He asked T & J to contact the GCH.

[59] It does not appear this was ever done, until the Beecham issue of a revised and engraved score for the Collected Edition in 1951. *Appalachia* was however engraved and corrected for the miniature score published by Universal (& Philharmonia) in 1927. In those days Philharmonia Edition re-engraved for the smaller page size. Reducing from a larger page would have been illegible.

I am giving you my orchestral material for the Cologne performance gratis,[60] only if you have the score of Appalachia & the score of Fennimore engraved.

If my works are not perfectly engraved by you and issued on good quality paper, you will receive nothing more from me. Just look at my scores published by Augener e.g. North Country Sketches – recently issued – how fine that is, then you will understand that I cannot give away my things under these conditions.

Our good understanding and our continued good relationship depend on these things.

With kind regards

PS Please let me know immediately about this & please send a vocal score of Appalachia at the same time – F. D.

No 155

Delius to Universal

9 February 1923
Frankfurt a/M

Dear Herr Direktor,

Thank you very much indeed for your kind wishes on my birthday. I am very pleased that the Cello Concerto enjoyed a success & I am pleased that I will be able to hear Herr Barjansky play it here on 1st March.

It was some time ago that you asked me to send you completely corrected copies of Seadrift, Appalachia and Paris for the purpose of a new engraving. In Seadrift, especially, there were an incredible number of errors & one passage was re-orchestrated. I revised these copies with the greatest care, then sent them to you, & I would ask you to look for them, because they are with you. If you have new engravings carried out according to the corrected copies of Seadrift and Appalachia, I will make concessions in the case of the Fennimore & Gerda score; but please send me a proof score from the new process, as you suggest. Of course the missing variation in Appalachia remains to be put back, with the remark that it may be omitted at will.

I have had the Hassan material sent from Darmstadt for correction & must admit that it is dreadfully shoddy. How someone is supposed to conduct from this awfully patched together score is a mystery to me. The copyist has done far too many string parts. Instead of the way it is composed, for just 6 solo violins, 2 violas, 2 cellos & 1 bass, he has done parts for a large orchestra. The work is composed for 26 solo instruments. We had the greatest trouble, because he mixed everything up in the strings. Also the text, in the choral parts, is so poorly written and with spelling errors that it might have been done by a foreigner. There are after all so many really good

60 *A Village Romeo.*

copyists, for ex. the one who copied the Cello Concerto. If you only knew how much time and energy must be spent on these corrections just to make them useable!

In the choral parts of the Song of the High Hills, the first choral passage is completely omitted. I never received a proof of it. The choral vocal score is all right (by Gardiner). These choral parts can not be used like this, so the choral vocal scores must be used instead. I hope and surmise that you have arranged everything with Klenau about the material for the Song of the High Hills & Cello Concerto, so that it arrives here on time.

We heard that Brigg Fair and Seadrift were performed extraordinarily beautifully and with great success in Krefeld.[61]

Percy Grainger's arrangement for 2 Pianos of the Dance Rhapsody is magnificent – quite splendid and brilliantly done – He performed it with Lippay at Simon's on my birthday; both played it splendidly. It is such a marvellous concert piece.

We have inserted the missing passage in the relevant parts of the Song of the High Hills for the performance here.
Kind regards

Yours

PS The Fennimore score must say

Dedicated to Sir Thomas Beecham Bart

When is the premiere of Romeo & J. to take place in Cologne. I am asked so often.

No 156

Delius to Tischer & Jagenberg

16 March 1923
Frankfurt-a/M

Dear Doctor,

I thank you very much for the quick dispatch of the piano arrangements of the small orchestral pieces. I had of course seen the arrangement before printing but never received the finished copies in print.

What you say in your letter astonishes me. You cannot possibly mean that you are going to pay my credits for the years 19, 20, 21, 22 in the present so steeply devalued currency. It is quite obvious that you owe me these sums at the rate of exchange ruling at the time. You have hesitated so long, in a way which is incomprehensible to me, – but that is your affair. I have asked you so many times to send me an account.

---

61 There is no specific record of these performances.

The same thing applies to payments from abroad. You have received them in foreign currency and you must, if you have changed them into Marks, reckon back again.[62]

I ask you therefore to let me have as soon as possible an exact and detailed account with this consideration in mind.

The content of your letter is in this sense grotesque and I can only conclude that some employee with no understanding of the matter wrote it and that you signed it without knowing what was in it?

Concerning Goodwin & Tabb, I hope you have arranged with them that material for the orchestral works is available for a specified fee, as is usual in England and has recently become quite simple to do in Germany.

Hoping for news of you soon,

Yours sincerely,

PS The small orchestral pieces are played a great deal in England and must bring in a great deal.

No 157

Delius to Universal

8 April 1923
Frankfurt a/M

Dear Herr Direktor,

As I told you in Frankfurt, Leuckart is still disputing the payment of the last instalment for the 6 works published by him, which you bought from him; that is to say, he says he is prepared to pay the final instalment with 4,000 paper marks instead of 4,000 gold marks.[63] My lawyer in London believes that if I could give the sum which you paid Leuckart for the works with the date, so that the value could be calculated in international currency, that would help my case a great deal. So please kindly inform me of it. Of course it will remain confidential between us, and will only be communicated to the lawyer in London.

Because of the travel difficulties[64] we have completely abandoned the plan to travel to France & are travelling from here straight to Bad Oeynhausen for a 6 to

---

62 It would be normal publishing practice to consolidate earnings outside the publisher's home territory into the home currency, but FD is correct in pointing out he could be losing money.

63 Earlier FD was complaining that Leuckart had only paid one of the 4 tranches of Mk 4,000. It seems that Leuckart had paid up. As to the final payment, under the 1913 contract, the last payment would only be made if FD had given Leuckart the 5 songs. These had gone to UE, but could possibly have been covered by UE's purchase of a 50 per cent interest in the Delius works in 1921.

64 According to Jelka, FD had been seriously ill through 1922 and was still weak.

8-week cure & from there to Norway. But I shall inform you of our dates of travel & address there.
Kind regards from both of us

Yours

PS Kapellmeister Scherchen was just here; he would like to play the Arabeske here and in Switzerland & asks you to let him know the orchestration for this work. We have no score here. So please send me the instrumentation as quickly as possible & I will then inform Scherchen immediately.

No 158

Delius to Tischer & Jagenberg

22 April 1923
Bad Oeynhausen

Dear Doctor,

Your registered letter with the account was sent on to me here, where I am taking the cure and I hasten to answer you.

Your objection that in most cases you receive payment in marks and cannot pay out in foreign currency is fair. Nevertheless you received so much in marks according to the rate of exchange at the time. You received this money and can account for it at its proper value. But now after years of selling my works you offer only Mk 6,542 – not as much as my wife and I could pay for one midday meal here. You never sent me the account for the instalments due.

Since I knew that I had to deal with an entirely honourable man and in consideration of the business difficulties I waited patiently. You are in error when you say that we had a comprehensive reckoning in Cologne last September. On the contrary you wrote to me from Norway that owing to the illness of your wife you would probably not be in Cologne. Also you did not book a room for us in the Dom hotel and in great distress we had to find lodgings for two nights. We concluded of course from that that you were not in Cologne. With regard to the payments, I would think it fair if you were to reckon according to the rate of exchange officially ruling at the time you received them. Herewith is a table of all the rates of exchange for those years;[65]

Since you have all the dates in your books, such a reckoning is a trivial matter for you. In your account I find no mention of the other songs, I mean the earlier ones.

Also I do not understand the account for the five songs.[66] Please give details of these. You write: 1920 five songs, 22.80. Is that for one copy? At the same time you make a deduction of 182.00 for two consignments of songs. What does this mean?

---

65 Not attached to translation.

66 The Five songs published by T & J in 1915.

Quite apart from that it is never the practice of other publishers to charge me if I ask for some songs for advertising purposes. I am therefore making a friendly request for further information.

I will apply to Goodwin & Tabb myself and take other steps to find out who is hiring the material for the small orchestral pieces, for that is quite inadmissible.

With best wishes,

No 159

Delius to Tischer & Jagenberg

10 May 1923
Bad Oeynhausen

Dear Doctor,
Before I answer your letter of the 23rd, I would like to ask you to send me a copy of the contract relating to my songs, from the first one (that is to say the passages directly referring to our agreement). I have not the contract with me and your demand that I should be liable for publication costs after so many years surprises me very much.[67] I should like to see once again the exact wording of the contract.

You have left unanswered my question regarding the deduction of Mk 182 for the songs. Together with a detailed statement of this sum, I require from you a detailed account of the sales of the songs which you put at the smallest possible figure, for example the 22.80 for songs sold in the same year that you deduct Mk 182 from me. I would like to draw your attention once more to the fact that I offered the songs to Dr Henry Simon who obtained the services of Helge Lindberg to sing them, which was very favourable advertisement for the publishing house. That you obtained Dr Simon's extraordinarily artistic translation of the songs for nothing makes the case even worse. Neither Universal Edition nor Harmonie made any deduction for a few extra copies, still less my English publishers. How can any advertising be done, if you act in such a niggardly way?

Naturally German paper money has gone up in proportion to the devaluation. A pair of boots which cost Mk 250 in 1921(?) now costs 80,000 or 100,000 – Every child knows that. It is incomprehensible that you take me to be so naïve!

I would like to remind you that up to now you have omitted to account for the songs at 2d a copy taken over at that time by Chester – Breitkopf & Härtel.

Looking forward to your quick dispatch of the contract copies.

Yours sincerely,

67 There is no such clause in the contract.

ꕥ

No 160

Delius to Tischer & Jagenberg

16 May 1923
Bad Oeynhausen

Dear Doctor,

Your three letters lie before me[68] and although you are attending to the matter, it is becoming still more complicated and I cannot accept the proposition that I should either accept a miserable Mk 6,000 for all these years without a proper account or that I should receive the sums that you owe me for the various years, which are noted in your three letters (but which never tally) at the rate of exchange ruling in March 1923 and so credit you with many millions of unaccounted royalties – with the addition of a whole list of sheet music which I am to pay for and which God knows who ordered from you. (Also neither dates nor figures agree in the different accounts).

Is it really so very difficult for you to make out a clear account in which the debits and credits for the songs are set out and which contains all the information in a few lines? Universal Edition does this twice a year and you are bound to do it by contract and you have only yourself to blame if I give your last three letters to an auditor. How can you charge me for music ordered by Herr Bernard? According to your list, you seem ....

REST OF LETTER MISSING

ꕥ

No 161

Delius to Universal

18 May 1923
Bad Oeynhausen,

Dear Herr Direktor,

I had a visit here from Mr Dean, director of the theatre which is staging Hassan in London. The performance is now definitely fixed for September & should be marvellous at His Majesty's Theatre. I shall go to London for it. Have you arranged anything definite with the theatre concerning sale of music? You have probably heard that Sir Thomas Beecham has conducted in London again, at a large concert at the Albert Hall where he also did the entr'acte from Romeo & Juliet. I would now like you to send the score of Fennimore & Gerda for engraving so that I can take

68 These are missing.

it to Beecham in September. The work is, as you know, dedicated to Sir Thomas Beecham and I would ask you to place in the score: Dedicated to

Sir Thomas Beecham Bart.

In addition, Grainger and I have inserted all the metronome marks in the Cello Concerto. I am sending you my copy with the request that these annotations are placed in copies sent out and also given to Mr Barjansky for insertion in his copy. I also ask you to send the Cello Concerto to Casals, if that has not already been done. Please return my copy back here. We are staying here until mid-June.

We have several songs, a Verlaine song[69] composed very recently & a few other songs. Would that interest you? The Verlaine song has a very lovely translation by Rudolf Binding. The other songs could poss.[ibly] form a single edition with the one by Holger Drachmann, which you took over from Leuckart with the Nietzsche songs.

With best wishes &,
because of devaluation, a request for prompt settlement

Cordially yours

I hear that Catherine Goodson played the [piano concerto] beautifully & impressively in London at the … & repeated it on 10 May in her own orchestral concert with Coates as cond.[uctor]

No 162

Delius to Tischer & Jagenberg

23 May 1923
Bad Oeynhausen

Dear Doctor,

I have received your letter of the 18th and, as you must have foreseen, I cannot accept the account on the following grounds:
1. The Old Songs

1. The count is unsatisfactory. You do not say how many copies have been bought and at what price.
2. You are quite out of order in charging me interest, as there is nothing in the contract about this.
3. You are also quite out of order in charging me annual expenses. For this, too, you have no contractual justification.

Reckoning by this erroneous amount, a sum of Mk 909.60 is outstanding for the songs, that is to say, after costs have been covered, Mk 909.60 remains as profit, of

69 *Avant que tu ne t'en ailles.*

which I receive 50 per cent. That pre-supposes that the payment for the sales and the sums credited agree, which considering your peculiar method of computation, I do not accept.

2. The small orchestral works and Five Songs.

I cannot accept this account either as:

1. The pound sterling on 15th March stood at 98,000 and not 90,000. Also you sent me no adequate account for this date.
2. The sums accounted for [in] your various letters do not agree with each other. (For example, you give me for 1922 a detailed account of my [sales] with Mk 6,452 to my credit, but in spite of that you account in your letter of 18 May for only Mk 4,000).
3. In addition I must know for certain the number and price of the sales, which do not appear in your inadequate account. Also the number of sales and the price of the piano edition.

It seems to me necessary to let an auditor examine the whole matter, in which case I bring it to your attention in advance that the costs for that would fall on you, because you have not fulfilled the conditions of the contract.

I have shown your accounts to a specialist who has assured me (and I was already certain of it) that from a business point of view you must be classed as unsatisfactory in every respect and that any subsequent auditing costs should fall on your shoulders.

I feel myself at the end of my patience and am tired of this hopeless, repetitive correspondence.

With best wishes to your dear wife for whom I wish the best of luck in the imminent event.

Yours

No 163

Delius to Tischer & Jagenberg

14 June 1923
Bad Oeynhausen

Dear Sir,

In reply to your letter of 6.6.23 I inform you of the following:

I am returning the cheque which you sent to me for Mk 8,372 in respect of the annual account for 1922 and indeed under the strongest protest.

I know that in the present chaotic state of Germany there still exists no direct legislation for the protection of authors.

It seems to me all the more regrettable that a self-respecting German publishing firm does not acknowledge its obvious obligation to send appropriate compensation to the composer whose work it has exploited. On 6 June 1923 Mk 8,372 was worth about 6 pence in English currency. On the same date you explain to me that for a single copy sold in England my 50 per cent net profit comes to 4d. According to your statement 2 scores of the small orchestral pieces, 13 piano arrangements, 1 set of orchestral parts and 9 'Five Songs' were sold abroad in 1922.[70]

That you think it enough to send me 6d for this year is quite incomprehensible to me. I will carefully preserve the relative documents among my papers for the edification of Posterity; also I will not fail to publish the matter shortly in a German musical paper, in order to give something of a surprise to our contemporaries.

Furthermore the judicial decisions in most analogous cases have not been arrived at according to the letter of an antiquated law but in accordance with a moral sense of justice, so that I would have nothing to fear from a court case. I have already won one case against Harmonie Verlag before the war, although Harmonie had not demonstrably offended against the Law and our contract, but on the grounds that their business methods in my case were immoral and unethical.

As for the accounts for 1919, 1920 & 1921, I am now awaiting the immediate remittance of Mk 182,220 the amount still due to me under our agreement. At the same time I want a clear assent in writing to my proposals for settlement. If you should delay any longer, you will force me to raise my demands according to the rate of exchange even up to four times as much.

I note from your letter that you agree to my separate proposals concerning the old songs; with the exception of the clause concerning the bill for expenses. These expenses according to my expert adviser should not exceed five per cent (five per cent) of the gross receipts. If I am to have anything to do with a new edition, I should require an exact account as to costs and the number of copies.

Lebenstanz You acquired this work by purchase before the war for 5,000 German Gold marks. So apart from the purchase price I get nothing from you, while during my lifetime and for thirty years after my death you are able to exploit this work gratis and for your sole benefit. Your reasoning by which you will not pay me in full the last instalment of 1,000 Gold marks still due after the 40th performance lacks therefore all logic and is quite untenable.[71]

In the case of both of the small orchestral pieces, piano arrangements and songs, for which I remain entitled to a royalty on sales, it is different and they can and should be sold at the peacetime price, multiplied by the official index figure of the music firm.

On reflection you must surely agree that the case is quite different here from that of a work obtained for one outright payment, like 'Lebenstanz'. That the last instalment is only to be paid after the 40th performance was purely a concession to you, protecting you against any risk, for if an orchestral work is performed 40 times, its future is assured.

---

[70] Added in a second hand. 'Not counting sales in Denmark'.

[71] The editors have only identified 6 performances between 1912 and 1921. The contract referred to the sale of the 40th set of material.

With regard to your remarks about the 1922 account I would point out that I did not mean orchestral sales but all sales, and that your account of 6 June does not agree with the one previously presented, even in the number of copies. What special pleasure you wished to give me by sending me an annual account which yields me a grand total of 6d, certain expenses apart, is not clear to me. Also the 6 pence have today already gone down to 3d!!

I will forgo my claim to the immediate payment of the smaller sums in foreign currency if settled quarterly and not converted into Marks, which I strictly veto and which you must prevent. Larger sums in foreign currency are to be paid to me immediately in accordance with your own proposals.

As a permanent address I give you
Westminster Bank
106 Finchley Road
London N.W.3, with the proviso that if I am in Germany when the time for payment is due I will let you know my address there in order that you may send it on.

Yours faithfully,
Frederick Delius
PS I have received with thanks the payment of 18 Danish Kroner for 1923.
F.D.
I am here until the 21st inst. after which my address is:
Lesjaskog Gudbrandsdalen Norway,
where I request you to send the account for the 1st 6 months of 1923. [Your]Enclosed cheque for Mk 8,372.[received]

No 164

Delius to Tischer & Jagenberg

2 July 1923
Norway

Dear Sir,
It was not possible to answer your letter of the 16th June before my departure from Oeynhausen. I received with thanks the cheque for Mk 190,592 and acknowledge receipt provisionally and under protest the Mk 8,372 for the 1922 account. I have noted the other contents of your letter and hope on the basis of this agreement to continue our business dealings without further trouble or argument.

Please send the account for the first six months of 1923, which you intended to send at the beginning of July, to my friend Percy Grainger, c/o Herrn Dr Schumacher, Grüneburgweg 129, Frankfurt-am-Main if it is ready in time. The latter is in Frankfurt until the 9th July and then he comes here to me and could therefore bring the foreign accounts with him.

If that does not work, please send me a postcard and I will ask the Westminster bank, London who their agents in Cologne are. In any case the amount itself must be sent to me here for checking and I will arrange about the cheque and foreign credits.

Because as a result of the catastrophic conditions in Germany so many restrictions and regulations prevail in German banks, I should much prefer it to come through Mr Grainger this time.

Yours faithfully,

No 165

Delius to Tischer & Jagenberg

18 July 1923
Norway

Dear Sir,

In reply to your letter of 7th inst enclosing your account for the first six months of 1923 and a cheque for Mk 83,537, I would like to inform you that I accept this cheque with reservations, as the amount is insufficient. The index figures, which are the key to the whole account, are nowhere quoted.

In one case alone, which I can check, the account is so strikingly incorrect, that I have no confidence in the other figures. I quote herewith:

The Bjornson set costs at the original selling price Mk 3.5. This, multiplied by the index figure valid on 15 June 1923, which (as published in the press) was 6,300, yields Mk 22,050 instead of the 7,920 that you use to account.

I must therefore ask you to send me the index figures for the first six months of 1923 so that I can check the account with them.

Furthermore I want a regular and businesslike account of the foreign currency paid in for me so that I can use this in my accounts instead of your mentioning these foreign currency payments as postscripts to a letter.

Also you have completely left out the entry of six dollars of which you informed me on the 12th and 18th May. You have made just as good an account of the foreign currency as you did of the income in marks. Have you not also forgotten the rest of the American income!!

When I have received the foreign accounts in a businesslike form and have declared them correct I will ask you to pay them into my account with the National Provincial and Lloyd's Bank Cologne. When you draw the amount from Goodwin & Tabb, you can have it paid through them.

Yours faithfully,

ꕥ

No 166

Delius to Universal

10 August 1923
Lesjaskog

Dear Herr Direktor,

Today I am returning the 4 Nietzsche songs[72] & the other song. I have corrected the music, but the English text is quite unusable & may not appear under any circumstances. No one in England would sing translations like this of such famous Nietzsche texts. The songs must either appear only with German text, or be translated by a true English poet. It would otherwise merely become a disgrace & laughing stock.

We are to leave Norway in a few days time because of the persistent bad weather & I would ask you to address everything to Grez-sur-Loing.

When may I expect the corrected orchestral scores of Fennimore & Gerda, Seadrift and Appalachia? We are heading straight for Grez where I shall check them. I have not yet received your settlement.

Percy Grainger was here for a few weeks & has just returned to America.

Hoping that things are well with you &

with kind regards

---

72 These songs were published in 1924 by UE with German words only.

ꕥꕥ

No 167

Delius to Universal

20 October 1923
Grez-sur-Loing

Dear Herr Direktor,

Today I received your letter of 16th Oct. and immediately wrote again to Mr Percy Fletcher head of orchestra at His Majesty's Theatre, that he must have the enclosed score fragments copied with minimum delay. In a few days Heseltine will be ready with his vocal score. He is already quite a way on with it. But of course you did well to re-issue the old one again, so that no break occurs.

This music & the simultaneous appearance of Heseltine's book[73] have made a colossal impression.

As far as the gramophone companies are concerned, I have, following the advice of my London colleagues, meanwhile become a member of the Copyright Protection Society in London and this society will now represent my rights. I have given permission to the Gramophone Company (His Master's Voice); this company is already in touch with Fletcher who, as a theatre conductor of many years' standing, has a great deal of experience; I therefore think that matters will now proceed according to the book. I hear from all sides that this company is by far the best & has the greatest coverage.

As far as Curwen[74] is concerned, I am happy to believe in his good will – but it is a shame that he has no shop. How much more will be sold when it is out in the shops & people see it & can buy it straight away.

It would naturally be very good if Heseltine's book, which has had a very positive reception in London & throughout England, could be translated into German. But it must be translated artistically & well.

How large is the run which you have made of 'Hassan'? In their statements, my English publishers always note the copies sold, the size of the print run & of the remaining stock.

I hear from Mr Grainger that he has already engaged halls for 2 concerts in Bridgeport & New York for the 28 & 30th April. I think he will play the Song of the High Hills & poss. some more of my works; he will conduct himself. I am very pleased about it.

All in all I am feeling rather better; in any case the lovely warm weather here & outdoor life has done me a great deal of good.

I hope you will visit us here one day, dear Director.

Kind regards from both of us,

Yours

---

[73] Heseltine's biography of FD.

[74] UE's agent after the 1914–18 war.

ꕥꕥ

No 168

Delius to Universal

3 November 1923
Grez-sur-Loing

Dear Herr Direktor,

I just received your letter of 30 Oct. & am sending back the criticisms enclosed.

Mr Heseltine is here at the moment & with my consent, he has completed the vocal score with the amendments. It will go off to you tomorrow. Of course you must pay Mr Heseltine a fee for this difficult task, £10 I should think. You must consider that he had to do this work in the theatre between d[ai]ly. performances. Heseltine might give you the piano score of 'In a Summer Garden' which you have had in your possession now for so long, if you bring it out without delay.[75] This piano arrangement is done as a piano piece with special respect for pianistic qualities & a reproduction of the impression of the whole piece & therefore of special value. (Grainger has put a similarly arranged piano score of 'On hearing the first cuckoo in Spring' in his concert programme & had great success with it).

Fletcher will send you the copy of the Hassan score as soon as it is ready. The copyist's bill will be sent to you with it.

As far as your wishes for fees for the Hassan music on the gramophone are concerned, I believe in this case that in England, the material belongs to the Reandean company, which alone has the say over it; mechanical rights belong to me. For a recording any of my other works e.g. 'Brigg Fair' etc. you would probably receive a hire fee for the orchestral material.[76]

Of course I am relying on you having the vocal score of Hassan produced with all possible speed. The serenade would be the most suitable as a solo piece & indeed for piano & violin. You can use the old plate which you have for tenor & piano for this, but you must send me a proof so that I can do some phrasings etc.

I fail to grasp why you did not immediately send
Mr Charles Kinsey
The Chicago North Shore Festival Association 624 Michigan Avenue
Chicago
my choral works: Mass of Life, Seadrift, Songs of Sunset, Appalachia, Requiem, which I requested.

Through this delay we have now missed the 1924 Festival; which is a pity for two reasons, as I am probably going to America around that time for Grainger's

---

75 It was ultimately published by Thames Publishing, in 1982.

76 This is the beginning of UE's campaign to receive a share of mechanical rights on Delius works, which eventually FD to some extent granted. He has a good point here, in that a record company wishing to record his orchestral music would have to hire the parts, with the possible exception of those for *Hassan*, which belonged to Reandean. These days publishers would charge a premium rate when hiring material for a recording.

concerts & could have done both together. Please send the works immediately if this has not already been done.

From all sides, people are asking me why there are no miniature scores of my larger choral works. I would advise you urgently to have same produced.

'Hassan' is enjoying great success as before & also Heseltine's book 'Delius', which is extraordinarily thorough and has had favourable reviews.

With best wishes from both of us

Yours

Please return the letter from Kinsey.

No 169

The Performing Right Society to Delius

27 Nov 1923
London

Dear Sir,
An unauthorised public performance of your sonata for violin and piano has been brought to our notice. We observe from our records that this sonata is published by Messrs. Forsyth Bros. Ltd. and we shall be grateful if you will inform us whether you retained the performing right on its publication by Forsyth Bros. Ltd. or whether you assigned that right to the publishers. As the matter is of some urgency and importance, we shall be obliged if you will favour us with an early reply. If you can furnish us with a copy of any Assignment or Agreement you made with Messrs. Forsyth Bros Ltd. in regard to this work, we shall be obliged.

In looking through our records of your compositions, we find that we do not have the dates of first publication on the continent. We enclose a list of these works and shall be obliged if you will place opposite the title of each work the date and place of first publication.
Yours faithfully

Secretary

ജ്ഞ

No 170

Delius to Universal

21 December 1923
Villa Raggio
San Ambrogio
Rapallo

Dear Herr Direktor,

We have just arrived here & found your ltr here ahead of us. I am also greatly astonished by the price of this copy [of Hassan] & will write to Fletcher immediately to protest.

However it is truly better to have a really good copy of the whole thing, because so many small changes have been put in here and there & also amendments so that the whole thing would have become very unclear & completely useless for a stage version. The entire final scene is more or less new & in many cases unorchestrated because of the speech. In Darmstadt the final scene was not played at all. But a price of £23 is unheard of. Because this piece will go all over the world it is indeed very important to have a good score engraved straight away.[77]

Please send Heseltine the £10 for the Hassan vocal score & his arrangement of In a Summer Garden.

I am now hearing that the Columbia Company has brought out the Dance Rhapsody on gramophone. The Copyright Society has written to me that the work is free because it was published before 1912. Is that correct? I don't have the contracts here. Did Leuckart really bring it out before 1912?[78]

With kind regards and Christmas wishes from both of us

Kind regards

---

[77] The orchestral score of the *Hassan* music was not engraved until 1978, for the Boosey 'Hawkes Pocket Score' series.

[78] 1910, the date of publication by Leuckart has been pencilled in on the original, probably by UE. The issue of musical works published before 21 July 1912, the commencement date of the UK 1911 Copyright Act, is covered in a separate section on mechanical rights. In brief, it was not necessary for the record companies to seek consent before recording such a work, and in the case of works published before 1 July 1910, no mechanicals were due on recordings until 1 July 1913, and then only at half rate.

ꟾ

1924

Such was the success of *Hassan* that Universal brought out a violin and piano arrangement of the Serenade and suggested an arrangement of the *Hassan* music for small orchestra. Delius pointed out that it was scored for a band of 26 players already. He was still short of cash and harangued Universal on a number of matters. There was still no sign of the engraved scores Universal had promised him. There was no London showroom; The prices of his printed music were too low in Germany and too high in London.

In Germany the rentenmark had been introduced in November 1923 and had become accepted, bringing inflation under control and with it a slump.

Delius, absorbed in his own music, was unsympathetic, but to encourage Universal, he was prepared to drop his royalty percentage in some circumstances, such as for the sale of vocal material for the London performance of *A Mass of Life*. Albert Sammons and Evlyn Howard-Jones recorded the second violin sonata.

In Britain the music publishers noticed a serious reduction in sales of printed music owing the growth of record sales and the coming of broadcasting, leading to more publishers joining PRS in order to benefit from broadcast fees.

No more big works would be forthcoming from Delius.

No 171

Delius to Universal

4 January 1924.

Herr Direktor

Enclosed I once again send you the bill from the Hassan copyist which as you will see through my intervention has been reduced to £17-17-6d. Fletcher did the work for me as a favour. I attach his letter. It will not have escaped your attention that the 10/- charged for the hire of the vocal score is thought too high. I would ask that you please settle the copyist's fees with all haste. Of course the material being required every night for performance at the theatre made the whole project fearfully difficult, including Heseltine's work.

As far as the Hassan Serenade is concerned it should be done for violin and piano as follows: It begins on page 5 of the vocal score (the printed one), bottom-most line, 2 bars of arpeggios before the violin comes in and is to be printed exactly as it is there down to page 6 at the 2nd bar after A. From here to the end the violin is to play one octave higher. The accompaniment remains as it is.[79]

[79] In fact, FD's suggestions were not carried out; a slightly different arrangement by Lional Tertis was published instead, dated 'copyright 1923'.

I find it most regrettable that you could not come to an agreement with Langen[80] regarding the Hassan music; isn't that after all the whole point of the publisher! I will however write to Mdme. Flecker once again although I expect she will reply that she is quite powerless to intervene and that you will have to pursue the matter with the publisher.

With kind regards

ꕥ

No 172

Delius to Universal

9 February 1924.

Herr Direktor,

I am most surprised to hear nothing from you concerning the newly engraved scores of Sea Drift and Appalachia, nor about the engraving of Fennimore and Gerda. These works should have been ready to print some time ago. May I request that you just bring out the Hassan vocal score as quickly as possible. In sales terms it is tremendously important that so long as it is being played it is available for purchase; I receive enquiries so frequently.

On to other matters, I have published in London several small pieces composed in the last year – 3 short preludes for piano with the Anglo-French Music Co. and a handful of children's songs and four part-choruses with Oxford University Press. Also a violin sonata with Hawkes & Son. Under the current circumstances I am earning so little from my works at Universal Edition that this seemed the natural path to go. Furthermore I am yet to receive my statement for the second half-year of 1923 and would ask that it please be sent.

Our stay here is very pleasant and we have enjoyed the splendid sunshine.

With best wishes from us both

ꕥ

No 173

Delius to Universal

23 March 1924.
La Napoule, Alpes Maritime

Dear Herr Direktor

80 Albert Langen, Munich, published the German translation of *Hassan*.

I should like to respond to your letter of 21 March,[81] receipt of which I hereby acknowledge, by reaffirming to you on the contrary that the firm of Universal Edition remains of prime importance to me. I am willing to state in plain language my reasons for not offering these small works to you.

1. Sea Drift. You promised to engrave this work as the current lithographed score is defective and full of mistakes; several passages have been re-orchestrated and improved and it is being performed time and again using the defective version.
2. You had promised to engrave Appalachia. The present autograph edition is not only less than satisfactory but also contains mistakes.
3. You gave a commitment that the full score of Fennimore and Gerda would be engraved. Apart from the copy of the score in your own possession you could always have recalled the copy lent to Cologne. What on earth is happening in Cologne to cause them to retain this copy for so long'?
4. You still have no showroom or window in London where my music can be displayed; consequently sales have been severely restricted and I am constantly bombarded with enquiries and complaints that my music is unobtainable in any music shop.

Besides, in comparison with other English prices your own are much too high thus detracting still further from sales.

Although you own almost all of my works my royalties from them are a mere pittance when compared with the income generated by the scant few published in England. Furthermore, it is my belief that the latter will contribute considerably to the public's awareness of my oeuvre. Of course I would never have imagined that the reissue of the Hassan vocal score would require quite the length of time it has – just think what sales may have been lost in the interim. Moreover, in London your only advertisements appear in Sackbut, a journal that no one actually reads.

You see, your prices in Germany and Austria are so low that my earnings are to all intents and purposes non-existent – a few Swiss francs for my entire published output with you. On top of that you charge such inflated prices in London that you actually hinder any chance of these works being performed and sales are far too low.

As soon as you show some willingness to fulfil the aforementioned conditions to the extent that I see some gain for myself I shall be more than happy to give you more works as well as smaller things.

I was deeply distressed to learn of your illness. It was certainly a very cold winter everywhere.

We are now here until the end of April and then we shall be taking the waters in Kassel. I shall notify you of the address once we are there.

With kind regards from us both

Cordially yours

81 This letter has not survived.

ཐྭཐྭ

No 174

Delius to Universal

22 April 1924
Grez-sur-Loing

Herr Direktor

I have received your letter of 16 April and can only repeat that you promised me, verbally in Frankfurt and later by letter, that Sea Drift, Appalachia and Paris would be engraved; not to mention Fennimore and Gerda which I was to have presented to Sir Thomas Beecham last September.

The current edition of Sea Drift is awash with mistakes and it lacks the later revisions. Circulation of this edition is detrimental to the piece and quite unworthy of a work that enjoys such a large degree of popularity. As soon as you fulfil your promises you can expect to receive new works from me, including works for the piano, but not before.

I am especially pleased that you have at last elected to reduce significantly the prices charged for my music in England. I have been recommending this course of action for many years now – we are sure to see a rapid change of fortune.

As far as the edition of my Hassan Suite is concerned, I would advise you to publish my score as it stands, i.e. for 26 instruments.[82] That will render it accessible to any orchestra. How would you differentiate between a medium-sized orchestra and salon orchestra? Of course I cannot have my works reorchestrated by just anyone; I would request therefore that you write to me with further details. To my mind it should be produced according to how it is performed in the theatre, leaving anyone free to perform whatever numbers they choose.

I received a letter from Heseltine a few days ago. On 4 April he wrote, 'I have only just received the last part of the Hassan proofs. Universal Edition has had my arrangement now for 5 months – one would hardly describe them as swift!!'

What is one to think? It is beyond me.

With best wishes

ཐྭཐྭ

No 175

Delius to Universal

12 June 1924

Herr Direktor

---

[82] This was not done until Boosey & Hawkes first issued a study score in 1978.

I have just heard from one of the directors of the Royal Philharmonic Society that a performance of my Mass of Life is planned to take place there under Klenau.[83] They are demanding however as a prerequisite to this performance a complete revision of the chorus parts.

You will no doubt recall that the chorus parts originally acquired from Harmonie are in a quite unbelievably poor condition and utterly useless in this state. They were produced by Harmonie in haste without my corrections or consent, and contain no orchestral cues. Also, the parts must be printed together, not individually, as is the case with the Song of the High Hills, to enable the singers to follow each other's parts. With such complicated choral works this is absolutely necessary[84]. Kennedy Scott, England's foremost choir master, would like to start rehearsing his chorus, however he has stated in advance his reluctance to do so in the absence of any workable material as he has already tried once with the present material and given it up as impossible. Apart from all this the material is riddled with mistakes. In one place there are even two bars missing. I must insist on your immediate reply on this matter for this major London performance is of the greatest significance.

I fail to understand why the lines of communication from your end are so quiet especially regarding Hassan. Is the vocal score finally ready yet? You had intended to send it to me. You have left unanswered all questions concerning the arrangements. Moreover I hear that Hassan is to go to America this autumn. For that vocal scores and instrumental arrangements etc. will have to be readily available if we are going to make any profit from this.

I gratefully acknowledge receipt of one copy of the Nietzsche Lieder but would ask you please to send me the usual five copies when I am back in Grez.

Cordially yours

No 176

Delius to Universal

29 June 1924
Grez-sur-Loing

Herr Direktor,

I gratefully acknowledge receipt of the vocal score to Hassan. It is a great pity of course that it was not ready before. It can only be regretted that my questions went totally unanswered by you. Self-evidently I was unable to give my consent to the Suite before knowing what sort of instrumentation was involved. You failed to

---

83 2 April 1925.

84 Separate parts, the soprano part on its own etc., would have been, and are nowadays, very unfriendly, and increase rehearsal time needed. See FD to UE 27 December 1925 re the *Song of the High Hills*.

answer me at the time – hence the delay. In your letter of 16th April you made no mention of instrumentation etc. For my part I am agreeable to the instrumentation as outlined.

Turning now to the chorus parts of A Mass of Life I doubt very much whether your proposal to use the vocal scores as chorus parts will be practicable. A choir standing shoulder to shoulder cannot handle the weight of these heavy scores. There is already more than enough for the orchestra alone to manage, without the soloists also having the encumbrance of constant page turning. Is it not possible to extract only those passages relevant to the chorus and print these from the plates on to lighter paper. To my mind the only way to proceed and one which will significantly improve the format is to produce once and for all sensible chorus parts containing all necessary cues. The Mass is also to be given in Vienna; furthermore we have the prospect of a number of other performances in Germany. In order to release you from some of the burden of the London performance I would happily forgo my 25 per cent royalty on the sale of chorus material and satisfy myself instead with 10 per cent. This accommodation though would be restricted to this performance only and, it goes without saying, to those copies supplied to the chorus. I would ask that you please first enquire whether the London Philharmonic Choir wishes to use these vocal scores and whether the concert society agrees to the price of 3/6d. Please then advise your findings without delay. I shall be here for another few weeks.

I hear that Brecher and Brueggemann are now employed by the Leipzig Opera. You might draw their attention to Fennimore and Gerda. Here in Germany awareness of my choral works is negligible, whilst...? Hagen, Elberfeld, Barmen, Cologne, Duisburg and many other towns could well host a performance of one of my works.

With best Wishes

ꙮ

No 177

Delius to Universal

7 July 1924
Grez-sur-Loing

Herr Direktor,

I received your letter dated 4th July today and am of the opinion that printing the chorus parts in this way ie. on lighter paper and without the solo and orchestral parts would indeed be a great improvement. It would merely be necessary to make sure that no cues were omitted anywhere. However with regard to the 10 per cent sales royalty proposed for the chorus material for the Mass, I am willing to give my consent only to the performance in London. I quite simply fail to grasp why you wish to reduce my sales royalty to such an extent since the vocal score contains fine engravings of all the chorus parts and these would only require simple transferal to inexpensive light paper. I have agreed to these terms for the London performance alone, but please recognise that this has involved a not insignificant concession on my part.

You see, my dear Herr Direktor, you always go to great lengths to highlight the promotional efforts you are undertaking on behalf of my choral and orchestral works, but I think in this context that your main priority should lie in the publication of a proper comprehensive catalogue including a price list. I did request such a catalogue and today you have sent me one that is quite incomplete. The following works are missing:

The Song of the High Hills A Dance Rhapsody In a Summer Garden Requiem
Songs of Sunset
Cello Concerto
Two Songs to be Sung of a Summer Night on the Water
Four Old English Lyrics
Hassan
Dance for Harpsichord

As will be apparent all works delivered since the war are missing.

Herr Laugs the music director here has demonstrated a great interest in my work but is quite unaware of my compositions since Sea Drift and moreover by whom they have been published.

It is very difficult for me to list all my works for him whereas I could simply have given him a catalogue. The same goes for Hagen where Weissbach would like to give one of my larger scale works if only he knew their titles. And that is only to mention two people with whom I happen to have come into personal contact. Others, in receipt of such an incomplete catalogue, must surely also be fumbling around in the dark. What mystifies me even further is that a healthy circulation of my works must also be central to your own best interest.

I am presently in correspondence with Dr Heinrich Simon whose dearest wish it is to stage a performance of A Village Romeo and Juliet.

I am no closer to knowing how matters stand with Hassan in America. Basil Dean, the London theatre director, wrote to me that he would in all probability be taking the work to America in the autumn. I have also heard from other parties that Hassan will be going to America.

To return once more to the subject of A Mass of Life, let there be no doubt over my own opinion that by far the best option would be to produce new proper chorus material which can then be used for every performance. Any conductor seeing the parts in their present state is certain to shy away from a performance.

I received a letter from the Wiener Philharmonischer Verlag requesting photographs for the miniature scores. The letter states that the Verlag also plans to publish Appalachia or'Sea Drift as part of this edition. I sent them two photographs and the address of the Munich photographer Hilsdorf-Mueller in Amalienstrasse. I should like to take this opportunity once more to point out to you that the score of Sea Drift is incomplete and peppered with errors and may not be reissued under any circumstances without incorporating the corrections and reworkings I originally sent to you. The missing variation must be reinserted into Appalachia along with everything else we previously discussed. Obviously I shall continue to receive my royalty in respect of these editions in line with the provisions of my contract.

I am returning the Hassan Serenade to you today with corrections. My wife joins me in sending you our very best wishes.

Cordially yours

No 178

Delius to Universal

25 July 1924
Grez-sur-Loing

Dear Sir,

I gratefully acknowledge receipt of your letter of 22 July.

I regret that your solution to the problem of the Mass chorus parts is quite unworkable for the simple reason that the worst obstacle, namely the continuous turning of pages, which in a large double choir gives rise to an ominous rustling, is not thereby eliminated. Mr Kennedy Scott is insisting upon new chorus parts with cues in addition to all the other things he raises in his letter. As matters stand he refuses to rehearse the work. His choir simply will not tolerate such poor material in this long and difficult work. I really would have thought that Kennedy Scott's letter in which he sheds light upon the reason behind the paucity of Delius performances in England really would have driven home the importance of this matter.

I would ask that you please correspond with Herr Direktor Hertzka immediately if you cannot act without his authorisation, for if the material is not available by 15 November, the rehearsals will have to be cancelled. Quite irrespective of the potential for performances to be generated in other cities on the back of this London concert, the fact that Mr Scott wishes to buy an extra one hundred vocal scores at 3/6d is in itself good business for you. I fail to understand why you insist upon being so shortsighted and petty!

I should be grateful if you would please forward the complete catalogue in German of my UE works as soon as this appears.

I have received no reply regarding the vocal score of Hassan where on page 38 the lower half of the whole should appear before the upper page. This amounts to an incredible mistake which must under no circumstances enter circulation. It must be corrected in all copies. As printed therein the closing section of the act ends with an open upbeat!!!

Could you please give these questions your earliest attention and address any correspondence including my statement to me here where I should be staying for approximately another two weeks.

Yours respectfully,

FD

PS I am not familiar with the paper used in printing bibles, but whatever paper you choose it must not be so flimsy and of such poor quality that difficulties arise in page turning. Above all the paper must be capable of enduring months of rehearsal.

No 179

Delius to Universal

5 October 1924
Grez-sur-Loing

Dear Herr Direktor,

Please accept my profoundest thanks for the two copies of the arrangement for piano and violin of Hassan. Can you please however send me the remaining three copies right away. I have received the chorus material for the Mass and will return this as soon as I have had the chance to check through it.

To my astonishment I hear from the committee of the Royal Philharmonic Society that they have been charged more for these chorus parts than for the complete set of vocal scores (as you informed me at the time). You intended to charge 3/- for the latter, even 2/6d if necessary. The vocal score contains 200 pages; there must be some mistake to cause you to charge 4/- for the 74 page choral score. The Philharmonic Society has placed an order for approximately 300 copies and you ought not to charge them at a higher rate than for the vocal score – that would be farcical. Clearly you will not be able to recover your costs through one performance alone; to enable the performance by the Philharmonic Society to go ahead I have forgone my 25 per cent and dropped my royalty to 10 per cent – you too must do your bit my dear Herr Direktor. Do not be so shortsighted! Rather, you should be ensuring that Curwen has sufficient stocks of the vocal score and in particular that copies are on sale at the concert venue itself.

Cordially yours

Please read the following addendum 05.10.24

I have just completed composition of five short piano pieces, including a few short waltzes, a lullaby and a Toccata. These could make up an album.

Like Forsyth, the Anglo-French Publishing Company would dearly like to publish these pieces. You are aware that Anglo-French has already published my three short preludes for piano which seem to have found a good market. Howard-Jones, who has given regular public performances of this work, was recently here. He plays the preludes quite delightfully and is now very keen to premiere the latest five pieces.

Before I deliver them over to a London publisher I wanted to enquire of you whether you would be inclined to publish these in collaboration with Curwen, in such a way that you acquire the rights for continental Europe and he for the territory of England. I will claim a sales royalty of 33 per cent.

If I assign these piano pieces to you I expect you to finally fulfil your commitments regarding Fennimore, Appalachia, Sea Drift and Paris. May I request that you please reply with all possible speed concerning the piano pieces. On 8 November a concert will be given in the Wigmore Hall of Delius chamber music[85] and in a few days my new violin sonata will be premiered at the Music Club. The preludes have just been played by Howard-Jones on the radio which is always the best form of publicity. The time is ripe!
In eager anticipation of your response

Yours

ꟷ

No 180

Delius to Universal

18 October 1924
Grez-sur-Loing

Dear Herr Direktor,

I gratefully acknowledge receipt of your letter of 10 October and following your advice have decided to assign the Five Piano Pieces to Universal Edition in accordance with the conditions as outlined by you. This is to say that I shall receive a sales royalty of 25 per cent of the recommended retail price of all published editions. I however would wish to stipulate that these pieces be published without delay and furthermore that if you engrave these pieces in their entirety that you produce both an English and a German edition.[86] Under no circumstances would I wish the English and the German to appear in the same edition. It is self-evident that my 25 per cent sales royalty applies equally in Curwen's territory.[87] As is the custom with my

---

[85] 2 violin sonatas with Sammons and Howard-Jones
Cello sonata
Songs
3 preludes for piano and 5 manuscript pieces.

[86] Presumably the 5 manuscript pieces played at the Wigmore Hall. German and English editions were produced.

[87] Good Point. UE probably agreed to pay FD 25 per cent of receipts in Germany from sheet sales outside Germany, which would have allowed Curwen to take a big commission on purchases for the UK to FD's detriment. Accounting for royalties earned in subsidiaries' or agents' territories has always been a thorny problem, when composers realised what was happening, as FD clearly did. It could not affect performing right income, which was paid direct to the composer, but it became more serious with mechanical income, where traditionally

other works the proceeds are to be accounted in pounds sterling and the remaining countries in their respective currencies. The pieces are presently with Howard Jones who will be performing them on 8 November as part of the Delius chamber music concert in London (in MS of course).

May I therefore request that you reach an agreement with Curwen as soon as possible and set everything in place.

The second Violin Sonata published by Hawkes & Son will also be performed at the concert on 8th as well as the first Violin Sonata which was published by Forsyth back in 1915. Incidentally why do you not obtain distribution rights to these works for Germany and Austria?

I was quite disturbed to hear from Howard Jones that you are continuing to supply the Piano Concerto in the flawed edition with mistake-ridden handwritten material. You are thereby preventing any hope of a performance. The whole work must now finally be reingraved. By the same token I am also depending on you to engrave the other works, namely Fennimore, Appalachia, Sea Drift and Paris. This has been a long-held commitment of yours. Incidentally it is just possible that Fennimore will be done next season in London. You will also recall that I delivered over to you the material to A Village Romeo and Juliet without charge on condition that there is a new engraving.

I see that Romeo and Juliet appears on the programme for Cologne and request that you inform me of the date of the performance and details of the conductor as soon as these are known to you. Similarly it pleased me greatly to hear that A Mass of Life is to be performed in Vienna, Prague, Berlin and Wiesbaden. Again please forward dates to me here along with the name of the conductor as I might possibly have to visit my doctor in Cassel again and might be able to attend a few of these performances.[88] I am assuming that Schuricht has remained in Wiesbaden. Klenau of course will be conducting in Vienna.

I was greatly relieved that the price of the chorus parts has been set at 2/- and do hope that Curwen will also be agreeable to your proposals.[89]

With best wishes from us both,

publishers moved royalties from one subsidiary to another, leaving 50 per cent at each stop and paying the composer his, say, 50 per cent share based on what eventually arrived in the home territory.

88 The editors can trace nine performancs of *A Mass of Life* in 1925 including some of the ones mentioned above. Vienna (Feb), Berlin, (Mar), Wiesbaden (Mar), but not one in Prague.

89 UE had reduced the chorus score prices in the face of FD's objection.

ꕥ

1925

Delius was by this time largely immobile. There appears to have been an increase in the number of performances. The editors' record of performances shows 25, including nine of *A Mass of Life*, possibly the first since 1914.

It is unlikely that he received any performing fees from the Continental ones, although he would have received hire fees. *Hassan* was broadcast in November, and Jelka insisted, quite rightly, that the broadcasting fee was all for Delius. He had received a grand right fee of £25 per week while the show was running and the BBC offered £5 per broadcast, not a bad fee. In September a neighbour in Grez-sur-Loing bought a radio and Delius was able in future to hear the many broadcasts of his music. He in turn obtained both a radio and a gramophone.

PRS had licensed the BBC to broadcast from 1922, and charged each station about £1,000 per year. In 1925, non-PRS publishers succeeded in negotiating much-improved fees, resulting in PRS combining with those outside to increase the fees paid for broadcasting. This had the effect of encouraging many more to join PRS.

Letters to Universal deal with what Jelka considered to be inadequate pricing and she had spotted how Curwen was making so much from Delius's music. Much to his irritation, Universal continued to print single line chorus material.

ꕥ

No 181

Delius to Universal

2 January 1925.
Grez-sur-Loing

My dear Herr Direktor

A happy and prosperous 1925 to you!

In swift reply to your letter of 29 December which I have just this minute received, you appear to have completely forgotten the vocal score of Fennimore and Gerda with English text that you published a few years ago (as far back as the early summer of 1920 I believe). You produced a separate edition with title pages in English (with illustrations by my wife). Can this have slipped your mind completely? I of course assumed that this vocal score would be placed on sale by Curwen in England? I am not aware of what you subsequently agreed with Mr Heseltine regarding the text.

It stands to reason that the score must be printed with German and English text.

Concerning your present letter, you can have the 5 Piano Pieces according to the conditions we agreed <u>when</u> I have received a firm commitment on your part to bring out an engraved edition of Fennimore and Gerda in 1925 and of Sea Drift and Appalachia in 1926.

I am also still awaiting your news concerning the prices that you have agreed with Curwen. Please send a new English and German catalogue with price lists.
I have returned the specimen print of Brigg Fair. I do not really understand why a new engraving of this miniature score should have been prepared when one previously existed by Leuckart?[90]

This letter comes with a request for your immediate attention and best regards from us both.

Yours

PS I am delighted that the London price for the Requiem has been confirmed at 6/-. But what price should the other works, in particular the Mass and Romeo and Juliet, now be set at?

ℵ೧ℵ೧

No 182

Delius to Universal

10 January 1925.
Grez-sur-Loing

Dear Herr Direktor

Your letter of 7 has just reached me. In error you have neglected to insert the clause relating to the new engraving of Appalachia and Sea Drift in 1926, which as I expressly demanded in my letter is a *conditio sine qua non*. I enclose said clause herewith and would request that you please forward a revised contract.[91]

I am relieved that the mistake with the English text of Fennimore and Gerda has now been clarified.

With best wishes from us both

ℵ೧ℵ೧

No183

Delius to Universal

15 January 1925.
Grez-sur-Loing

---

[90] It was re-engraved for the smaller page size of the Wiener Philharmonischer Verlag miniature scores. (See also letter to UE date 27 April 1925.)

[91] FD did not include *Paris* among the works to be re-engraved, though he had previously done so. In fact, UE did not engrave *Paris* until 1965.

Herr Direktor

Mr Howard-Jones (the pianist who played the Five Piano Pieces in London and then sent you the manuscript) has just written to me advising that he would be very keen to complete the thorough correction and insertion of dynamic markings of the pieces for me. This would be most welcome as he would do it superlatively and also just at the moment I am neither keen nor able to do it myself. He asks therefore that you send him as soon as possible 2 copies of my corrections. He would then play the work in his two February concerts in Paris for which he would have to retain one copy of the corrected score. There is much at stake here for me; so you see this is of the utmost urgency. His address:

E. Howard-Jones
37 Eaton Terrace
London SW1

I trust that you received my letter of a few days ago and will be sending me as soon as possible the definitive contract so that we have everything in order.

I urgently request you to sort out matters promptly.

When he has completed his corrections Howard-Jones will then send me the pieces for final checking before publication and I will forward them straight on to you.[92]

Kind regards

PS H-Jones writes:

Those new piano pieces are to my mind some of the best things for piano that I know, short as they may be.

No 184

Delius to Universal

25 January 1925.
Grez-sur-Loing

Dear Herr Direktor

Thank you for your letter of 21 which I received yesterday.

In my opinion Lullaby for a Modern Baby must be included in the album of piano pieces at any cost. It is definitely not a piece for violin and piano. The melody

[92] In fact, the printing was in some places garbled – the instructions for corrections of errors, relating to the disposition of left and right hands, were printed, instead of being carried out. Only in the Boosey piano album of 1978 and in the Collected Edition, volume 33, published in 1988, were these set to rights (and H-J's dynamics fully included from his copies then in the Trust's Archive).

should only be hummed.[93] I suppose that it might easily be possible to play it on a violin as well; but that is not my intention. As such it suits the album perfectly and may not be excluded.

At the same time as your own letter arrived I received another from the young pianist Hans Levy Diem, who has just played my Piano Concerto under Schuricht in Wiesbaden, and I have heard, done so with overwhelming success. He has written to me now to tell me that you have sent him a declaration to sign which binds him to performances of the work exclusively within Germany. There must be some mistake. Levy is Swiss and would like to give the Concerto in March as part of his Swiss series of concerts, something which would obviously bring me great delight. It is therefore utterly incomprehensible that you are unwilling to permit this. You have always treated this work as second-rate; the old error-ridden Harmonie-Edition is to this day the only one in existence and it is indeed a miracle that a pianist has taken it up, and now you are prohibiting the performance. I would appreciate a response on this, as would Levy.

I am furthermore still awaiting your reply on the matter of the present prices being charged by Curwen for my works, particularly for the vocal score of the Mass of Life. Please forward the 5 Pieces to Howard-Jones as soon as possible. He will decide upon the sequence.

Respectfully yours

No 185

Delius to Universal

27 April 1925
Cassel

Dear Herr Direktor

My good friend Gardiner is making the corrections to Fennimore and Gerda[94] as I myself would not have been able to do them at the moment. I have already despatched the first consignments to you (under one cover); the others Mr Gardiner anticipates he will be sending from Munich where he is presently staying. In the interests of producing an immaculate edition he asks that you send him a further proof but this time to his permanent address in Ashampstead, Pangbourne, Berks. England.

Please do not neglect to do this as there were still numerous errors in certain places, in addition to various small corrections and ambiguities in the score. It is in fact to our mutual benefit that we produce a score totally beyond reproach.

---

93 By the pianist.

94 Published by Universal in 1926.

Many thanks for the study score of Brigg Fair. It is most attractive and easy to read despite its small format.[95]

You will certainly have heard from all quarters that the Mass of Life enjoyed a great success in London against all expectations. The work would be performed several times over in England if it were not for such prohibitive hire fees. You will recall that I promised to forgo my royalty of 25 per cent and accept 10 per cent, but only on the proviso that you too compromised by setting the sales price of the chorus parts at no more than 2/6d. I am now astonished to learn that you fixed the hire fee at 2/6d and with further payment due upon repeat performance. This is unacceptable and I would ask you to amend this situation without delay. It is preposterous that the cost of the vocal score to the Mass is Mk 10 here and yet 18/- in England. How can you justify this? The Philharmonic Society intends to repeat the Mass as does Kennedy Scott in his own concerts. As a result of the tremendous fees set by you orchestras are now incurring a considerable loss even in the event of a sell-out. Your shortsighted policies are making things impossible for them. If Curwen charged reasonable prices his sales would not merely be doubled but at the very least quadrupled which could only be to his own advantage. Oxford, for example, is also planning to programme the Mass of Life but a town like that will never be in a position to afford it with fees as they stand at present.

I am considering a trip to Grez soon, a place I like so much – I have had enough of Cassel.

With best wishes from us both

No 186

Delius to Universal

11 May 1925.
Cassel

Herr Direktor

Thank you for your letters of 6 and 8 May, both of which arrived today. With the state of my eyes at the moment any proof reading of the Dance Rhapsody is unfortunately quite impracticable.

If there is somebody there in whom you have absolute confidence then please tell me and I will return them to you. Otherwise I shall take them to Grez with me; Mr Heseltine will soon be visiting me there and he might take it upon himself to do the proof-reading. At any rate it will require a few weeks work.

I am at a loss to know what to make of the other letter regarding the Mass performance material, having discussed the question of prices at considerable length with you last autumn. Consent to lower my share from 25 per cent to 10 per cent was

95 See letter of 2 January 1925. FD to UE.

granted on the condition that the price of the performance material be reduced and I have your written confirmation that the chorus parts were to be sold at 2/6d. If you are now declaring this commitment null and void then I too withdraw my consent to a 10 per cent royalty. I fail to see why I, the creator of the work, should receive 10 per cent in respect of sheet music sales whilst Mr Curwen in London takes 50–60 per cent.[96] Can you imagine for one moment the result? Income from the vocal score will be as good as nullified and any further performances will be placed in jeopardy.

I am certainly not looking to initiate some whispering campaign to undermine your credibility. We are dealing here with the facts and you yourselves would be ill advised to allow the firm of Curwen to dictate the running.

We are still awaiting a visa for my nurse from the French consulate and until that arrives we will not know our date of departure. In any event we will travel directly through Paris and then on to Grez but probably not until after the 19th.

With best wishes

No 187

Delius to Universal

28 July 1925.

Dear Sir

In reply to your postcard of 15 July I hereby inform you that Mr Balfour Gardiner has begun the job of correcting the score to Fennimore and Gerda. I would ask you please to write to him once more, as I have no wish to be the one forever plaguing him.

The question of Curwen's agency agreement has always been and still remains a disaster. What we needed in London was merely a well-frequented music shop that could sell my works. Not only does Curwen possess no shops and yet lays claim to a high percentage of the income but neither does he handle all my works. It is inconceivable that he does not have a single copy of the vocal score to A Village Romeo and Juliet?! And yet, this is the current situation! In the case of other works he has only a single copy in stock. Is this any way to run a business?

Even you could vastly improve the commercial prospects of my music if you were somewhat more enterprising. The Intermezzo from Romeo and Juliet, so beloved of concert programmers of late, is a prime example of a work which should undoubtedly appear as a separate edition. Has Howard-Jones returned the Piano Pieces to you yet? This must be considered a top priority – I am sure you will agree they are already long overdue for publication.

---

96 Curwen seems to be the problem. He is buying the vocal material from UE in Vienna at a big discount and then marks up the sale price significantly. FD, who receives his royalty on UE's receipts shrewdly sees that he is losing out.

Herr Slivinsky (5 rue du Cherche Midi, Paris), the proprietor of the Parisian music and art showroom 'Au Sacre du Printemps', would very much like to promote my works there and for this reason requests that you send him a display copy of each of my works for his shop. I believe this to be a very good idea as his regular patrons are the very people who claim an interest in the Modern. Moreover, he even organises concerts there. I would appreciate your comments on this arrangement. As far as your catalogue is concerned, I consider the two choral songs (On the Water) too expensive and disproportionate to the rest and for that reason will never be sung.

Yours faithfully

From Jelka Delius:

I cannot help but mention to you that in my opinion you should propose an arrangement for orchestra of the Hassan Suite to my husband. Heseltine could possibly do the arrangement as my husband unfortunately is himself unable to do it on account of his eyesight. If you were to make definite proposals perhaps Delius would give his consent.

Respectfully yours

J.D.

No 188

Delius to Universal

23 November 1925.

Dear Sir

Thank you for your letter of 18 November concerning Hassan.

May I point out that the radio broadcast has already taken place and without my knowledge.

Of course the broadcast medium did not exist when our contract[97] was made. However it does state the following:

(Para. 3) In respect of all performances of the said music the manager shall pay to the Composer a royalty of etc.

(Para. 5) So long as this agreement lasts (5 years) the said manager shall have the sole license to perform the music of the said play on theatre or music hall stage in the British Empire and Dominions and U.S.A.

(Para. 8) The Manager agrees that in the West End of London and in N. York the orchestra shall never consist of less than 23 players without the consent of the Composer.

97 'Our' refers to UE.

(Para. 5 (II)) All rights other than the licence to perform the music with the play to be the exclusive property of the Composer.

I should like to make the following observations: From the performances at His Majesty's Theatre I received £25 per week. I have no idea how much Mrs. Flecker was remunerated. It would only be fair if my share in respect of the broadcast right was calculated in proportion to the share she received in respect of the performing right. If she also was paid £25 per week then we would have equal rights in the broadcast. Paragraph 5 should be interpreted as meaning that radio broadcasts are neither stage performance nor Variety Theatre, that the work is not to be performed but only to be read. Furthermore, I was entitled to mechanical income. I wonder whether an orchestra of 23 members participated?

I heard the performance on the radio here in Geneva. On the whole the music was reduced right down to background volume and was barely audible although the spoken word was crystal clear; the music to the entire ballet and much else besides was omitted.

Can you please tackle Curwen about this right away and forward your comments to me.

From Para. 5 (II) it is self-evident that I am entitled to the rights since broadcasting is neither Theatre nor Music Hall.

I myself have not written to Basil Dean. I have only enquired of the MCPS whether they were somehow consulted.[98]

Yours faithfully

Please convey my best wishes to Dr Hertzka. Delius is now somewhat recovered.

Yours

J.D.

No 189

Delius to Universal

9 December 1925.
Grez-sur-Loing

Dear Direktor,

Reandean has forwarded me a letter from the B.B.C. offering me £5 in respect of the performing right in the music to which I am naturally entitled. I have not given

[98] PRS did not control grand rights. See FD to UE. 9 Dec 1925. A mechanical fee would only be due if a recording was made from which the music was broadcast.

them any response yet as I am not sure whether it is enough.[99] You told me that when you questioned Curwen he replied that he had nothing at all to do with it.

May I request that you please send by return two German and two English copies of the Mass of Life. There is a chance of a performance in P[?]. On another matter, Mr Gardiner tells me that he has not received a complimentary copy of his excellent English translation!![100] Please rectify this situation immediately.

Respectfully yours

ꕤ

No 190

Delius to Universal

27 December 1925
Grez-sur-Loing

Herr Direktor

Kennedy Scott and Gardiner have just left. The latter has now carefully completed the corrections to Fennimore. I would ask you to put the title page illustrated by my wife on the outer jacket and simply leave Fennimore and Gerda as it is. On the inner title page you may do as you wish and print the German-English.

I learnt from Kennedy Scott that you have now printed the chorus parts of Song of the High Hills separately. I cannot grasp why you have done this since it makes life much more difficult when the singer does not have the harmonies in front of them. The present mini score is I believe so handy and I beg you please to reprint it without delay and deliver it to Mr Kennedy Scott for his London performance. <u>Under no circumstances is he willing to work with the separate parts</u>.[101] I could have told you that on the spot if you had asked me. We simply have a repeat of the situation with the Mass.

Many thanks for sending over the vocal score of the Mass and the Haym programme note.

With our very best wishes for a Happy New Year.

Respectfully yours

F.D.

PS My two friends played me the Song of the High Hills arrangement for 2 pianos again. I am thrilled with it and sincerely hope that you will be publishing it <u>promptly.</u>

---

99 Presumably £5 per broadcast. FD does not seem inclined to share it with UE.

100 Gardiner's English translation of Hans Haym's analysis.

101 UE published separate (single line) parts and a choral score, but as the latter was inaccurate it was withdrawn and re-printed.

ജ്ജ ജ്ജ

1926

Frustrated by the lack of performing fees, Jelka took advice from Universal, who advised that Delius should join AKM or GEMA. She put this to PRS, who were able to tell her that agreements had been concluded in September with AKM and GEMA, back dated to 6 April 1926.

Accounting records for the period have not survived, so we will never know whether Universal received fees for performances in Central Europe, while Delius, caught in the post-war chaos, did not.

Beatrice Harrison and Harold Craxton recorded the Cello Sonata.

The letter to PRS from Augener is interesting, showing why so many publishers of classical music continued to stand outside PRS, even though printed music sales were falling fast. If Universal's UK agent had been assigned performing rights, it might have been to Delius's advantage. It is strange that Universal apparently did not know to which performing right society Delius belonged.

ജ്ജ ജ്ജ

No 191

Delius to Universal

17 February 1926.
Grez-sur-Loing

Dear Sir

I wonder if I might politely request that you forward some explanation for the total absence of sales royalties and income in respect of hire fees in England for the last half-year. I cannot accept that they have suddenly ceased in view of the considerable sales that have shown up on every half-year statement to date. And what is the situation with Sea Drift? There must surely be German sales to be accounted.

Furthermore, on the German statement you have accounted 621 Rentenmarks in respect of 207 chorus parts – representing a rate of 10 per cent instead of 25 per cent. This is doubtlessly an error as in other places for the same chorus parts you have accounted my due share of 25 per cent.

It also remains a mystery to me why for purely commercial reasons you keep yourself informed only about those works of mine which are published by yourself. And yet it would be in your own interest to see my music enjoy the widest circulation and to know where to obtain it if so demanded.

Herr v. Klenau has arrived here without the score of the orchestral work which he was to conduct with the London Philharmonic.[102] This, I believe, is because you

---

[102] Jelka Delius wrote to PH on 8 Dec 1925 to say that a French friend was prepared to put up money for a Delius concert in Paris. FD wanted *A Mass of Life*, conducted by Klenau. The

first had to make enquiries of me regarding its whereabouts instead of obtaining the score directly from the publisher. As a result I have been forced to loan my own score to Herr v. Klenau.

I am enclosing a list of all my significant works, which I would ask you to file safely, so that in future you will be fully apprised of their location.

It could only be to the good if at some point you were to acquire the sales rights to these works in Germany. I am thinking chiefly of the second Violin Sonata and the Augener works.

I have heard that a performance of A Village Romeo and Juliet is planned in Hagen. Please advise how matters are progressing, what arrangements you have made and what forces are available in Hagen. What has become of Cologne?[103]

Please send two copies of the orchestral score to Fennimore and Gerda when they come out. I would of course like to forward one copy to Sir Thomas Beecham.

With best regards to Herr Dir. Hertzka

Yours faithfully

I look forward to your earliest reply.

No 192

Delius to The Performing Right Society

24 April 1926
Grez-sur-Loing

Dear Sir,

Lately a number of performances of my large and small works have taken place in Germany. Some of these have come to my knowledge and naturally it is very important for me to have my royalties duly collected.

Have you a definite arrangement with the central powers now, as also with France and USA, where also a number of my works are being performed.

I will list a few performances of which I have heard[104]

---

plan was for the Philharmonic choir (+orch?) to go, but it came to nothing. Klenau conducted *A Mass of Life* at an RPS concert in London on 25 February 1926.

[103] Nothing came of either.

[104] PRS replied on 30 April 1926. It had not yet a contract with Germany, Austria or the USA, although there was a long-standing contract with France. PRS asks FD to let them know where and when the performances took place abroad, for, as it writes elsewhere, it can't act without knowing the details of a performance.

The list of performances equates roughly with the known list of performances, with some omitted and insufficient details for PRS to check, even if it had an agreement with GDT/

Mass of Life (evening filling work. Orch. soli. chorus)
Wiesbaden 16.3.25
Coblenz December 25
Hagen 13.3.26
Duisberg
Darmstadt
Wiesbaden
Frankfurt

Seadrift
Wiesbaden
Gotha

Cello Concerto

Carlsbad 25
Wiesbaden

USA

Song of the High Hills
(New York and California)
Dance Rhapsody
North Country Sketches
Cello Concerto Dec 25

Song of the High Hills
Athens

Piano Concerto
Wiesbaden 25
Munich
Tour in Switzerland

I should be grateful to you to send me a detailed account next time, as I could ill afford to lose all these royalties. I cannot follow the smaller works, as Cello and Violin Sonatas, which are being played frequently also on the Broadcasting.

Yours faithfully

No 193

Delius to The Performing Right Society

29 May 1926
Grez-sur-Loing

GEMA, which it did not. Under the soon-to-be-signed agreement GEMA and AKM would pay out on performances in their territories from 6 April 1926.

Dear Sir,

I duly received your letter of April 30th. In reply I wish to say that the war being ended more than seven years I can see no reason for your not having a contract of Affiliation with the central powers – not to speak of America.[105]

May I remind you that when I became a member of your society I belonged to the Genossenschaft Deutscher Tonzetzer who collected all my royalties for Germany Holland Austria Russia Switzerland Italy and USA. At that time you made it a condition that I should resign my membership of the Genossenschaft, giving me the understanding that you would be collecting all these royalties for me. Your promising to do so all these years c… a very anxious financial loss to me, as my largest works like The Mass of Life are so frequently performed there.

You reproach me for not obtaining the exact name of concert society and dates of performances. But it is for <u>you</u> and not for <u>me</u> to find out these things. It is only casually that I receive news of such performances.[106]

I beg you to consider the situation carefully. Either you must undertake to collect all continental and American performing fees for me or you must authorise me to become once more a member of the Genossenschaft so that I retain your services only for the British Isles and Dominions.

Hoping to hear from you soon about this.

I remain,

Yours faithfully,

No 194

Delius to Universal

1 August 1926
Grez-sur-Loing.

Dear Sir

I have just been studying your statements and have come across a few points that I fail to understand and I would therefore appreciate some clarification.

1. You have accounted £5 in respect of hire material for the London performance of the Mass. This fee is much too low. Insofar as I recall the Philharmonic Society paid £20 or more.

In total you have accounted:

---

105 PRS had an agreement with ASCAP in the USA from 1919.

106 It is unlikely that GDT managed to collect from the USA before the 1914–18 war and certainly not from Russia. There were only about ten known Delius performances in the USA before the war and only one in Russia.

Piano Concerto	3-7-3d
Mass of Life (Hire)	5-5-0
Sea Drift	2-2-0
Sea Drift	6-0-0
	———
	4-14-3d
while this should read	£16-14-3d

of which my 25 per cent share amounts to £4-3-9d instead of £1-3-7d. Can I assume that this is just a simple accounting error? I herewith enclose the relevant statement.

In accordance with your contractual obligations I am hoping that work on engraving Sea Drift and Appalachia has begun.

Please attend to these matters at the earliest opportunity, as I would like to be able to put my accounts in order.

Yours faithfully

PS One further matter – in the English statement there is no mention of the 5 Piano Pieces which according to the contract are to be settled directly from England.[107]

No 195

Augener to The Performing Right Society

4 Aug 1926
London

Dear Sir

Re-Mr F. Delius

Thank you for your letter of the 26th ulto., which confirms my opinion of the present position.[108]

The disadvantage to Mr Delius lies in the fact that every performance of these large works has to be specially arranged for, and, in the majority of cases, the

[107] This is correct. Under the contract for the 5 Pieces, Curwen was to pay a royalty on sales of 25 per cent of the English retail price, thus getting over FD's objection to Curwen buying sheet music from UE at a discount of about 50 per cent and accounting for sales through UE in Vienna.

[108] The PRS letter has not survived.

performing fee and the charge for the hire of the orchestral material have to be dealt with together, and probably adjusted to meet the circumstances of the case.

Quite recently we had an application to arrange for a series of performances of [the] Delius Violin Concerto, but, because we were not in a position to settle terms on the spot, the project was abandoned, with the result that Delius lost at least £30 in fees and we about £25 for hire of the material.

This illustrates the point which prevents Messrs. Novello from becoming members of PRS, as they have a very considerable number of works, each performance of which has to be specially arranged for.[109]

Yours faithfully

Augener

No 196

Delius to Universal

28 August 1926.
Grez-sur-Loing

Herr Direktor

I have just heard that entries to the 1927 Essen Music Festival [Tonkünstlerfest] must be completed by the beginning of September. I would advocate you enter my Song of the High Hills. Or, if relations with the theatre establishment in Essen are good and the festival is to include operatic performances then possibly Fennimore und Gerda.

But this should come from you as the publisher.

Barjansky was recently here. Playing exactly as I would have wished, he produced quite wonderful, truly masterful performances of both the Cello Sonata and the Cello Concerto. All tempi are now fixed. What a delight it would be if he could now make a gramophone recording and even take the works on tour. He is such an accomplished interpreter.

Naturally I would welcome any undertaking on your part to publish miniature scores of Appalachia and Sea Drift as well as Song of the High Hills; I do think this is most important. Nevertheless, you are still aware that you have agreed to engrave full size scores of Appalachia and Sea Drift. I could not hope for a more apposite moment than now for their publication.

Furthermore, you also have the transcription of Song of the High Hills for 2 pianos by Grainger. To bring that out would not strain your resources. In addition you have in your possession the Summer Garden transcription for solo piano by

[109] Publishers who were not members of PRS and hired material out would be able to charge a joint performing/hire fee and negotiate.

Heseltine which has lain finished for years. I beg you, my dear Herr Direktor, to bestir yourself without delay. I am so overjoyed with the Fennimore und Gerda score; by your efforts I do hope that the work will soon be engrossing the attentions of a good theatre.

The statements sent are probably quite correct, but they are so unclear that we could be forgiven for misinterpreting the deductions from Sea Drift. Curwen has meanwhile sent me the accounts concerning the Piano Pieces. Everything is now in order.

You enquired of me recently, whether I was still a member of the Genossenschaft.[110] As far as my position stands, towards the end of the war when Augener had published several of my compositions I became a member of the English Performing Right Society. It was made a condition of membership that I give notice to GDT for the PRS had imminent plans to spread its licensing activities to include continental performances. Unfortunately, to date these intentions have not come to fruition although they do collect royalties in France and the British Commonwealth. I have incurred great financial loss because they do not collect in Germany, Austria and Switzerland. What is your feeling on the matter and what would you counsel me to do?

I shall need the monies owing on my statements in a few days time.

On the whole my health is improving. I hope that you are well.

My wife joins me in sending very best wishes.

Sincerely yours

No 197

Delius to The Performing Right Society

13 September 1926
Grez-sur-Loing

Dear Sir,

I must again draw your attention to the fact that many performances of my works are continually taking place in Germany, and in fact on the continent, and naturally I can not go on losing all the royalties due to me and which before the war the Genossenschaft Deutscher Tonsetzer collected for me.

In your last letter you wrote to me that I ought to inform you of the projected performances with the exact dates and names of the concert societies. That of course is quite impossible, as they are generally not known to me. My Austrian publishers, the Universal Edition urge me to become a member of a German or Austrian Society

[110] The two German Performing Right Societies, GEMA, founded in 1915 and GDT, (1903) merged in 1922. From the letter dated 12 July 1928 from GDT to PRS, not included in this book, it seemed that the two societies continued to exist within the merger for a time. It was not possible until recently for a publisher or composer to belong to more than one performing right society.

of Authors unless you can promise to follow up all these performances for me and I put it to you, that I cannot go on like this.[111]

The other night – quite by chance I heard a performance of my violin concerto at a Symphony Concert – Leipzig, on the wireless. My Mass of Life will be given a number of times in the coming season in Germany. My cello sonata will be given many times as well as the cello concerto. I have already lost the fees over all past performances over there of my large works like Mass of Life, Song of the High Hills, Seadrift, piano concerto, many performances of chamber music, songs. I must beg you to allow me to use your Society for England and Dominions and to have my continental fees collected over there as I really cannot afford to lose them.

I live in great retirement and very often hear of these performances long after or not at all.

Hoping for an early reply.

Yours faithfully,

PS Please find enclosed the subscription fee for your journal.

No 198

The Performing Right Society to Delius

15th September 1926
London

Dear Sir,

In reply to your letter of the 13th inst you will be pleased to hear that we have now concluded contracts of affiliation with the Genossenschaft für Verwertung musikalischer Aufführungsrechte, of Berlin, and the Gesellschaft der Autoren Komponisten und Musikverleger in Wien, whereby fees will be collected by those two Societies in Germany and Austria respectively in respect of performances of our members' works taking place from April 6 1926 onwards. In addition we would refer you to the Editorial on page 99 and to the third paragraph of 'Variorum' on page 106 on the last (July) issue of the 'P.R. Gazette' where this Society's other foreign affiliations are referred to in detail, including the recently concluded contracts with the Societies of Hungary and Czecho-Slovakia. Under these circumstances you will see that the question of your applying for membership of any of these European Societies does not arise, as fees for performances of your works in their respective territories will in future be collected by them and remitted to us on your behalf.

---

[111] The PRS/GEMA/AKM agreements took effect from 6 April 1926. From then on GEMA/AKM would have been policing on behalf of both composer and publisher. As a long time member of AKM, UE may have been collecting its share of German/Austrian performing fees, and if so there is no mention of it passing a share to FD.

We will draw the attention of the Societies concerned to the works which you state are performed on the Continent, but in the absence of particulars as the actual dates and places of performance, we can only leave it in their hands to account to us for the fees which may be due to you.

We thank you for the cheque value 2/6d being renewal of your subscription to the 'P.R. Gazette' for four quarterly issues commencing October next, and have pleasure in enclosing herewith receipt for that amount.

Yours Faithfully,
Woodhouse
Controller

No 199

Delius to Universal

18 September 1926.
Grez-sur-Loing

Dear Herr Direktor

In response to your kind letter I would like to advise you of the following. Under no circumstances would I be willing to sacrifice the engraving of Sea Drift and Appalachia thereby releasing you from your firm commitment to the above. Nevertheless, in view of the difficult times I would be prepared to accept a postponement of 1 to 2 years. These however are my conditions:

Firstly, that the miniature scores of both works, in addition to the miniature score of Song of the High Hills are put to press right away. Secondly, that these miniature scores are supplemented by detailed errata lists, encompassing all changes and corrections, until the large format scores appear in print. My main concern here is the reorchestrated part of Sea Drift which appeared to have been performed using the old version at the concert in Cassel. Please forward these errata lists for my own inspection.

As you have not responded regarding the Mass and the right of exclusivity that I granted to Schuricht for the 1926–27 Berlin season, I am going to assume that you have no objection.[112] Please confirm this however with Herr Schuricht as he is awaiting an answer. Also, I still have not received the score of [the] Song of the High Hills.

After repeated representations I received news yesterday from the English Performing Right Society that they have at last concluded an agreement with GEMA in Berlin and AKM in Vienna whereby these societies will collect my royalties on

[112] FD had written to UE on 8 September to say that he had granted Schuricht the exclusive right to perform *A Mass of Life* in Berlin for the 1926–27 season. As a published work it was UE's decision. Schuricht duly performed the Mass in October 1927.

behalf of the PRS; furthermore, these will be backdated to April 1926. I am no longer required to be a member of these societies either.

My wife joins me in sending our best wishes.

Respectfully yours

ഇ൬ഇ൬

No 200

Delius to Universal

16 October 1926
Grez-sur-Loing

Dear Sir

I am in receipt of your letter of 5 October and would hasten to inform you that I am not prepared to accommodate your wishes. It is my intention temporarily to forgo the new engravings of the performance scores of Sea Drift and Appalachia in favour of the miniature scores.[113] Producing these scores will in themselves be a difficult task being so riddled with errors. By meeting you halfway like this, however, I do hope to demonstrate my good will towards you and furthermore to urge you to make an immediate start on the production of the three miniature scores.[114] It has not yet been possible for me to review the scores which only arrived yesterday; I shall however do it straight away, by which I mean in so much as I can. I may ask Gardiner to look through everything for me once again.

I shall write with more precise details over the next few days.

With my very best wishes to Herr Dir. Hertzka – I was most sorry to hear of his ill health.

Respectfully yours

PS Have you forwarded the balance of my account to the Darmstadt National Bank in Frankfurt as I requested? (It is the same bank as Handel u. Industrie.)

PPS When looking through the two scores I noticed that the Sea Drift score is my own copy and that a page of music written by me which should have been enclosed is in fact missing. This is now of the utmost importance and I would ask you please to check your files as I am sure that I gave you this music. No doubt you have put it away somewhere for safekeeping.

Regarding Appalachia, the one unused variation should be reinstated, just before ‘Oh Honey’. When I come to the more detailed scrutiny I shall ask Mr Gardiner to assist me, but for that purpose I must have the score of Sea Drift.

---

[113] The engraved full scores of *Appalachia* and *Sea Drift* (and the Piano Concerto) did not appear until 1951, as the first volumes of Beecham’s Collected Edition, from Boosey & Hawkes.

[114] *Appalachia*, *Sea Drift* and *The Song of the High Hills.*

We can pick up Vienna very well on the radio. We heard the recent performance of In a Summer Garden which afforded me great pleasure. The interpretation was very good.

ᘓᘏᘓᘏ

1927

Only seven performances and broadcasts are definitely known, and Delius began to receive his PRS fees based on known performances rather than the class system. Initially he seems to have lost out. Under the class system he had received about £80 a year in 1924–26. In 1927, under the new distribution system he received only £50, although this increased rapidly, so that he was receiving £300 a year by his death. Performance income from Germany and Austria took time to come through and in her frustration, Jelka wrote direct to AKM asking for information. AKM passed the letter unanswered to PRS, who told Jelka that some money, although not much, had been received from AKM. Delius was probably also badly affected by the low priced agreement that PRS had with the BBC and by the fact that more members had joined PRS, so that the pot had to be shared between more mouths.

Jelka was obviously worried about the availability of Delius works as well as money. She studied the Universal royalty statements carefully. Why, she writes in February, had five guineas been deducted from income from hire fees for *Sea Drift*? Universal explained that Delius had erroneously been credited with two performances of both *Sea Drift* and *A Mass of Life*, where there had only been one, and apologised that the statements had not been clearer. She continued to be suspicious of Curwen and, as she wrote on 27 January to Heseltine, (a letter not included in this book) was irritated that in the case of works published in the UK by Augener, which Augener had sub-published for Germany with Universal, a share of royalties was kept by Universal, meaning that Delius only participated in royalties returned to London.

In June she enquires from PRS as to whether PRS is collecting for the use of the Lullaby in the Beau Stratagem at the Lyric Hammersmith. PRS confirms that it is. The use of a single musical piece in a play would have come within the PRS remit.

Hertzka attended a performance of *A Village Romeo and Juliet* in Wiesbaden in December and wrote to Delius with suggestions for further performances on small stages, to which Delius replied.

Columbia recorded *On Hearing the First Cuckoo in Spring* and *The Walk to the Paradise Garden* conducted by Beecham. On 30 January the BBC broadcast a one hour programme for his birthday.

ꕥ

No 201

Delius to Universal

7 January 1927.
Grez-sur-Loing

Dear Sir

Mr Gardiner has just informed me that unfortunately you have not sent him the promised Sea Drift score necessary for his corrections. It is regrettable that you have made him wait like this especially when you consider that he has carried out such a wearisome task for you.

I would request that you forward the score to Mr Gardiner's address at Ashampstead, Pangbourne, Berks. post haste.

I am hearing report after report of Sea Drift rehearsals floundering in a myriad of troubles directly attributable to the chorus parts. This resembles rather closely past experiences with the Mass of Life. I must prevail upon you the necessity of reprinting these parts the same way as those of the Mass and the Song of the High Hills; this is scarcely the first time I have had to mention this. All the parts must be printed together and with sufficient cues so that everybody can use the same parts.[115] This will indeed be less bothersome. Mr Gardiner might undertake to produce these chorus parts with the exact dynamics but would then expect a fee for his efforts. I would appreciate your thoughts on this soonest. To illustrate my point, the Philharmonic Choir is going to have to abandon any hope of rehearsing Sea Drift this winter because it is too irksome and prolonged with these parts as they stand. Thus what promised to be a rousing performance under Sir Thomas Beecham before his move to America, which had been fixed in the diary, has now as a result had to be cancelled.

Please convey my best wishes for a Happy New Year to Herr Direktor Hertzka and please send the Sea Drift score to Mr Gardiner immediately.

Yours faithfully

---

[115] See footnote to 27 December 1925. The choral score was inaccurate, withdrawn and then re-issued corrected.

No 202

Universal to Delius

22 January 1927
Vienna

Maestro Delius,

We beg you please to excuse the slowness with which we respond to your letter of 7th instant. Which is due to the extraordinary demands placed upon us at this time. We wish to inform you that Mr Gardiner was already in receipt of the score of Sea Drift at the time you sent the previously mentioned letter to us and we now await the return of the page proofs.

We were distressed to learn that difficulties have arisen during the choral rehearsals of Sea Drift and all the more so considering that the chorus parts were only produced a short time ago. Of the many other similar choral works in our catalogue we have encountered no unsatisfactory feedback and in consequence we are generally disinclined to produce choral scores for the reason that we must always charge a higher price in comparison with the individual parts. In view of the large stocks that we still possess it is not our intention to print a choral score in the short term. To assist rehearsal we will however give an undertaking that with every contract we shall supply to the choral society in question a corresponding number of vocal scores, in which the chorus parts are contained in score format, at a reasonable cost. This will enable the chorus to rehearse from the score at an affordable price.

We are not aware of any enquiry from the Philharmonic Choir regarding Sea Drift. However we will consult them without delay and hope that by furnishing the choir with vocal scores any difficulties they have encountered will be eliminated and the performance will be able to proceed.

Herr Direktor Hertzka would like to express his belated thanks for your New Year's greeting and heartily wishes me to convey his to you. He will soon be taking a few weeks vacation in the south.

Yours faithfully

No 203

Delius to Universal

8 February 1927
Grez-sur-Loing

Herr Direktor

I have written to your firm, Universal Edition, to protest in the strongest terms about my statement.

My complaint rests with the sterling accounts in respect of London sheet music sales. According to this statement there have supposedly been zero sales of my works in England for the second six month period in succession. Furthermore the sum of £5-5-0d is to be deducted against the orchestral hire fees for Sea Drift just as £6-0-0d was deducted in the previous half-year. Taking all this into account my earnings over six months in England amount to 4/5d. The whole business is preposterous. An error must have occurred somewhere. Could it for example be the case that Curwen does not provide detailed statements and as a consequence the sales are not being accounted individually. In a recent press feature on myself prompted by Sir Thomas Beecham, interviews were conducted with the publishers in which Curwen stated that sheet music sales had consistently and most satisfyingly surpassed expectations. How am I supposed to reconcile that with the statement? The newspaper was sent to me.

I beg you, Herr Direktor, to investigate this matter with the utmost urgency for I cannot and will not allow this to go unchecked. The balance I would ask you to pay into my account with the Frankfurt a/M branch of the Darmstaedter und Nationalbank. Could you convert the Dollars into Reichmarks; as matters stand I cannot accept the sterling.

With best wishes

No 204

Delius to Universal

8 February 1927
Grez-sur-Loing

Dear Sir[116]

I today received your statement for the second half-year of 1926.

You will recall that following the statement to 30 June 1926 you informed me that you had received no further English statements from Curwen. I then queried the deduction in respect of hire material for Sea Drift; today to my astonishment another deduction of £5-5-0d has been made for Sea Drift meaning that I am to receive only £4.

I must now ask you earnestly to fully resolve this matter with London. I have all your earlier statements to hand and cannot find any explanation for this duplication.

Furthermore, it is an impossibility that no sheet music has been sold in London. An incredible error has occurred somewhere which is happening repeatedly with

[116] Both the letters dated 8 Feb come from the Universal archives, so were definitely sent.

every statement and with the result that income from all London sales is being withheld.

I know for certain not only that sales are increasing at a considerable rate (in spite of the high prices for which I am frequently castigated by the customers) but also that Curwen himself in a recent interview in London expressed the view that sales are rising consistently and in a most pleasing manner. This newspaper was sent to me.

Matters have now reached a point where they cannot be allowed to continue unchecked and I would request that you please get to the bottom of this and assert my rights.

It may be that Curwen will send a rough estimate of his accounts and goodness knows what else: I demand to see a detailed statement of Curwen's sales covering the whole of last year and I want no more excuses.

Yours sincerely

No 205

Universal to Delius

15 February 1927
Vienna

Dear Sir

We are in receipt of your letter of 8 instant. We beg to respond to your queries as follows:

You complain in your letter that once again the sum of £5-5-0d has been deducted from your statement. This deduction refers to orchestral material for A Mass of Life. You will notice that your two statements to 30 June 1925 and 30 June 1926 also showed fees accounted in respect of A Mass of Life. In fact there was only one concert given in London, i.e. through Curwen. The duplicate fees charged to Curwen and the credits to your account arose because Curwen ordered the material from us and then after a gap of some time informed us that a performance was taking place. Our invoice clerk made the erroneous assumption that a second performance had taken place and accordingly invoiced Curwen for a second set of orchestral material. It was not until Curwen queried this second invoice that it was cancelled. By then however the fees in respect of the second set of orchestral material had already been accounted to you and for this reason the credit from June 1926 had to be cancelled on your last statement to December 1926. '30 June 1926' has no doubt been stamped in the deductions column. However we would concede that a clearer explanation in the relevant place would have been helpful.

As regards your other remarks on Curwen's statements in relation to A Mass of Life we should like to point out that the figure of £5-5-0d represents only orchestral hire fees and that we issue separate invoices to Curwen for chorus parts. Any sums received are accounted separately and in this instance were settled as per your statement of 30 June 1925.

With reference to sales in England we beg to inform you that in accordance with our agreement Curwen has been purchasing all his music from us in Reichmarks since March 1925 on the basis of the German catalogue with the result that any orders are settled in Marks as opposed to Sterling. By comparing earlier sales in Marks with the current figures, you will recognise an apparent upswing in sales even when allowance is made for the fact that 1926 was a poor year for music retailers in general and particularly in Central Europe. Attached to this letter please find a copy of Curwen's order forms for 1926.

Hire fees on the other hand will be settled in Sterling as they always have been.

Incidentally we are always happy to provide you with more detailed information, as it can only be to our benefit that you receive full explanation whenever you come across an ambiguity.

Yours sincerely

FD
encl.

I. £20-0-0 not paid by Philharmonic Society (letter from Curwen of 10/8/26) £5-5-0 (hire material A Mass of Life) paid and accounted 30/6/25 The sum of £37-10-0d minus £22-10-0d for chorus parts E 3908a[117] from the total (30/6/25)

II. Sea Drift, was accounted London 2 set(s) of material — £11-5-0 (30/6/25)
London 1 set(s) of material (Radio) — 2-2-0 (30/6/25)

£13-7-0d

Deductions as per statement 30/6/26 — £6-0-0d
(invoiced twice in error, only one perf).

A Mass of Life, was accounted
London 1 set(s) of material — £5-5-0 (30/6/25)
London 1 set(s) of material — £5-5-0 (30/6/26)
(cancelled as per statement 31/12/26
as invoiced twice in error, only one perf).

III. Hire material only is invoiced to London in Sterling. Sheet music sales however have been invoiced to London since 25/3 in Reichsmarks and appear

[117] This is the choral score of the *Mass of Life*.

on the Reichsmark statement.

IV. Comparison between the Reichmark statements up to and including 2nd half-year of 1924 & later statements.

ꕥ

No 206

Universal to Delius

17 February 1927.
Vienna

Maestro Delius!

As our accounts department has already painstakingly explained to you your supposition that there have been no sales of your music in England or more precisely that sales have not been settled in your statement is ill-founded. Please find attached details of those works which have been ordered and paid for by Curwen. The reason it was twice necessary to claim back fees on material which had shown up on your statement as fully executed transactions can be attributed to our procedure for settling orchestral hire fees with Curwen (I have deliberately not used the word 'blame' for there is nobody at fault here). I have satisfied myself that these reimbursements were perfectly in order since our hire library was convinced from the correspondence with Curwen that in both instances he was giving separate instructions for the material to be released. It transpired from the statements which Curwen then delivered that only one set of material had been required which of course left the accounts department with no option but to claim back the overpaid fees. As a consequence of this decidedly unpleasant incident a special control mechanism has been introduced which it is hoped will avoid the reoccurrence of duplicate payments of this nature.

Our office has probably already imparted the news that A Village Romeo and Juliet is to be staged next season by Paul Bekker in Wiesbaden. I have pinned great hopes on this performance and am delighted that we shall at last witness a serious revival of this work.

My health which over the preceding months has left much to be desired (I am plagued by a heart condition) has improved and I shall be travelling soon to the Riveria for a few weeks stay.

In the hope that you are enjoying the best of health I send my best regards to you both

Yours respectfully

Hertzka

ꕥ

No 207

Delius to Universal

28 February 1927
Grez-sur-Loing

Dear Sir

I am in grateful receipt of your letter of explanation and also that of Herr Direktor Hertzka. Do not regard this matter with any surprise – firstly, why did you not explain the deduction of the hire fees in a footnote. Secondly, when I made enquiries of you concerning the previous statement and the sales figures in England you merely stated that no sales had been made. You should have advised that Curwen's sales were to be found in the German statement.

Once again I reiterate my urgent request that no reprints or new editions be undertaken without my prior knowledge as nothing currently exists which is without error. You will receive Sea Drift in the next few days from Mr Gardiner.

Please pass on our best regards to Herr Direktor Hertzka; we both hope that he will soon be totally recovered and that his stay on the Riviera will be beneficial to his health.

Should the performances of A Village Romeo and Juliet in Wiesbaden and A Mass of Life in Darmstadt be fixed please forward the details. I am delighted about Wiesbaden.

Yours faithfully

F.D.

PS I should be grateful if you would please pay my balance into the Frankfurt branch of the Darmstaedter and Nationalbank and at the same time convert the Sterling and Dollars into Marks.

ജ്ഞ

No 208

Universal to Delius

4 March 1927.
Vienna

Dear Sir

We hereby confirm receipt of your letter of 28 February and further that the sums owed in your last statement (listed below) were transferred yesterday to your account at the Darmstaedter and Nationalbank in Frankfurt:

$ 15.31	= M 64.61
4/5d	= M 4.30
	= M 660.43
	Total M 729.34

We would request that you please acknowledge receipt at your earliest convenience.

Our publications department has taken note of your wish to be advised prior to any reprints and new editions being scheduled.

Sea Drift has already arrived and the engraving in 16mo will soon commence.

We will advise you of the performance dates of the Wiesbaden A Village Romeo and Juliet and the Darmstadt Mass of Life as soon as they are known to us.

We will forward your kind regards to Herr Direktor Hertzka who is relaxing on the Riviera.

Yours faithfully

ജ്ഞ

No 209

Delius to The Performing Right Society

19 June 1927
Grez-sur-Loing

Dear Sir,

I have duly received my warrant for 9 months and have also read the enclosed explanations. Yet, granting all that, it does not seem possible that this fee (half of what I got last year) can include the continental fees due to me thro' the agreement with the Weiner Autoren Gesellschaft about which Mr Volkert specially informed me as his last achievement while on your committee.[118]

Kindly inform me on this point.

Yours faithfully.

PS Can you tell me if fees for a short piece of music played for a long time during the performance of The Beau Stratagem [at the] Lyric Hammersmith have been collected and are included? The piece is called Lullaby for a Modern Baby, written for piano and adapted for their small orchestra. My name was given.[119]

PRS footnote:

Fees

(5/1/27)	This year (9 months)	£44-11-8 (includes £40 special allocation)
(5/4/26)	Last ¨	£89-8-11
		B'casting £4-9-11

Points

(5/1/27)	This year	708	(9 months)
(5/4/28)	Last ¨	207	

No 210

The Performing Right Society to Delius

23 June 1927
London

Dear Sir,

In reply to your letter of the 19th inst. No fees in respect of performances of your works in Austria and Germany have been included in the amount of the warrant sent to you, as no such fees were received on your behalf from the respective Societies during the period accounted for.

In answer to your further question, performances of your work 'Lullaby' during the run of 'Beau Stratagem' at the Lyric Theatre, Hammersmith, have been recorded from the 20th January to the 10th April, 1927. No fees, however, have yet been allocated to you in respect of these performances, as they took place after the period accounted for, viz., the nine months ended 5th January last.

Yours faithfully
Secretary.

---

118 Hand-written note by PRS. 'No it does not. – approx £2-10-0 on statement recently sent from Austria.'

119 'Yes. 20th Jan to 10th Apl 1927.'

No 211

Delius to Tischer & Jagenberg

23 June 1927
Grez-sur-Loing

Dear Sir,

I have received with thanks your account and cheque for Mk 233.45. I only regret that Life's Dance did not figure in it. I can only conclude that that sort of contract for this work is at fault.[120] If you could make some suggestion how in some other way [I] could share in the profits, please write to me about it.

Yours sincerely,

No 212

Delius to Universal

2 August 1927

Dear Sir

Yesterday I posted to you the Sea Drift corrections which have been so ably undertaken by Mr Gardiner. Any ambiguities have already been discussed by us and therefore I shall not need a copy. However Mr Gardiner asks that without fail you send him the proofs for further checking once the corrections have been made. Please do not forget this, as it is most important.

In the next few days we are expecting a visit from Mr Percy Grainger; will you now at last be proceeding with the production of his splendid arrangement of Song of the High Hills? He would certainly see to it that it was issued on the Duo-Art label and thereby guarantee it the widest circulation.

With very best wishes to Herr Direktor Hertzka, I remain

Yours faithfully

---

[120] The contract for *Life's Dance* was a buyout. Mk 5,000 was paid, in instalments. 1,000 in each of 1913 and 1914 and 3,000 on the sale of the 40th set of orchestral parts, on which interest at five per cent was due to FD. The contract refers to sale, but in his letter to T & J dated 14 June 1923, FD thought that the final Mk 3,000 was due on the 40th performance.

ꕥ

No 213

Delius to AKM

18 August 1927
Grez-sur-Loing

Dear Sir,

As you no doubt know, I am a member of the English 'Performing Right Society'. That Society, I am informed, concluded an agreement with you some years agoa in order to collect fees for its members from the continent. I have, however, received my warrant, and the PRS informs me that it has received nothing for me from you. As quite a number of performances have taken place both at concerts and on the wireless, I would ask you to kindly let me know how matters stand. You of course know yourself what a great pecuniary loss I am thereby sustaining. I am very anxious to obtain a satisfactory explanation of the position.

Hoping to hear from you very shortly,

Yours very truly.

FD
Composer.

ꕥ

No 214

The Performing Right Society to Delius

2 September 1927
Grez-sur-Loing

Dear Sir,

Your letter dated 18th ult. addressed to the Austrian Society has been forwarded by them to us for reply, as their contract with this Society requires that each Society shall communicate direct with its members only.

We observe that in your letter to them you refer to our having concluded an agreement with the Austrian Society many years ago. It is true that we had a contract with the Austrian Society in 1914, but this terminated on the outbreak of war, and the present contract between us only commenced to run from the 6th April 1926. We find that we informed you on this point in our letter of the 15th September last to which we beg to refer you.

It is not correct to state that we have informed you that this Society has received nothing from you from the Austrian Society. You will bear in mind that the last distribution of general fees was for the period of nine months ended 5th January

1927. Since that date we have received from the Austrian Society a statement of fees for the year 1926 in which the following of your works appear.

Serious Music:	
'In a Summer-Garden'	1 performance
'Sonata'	1 "
Broadcasting, Serious Music:	
'In a Summer-Garden'	1 "

We have also received an account for the year 1926 from the German Society (Gema) in which the following of your works appear:-

Serious Music:
'Kuckuksruf im Frühling'
'Sommernacht am Flüsse'
Broadcasting:
'In einem Sommergarten'
'Sonate No.2 C-Dur'

The fees in respect of these performances of your works will be included in this Society's next distribution of general fees.

Yours faithfully

Controller

No 215

Universal to Delius

14 December 1927
Vienna

Maestro Delius!

A few days ago I traveled back from Wiesbaden where I attended a performance of A Village Romeo and Juliet.[121] As far as the music is concerned, the work enjoyed outstanding success and was received rapturously by the audience. Musically the performance was also quite superlative, the orchestra produced a beautiful sound and the main roles were cast most befittingly. I was not quite so overwhelmed by the staging and direction although it must be said that the Wiesbaden Theatre embarked upon these with the greatest diligence. I found that the problem of the stage design was not satisfactorily resolved. The stage at Wiesbaden is very large and the scenes in which the action revolves around two characters on stage lost the charming and intimate lyricism demanded by the music. As I see it A Village Romeo and Juliet

[121] The opening night was 4 December.

should only be performed on a small stage. However, in those places where only a large stage is available the same effect could be achieved by installing a second smaller stage. Having said that, a small or diminished stage would present certain difficulties in the funfair Act since it is the very one which does require an ample stage area. Of course this question of the smaller stage is far more easily resolved than the question of the reduced orchestra demanded by such a stage. I would therefore like to ask how you would react in principle to an experiment which I have in mind to facilitate the staging of Romeo and Juliet in other theatres. I would like a well-trusted Kapellmeister, familiar with musical works of this genre, to make substantial revisions to the score and ideally if at all possible within the range of a Mozart orchestra. I am very well aware that by doing this a good degree of the music will be lost. But it could well be that what is retained could work very successfully on the small stage. It is after all merely an experiment that should be attempted and if it does not meet the grade then nothing will have been lost in the process. On the other hand if it were to fulfil our expectations, then far more opportunities would present themselves for performance than is currently the case. I would strongly question whether the opera shows any sign of a promising future in its present form.[122]

I look forward to receiving by return your comments on the above along with news of how you are. With best regards to you and your wife

Respectfully yours

Hertzka

1928

Eric Fenby wrote to Delius in June, arrived at Grez in October and was soon hard at work with Delius.

Delius was still keen to spot promotional opportunities, writing to Universal in February to suggest that *The Walk to the Paradise Garden* be published separately for orchestra and possibly piano. Universal replied, agreeing, but suggesting a reduced orchestration for their salon orchestra series. Delius did not reply, but when Universal asked permission to include two items from the *Five Piano Pieces* in one of their albums in the 'Music in Time' series, against a buyout of Mk 100, he agreed but asked for 200, about £10.

The new PRS distribution system, whereby fees were allocated against known performances caused Jelka to query the distributions. PRS painstakingly and rather quickly, answered her questions.

In July GDT wrote to PRS regarding Tischer & Jagenberg's claim to a share of performing fees. This correspondence is spread over the next two years. The gist of it is that Tischer & Jagenberg were in the process of licensing OUP to print their

[122] FD replied on 29 December. He was not averse to reducing the orchestra, after all only 26 players were needed for *Hassan*, but it would have to be done carefully. (Carley/2/515)

Delius works. OUP did not join PRS until 1936. GDT claimed at first that Delius had assigned his performing (and possibly his mechanical rights) to GDT and couldn't take them away, even if he had resigned. Delius countered by saying that when he resigned from GDT and joined PRS he had retrieved his performing right and assigned it to PRS. He also pointed out that if, as GDT maintained, it still had the performing right, why had GDT not paid him any fees?

A PRS file note, dated 18 July 1928, confirmed that it considered that Tischer & Jagenberg were entitled to one-third of fees collected by PRS, which would be sent to GDT, which apparently now accepted publisher members. The agreement between Delius and OUP dated 11 April 1931 clarified the issue. Delius kept mechanical rights. He reserved his performing rights, but after OUP joined PRS it received the publisher's share of performing fees.

Beecham recorded *Sea Drift*, *Summer Night on the River* and *Brigg Fair*. Geoffrey Toye recorded *On Hearing the First Cuckoo*, *Brigg Fair* and *In a Summer Garden*.

No 216

Universal to Delius

9 January 1928
Vienna

Maestro Delius,

I gratefully acknowledge receipt of your letter of 29 December. It affords me great pleasure to discover that my impressions of Romeo and Juliet echo your own findings. I note with interest that you agree in principle to a possible orchestral reduction. Rest assured that if we proceed with this project it will only be undertaken by a musician who demonstrates a true understanding of your compositions. I shall endeavour to contact you in good time regarding the instrumentation and other matters besides. I shall have to ascertain of course before embarking upon the toilsome and costly re-orchestrations that a stage can be found. I will in particular approach those theatres known to have small stages and which are on the lookout for a suitable work.

I am aware that A Mass of Life is being performed in London on 16 May and we are making all the necessary arrangements.

Mr Gardiner will be receiving the final proofs to Sea Drift in the very near future. In any case we shall have the preface checked by one of your English friends beforehand for you are totally right to urge that we take the greatest care to avoid possible blunders in the translation.

I wish you and your wife in turn a Happy New Year and remain

Respectfully yours

ჩ෬ჩ෬

No 217

Delius to Universal

11 February 1928
Grez-sur-Loing

Dear Herr Direktor

Mr Gardiner has the corrections to Sea Drift in hand. He has however sent me back the introductory words for they really are unusable. Among other things they mention that 'Delius lives in Germany but should be viewed as an English composer for his experiences on a Florida orange plantation strongly influenced his musical horizons.' Neither is Florida to be found in England nor do they grow oranges there!

They go on to say that he is self-taught whereas it is common knowledge that he spent the three years between 1887 and 1889 studying music in Leipzig. Further on we read that 'a predilection for triplets is in general an idiosyncrasy of English composers'. The afore-mentioned constitutes a mere handful of examples in illustration of the utter nonsense which has been written.

I fail to understand the justification for these explanations and I can only plead that you omit them in their entirety. Whoever wishes to know that sort of thing about my life need only refer to a musical lexicon. My name is continually in the newspapers and it is a well-known fact that I have been living in Grez-sur-Loing for thirty years. No work – especially one with text, requires explanation. I beg you not to print this under any circumstances. For this reason I shall not be bothering to go into all the translation errors.

Moving on to other business: My Czechoslovakian friend, Oskar Klemperer, wrote to me that a short while ago he had a very involved discussion with Mons Krapil,[123] the directeur du theatre Municipal de Prague concerning my Hassan. The latter is most interested in it; although it will have to be translated into Czech he does not consider this to be an impediment.

I would now ask you as my publisher to make contact with this gentleman and send him the music and German text on perusal. We must somehow ensure that this work receives a performance. You may also draw upon the HMV boxed set which reproduces parts of the work very well.

And now on to my third point: Beecham has just celebrated a great triumph in America. He gave performances there of Paris, On Hearing the First Cuckoo in Spring and the Interlude to A Village Romeo and Juliet (between the penultimate and final scene.) This last piece in particular enjoyed a very favourable reception. In view of its general popularity I would like to impress upon you the need to publish it as a separate edition. It would certainly be played frequently for it is so well loved. It would also be suitable as a piano reduction and indeed was released before the war

---

123 JD clearly wrote Krapil; but should it not be Kvapil?

as a piano roll without my knowledge. But its primary importance is of course as a short work for orchestra.

I have not yet had the opportunity to properly study my statement and will write back to you on this subject at a later date.

Best wishes as always

No 218

Universal to Delius

25 February 1928
Vienna

Maestro Delius,

We beg you please to excuse the tardiness with which we today respond to your letter of 11th instant due to our first having had to contact the author of the preface, Herr Dr Paul Amadeus Pisk, a most learned writer and critic. We enclose herewith a letter from Herr. Dr Pisk[124] in which you will see that his introduction was not conceived of arbitrary invention although we should point out that we did ourselves double-check your place of residence in order to make corrections, which would have happened in any case prior to printing. In line with your wishes regarding Hassan we have contacted Herr Krapil[125] in Prague and hope that something positive results.

It is our intention to promote to conductors the interlude before the final scene of Romeo and Juliet. However we fear there may be problems as it demands a large instrumentation. We are also considering having a new arrangement made of this work for salon orchestra for inclusion in our new 'Vindobona-Collection'. It is to be hoped that through this that the interlude will achieve wider circulation.

Respectfully yours

enc.

---

[124] No such enclosure has survived.

[125] Kvapil?

No 219

Universal to Delius

1 June 1928
Vienna

Maestro Delius,

In the original assignment in respect of the Five Piano Pieces you granted us the right to reprint single pieces from the afore-mentioned work in periodicals and journals for which no remuneration or royalty would be payable. However you reserved the right to be consulted on their inclusion in albums. Universal Edition is now planning the publication of a series of six albums of modern piano music under the title Music of our Time. Our aim is to popularise the modern piano repertoire and we should therefore like to include in the first album the Waltz and Mazurka from the Five Piano Pieces. We should emphasise that the purpose of this collection is to breed a sense of familiarity among those musical enclaves that have hitherto held at arm's length the modern piano repertoire. If the end product is to be the broadest possible survey of the repertoire then the albums have to be produced cheaply and without the incurrence of hefty royalty payments. In recognition of this reality every author has granted us a gratis permission to reprint single compositions in the forthcoming albums unless provision for this type of exploitation already exists in their contract.

We should be most grateful if you would please consider giving your approval to the reproduction of both the above-named pieces against a lump-sum royalty of RM 100. I am confident that you will appreciate the huge promotional value to be harvested from an enterprise of this nature.

In eager anticipation of your response, we remain

Yours faithfully

No 220

Delius to The Performing Right Society

7 June 1928
Grez-sur-Loing

Dear Sir,

I am greatly astonished that my fees for the year 1927 should only amount to £11-18-5d.

My fees always came to about £80. Last year owing to certain adjustments and for nine months only, they were £44.

My music from all accounts has been increasingly performed and even the separate accounting of BBC fees would not make it right.

There are all my performances in the Dominions, US and the Continent of Europe, all of which you tell me you now collect.

I should be very grateful to you for a detailed account, as, I think there must be omissions.

Thanking you in advance,[126]

I remain,

Yours faithfully,

No 221

Delius to Universal

8 June 1928
Grez-sur-Loing

Dear Sir

In answer to your letter of 1 June I hasten to inform you that I am inclined to grant you permission as requested to reprint the Waltz and Mazurka from the Five Piano Pieces in the forthcoming piano albums. Nevertheless I shall insist upon a royalty of at least RM 200 (two hundred Marks.) A collection of this kind will doubtlessly yield high profits, ignoring any promotional advantage that you might gain. My reputation will contribute to the success of these albums especially in consideration of the fact that I have penned so few compositions for the piano and so those that do exist will be valued for their rarity.

It is my view that I am making a large concession here which I in no way begrudge since you are the most prominent publisher of my works.

With very best regards to Herr Dir. Hertzka

Yours faithfully

PS When will the miniature score of Sea Drift eventually be appearing? We are all impatiently awaiting its arrival.

[126] This letter, not in the PRS archives, came to light from another source in 2005.

No 222

Universal to Delius

8 June 1928
Vienna

Dear Sir
Your Three Preludes have just appeared in print[127] we have pleasure in enclosing three complimentary copies.
With best wishes

Yours faithfully

No 223

The Performing Right Society to Delius

12 June 1928
London

Dear Sir,
In reply to your letter of the 7th instant, the fees allocated to you have been arrived at in accordance with the Constitution and Rules of this Society, that is to say on the basis of recorded performances of your works appearing in programmes. I believe you are aware that this system is followed by the similar Societies on the Continent, and in particular the French Society, which has been established for over 70 years. This system has recently been adopted by our Society, and as is perhaps only to be expected, the fees now receivable by some of our members differ from those which they received under the previous system of allocation by the Board.

The task of obtaining from our licensees complete and accurate returns of music performed is, as you will no doubt appreciate, a very considerable and difficult one, and our members can materially assist the Society by forwarding to us any programmes which may come into their possession. In your case for example, if you happen in the future to obtain programmes recording performances of your works, and will forward them to this office, it will help us in checking our records and at the same time serve your own interests.

Included in the amount of the Warrant recently sent you are fees from South Africa, Australia, Germany and Austria, for, as you correctly observe, the Society is

[127] Originally published in 1923 in London, by the Anglo-French Music Co. This re-engraved edition issued 'for the Continent of Europe' by Universal in 1928 is a more accurate text in many respects.

now collecting through its Agents or affiliated Societies, fees in those countries and dominions. There are, however, no fees credited to you in respect of performances in America, for we have at present no contract of affiliation with the American Society, although the matter has for some time past been in negotiation, and is still receiving the close attention of the Board.[128]

I may also say that the performances of your work 'Hassan' which were fairly numerous during the year 1926,[129] appear to have ceased during the year 1927 according to our records, which has further affected the amount of fees recently credited to you.

I trust the foregoing gives you the information you desire, and shall be happy to furnish you with any further particulars in my power upon hearing from you.

Yours faithfully,

Secretary

No 224

PRS File Note 11 June 1928

Frederick Delius

Year ended 5/4/26	
General Fees (Class 5)	87-0-0d
(23 performances)	
Broadcasting Fees	2-1-6d
Foreign & Colonial Fees	7-5d

	£89-8-11d
9 months ended 5/1/27	
54 perfs = 708 points	1-3-2d
Colonial & Foreign Fees	6d
Special Allocation by the Board	40-10-0d
Concert Halls	2-18-0

	£44-11-8d

128 ASCAP had been founded in 1914. C.F. James in *The Story of the Performing Right Society*, pub.1951 writes that in 1932 'a new contract of affiliation was entered into with the American Society providing, *inter alia*, for the allocation of fees by ASCAP on the basis of the analysis of broadcasting programmes'.

129 On stage in London in 1923. Ran for 183 performances.

Year ended 5/1/28	
49 performances = 244 points	12-11d
Colonial & foreign fees	7-19-9d
Minimum allocation	10-0d
Concert Halls	2-15-9d

	£11-18-5d
Broadcasting Fees	
6m ended 30/6/26	4-9-11d
·· ·· 31/12/26	1-9-11d
·· ·· 30/6/27	16-12-3d

No 225

Delius to The Performing Right Society

28 June 1928
Grez-sur-Loing

Dear Sir,

I thank you for your letter of explanation, dated June the 12th.

I think you know, that I was a member of the German 'Genossenschaft Deutscher Tonsetzer' for years before the war. This society worked on the system you have adopted now. But I always obtained very adequate fees.
My evening-filling work 'A Mass of Life' brought me Mk 100 to 120 every performance,[130] so that the 3 performances of this work in 1927 (Utrecht, Berlin, Frankfort) would have far exceeded your entire amount for the year.

I enclose a little list, naturally very incomplete, of performances in 1927, which happened to come to my notice.[131] I rarely receive programmes but, possessing a wireless set, naturally I see the programmes in the Radio Times.

Let me only mention that my Viennese Publisher, The Universal-Edition, published in a Musical Journal that they had made arrangements for 29 orchestral performances of my works for 1927.[132] Of these I have only mentioned very few on my list.

---

130 PRS note on letter reads. '£5 to £6'.

131 The list was duly analysed by PRS, each performance/broadcast being marked with the name of the relevant society. Attached to the PRS letter to FD dated 18 July is the result of the PRS analysis.

132 The editors can only locate ten performances in 1927 in total of all Delius works.

I beg you now to send me a detailed list of the works you have checked with the sum you have allotted to me for each.[133]

My list, however incomplete will, I am sure, convince you of the utter inadequacy of your distribution to me, even if you include the fees you sent me for broadcasting.

I am determined to see this matter through, even if I should have to draw publick (sic) attention to the way in which your funds are distributed.

Yours faithfully,

FD

PS Besides Univ. Edition I have published works with Tischer & Jagenberg, Cologne, and in London with Augener, Hawkes and Oxford Univ. Press. Curwen represents Univ. Edition in London.

PPS At the end of the half-year I will send you a list for first half of 1928

[There follows a list of performances in 1927 which is later analysed by PRS. Perhaps this letter was the cause of the special allocation by the Board of £40 10s 0d?]

No 226

GDT to The Performing Right Society

12 July 1928
Berlin

Dear Sirs,

Re Frederick Delius

Arising out of a claim by the Publishers Tischer & Jagenberg, we have ascertained that in the case of the following works by Frederick Delius:

1. His first 13 Songs
2. His last 5 Songs
3. The Orchestral Work 'Lebenstanz' (Dance of Life)
4. 'Beim ersten Kuckuksruf' and 'Sommernacht auf dem Flusse' (On Hearing the first Cuckoo – Summer Night on the River)

The Performing Right and Mechanical Copyright are, according to the contract of publication, assigned to and controlled by our Society. Mr Frederick Delius

133 PRS note 'We do not do this for general fees – only broadcasting'.

assigned the 'Performing Right and Mechanical Copyright' in these works to us, and to our regret resigned from the Society as a member and as a person entitled to fees. By virtue of the contract of publication, however, he cannot wholly withhold the 'Performing Right and Mechanical Copyright' from us. We claim, therefore, now as previously the 'Performing Right and Mechanical Copyright' in these works, and have given Herr Delius notice accordingly that we control such rights, now as previously, for Germany and the territories for which we have contracts of affiliation. We are, however, quite willing that you, in respect of performances taking place in your territory, should settle direct with Mr Delius, but with regard to the share of the publishers, Messrs Tischer & Jagenberg, we would ask you to settle with us.

We should be much obliged for your confirmation of the foregoing, and would ask you to let us have a correct account of any sums which may, in accordance therewith, be accountable to us retrospectively on behalf of Messrs. Tischer & Jagenberg

Yours very truly,

No 227

PRS File note

18 July 1928
To:
Mr Trevelyan
Miss Coker

Memo

re Mr Frederick Delius

Please take note of the attached letter from the GDT of the 12th July, and our reply of the 18th July 1928, and make the necessary entries to ensure the publishers, Tischer & Jagenberg, being credited with one-third of any fees due in respect of the works mentioned. In connection with this composer you should thoroughly examine his notification file, for you will see that many of his works are published by publishers who are members of affiliated foreign Societies, e.g. Tischer & Jagenberg, members of GDT, and the Universal Edition, members of AKM. You should make the necessary entries on your records in order that these publishers may receive their proper share of the fees.

No 228

The Performing Right Society to Delius

19 July 1928
London

Dear Sir,

1. I duly received your letter of the 28th ultimo, enclosing a list of performances of your works during 1927. This list has been carefully examined in conjunction with our records, with the result shown on the accompanying statement.[134] Generally speaking, you will see that we have a record of most of the performances in British territory mentioned in your list, and that you have been duly credited with the corresponding fees. Where we have no record, you will see that there is a good reason for its absence.

2. In the case of British Broadcasting fees you should bear in mind that these have only been distributed up to 30th June, 1927, so that fees for the performances after that date, of which there are a number on your list, have naturally not been included in the payments made to you up to the present. The performances referred to are Nos. 6 to 17 in Para 2(a) of the enclosed statement.[135]

3. It appears that you have obtained most, if not all, of the Broadcast performances from the 'Radio Times'. Accordingly, I would point out that that journal gives particulars of performances which have been arranged to take place at some future date, but it very frequently happens that the actual programme for any given day differs materially from that projected in the 'Radio Times', as you have no doubt observed yourself when using your wireless set. The B.B.C. in accordance with the terms of its contract with us, renders official programmes to the Society which give particulars of the performances after they have taken place, and it is on the basis of these official programmes that the Society collects and distributes Broadcasting fees.

4. With regard to some of the foreign performances, you will see that the affiliated Societies concerned have either accounted to us for them after the close of the Society's financial year on 5th January last, or they have not yet accounted for them at all. In the former case the fees would not of course be included in the amount of the last Warrant issued to you; and in the latter case we will communicate with the Society concerned with a view to getting the matter attended to.

5.Dealing now with the various points in your letter, I may say we are aware that you were at one time a member of the GDT and I note what you say with regard to the fees you received from that Society under the programme system. The adoption

---

[134] This follows. The original is dated 19 June 1927, which must be a mistake as Jelka's list was not sent until 28 June. Assume 19 July.

[135] Broadcasting fees could only be distributed in arrears, when the annual licence fee paid by the BBC could be spread across the known uses of copyright music under PRS control.

of that system by this Society, however, is not by any means the only factor which has affected the last two distributions of general fees. One of the other most important factors which I have again to emphasise is that the very considerable influx of new members in 1926 necessitated the division of the society's revenue amongst a much larger number of members, before we had any opportunity of increasing the revenue so as to be more in proportion to the larger repertoire under the Society's control. I also have to point out that you are affected by these changes, but in most cases we have the advantage or being able to explain matters to them at a personal interview or at the Annual General Meetings, and had you been resident in this country, I should been glad to have had a similar opportunity of discussing the question with you in person, which would have been a much more expeditious and satisfactory means of dealing with it than by correspondence.

6. I note the fee which you state you were accustomed to receive for a performance of your work 'A Mass of Life' and will pass this information on to the 'GEMA' and the French Society, in whose territories the performances you refer to are said to have taken place. As you will see from the enclosed statement, we have received no fees from abroad in respect of this work up to the present, and we will ask the Societies concerned to look into the matter. If you can state the name of the premises at which the work was performed, will you please do so, as without that information it will probably be difficult to carry the matter very far.

7. I also note what you say with regard to arrangements made by the Universal Edition for orchestral performances in Vienna. You will see from my letter of 2nd September last that we have received fees from the Austrian Society for three performances of your works in Vienna in 1926, and these have been included in the amount of the general distribution warrant No. 178. Fees for performances of your work 'Paris' and 'Brigg Fair' in 1927 have since been received from the Austrian Society, but they did not reach us until after the close of our financial year on 5th January last, and have therefore not yet been distributed.

8. With regard to your request for a detailed list of all the fees credited to you, it is not the Society's practice to issue statements in respect of general fees, but only in respect of Broadcasting fees, and the latter have already been sent to you, but I have no doubt that the very full details I have given you in this letter and the accompanying statement will afford you the desired information. The performances of your work 'Lullaby for a Modern Baby' at the Lyric Theatre, Hammersmith, in the early part of 1927, were duly credited to you and included In the amount of Warrant No.178, as I intimated they would be in my letter of 23rd June 1927. I may add that numerous other performances of your works have been credited to you, of which you make no mention, but I note you propose to send a further list of performances for the half year of 1928, which shall receive due attention when it comes to hand.

9. When you have fully considered all the points set out in this letter and the accompanying statement the preparation of which has entailed very considerable labour and investigation, I think you will appreciate that the remarks contained in the last two paragraphs of your letter are unjustified. The manner in which the Society's revenue is distributed is determined by the Rules laid down by the Board, and as to your suggestion to draw public attention to the matter, may I point out that the question is hardly one to interest the general public. It is the members of the Society

who are concerned, and inasmuch as the plan of distribution as recommended by the Board was approved by the members in General Meeting, I do not see what purpose would be served by your taking the step to which you refer. I have dealt somewhat exhaustively with the points you raise in the desire to make the position clear to you, and shall now be obliged it you will kindly pay your Warrant into your Bankers without delay, as its period of currency expires within three months from the date thereof.

Yours Faithfully

Woodhouse
Controller

No 229

19 July1928
[This schedule answers the analysis sent by Jelka with her letter dated 28 June. It would have taken several weeks to complete the investigation.]

PERFORMANCES OF THE WORKS OF
MR FREDERICK DELIUS

Statement showing the result of the analysis of the list of performances enclosed with Mr Delius' letter to the Society dated 28th June 1928.

1. BRITISH GENERAL PERFORMANCES

(a) Performances traced 1927

1. Brigg Fair — Queen's Hall London 19th March
2. Brigg Fair — " " " 17th Sept
3. Eventyr — Beecham orchestra 17th Oct
4. Violin Sonata — Wigmore Hall 10th Nov

Fees for these performances duly credited to you, and included in the amount of the General Distribution warrant No. 178 dated 5th June 1928, in respect of the Society's financial year ended 5th January 1928.

------

5. Cello Concerto — Three Choirs Festival — 7th Sept

The fee collected for this performance will be credited to you at the next Distribution of general fees.

(b) Performances not traced

1. Seraglio	Sheffield	25th Feb
2. I Brasil	..	..
3. So White, So soft	..	..
4. Spring, the sweet spring	..	..
5. La Lune Blanche	..	..
6. Il pleure dans mon jardin	..	..
7. It was a lover	Bradford	5th Dec
8. So white, so soft	..	..
9. Minstrels	..	..
10. Spring, the sweet spring	..	..
11. Cello Sonata	..	..
12. Paris	Liverpool	13th Dec

These may be amongst the numerous performances credited to you, but we cannot tell unless we know the name of the establishment at which the performances took place. If 'Sheffield', 'Bradford' and 'Liverpool' refer to British Broadcasting Stations, see our remarks in paragraphs 2 and 3 of the accompanying letter.

14. Piano Concerto	Royal College of Music	4th Jan 28

It is not the present practice of the Society to charge fees for educational performances such as those held at the Royal College of Music.

2. BRTISH BROADCASTING PERFORMANCES

(a) performances traced	1927
1. On hearing the first cuckoo	18th Jan
2. The Splendour falls	19th
3. Brigg fair	30th
4. In a Summer garden	30th
5. Dance Rhapsody	30th

Fees for these performances duly credited to you, and included in the amount of the Broadcasting Distribution Warrant No.187 dated 27th February 1928, in respect of the six months ended 30th June 1927. See the statement of account sent to you with the warrant.

6.	Violin Concerto	30th Jan
7.	Dance Rhapsody	25th Aug
8.	Indian Love Song	29th Aug
9.	Cradle Song	29th Aug
10.	Brigg Fair	30th Sept
11.	Dance Rhapsody	5th Oct
12.	On hearing the first cuckoo	2nd Nov
13.	Summer Night on the river	2nd Nov
14.	Brigg Fair	16th Dec
15.	I Brasil	27th Dec
16.	On hearing the first cuckoo	29th Dec
17.	Summer Night on the river	29th Dec

Fees for these performances duly collected, but not yet distributed. They will be included in the amount of the next warrant for broadcasting fees which will be sent to you during the next few weeks.

(b) Performances not traced

1.	Dance Rhapsody	Sept
2.	Two Preludes	21st Dec

With regard to 1, we can trace no broadcast performance of the work in September 1927, although there are several performances in other months.
With regard to 2, the work is published by the Anglo-American Co; who are not members of the Society, and assuming you have assigned the performing right in the work to the publisher in the usual way, the Society is not in a position to collect fees for same.

3. AUSTRIAN PERFORMANCES

(a) performances traced 1927

1.	Paris	Vienna	6th Jan
2.	Paris	Vienna Broadcasting	13th Feb

Fees for these performances not received from the AKM until after the close of the Society's financial year on the 5th January 1928. They will be duly included in the amount of the next General Distribution Warrant to be sent you about June next.

(b) performances not traced

3.	On hearing the first cuckoo in Spring, Vienna Broadcasting	6th Nov
4.	Summer Night on the river	"

In the statements we have received from the Austrian Society for the year 1927 there are no fees credited in respect of the above performances. We will take up the matter with them.

4. GERMAN PERFORMANCES

(a) performances traced 1927

1.	In a Summer Garden Frankfurt Broadcasting		14th Feb

A fee for this performance received from the GEMA and duly included in the amount of the General Distribution Warrant No. 178 dated 5th June 1928, in respect of the Society's financial year ended 5th January 1928.

2.	Brigg Fair	Hagen	6th Jan
3.	On hearing the first cuckoo	Stuttgart Broadcasting	21st Sept
4.	"	Bremen Broadcasting	31st Oct
5.	Summer night on the river	Bremen	31st Oct

Fees for these performances not received from the GEMA until after the close of the Society's financial year on the 5th January 1928. They will be duly included in the amount of the next General Distribution Warrant to be sent you about June next.

(b)performances not traced 1927

1.	Summer night on the river	Stuttgart Broadcasting	26th Sept
2.	Mass of Life	Berlin	2nd Oct
3.	Mass of Life	Frankfurt	16th Nov
4.	Piano Concerto	Wiesbaden	9th Dec

In the statement we have received from the GEMA for the year 1927, there are no fees credited in respect of the above performances. We will take the matter up with them.

5. CZECHO-SLOVAKIAN PERFORMANCES 1927

1.	Paris	Prague	10th Dec

The Czecho-Slovakian Society have so far only accounted to us for the period ended 30th June 1927, and the above performance took place after that date.

6. PERFORMANCES IN TERRITORY ADMINISTERED ON OUR BEHALF BY THE FRENCH SOCIETY

1.	Mass of Life	Utrecht
2.	Song of the High Hills	Athens

In the statement we have received from the French Society for the year 1927, there are no fees credited in respect of the above performances. We will take the matter up with them.

7. PERFORMANCES IN THE USA

1. Brigg Fair	Minneapolis	18th March
2. Song of the High Hills	Los Angeles	30th April
3. Dance Rhapsody	Chicago	7th July

We do not at present collect fees in respect of performances in the USA. See paragraph 3 of our letter of 12th June 1928.

ꕥꕥ

No 230

Delius to Universal

5 September 1928.
Grez-sur-Loing

Dear Sirs

In response to your card of 29 August may I please request that you allow me the flexibility of a few days delay as I would like to be able to pursue a few possible corrections to the Mass vocal score in London. In any event I would ask you not to proceed with the reprint before you have heard from me again. Furthermore, I must insist that the Keith Douglas arrangements are not printed under any circumstances until they have been given my approval.[136] Please forward the manuscript; I shall inform you of my wishes once I have been able to scrutinise it for myself. As I mentioned to you in my letters in the summer it would be a source of great delight to me were you to publish in a separate edition the Interlude as it is written in the opera and with which Beecham has enjoyed so much success in the concert hall.

Yours faithfully

ꕥꕥ

No 231

Delius to The Performing Right Society

16 December 1928
Grez-sur-Loing

Dear Sir,

I have just received your account and I regret to say that there are some obvious mistakes and omissions.

[136] FD wrote to UE on19 September approving the Keith Douglas arrangement of the 'Interlude to Romeo and Juliet'. It is interesting that he did not refer to it as the '*Walk to the Paradise Garden*'.

For example you allow me ¼ [of the length] for Seadrift an orchestral choral work playing 30–35 minutes.[137]

You would oblige me very much by telling me roughly what you allow for an orchestral work playing 20–25 minutes, for a choral work[138] 30–35 minutes, for a violin sonata (15–17 minutes), for a shorter orchestral work (10 minutes), for a concerto with orchestra.

With these approximate data it would be possible for me to see whether all has been accounted so far.

Thanking you in advance for [your] kind information.

Yours sincerely

ꙮ

No 232

Delius to Universal

17 December 1928
Grez-sur-Loing

Dear Sir

The Aeolian Company Duo-Art (London) is proposing to produce an illustrated biography of my life on 2 rolls. These rolls are to contain the Dance for Harpsichord and a handful of other demonstrative works from my oeuvre. To prevent any misunderstandings I would like to clarify your position on this proposal now. Basically it will serve as a good piece of advertising. I should be grateful for a favourable response.[139]

Yours faithfully

ꙮ

No 233

The Performing Right Society to Delius

28 December 1928
London

Dear Sir,

---

137 PRS note says 'shown on BBC programme as 6 minutes'.

138 PRS did not control choral/orchestral works lasting longer than 20 Minutes, but at this stage Jelka, whether or not she had been told by PRS, had not taken this in.

139 UE replied on 22 December that they had no objection. As they did not own mechanical rights they could not have objected to the project.

In reply to your letter of the 16 inst. We have now had the opportunity of referring to the official programme rendered to us by the BBC and find that the performance of your work 'Sea Drift' from the Liverpool Relay Station on 21 February last, is shown as having occupied six minutes. This appears to indicate that a portion only of the work was performed, and the fee was charged accordingly, but as I observe on reference to previous correspondence with you that you have a Wireless Receiving Set, I shall be glad to learn whether you happened to have listened to the performance in question, and whether you can state how much of the work was performed. If it was performed in its entirety, we shall be pleased to take the matter up with the BBC and adjust the fee on your next account.

In reply to your further enquiries, the charges made by the Society under its existing contract with the BBC for works of the nature to which you refer, are as follows:

Duration of performance	Charge per item per Mainstation per programme
Items not exceeding 7 minutes in transmission	4/-
Exceeding 7 min: but not exceeding 10 mins	7/6d
" 10 " " " 15 "	11/3d
" 15 " " " 20 "	17/6d
" 20 " " " 30[140]	22/6d
" 30 " " " 40 "	30/-

The charges for items originating from Relay Stations are one-half of the above. Where an item is simultaneously broadcast from other main stations, the charge is multiplied by the total number of Main Stations from which the item is transmitted.

You will bear in mind of course, that the fees collected are divisible according to the Society's rules in the proportions of two-thirds to the composer and one-third to the publisher.

I may mention that the Society is at present in negotiation with the BBC with a view to the conclusion of a new contract on terms which it is hoped will prove more advantageous to our members than the foregoing. Meantime, it will be of assistance to our department concerned if you would kindly indicate on the attached list of your works the time which each of them takes to perform. Perhaps, therefore you will be good enough to complete the list accordingly, and return it to me at your early convenience.

Yours faithfully,

Woodhouse
Controller

---

[140] Choral works accompanied by an orchestra lasting more than 20 minutes were outside PRS control.

ꙮ

1929

Much of the correspondence for the year concerns financial matters. It is clear that Universal are in trouble. As the company writes in December, the growth in record sales and broadcasting 'has caused sales to plummet in the printed music sector'.

Universal are using shorter print runs, printing separate songs rather than albums and are loath to embark on unnecessary reprints. The Grainger 2-piano version of *The Song of the High Hills* is not a practical proposition. Universal again asks for a share of mechanicals. Delius says that he is earning so little that he cannot afford to give anything up. It doesn't seem that Universal are aware of the Delius recordings available until Delius tells them in October or that they are active in encouraging record companies. *A Song Before Sunrise* was recorded by John Barbirolli and *Seadrift* by Anthony Bernard with Roy Henderson as the baritone soloist. May Harrison and Arnold Bax recorded the Violin Sonata No. 1. The *Serenade from Hassan* was recorded twice, once by Beatrice and Margaret Harrison and once by Lionel Tertis on the viola, who also recorded his own arrangement of the Violin Sonata No. 2. Thomas Beecham and Dora Labbette recorded three songs and Evlyn Howard-Jones some piano pieces.

Performances are dropping off and few performances of major works are scheduled. There are high hopes of the October London Festival.

Universal, which is obviously occupied with performing rights complains that it has been told by AKM, its performing right society, that PRS will only pass shares back to AKM if the composer is a member of the society. This goes against the PRS file note of July 1928. There is however the willingness between Delius and Universal to exchange information on broadcasts and performances, to enable Universal to put pressure on the societies.

The London Festival takes place in October. Delius was made a Companion of Honour.

ꙮ

No 234

Universal to Delius

9 January 1929

Maestro Delius,

We are in the midst of launching a new English catalogue and once again we are obliged to bring to your attention the difficulties we are experiencing in fixing the price of your choral works Der Wanderer, Midsummer Song and On Craig Ddu. These prices are based on their equivalent German retail price which, as our English agent repeatedly reminds us, results in exorbitant prices that make wide distribution impracticable. The sole reason for these high prices is your 25 per cent royalty which we must always account for in our calculations. Our English agent informs us that generally no composer derives more than one-third of the retail price in royalties.[141] To allow us to reduce the English retail price we would be most grateful, Maestro, if you could accept a royalty rate of 15 per cent on sheet music sales of the afore-mentioned works. Trusting that these terms will meet with your approval we remain

Yours sincerely

No 235

Delius to The Performing Right Society

Editorial comment. This is printed as on the original which is in Jelka's hand.

10 Jan 1929
Grez-sur-Loing

Dear Sir,

I regret that I was unable TO answer Your letter of Dec.22 at an Earlier Date. But I had to procure the duration of performance of all my works, Which took some time.[142]

Regarding 'Seadrift' let me tell you That it was given in its entirety at Liverpool; I listened in myself: The duration is 30 minutes.

I notice the 'Seadrift' is altogether omitted on your list of my works. As it is my best known and oftenest played Choral work this is very regrettable. Owing to your System of not giving detailed accounts[143] I have been unable to detect this omission before. If indeed you have never recorded the performances of this work, or Counted it as a song, as on the last bill, that alone would cause me serious prejudice.

On your list of works you further mention 'Sonata' & 'Sonata for Violoncello & Piano'. But Beside this latter I have written 2 Sonatas for Violin & Piano: Sonata Nr. 1, playing 21 min. & Sonata Nr 2, Playing 12 min. As you will see on the list I include each of these Violin sonatas has had 5 BBC performances from Main Stations During the first half year from 1928. For these no adequate fees are allowed.

Omitted from your list of works are also 'Five Pieces' for piano.

---

141 The editors do not understand the mathematics, but this is a correct translation of the original letter. The correspondence with UE shows that UE were constantly trying to reduce the royalty rate, partly because to build in a 25 per cent royalty as well as recovering their costs would result in a higher than ideal retail price.

142 The faults are on both sides. PRS had obviously omitted some performances and broadcasts as well as making an error over the length of *Seadrift*. One factor working against Delius was that Universal Edition were not PRS members, although as members of the Austrian Society UE should have been pursuing PRS for the publisher's share.

143 This is a good point and one still not always adequately dealt with on Performing Right Society statements even today.

I again emphasise that the list of performances I enclose is quite incomplete, it Contains Just what I heard myself on the Wireless, or performances I happened to hear about On the other hand I am absolutely Certain, that these Perfs. Have actually taken place.

It is not Possible with the casual data at my disposal to exercise any adequate control. But the mere facts of the Violin sonatas just mentioned, of Seadrift and of Brigg Fair Performed in Ireland Wireless & being given Only 5/8, Shows that all is not well with the accounts of Your Society.

As regards the further Outstanding points, as f. ex. The Mass of Life I must await the Next general account. I sincerely hope You will assist me by sending me a detailed account.

I remain Yours Faithfully

No 236

Delius to Universal

12 January 1929.
Grez-sur-Loing

Dear Sir

I feel sufficiently compelled by the contents of your letter of 9 January, of which I gratefully acknowledge receipt, to furnish you with an immediate response.

I am prepared to satisfy myself with a 15 per cent royalty on sales of my 3 a cappella choral works through Curwen. In return however I must make the proviso that you publish without further ado the Percy Grainger arrangement for 2 pianos of Song of the High Hills.

You must concede that the availability of this arrangement would aid the public's familiarity with this work which, by any yardstick, ranks amongst the greatest of my creations. In a display of great generosity Percy Grainger has furthermore assigned the work to you without expecting to derive any income from it; it would therefore only be a common courtesy to publish the said work.

In addition to this I am in possession of the manuscript of a splendid piano reduction by Heseltine of In a Summer Garden which you should be itching to publish. Enquiries are frequently made of me concerning these arrangements and I think they would be of great assistance to a student of this work and could even become a best seller.

I am relieved to be able to pass on to you the happy news that my health is somewhat better and, with the aid of a young musician, have taken up work again on my compositions. Presently I am in the process of writing an orchestral suite based on the music from Hassan which I believe contains the makings of a very worthwhile and effective orchestral piece.

To move on to other matters, I hear from London that various vocal scores of mine, for example A Village Romeo and Juliet, are to appear very soon in new editions. If this is the case, as with all reprints I would ask that you keep me abreast in order that I might correct possible errors. If, for example, a reprint of the Five Piano Pieces was planned I would wish to remove the Lullaby for a Modern Baby and issue it separately as a song without words or scored for violin con sordino. Sales would certainly improve in this format.

How do matters stand with the H. Drachmann Song which I believe was originally bought from Leuckart with the 4 Nietzsche Lieder. Can I dare to hope that you have published it? I still have in my possession an unprinted Verlaine song and might possibly be able to lay my hands on another one or two. This should be done – if at all – whilst I still have my young friend here. The Douglas version of the Intermezzo from Romeo and Juliet has made quite an impact on concert halls in England. Might you not launch in Germany as well? Schuricht I know would certainly jump at the chance to play it.

My wife joins me in sending our best wishes to Herr Dir. Hertzka
Respectfully yours

F.D.

PS With reference to the reprint of Romeo and Juliet, I would appreciate it if you could please reuse the colourful title page designs acquired from Harmonie for the jacket.[144]

No 237

Universal to Delius

16 January 1929
Vienna

Maestro Delius,

Before I go any further may I express my great pleasure at the news that your health has improved and that you are once again able to resume composition, albeit with assistance of a young musician. Few will dispute the claim that an orchestral suite from Hassan will be anything but a worthwhile addition to the orchestral repertoire and we look forward to the moment when we can include it in our orchestral catalogue.

Regarding reprints, you may take it for granted that we shall do our utmost to notify you promptly in advance to allow you ample time to undertake any correction work. I have noted you desire to remove the Lullaby for a Modern Baby from the Five Piano Pieces and will ensure that this change is effected at the next reprint. The

144 This was never carried out.

Lullaby will then be published as a song without words or for violin con sordino.[145] I am also keen to publish the Leuckart Drachmann Song along with the new Verlaine Song, possibly with one or two other songs should they become available.[146] In this connection we presently have designs to publish an English song collection (possibly with German or French texts) exclusively for the English and American territories. The presentation has been deliberately conceived to fit English tastes and could perhaps lead to our accessing new markets. Separate editions of your previously published songs are envisaged as part of the collection and we can likewise include the new ones mentioned before. In response to ever-decreasing sales of song anthologies, indeed of most music forms that you might care to mention, and the worsening crisis in the publishing establishment it is imperative that we be indefatigable in our endeavours to attract new custom by reducing our overheads. Since we can however only afford small print runs due to declining sales and production costs are always substantially higher per copy when compared with larger runs, the publisher, who in previous times was able to guarantee himself a level of income by virtue of less expensive anthologies, has been forced to fall back on the age old practice of publishing every piece in separate editions. For this reason it is now our policy to publish not only songs but also most other compositions individually because the public is much more inclined to purchase a title or song for RM 1 than five songs for RM 3.

With these facts to hand you will understand that it is really not practicable at the moment to publish the Grainger arrangement for 2 pianos of the 'Song of the High Hills' as well as the Heseltine arrangement of In a Summer Garden as you requested.[147] I hope that the situation can be reversed in the not too distant future and in the meantime I shall contact the firm of Curwen in London and enquire whether they can facilitate the publication of the arrangements by agreeing to purchase a certain quantity. If any public interest is shown in these arrangements then it will undoubtedly arise in England where Curwen is our agent. If he can declare himself willing to make a not insubstantial order then we may be able to consider pursuing a publication.

Regarding the reprint of the vocal score to Romeo and Juliet we have at this point in time no cause to contemplate such a venture; as soon as we have one your comments will be given due consideration.

We shall make strenuous efforts to bring about a German performance of the Intermezzo from Romeo and Juliet in the K. Douglas version. In accordance with your instructions we shall forward the material to Generalmusikdirektor Schuricht as soon as it is returned from London.

---

145 Although the Lullaby was published separately, as FD had requested, no subsequent editions of the *Five Piano Pieces* omitted it.

146 The Drachmann song, which had been engraved by Leuckart, remained in UE's safe until 1981, when it was issued in the collection of Four Posthumous Songs. The Verlaine song (*Avant que tu ne t'en ailles*) was published by Winthrop Rogers in 1932.

147 Neither of these two arrangements was ever published by UE. The Heseltine arrangement of *In a Summer Garden* for piano solo appeared in 1982 from Thames Publishing; the Grainger arrangement of *The Song of The High Hills* remains unpublished to this day (2006).

In offering our New Year's greetings may I take this opportunity on behalf of my colleagues to express our sincere hope that you maintain your vigour and that you are soon able to return to your compositions without impediment
I remain

Respectfully yours

ജ്യങ്ങ

No 238

The Performing Right Society to Delius

30 January 1929
London

Dear Sir,

I am obliged for your letter of the 10th inst. And for the accompanying list of your works, showing the time each work takes to perform, which will be of assistance to us.

The omission of the work 'Seadrift' from the list of your works sent with my letter of 22 December last, was due to a typist's error, which is regretted. You had duly notified the Society of this work, and the fact that we had previous correspondence with you with regard to it will show you that it had not been overlooked. On the other hand, your 'Five Pieces'(Mazurka, etc.) were not included in the list we sent you, as you had not previously notified the Society of them, but particulars have now been entered on the Society's records.

We note what you say with regard to the length of the broadcast of your work 'Seadrift' from the Liverpool Relay Station on the 21st February last, and acting upon your statement, we are arranging to collect a supplementary fee from the BBC in respect of this performance.

We now have pleasure in sending you herewith supplementary accounts for the three half years ended 30th June 1927, 31st December 1927 and 30th June, 1928 respectively.[148]

The works appearing thereon are, you will observe, the publications of Augener Ltd., concerning which there has for some time past been a difference of opinion between that firm of publishers and the BBC. The points at issue having now been settled, we have collected and are now able to distribute the corresponding fees. We also enclose a further account in respect of the half year ended 30th June, 1928, whereon you will see you have been credited with supplementary fees in respect of the works mentioned in your letter, and the broadcast performances indicated on the lists accompanying same. The remaining broadcast performances which took place during the last six months of 1928 will be duly accounted for at the next broadcasting distribution. We are also investigating the performances of your works other than broadcasting referred to on the lists in question.

[148] Delius was vindicated.

You will see that the total of the four accounts mentioned amounts to £15-8-11d, and we now have pleasure in sending you herewith a supplementary warrant, which please pay into your account at your early convenience.[149]

I may mention that the fees collected in respect of broadcast performances in the Irish Free State and Australia are not based on the scale set out in my letter to you of the 22nd December last, which for the present applies only to the BBC here.

Will you be good enough to let us know whether you have assigned the performing right in your work 'Three preludes' to the publishers, the Anglo French Music Co. for if so, the Society will not be in a position to collect fees in respect of this work, the publishers not being at present members of the Society.

Yours faithfully

No 239

Universal to Delius

4 February 1929
Vienna

Maestro Delius,

As you have probably already discerned, the performing and mechanical right have in recent history assumed a considerably enhanced profile in our musical lives. In recognition of this development we have devoted intense study to the administration of these rights and to the matter of performance promotion, mechanical reproduction and distribution and sale of copies of your works. Most work assignments to Universal Edition reflect a publisher participation in the division of these shares, in particular, revenue derived from the mechanical right, whilst your contracts show no consideration of the mechanical right whatsoever. You will understand our reticence in promoting your music and administering the mechanical right if we are not to enjoy the usual publisher share. We should therefore like to propose that in respect of the works published by Universal Edition you grant us a share entitlement in accordance with 'AMMRE'[150] rules, in other words a 50/50 split of mechanical income between publisher and composer less commission deducted at source by the collecting society.

(rest of letter missing)

---

149 PRS records of distributions to Delius show £5-17s-9d distributed in 1927, the first broadcasting distribution: In 1931 £108-2s-5d from the UK and £41-19s-1d from the colonies. For 1932 it was £147-0s-5d from the UK and £13-7s-1d from the Colonies. There is no specific reference to Broadcast fees from Continental Europe.

150 AMMRE, the Anstalt für mechanisch-musikalische Rechte GmbH (Institute for mechanical musical rights) was founded in Germany in 1909 for the exploitation of the so-called mechanical reproduction rights for phonograph records. Became part of GEMA.

ཀྵཀྵ

No 240

Delius to Universal

20 February 1929
Vienna

Dear Sir

I gratefully acknowledge receipt of my statement enclosed with your letter.

From the attached list of performances of my UE works you can see for yourself just how little income I earn in respect of performing rights.[151] Mostly the list consists of works where the material has been bought outright from you.[152] The Cello Concerto must also be omitted from any calculations since the material seems to be under the ownership of B. Harrison, as must the Intermezzo from Romeo and Juliet and Sea Drift for which Beecham has retained his own material. What is the position however with regards to Sir Henry Wood who twice performed Sea Drift in Liverpool during the winter/spring season?

The net result is a level of income so modest that I dare not even contemplate what would remain were I to divide my mechanical rights with you.

You must yourself concede that my musical reputation is slowly but surely gaining ground, that you own outright a vast majority of my compositions and earn a healthy sum from those that you do not. It is indirectly of enormous advantage to you that the gramophone record etc. is now a cornerstone in kindling understanding of my works and I must say it is tremendously shortsighted of you not to maximise this indirect advantage and launch yourselves wholeheartedly into the mechanical exploitation of my works in Germany.

As far as my performance income is concerned in Central Europe, I have to admit that the Vienna Autorengesellschaft[153] has to date been particularly idle on this point and that no significant performance to have taken place in the last year, especially of the Mass of Life, has been accounted. I am therefore forever tangled up in lengthy discussions with the English PRS which has somewhat soured my relationship there.

Sir Thomas Beecham is intending to organise a large Delius Festival in London for next October. I cannot begin to estimate the good he does for my music day in, day out and I do hope that you will place yourselves unquestioningly at his disposal. To this extent on 8 February he gave an enchanting radio concert of my works that I listened to most excitedly on my wireless here. I also heard Barjansky's gleaming account of my Concerto with the London Philharmonic.

May I make the suggestion that you arrange a small paragraph on the subject in Pult und Taktstock.

---

151 The list has not survived.

152 There is an assumption here that if a performer has bought the performing material, no performing fee is due. This is wrong.

153 AKM.

Barjansky wanted to draw your attention to the exquisite cello sonata by Frederic Austin, an English composer of acute sensitivity. You will recall that Austin among others has composed music to John Gay's Beggar's Opera and that this opera was performed daily for three and a half years and still enjoys regular performance to this day. I should be delighted were you to take an assignment of this work!

In my statement I fail to see any mention of the Appalachia performance in Seattle (U.S.A). Moreover the English sales figures in respect of vocal scores seem all too low to me, equally A Mass of Life. These two vocal scores were sold in bulk quantities for performances in London, as was Sea Drift for a performance in Leeds.

With best wishes to Herr Dir. Hertzka
Yours respectfully

F.D.

Please find overleaf the programme from the recent Delius Concert given by Sir Thomas Beecham.

No 241

Universal to Delius

26 February 1929
Vienna

Maestro Delius,

We gratefully acknowledge receipt of your letter of 20 February and also the list pertaining to performances of UE works which, inasmuch as we had no record of them, we have forwarded to AUME. Since we operate a tight checking procedure of all radio listings magazines we were already apprised of the performances given by the BBC in London.

In reference to performing rights income, for some time now we have been engaged in considerable efforts to increase the income derived from licensed performance. Recently we have been involved in protracted negotiations with AKM,[154] which is regarded generally as a well organised collecting society, the outcome of which has been an augmentation of income in respect of serious music compared to light music. Additionally, pledges have been made to improve the control and registration of performing rights abroad. It is our hope that our efforts will be rewarded with some success. Not one single Delius performance for the whole of 1927 was accounted to us by the P.R.S. and when we lodged a complaint we were informed that P.R.S.

---

[154] This should be AKM, founded in 1897,which collects performing rights in Austria. AUME is Austro-Mechana, the mechanical rights organisation.

will only forward monies to us if the composer is also a member of AKM.[155] As a result we were deprived of the opportunity to check performances of your works in England although this is a situation unlikely to remain unchanged. On the one hand we have been promised payment on all future foreign performances and on the other we hope to find a way forward that will not only guarantee in the long term the control of rights but also provide us with a platform for the energetic promotion of your music in England. Should you fail to receive any payment on the part of P.R.S. in respect of German performances we ask you in future to furnish us with the details in order that we might be able to pursue the matter. After due processing those performances that took place in 1928 will not be accounted until 1929 and we do not envisage remittance on performances from November and December 1928 until 1930 as the reciprocal accounting procedures of the individual societies are very time consuming.

From the evidence before you, you will find it hard to dispute our claim that we have made strenuous efforts to increase the income of our composers and we say this in the hope that in future you will have no further occasion to express your dissatisfaction whilst keeping in mind that the direct governorship of performing rights has been ceded to the collecting societies.

We regret all the more that you lend little weight to our viewpoint that the publisher should be participant in mechanical rights for such a participation is provided for in the statutes of every collecting society. However we are willing to make an exception in this instance and will therefore not be claiming a share of mechanical income in respect of your works published by Universal Edition.

We are happy to arrange an item in our journals on the radio concert of 8 February and note with interest that Sir Thomas Beecham is minded to organise a large Delius Festival in London in October. We shall insert a notice in Anbruch.

Please accept our thanks for your rapturous recommendation of the Cello Sonata by Frederic Austin, a name already well known to us. Unfortunately we are over-stretched to an extraordinary degree and must prioritise the publication of works by composers under contract with the result that for some time to come we shall be obliged to refrain from any new assignments.

You should receive separate correspondence with regard to your statement queries.

Yours sincerely

[155] This goes against the PRS internal note dated 18 July 1928, which states that if a publisher were represented by a foreign society, PRS would pay the publisher's share to that society. There is also a PRS note to the effect that even though UE was not represented by PRS, PRS had stretched their rules to collect the composers' share for FD. It would be interesting to know whether UE were paid both composer and publisher shares, prior to the PRS/AKM contract, when Delius was represented.

ꕥ

No 242

Delius to Universal

11 March 1929
Grez-sur-Loing

Dear Sir

Of the progress to date on the printing of Mr Keith Douglas's score of A Walk to the Paradise Garden (from A Village Romeo and Juliet) I am not cognisant.

However, in case preparations are already underway I should like to request that a copy of the proofs be sent to

Sir Thomas Beecham Bart
Hyde Park Hotel
Knightsbridge
London S.W.

Sir Th. B., who has graced us with his performances of peerless beauty, would like to insert extra dynamics and bowing marks in certain places. Naturally it is of the utmost importance to me that I have his input on this.

In the event of further reprints of my works Sir Th. B. as a rule would like the opportunity to revise these works and provide exact markings. May I request that you inform me of every reprint in advance.

On Friday evening I am hoping to hear the Piano Concerto given by Catherine Goodson as part of a national concert. How is the new edition progressing?

With best wishes to Herr Dir. Hertzka.

Yours faithfully

ꕥ

No 243

Universal to Delius

16 March 1929
Vienna

Maestro,

We acknowledge receipt of your kind letter of 11 March and beg leave to inform you that the score to Walk to the Paradise Garden[156] by Keith Douglas has not yet

---

[156] This is the first time that the title to the interlude is given, although it is referred to as such in the UE score published in 1921–22.

gone to press as we are striving to secure German performances on the basis of the present material. We shall again be recommending the work to eminent conductors. We have however noted that the proofs are to be sent to Sir Thomas Beecham should a printed edition become a definite prospect.

On the matter of the Piano Concerto we have pleasure in informing you that the new edition appeared back in December. May we express our profoundest thanks for your greetings to Herr Direktor Hertzka which we have forwarded to him as he is presently on vacation.

Yours respectfully

ഇരുഇരു

No 244

Delius to Tischer & Jagenberg

12 May 1929
Grez-sur-Loing

Dear Doctor,

I send you the improved songs today.[157] They are our only copies so will you kindly send them back? Also we would like to read the proof of the new edition's English words. We could also improve the English version of 'Verborg'ne Liebe' when it is sent back. As it is less popular, it is not so urgent as the others.

Please pay the money due to me into my account with the Darmstadt and National Bank, Frankfurt Branch, and send me the account here.

What you write to me about the performances of the small pieces is most regrettable.[158] I should think however that OUP could settle the matter. They could enquire who has used the stolen music, and prosecute them. I almost think that the firm of Chester (formerly Breitkopf & Härtel) either held back a number of copies when they lost the agency, or has since acquired a number of others. I am not in a position to judge, but I think that this affair starts with Chesters. If you had an English agency, then of course the affair, which has greatly injured me during all these years, would have been much easier to deal with. When OUP suspects that a performance is to be held, it must demand to know where the music comes from. The Five Songs need no further correction.

With best wishes from my family to yours,

---

[157] *7 Norwegian Songs*. Originally published Augener 1892 with English words. Re-issued by T & J 1910 and later re-engraved by them. Further alterations to the English words were made in 1929. Transferred to OUP 1930.

[158] It seems that performing material for the small pieces had got out and that performances were taking place without hire fees being paid. This would not affect performing fees through PRS.

ꕥꕥ

No 245

Delius to Universal

27 May 1929
Grez-sur-Loing

Herr Direktor,

The Hassan Suite is now finished. In its instrumentation it is identical to the stage music, i.e. for small orchestra, 26 instruments and small chorus. The solo parts are to be sung by members of the chorus.

Because I have already received enquiries from various parties regarding the Suite may I suggest that it is published without delay. Of course the orchestral and chorus parts must go into production immediately.[159]

The score which you recently sent us in order to arrange the suite is peppered with errors[160] and I fear too that the orchestral material is in the same condition unless you have material in manuscript. I recommend that the score undergo thorough revision according to the instructions of my young friend followed by the production of new material.

You will doubtlessly be aware of Sir Th. Beecham's plan to organise a large Delius Festival in London. Everything should now be held in a state of readiness as the Festival is due to open at the beginning of October. Please inform me directly how you mean to proceed and how much time will be required. Some further news – we have made an arrangement of the Serenade from Hassan (solo cello and small orchestra) especially for Miss Harrison; it should prove a most worthwhile piece and she intends to take it with her on her American tour which she is embarking upon with a small orchestra in late autumn.

With best wishes

ꕥꕥ

No 246

Delius to Tischer & Jagenberg

17 June 1929
Grez-sur-Loing

---

159 This Suite, for small orchestra and chorus, does not appear to have ever been issued. See also, however, FD to UE 16 July 1932, where mention is made of a similar arrangement by Sir Thomas Beecham.

160 UE replied on 29 May, asking for the *Hassan* suite and the cello arrangement of the Serenade and saying that they would take great care with the performing material.

Dear Doctor,

I received your letter of the 15th. In no case could I suggest or accept an outright payment. You have no idea how widespread in England, America or the Colonies, these modern organs are. Every good cinema has one and a good sale is to be had from them.[161]

For your sake as well as for mine it is better to have a percentage share. Lets try to arrange it so that I get 20 per cent and you 10 per cent of the selling price. In that way the OUP retains 70 per cent. For you the 10 per cent is clear profit for you have no expenses.

The translations of the songs will go off tomorrow.

In haste to catch the post.

Yours,

No 247

Jelka Delius to Universal

19 September 1929
Grez-sur-Loing

Herr Direktor

As you are probably aware the Delius Festival will be opening on 12 October. I would remind you it is in your own interest to ensure that Curwen has sufficient stocks of all UE Delius works, as well as the Haym analyses which have been translated into English. Please be certain that everything is arranged without delay. No expense will be spared by the promoters and there will certainly be vast amounts of sheet music sold.

Excellent gramophone recordings have been made of a number of the songs.

I do hope that you will be able to exploit the full promotional potential of the festival. It is somewhat seldom that such a large festival, comprising concerts by four large orchestras and choruses and chamber groups, is put together featuring a living composer.

We shall leave as soon as everything is organised. As you will see from the programme there will be a few new works in MS there.

With best wishes from my husband,

Respectfully yours,

J.D.

[161] Was this an organ arangement of the small pieces? There would have been PRS from cinema performances. OUP published an organ arrangement of no. 1 by Fenby in 1934.

PS At the same time as the festival a performance of Song of the High Hills will be given by another conductor.

ꟷꟷ

No 248

Universal to Jelka Delius

25 September 1929
Vienna

Dear Madam

You may take it for granted that I am fully aware of the Delius Festival beginning on 12 October and that I am looking forward to it with eagerness. We have been in constant contact with Curwen and have already offered and supplied to him sufficient material for every work. May we dare to hope that these concerts will usher in a period of bumper sales. It would be of great interest to us if you could provide a list of those works which exist on gramophone, especially the songs, as we have scant details of the song recordings. According to our files there are records of Brigg Fair, Sea Drift and the Cello Sonata. Poring over the programmes it whets the appetite to see that there will be new manuscript works at the festival and also that at the same time as the festival the Song of the High Hills will be performed by another conductor. Your gratifying news that you and Maestro Delius will probably travel to London for the Festival attests to the improved health of the Maestro and I assert with sincerity my ardent desire to meet with him again. As there is a fair chance that I shall be going to Paris in October I shall self-evidently grasp the opportunity and travel on to one of the concerts in London in order to see you both.

In the meantime may I extend to you and Maestro Delius my best wishes.
Respectfully yours

Hertzka[162]

No 249

Jelka Delius to Universal

2 October 1929
Grez-sur-Loing

Herr Direktor,

[162] It was rare for Hertzka, who was usually on holiday when FD wrote, to sign a letter.

I do hope that you will come to the Festival in London. God willing, we shall be setting off tomorrow and will stay at the Langham Hotel (opposite Queen's Hall).

The main gramophone records of your Delius works are:

Brigg Fair	)	
In a Summer Garden	)	Gramo
Sea Drift		Decca
Intermezzo 'Walk to the Paradise Garden'		Columbia
Cello Sonata		Gramo

In time for the Festival, Columbia will be releasing a quantity of songs, among them Irmelin, and also intends to record all the works that Beecham wishes to conduct.

There will of course be much to confer upon with regard to the new works; in addition Beecham has drawn up detailed plans for a complete edition.

I must unfortunately bring a premature close to this letter as there is still plenty to organise for the difficult journey ahead.

Respectfully yours

No 250

Universal to Jelka Delius

10 October 1929
Vienna

Dear Madam,

I am afraid that the chances of making it to London have become considerably slimmer. I may still have the good fortune of being present for the festival finale of A Mass of Life. I shall of course do everything in my power to bring this about.

Profoundest thanks for your advice concerning the works of Delius recorded on gramophone. I would be grateful of news of any other recordings as soon as you hear of them.[163] I was extremely interested to learn of Beecham's extensive plans for a complete edition of the works of Delius.

With best regards to you and Maestro Delius I remain

Respectfully yours

---

[163] UE had no mechanical rights.

ꝏ

No 251

Universal to Jelka Delius

30 October 1929
Vienna

Dear Madam

To my great regret my plans to come to Paris in October and then travel on to London unfortunately fell through due to the poor health I had been suffering from in the previous few weeks. This saddens me deeply as I sincerely wished to see Maestro Delius and yourself again and to attend at least a part of the Festival. To date I have been unable to brief myself on how the festival went off as the German press devoted no coverage to proceedings in London and unfortunately I have not seen an English paper for some weeks. I should be most grateful, Madam, if you would send me any spare newspaper reviews that you might have and furnish me with your personal impressions on the audience reaction and the performances. In any event we would like to include in our review journals a summation of the Festival prepared by an authoritative source. Perhaps you could yourself recommend somebody who might be willing to undertake a report of this nature.

May I extend to you my warmest thanks in advance for your cooperation and with best wishes to you both I remain

Respectfully yours

ꝏ

No 252

Delius to Universal

5 December 1929
Grez-sur-Loing

Dear Sir

In response to your two cards of the 28 November may I request that you kindly inform me whether you now propose to publish the Suite for orchestra and choir from Hassan which is now complete. Should this be the case I could send it to you along with the old score which has undergone thorough correction and is now free of error. RSVP.

With regard to the payments made by Curwen in respect of the Five Piano Pieces may I suggest that you send Curwen's statements to me at the above address.

Furthermore I today received a letter from the Glasgow Orchestral and Choral Union. They intend to perform the Intermezzo from A Village Romeo and Juliet but are unable to obtain the material.

I have written telling them to contact you.

I should like to enquire whether you are hiring the Keith Douglas version for performance and also whether Curwen has orchestral material at his disposal.

Clearly this concert piece which has proved so popular should be published as an offprint from the opera.

I would gladly volunteer to do the proofreading myself.

That aside I should be most grateful if you would supply the material to the Glasgow Concert Society without delay.

May I take this opportunity to re-emphasise that no new editions are to appear without my foreknowledge as with every new edition I wish to include all the amendments, dynamic changes and metronome marks annotated since the publication of the previous edition. I am thinking here of the painstaking corrections by Sir Thomas Beecham.

With best wishes to Herr Dir. Hertzka

Yours respectfully

No 253

Universal to Delius

17 December 1929
Vienna

Maestro Delius,

We gratefully acknowledge receipt of your letter of 5 December and take careful note that you have now completed the Suite for orchestra and choir from Hassan. It would of course be our pleasure to publish the work; however we would firstly like to discuss a preponderating question that has been troubling us for some time.

As you may be aware the growth in mechanical media, by which I mean radio broadcasts, gramophone recordings and not least motion pictures, that we have witnessed over the past one or two years has caused sales to plummet in the printed music sector. For this reason publishers like composers have increasingly come to depend upon the income from the so-called small rights without which the future for all publishers would look extremely bleak. We have now concluded agreements with our numerous composers to the effect that we shall in future receive the normal publisher's share in respect of small rights; it is only your works where no provision exists for the publisher to participate in mechanical income. Were we still living in a time when sheet music sales enjoyed a bull market we would not attribute such importance to small rights and we probably would not feel the need to raise this question. In the present climate, however, we believe that even you will acknowledge our rightful claim in this respect and we therefore beg leave to ask that you assign to us your mechanical rights in which case AUME or its sister societies abroad (Edifo, Mecolico) will distribute the normal composer share. Alternatively, may we at least ask that you agree to allow the collecting societies to account the publisher's share directly to us. We do hope that you are suitably disposed to reach some accord with us in this matter.

As far as our remittance in respect of the Five Piano Pieces is concerned, the sum of 3/3/0d. paid to you refers to the 84 copies (@ 9d each) invoiced to Curwen.[164]

We have placed in the diary the performance of your Intermezzo from Romeo and Juliet by the Glasgow Orchestral and Choral Union on 21 January and we shall ensure that the material is delivered in good time. Regarding the printing of the Intermezzo please note that the afore-mentioned applies equally in this instance.

Your wish to be forewarned of new editions of your works to allow for possible corrections has been duly noted. We think it would be simplest if you gradually send us copies of all corrections as they occur; then we can transfer all the corrections on to the plates, irrespective of any plans to reprint the work, which will guarantee that no changes or corrections are ever overlooked.

In anticipation of your news, we remain

---

[164] Under the contract for the 5 pieces, Curwen was to account directly on UK sales. Nevertheless this seems the correct royalty.

1930–1934

1930

Although often in pain, Delius was still able to compose, with Eric Fenby's help, and in June wrote to Universal offering the company *Cynara*, *A Late Lark*, and *Air and Dance*. Universal appear to have rejected them, as all three were published by Boosey & Hawkes. *Songs of Farewell* and the *Caprice and Elegy* for cello and chamber orchestra were completed with the help of Eric Fenby, who left in October and recorded the *Caprice and Elegy* with Beatrice Harrison. The Fenby works, which could not have been finished without his help, had all been sketched, albeit briefly, by Delius.

For her part Jelka Delius, whom Oskar Klemperer found 'overwhelmed by her responsibilities' continued to write detailed letters in search of royalties and clarification. In June she remonstrates with PRS over payment in General Distribution 14 of only £56-9s-5d, received in June 1930 and covering general fees received by PRS in the year ended 5 January 1930. Surely the 1929 Festival must have produced more? A PRS margin note shows that the concerts at the Queen's and Aeolian Halls produced £9-9s-6d for four concerts, although broadcast fees would be distributed later. PRS had previously made two distributions in respect of fees received in 1929, giving a total of £275-15s-8d, from which income tax of £56-19s-7d had been deducted at source, perhaps because Delius was a British subject living in France, leaving £218-16s-1d. This compared with £83-7s-1d net in respect of 1928 activity, received in 1929. The deduction of tax at source seems only to have started in 1930.

Elgar received £295 from PRS in 1930, bearing in mind that Novello were not members, Frank Bridge £168, Gustav Holst £119 and Arnold Ketèlby £1630.[1]

In August Delius finally agreed to give Universal a 20 per cent share of mechanicals from Germany, Austria, Czechoslovakia and Switzerland, but not Great Britain or the Empire. Were the Leuckart works excluded? The agreement seems to have been incorrectly registered with MCPS, resulting in apologies. It also transpired that Universal had written their share of mechanicals into the contract at 25 per cent. The Trust does not have a copy of the subsequent agreement, so we do not know whether the 20 per cent was payable on sales of records in the countries concerned, or records pressed there, although from Universal's letter to Delius of 15 June 1931, it seems likely that Universal were entitled to mechanical royalties on pressings in their territories. Before the coming of the European Economic Community this was an important contractual point.

PRS dealt with Tischer & Jagenberg's claim to performing fees on the Delius works licensed to OUP, which did not join PRS until 1936. The publisher's share

---

1 *Harmonious Alliance, A History of the Performing Right Society* by Cyril Ehrlich. Published OUP 1989.

would be passed back to GDT, which still existed within GEMA, and of which Tischer & Jagenberg was a member.

ꙮꙮ

No 254

The Performing Right Society to Oxford University Press

13 March 1930
London

Dear Sirs,

We beg to acknowledge receipt of your letter of yesterday's date and hope to be in a position to reply to your letter of the 13th ultimo in a short time.

The matter is one upon which it is necessary that we should have the views of the Genossenschaft Deutscher Tonsetzer, of which Messrs Tischer & Jagenberg,[2] are members, for the position as it presents itself to us at the moment is as follows:-

The collection of any performing right fees in respect of works published by the firm in question is entrusted to our Society by virtue of a contract of affiliation which we have with the GDT, and such being the case that firm is not at liberty to seek to obtain such fees through any other channel. As a matter of fact, we understand that the performing rights in the works remain vested in the composer, Mr Frederick Delius, who is a member of our Society, and under the circumstances it is only by virtue of their membership of the GDT that Messrs Tischer & Jagenberg are entitled to any share of the performing right fees collected. We will, however, communicate further with you on the matter as soon as we are in a position to do so.

Yours faithfully,

Secretary

---

[2] OUP did not join PRS until 1936. It appears from the correspondence re the Tischer & Jagenberg Delius works that either they didn't want to charge performing fees, or that they wanted to handle them themselves. See PRS to BBC 25 March 1931.

ꕥꕥ

No 255

Universal to Delius

17 March 1930.
Vienna

Maestro Delius,

The firm of Curwen has forwarded an enquiry to us from the London music journal Music and Youth which is seeking a licence to reprint the second of your Five Piano Pieces. This piece is to be assessed by the pianist Harriet Cohen for its teaching value in a manner similar to the recent review of a Bach sonata. Curwen is confident that in promotional terms exposure of this kind can only be beneficial. We indicated that permission would only be granted on condition that a full-page advertisement of your works appeared free of charge in the respective edition whereupon we received the enclosed response from Curwen. We would not wish to give approval without first consulting you and we would request therefore that you indicate by return post whether you are agreeable to the reprint of said work in Music and Youth. We share Curwen's belief that a rich promotional opportunity lies before us and we would therefore recommend that you yield assent.

In anticipation of your earliest consideration we remain

ꕥꕥ

No 256

The Performing Right Society to Oxford University Press

24 April 1930
London

Dear Sirs,

Further to our letter of the 13th ult. We have now inspected copies of the agreements between our member, Mr Frederick Delius, and Messrs Tischer & Jagenberg.[3] These are dated 10th September 1910, 24th June 1912, and 9th December 1913, and it is clear from all of them that the composer did not assign to the publisher the public performing right in any of the works which are the subject of the agreements, as set out in the lists accompanying your letter to us of the 13th February last. That right is, in fact, expressly reserved in all the contracts.

We have also received a call from one of the officials of the Genossenschaft Deutscher Tonsetzer, of which Tischer & Jagenberg are members, and he confirms, as we anticipated, that they are not at liberty to collect fees in respect of broadcast or

---

[3] PRS had asked FD to send them.

other public performances of the works, so far as British territory is concerned, that is a matter for our Society, and, as mentioned to you in our letter of the 13th ult., it is only by virtue of their membership of the Genossenschaft Deutscher Tonsetzer that Messrs Tischer & Jagenberg are entitled to any of the fees which we may collect. If they were not members, the whole fees would be payable to the composer, from whom our Society derives its title to the performing right in the works.

A similar question has arisen with regard to the works of Kodaly, published by the Universal Edition A.G., of Vienna, who are members of the Gesellschaft der Autoren, Komponisten und Musikverleger (A.K.M)., with whom we have a contract of affiliation. We are informed by the Austrian Society that the Universal Edition A.G., have appointed you their Agents for the sale of these works in this country, but have not assigned any performing right in the works to you. Under these circumstances, the collection of broadcasting or performing right fees in respect thereof is again a matter for our Society to deal with, such fees being accounted for in this instance to the Austrian Society, of which both the publisher and composer are members.

Yours faithfully

General Manager

No 257

Delius to Universal

5 June 1930
Grez-sur-Loing

Dear Sir

I received the enclosed letter yesterday from a friend in Paris. You will see from it that he has been negotiating with the conductor Alb Wolff to obtain performances of my works in Paris.

With relations the way they are in Paris it would be best if you follow his instructions to the letter and send Herr Wolff the scores along with details of the hire fees. Please send Brigg Fair and Sea Drift and tell me when you have done so, so that I can then write to him.

On another subject I should like to inform you that I now have several new works ready for publication in which you might possibly be interested. They are: -
Cynara – baritone & orchestra (short work)
A Late Lark – tenor and orchestra (equally short)
Air and Dance – for small string orchestra
These three works were premiered at the Delius Festival.
Furthermore I have
A Song of Summer (Ein Sommerlied) – short orchestral work, brand-new and a Sonata for violin and piano (duration: 16 mins)

The translation of Cynara is a particularly natural, eminently singable one and indeed without music it still reads like an original piece of poetry.

A Late Lark (Eine spaete Lerche) is presently being translated into German. Air and Dance should prove a particularly popular short work and be well loved. If you have any interest in these works I would be delighted to send them to you for your perusal.

With best wishes to Herr Dir. Hertzka who I hope is enjoying the best of health.

Yours respectfully

F.D.

PS May I kindly request that you return the enclosed letter.

No 258

Universal to Delius

12 June 1930
Vienna

Maestro,

May we extend to you our profoundest thanks for your kind letter of 5 June and express our delight at the announcement that Monsieur Albert Wolff will be performing your works in Paris. In accordance with your wishes we have dispatched to him complimentary copies of
Sea Drift
Brigg Fair
and informed him of the hire fees.[4] Moreover we have made it known to him that we would be happy to sell the works.

In the same degree may we also acknowledge kind receipt of the news concerning your new works which has provoked tremendous excitement. We should be grateful if you would in the meantime please forward the MS for our perusal.

Herr Direktor Hertzka is presently away on vacation and we shall forward your best wishes to him as soon as he returns.

Please find enclosed Herr ....'s [friend in Paris] returned letter.

Respectfully yours

---

[4] FD wrote back to UE on 29 June 1930 asking them to let M. Wolff have the sale price of the orchestral material. He felt that French orchestras would require a substantial discount on the purchase price, or to have the material free.

On 10 July UE replied that they had informed M. Wolff that they would sell the *Brigg Fair* material for FF800, and supply *Sea Drift* gratis. Presumably this would have included the chorus material?

No 259

Delius to The Performing Right Society

21 June 1930
Grez-sur-Loing

Dear Sir,[5]

I have just received my annual distribution cheque and I must tell you that in view of the numerous performances of my works in the year in question this sum of £56-9-5d seems absolutely inadequate.[6]

If one only takes the Delius Festival, composed of six large concerts composed entirely of my music and all of them with especially long programmes this is only too evident.[7]

I therefore beg you kindly to send me a detailed account of that so that I can judge whether any mistakes or omissions have been made.

Have you now been collecting my American fees and are they also on this account?[8]

You must realise that I have been a staunch defender of your Society, but I should like to be fairly dealt with.

Awaiting a prompt reply,

I am yours truly,

---

5 PRS note states 'total fees last year £15 11s 3d. Re General Distribution No 14'.

6 PRS margin note. 'includes £35 special allocation, increased from £10'.

7 PRS margin note. 'Aeolian & Queens £9-9-6d for 4 festival concerts. Two others were broadcast and were therefore not charged for.' Presumably there would have been a separate broadcasting fee. Nowadays there would have been two performing fees, one for the concert and another for the broadcast, as well as a mechanical fee if the programme was recorded in order to be broadcast later.

8 PRS margin note. 'No, and it is improbable that ASCAP will collect on his works'.

No 260

The Performing Right Society to Delius

26 June 1930
London

Dear Sir,

re General Distribution No. 14.

I beg to acknowledge receipt of your letter of the 21st instant, and note what you say with regard to the amount of the warrant issued to you in respect of the above distribution. I find that you have been duly credited with all recorded performances of your works during the period in question, and may observe in passing that the amount represents a substantial increase over your fees for the previous year.

Possibly your observations are the result of an impression that the scale of fees charged by the Society is higher than is actually the case, and your acquaintance with the operations of Continental Societies may perhaps have confirmed this impression. Actually, however, the amounts which the Society collects are on a modest scale, its tariffs, generally speaking, being considerably lower than those of similar Societies abroad.

As an example, we may say that the total fees collected by the Society in respect of four of the six Festival Concerts at the Queen's. Hall and Aeolian Hall in October and November last, when your works were performed, amounted to £9.9.6d. The remaining two concerts of the series were broadcast, and are therefore subject to our agreement with the British Broadcasting Corporation, the fees in respect thereof having been included in the amount of the warrant sent to you at the Broadcasting Distribution in April last. It is not practicable to issue detailed statements for general fees allocated to members, but you will have seen the statement which accompanied your Warrant for broadcasting fees. It is possible to furnish statements in respect of the latter as the system of collection and distribution is different from that which applies in the case of general fees.

In comparing the fees collected by our Society with those collected by similar Societies abroad, it has to be borne in mind that the principle of performing right has only been introduced in this country in comparatively recent times and not as is the case of France for example, something like 80 years ago. You yourself have seen something of the recent attacks upon the Society under the guise of the Musical Copyright Bill, for we have not failed to note that you added your voice in support of the Society and in condemnation of that measure and we take the opportunity of expressing our appreciation of your action in the matter.

The point we desire to emphasise is that the modest fees at present charged by the Society have been referred to as 'extortionate', and a great deal of insidious propaganda has been carried on by the wealthy music users of this country under cover of which this allegation was frequently made. Whilst there is, of course, no truth in these assertions, it indicates that the Society's task of educating public opinion in the matter of performing rights is by no means light.

As already stated, the amount of fees credited to you has been correctly allocated in accordance with the Society's Rules and you may rest assured therefore that you have been 'fairly dealt with'. With regard to America, you will have noted from the January 1930 issue of the PR Gazette that this Society's agreement with the American Society came into operation on 1st January last, and as the general distribution recently made is in respect of the year ended 5th January last, it does not include fees from America. It will of course be some months yet before we receive any fees from that source.

Yours faithfully,
Secretary

No 261

Delius to Universal

14 July 1930
Grez-sur-Loing

Dear Sir

Before I respond to your letter of 30 June which I did not receive until a few days ago may I first turn your attention to the matter of motion picture rights and what you understand by them. Are compositions to be used in a motion picture in their present state or do you propose to arrange them for reduced forces etc? I would not grant permission for this. R.S.V.P.; can you also explain to me the relationship of gramophone records to motion pictures?[9]

I should like to respond to your letter of 10 July[10] by sending you a photograph taken in London. You may not however publish this without obtaining the approval of the copyright holder. Unfortunately there are otherwise no new usable photographs, only small yet good amateur ones taken in the open air. Could you possibly make use of these?

As regards Herr Alb. Wolff, may I express my delight that you have supplied the material to him so smoothly and speedily.

On another matter may I enquire to what degree you had considered participating in the royalties accruing from gramophone sales of my works. It is not beyond the realm of fantasy that I would grant you a certain percentage but only if I were guaranteed that recordings of my works would be made in Germany or Vienna.[11]

---

9 If UE did not have mechanical rights, they did not have film synchronisation rights.

10 We do not have the photos.

11 FD was ready to drive a hard bargain and give rights only if Universal would actively get recordings in Germany and Austria. Elgar took the same view with Hawkes & Co.

In reference to the publication of my new works, I can only send them to Vienna if you can pinpoint exactly when you will check through them. In any event I do not want them left abandoned in Vienna over the summer holidays.

With my best wishes to Herr Dir. Hertzka

Yours respectfully
F.D.

PS I must insist that the Hassan Serenade for small orchestra and cello be published without delay bearing in mind the monumental success Miss Harrison has enjoyed playing this MS work on her American tour which in turn has stirred up much demand. I could send you this immediately.

No 262

Universal to Delius

21 July 1930
Vienna

Maestro Delius,

We gratefully acknowledge receipt of your letter of 14 July and should like to respond as follows.

As we understand it 'motion picture rights' should be defined as the incorporation of a synchronised musical accompaniment within motion picture production in a manner similar to the role live music has played to date in the accompaniment of silent films. One may take it for granted that any music synchronisation will entail some arrangement or alterations to suit the designs of the production. There are two main technical processes that exist within the field of motion picture production, namely the 'sound-on-disc' (or disc-sychronisation) process and the 'sound-on-film' system. With the 'sound-on-disc' process the complete film soundtrack is recorded on to gramophone which is played back in time (synchronised) with the relevant frames. These gramophone recordings serve only the cinematographic process and are not destined for general release. Correspondingly the usual licence fees are not remittable on these recordings as synchronisation fees are charged to the film's producers.[12] The afore-mentioned synchronisation fee is calculated according to either the duration of music used or else against tariffs which vary from country to

---

12 'Usual licence fees' refers to the royalties on retail sales. In the UK, the compulsory licensing procedure on records made for retail sale did not apply to recordings made for films. Retail licensing procedures in continental Europe, where there was no compulsory licence, would also not have applied to films.

Synchronisation fees were a one-off fee to license a producer to add music to a sound track, the level of the fee being related to the type of exposure, i.e. films for general release or films to be shown to clubs. It would be usual to specify the number of copies to be made.

country. In the case of the 'sound-on-film' process the film soundtrack is dubbed on to a sequence of shots and when played back the pictures and sound are reproduced simultaneously (the latter by means of complex apparatus involving loudspeakers).

Please accept our most heartfelt thanks for the photograph taken in London which you sent us. If we should publish this we will secure permission to do so. We would in any event be most obliged if you would send us the amateur shots.

With regard to our participation in the distribution of mechanical rights we shall do everything within our power to bring about recordings of your works in Germany and Austria. However we can offer no guarantees as decisions of this nature do not fall within our jurisdiction but are exclusively the prerogative of the recording companies and conductors. We remain convinced that no other publisher, despite every last one of them participating in mechanical rights, could give a composer such guarantees and we would be most obliged if you could modify your present stance in line with current practice.

As far as your new compositions are concerned, it would in fact be better if they were not sent to Vienna at this stage as a large proportion of our employees are on vacation. We shall look forward with much pleasure to receiving the manuscripts during the month of September. However we would be grateful if you could kindly send the Hassan Serenade.

Respectfully yours

No 263

Universal to Delius

31 July 1930
Vienna

Maestro,

We gratefully acknowledge receipt of the Fenby arrangement of the Hassan Serenade. We are prepared to print the reduction for piano and solo cello immediately on condition that Mr Fenby gives up any claim to royalties in respect of his arrangement.[13] We would ask you please to furnish us with confirmation of this whereupon we shall proceed with the printing.

Respectfully yours

[13] Music publishers do not normally allow an arranger of a piece of their copyright music a share of royalties. However, once the original work is in the public domain, now 70 years after the composer's death, the arranger or his estate may be able to claim copyright royalties on his arrangement for the balance of the arranger's copyright period. FD confirmed to Universal on 4 August that no royalties would be payable to Fenby, but asked if Fenby could be sent a couple of Strauss's scores.

No 264

Delius to Universal

21 August 1930
Grez-sur-Loing

Dear Sir

I have just completed my corrections to the performance scores of A Mass of Life and the Songs of Sunset and inserted the dynamic marks annotated by Sir Thomas Beecham. I would suggest that these corrections be incorporated into the copies that you have there. To this end I could either lend you my copy for a short time or you could send copies of each to me in Grez-sur-Loing so that we can carry out the remarking and correction work here.

The same applies to Appalachia and Arabesque to which we shall be turning our attention in the course of next week.

We seem to be lacking any orchestral scores of both the Piano Concerto and the Cello Concerto. As I am frequently bombarded with questions concerning the ambiguities in both scores – indeed I received one only today about the Piano Concerto – may I request that you please send me copies by return.

If you wish to borrow my scores I must insist that you return them as quickly as possible as I do often need them for reference.

Further to our earlier correspondence and in view of your present commercial malaise I should like to grant you a 20 per cent (twenty per cent) share of income derived from the mechanical exploitation of my UE works for the territories of Germany, Austria, Czechoslovakia and Switzerland. Please send me a contract in this respect.

With best wishes to Herr Dir. Hertzka

Yours respectfully

No 265

Delius to Universal

2 September 1930
Grez-sur-Loing

Dear Sir,

The copy of A Mass of Life sent to us in order to insert the corrections and dynamic markings has been tampered with – by whom I do not know, but the alterations as I read them are for the most part quite incorrect and do not correspond to my original score. It would simplify matters greatly for my colleague if he could incorporate his handwritten amendments into a printed copy. Could you please send one by return?

From the enclosed examples[14] you will be able to see for yourselves what form the alterations take. Who would have done this? And for what reason?

How could one for example remove completely two bars of the baritone solo?

There are other examples too where notes have been shortened and pauses introduced upsetting the flow of the music which have not been approved by me.

These copies are not legitimate and are never to be issued for performance.

I should be grateful if you would provide some explanation of what has occurred here; please also forward one clean copy.

Yours faithfully

No 266

Universal to Delius

5 September 1930
Vienna

Maestro,

Thank you for your letter of 2 September.

We have enclosed one clean copy of A Mass of Life into which we would ask you to insert your corrections. Without viewing the copy that was sent to you it will not be possible to determine whose amendments it contains but we would hazard a guess that what we are dealing with here are corrections that have been pencilled in by a conductor for a performance. However we can assure you they have not found their way into other copies.
We remain

Respectfully yours

---

14 The 'enclosed examples' are in Fenby's hand, annotated by JD, and are as follows:

(1) Cellos and basses on p. 26 & horns on p. 27. The added rests in place of sustained notes were specifically called for in the list of corrections later issued by Harmonie (but by now overlooked evidently by FD – or by Fenby, reading the score for him).

(2) 2nd chorus sopranos on p. 42. Similar breathing rests were not in the correction list, and therefore were a conductor (or chorus master)'s practical insertion.

(3) The [three] bars of the baritone solo part evidently deleted on p. 65 had been criticised by Hans Haym in a letter to FD of 16 June 1909 as 'meaningless as they stand': hence they were omitted, presumably on FD's authority, from the later UE vocal score (again evidently overlooked by FD or EF).

ꕥ

No 267

Delius to Universal

2 October 1930
Grez-sur-Loing

URGENT! URGENT!

Dear Sir

We received the enclosed letter today from our friend in Paris who as you know has been acting as an intermediary in the discussions with Abi Wolff. I leave it to you to act according to your best judgment. All I ask is that the matter be resolved as soon as possible.

I also enclose the signed agreement with respect to mechanical rights.

In reference to my questions regarding motion picture rights, am I to understand from your letter that you would have every entitlement to arrange my music in whatever form you wished for the purpose of film sychronisation? This I would never permit.[15] I would only consent to my works being exploited in this way as they exist now. Any changes or reductions might be approved in special circumstances but I give no guarantees and I reserve absolutely my right to personal consultation. Were you to send me documentation to this effect I would be willing to place my signature thereupon, otherwise I would rather let the whole matter drop.

With my best regards to Herr Dir. Hertzka

Yours respectfully
F.D.

PS The half-yearly statement due on 1 July has not yet arrived.

---

[15] Under the terms of the compulsory licence on records for retail sale, the record companies were able to alter or abbreviate works published before 1912. This did not apply to film synchronisation.

As Universal did not hold synchronisation rights on his works, FD would have referred requests to MCPS, which had formed a separate company, The Sound Film Bureau, which existed until the 1990s, to handle synchronisation licences.

No 268

Delius to The Performing Right Society

23 October 1930
Grez-sur-Loing

Dear Sir,

I have duly received the distribution warrant of my Broadcasting fees for the 6 months ending 30.6 of this year, together with the Irish Broadcasting fees for 1929.

In the latter there are several obvious mistakes in fees. For my Double Concerto, a piece playing 30 minutes only 1/6d is allotted, for Seadrift 4/- (this also plays 30–35minutes). Summer night on the River (8 mins – 3/-). Kindly go into this and readjust.

The pieces you marked are all by myself, some go by different names and I have written all the explanations on a separate sheet. I also enclose a list of my new manuscript works, in case they are not on your lists already.

I further mention that all the works published by Tischer and Jagenberg have been purchased from them by the Oxford University Press. As soon as arrangements with me are completed I will advise you of it.

Then there are my USA and Dominions fees. Numerous pieces have been played on tour there last winter and will be played this coming season. Some of my large choral works have been given lately. Seadrift, orchestral works: Brigg Fair etc.

There are also the German and Austrian and Dutch broadcasting fees. Quite a number of important performances of long works for orchestra have taken place. How are you going to account for these.

I could, if you wish it, send you lists of a few of these performances which have come to my knowledge. Performances have also taken place in Holland etc. But up to now you have not informed me of any practical results.

Thanking you in anticipation for an early reply.

Yours truly

ꕥ

No 269

Delius to Universal

3 November 1930
Grez-sur-Loing

Dear Sir

I today received a letter from the Mechanical Copyright Protection Society of which I am a member. This society informed me to my astonishment that you are claiming 20 per cent of the income derived from my works in England.

I cannot understand how such an error has occurred. Our agreement states quite plainly that I am granting you 20 per cent for Germany, Austria, Czechoslovakia and Switzerland only.

Whether this misunderstanding stems from GEMA[16] or G.D.T. I do not know. I must insist however that you cancel your claim immediately and also inform the MCPS of our exact agreement. I look forward to receiving by return your confirmation of what action has been taken.

Yours faithfully

ꕥ

No 270

Universal to Delius

6 November 1930
Vienna

Maestro Delius,

We acknowledge receipt of your letter of 2 October and beg leave to inform you that we have offered to supply Brigg Fair to M. Albert Wolff against payment of a hire fee in the amount of FFR 350.00 or the purchase price of FFR 800.00. These are prices which are perfectly reasonable for France. Bearing in mind the promotional opportunity that this concert in France represents we are willing nevertheless to make a special concession and reduce the cost of purchase to a nominal fee of FFR 400.00.

We extend our warmest thanks to you for receipt of the agreement in respect of mechanical rights and we enclose herewith your personal copy. We have noted your remarks concerning motion picture rights and enclose herewith an amended agreement to reflect your wishes. It is probable that your strict stipulation pertaining to the synchronised usage of your works in their original version only will severely

16 FD means AMMRE. The Anstalt für mechanisch-musikalische Rechte GmbH.

limit licences of this type. We however respect your viewpoint and if you could return to us the agreement signed we will ensure that any applications will be subject to the stipulations as laid down by you.

We beg you please to accept our sincerest apologies for the late arrival of your statement. Our accounts department that prepares the statements has been hit by lengthy illness as a result of which we now have a backlog of statements. However you should have received by now both your statement and all monies owing.

Respectfully yours

ꕥ

No 271

Universal to Delius

11 November 1930
Vienna

Maestro Delius,

We acknowledge receipt of your letter of 3 instant and beg leave to pass to you a copy of our complaint lodged with AMMRE which makes clear our bewilderment at MECOLICO's actions since we notified our interest quite correctly with AMMRE. We are working on the assumption that some sort of misunderstanding has occurred, either at AMMRE or MECOLICO. We shall keep you abreast of all developments. Meanwhile we remain

Yours respectfully

ꕥ

No 272

AMMRE to MCPS

15 November 1930
Berlin

Dear Sirs

Ref. DELIUS

The firm of Universal Edition (Wien) A.G. has today presented us with a copy of a letter received from Mr Frederick Delius in which it emerges that you wrote to

Mr Delius to the effect that Universal Edition were claiming 20 per cent of monies accounted in respect of his compositions.[17]

We should draw your attention to our letter of 9 October in which we enclosed a copy of a letter sent to us by Universal Edition. This states that Universal Edition are claiming a 20 per cent interest in all income for the territories of Germany, Austria, Czechoslovakia and Switzerland. The territory of England is not under discussion. We would kindly request that you clarify this error with Mr Delius and remain

Respectfully yours

No 273

The Performing Right Society to Delius

20 November 1930
London

Dear Sir,

We are in receipt of your letter of the 23rd ultimo,[18] and have now had an opportunity of investigating the errors referred to, which have arisen partly owing to incomplete details on the programmes received from the Irish Broadcasting Stations. We will make the necessary adjustments at the next distribution of broadcasting fees.

You will of course be aware that the scale of fees applicable to broadcasting performances from the two stations in the Irish Free State is lower than that applicable to the stations operated by the British Broadcasting Corporation.

We note that the works published by Tischer & Jagenberg are about to be purchased by the Oxford University Press, and that you will advise us when this transfer takes place. We understand that the Oxford University Press would only acquire a licence to print and publish the Tischer & Jagenberg publications, and that you have retained ownership of the performing rights therein. Will you kindly confirm this?

With regard to the performances of your works in the Dominions and foreign countries, the fees for these are included in the General performing fees, for which a separate warrant is sent to you about June each year, when the distribution of general fees takes place, but it would facilitate us if you will, as you suggest, advise us of any of these performances, in order that we may check returns from the foreign Society which accounts to us for that particular territory.

Yours faithfully,
Secretary

---

[17] A genuine error by MCPS, put right before any mechanical royalties were incorrectly claimed.

[18] A fairly quick response.

ꕥꕥ

No 274

Delius to Universal

4 December 1930
Grez-sur-Loing

Dear Sir

Enclosed I return to you the assignment in respect of the Nietzsche-Lieder.[19] It is on the whole satisfactory however I did feel compelled to strike through a number of clauses.

Of course I cannot accept any responsibility for the policies of some of these societies.[20] As a large company you are much better equipped to intervene in the protection of your rights. Furthermore no alterations etc. etc. to my works may be undertaken in the absence of my granting consent; by the same token I have excluded the passage relating to albums and anthologies. Also your specification of mechanical rights is badly worded; on this subject please bear in mind that I have only granted you a 20 per cent consideration, not 25 per cent. I am at a loss to understand the closing passage relating to copyright. I shall willingly entertain an application of this nature but only at my convenience. I myself cannot attend to this matter alone.

I do hope that we can reach some accommodation on the matters I have raised and in this vein I look forward to receiving an amended agreement.

On looking through your statements it has suddenly struck me that no monies at all have been paid in respect of miniature scores. Did you simply forget or can I look forward to receiving some explanation? Also I would like to request that all future statements show detailed figures of sheet music sales in England for every work. Please do not omit to do this in your January statement.

Yours faithfully
F.D.

Can you please send me a price list of Wagner and Brahms scores in addition to the 2-handed and 4-handed piano compositions by Schumann and Grieg as I have them in mind for Christmas presents. Do not delay therefore.

---

19 UE had written on 28 November to say that they did not have an assignment for the Nietzsche-Lieder.

20 This paragraph refers to the agreement on mechanical rights, of which the Delius Trust does not have a copy.

ꙮ

No 275

Universal to Delius

13 December 1930
Vienna

Maestro Delius,

We acknowledge receipt of your letter of 4 December and confirm that we have dispatched to you by return post the requested Wagner and Bruckner price lists.

In line with your wishes we have amended the work assignment in respect of the Nietzsche Lieder and have pleasure in enclosing the copies herewith. May we request that you please sign and return them to our Vienna office. We do not believe that you should have any cause for concern arising from the term 'copyright renewal', for it states in the contract that a copyright renewal petition should only be signed by the composer 'at the invitation' of Universal Edition.

In reference to your query regarding miniature scores, we regret that in fact an error has occurred on the part of our accounts department. Their files erroneously indicate that this work is to be accounted through Curwen.

We beg you please to forgive any inconvenience and accept our assurance that we have not delayed in rectifying the situation. All monies will be paid in the December statement.

We shall gladly accommodate your request to provide itemised lists of all English transactions on your future statements.

Yours respectfully

1931

While Delius remained in reasonable health, Jelka was not well and feeling the strain of looking after Delius. Fenby was also unwell, and stayed in England where he was able to correct the proofs of the three works to be published by Hawkes. The *Irmelin Prelude* and the *Fantastic Dance* were completed; *A Song of Summer* had its first performance, at the Proms on 17 September.

There continued some confusion over Tischer & Jagenberg, with the BBC unsure as to whether it could broadcast the Delius works, without permission from OUP. PRS assured the BBC that Tischer & Jagenberg were members of GDT, with which PRS had an agreement, so the Delius works came within the PRS repertoire.

In June comes an incident that the editors cannot explain. Universal wrote to Delius saying that it was claiming mechanical rights in Great Britain on *Brigg Fair*, through what appears to be a German small-claims Court. Was this perhaps on records of *Brigg Fair* pressed in Germany and exported to Great Britain? Universal proposed to charge Delius with a share of the costs and hoped for a share of any resulting income. *Brigg Fair* was of course a Leuckart work, and Delius had not granted a share on the Leuckart works. As he writes on 20 June, he believed that Universal had no claim to mechanicals on the work.

There is correspondence with PRS on the problems caused by the incorrect reporting of titles, which PRS try to address. Then, in October 1931, PRS write to point out that, under its rules, it does not control choral & orchestral works lasting more than 20 minutes. PRS listed the works outside their control, which Jelka queried. *Appalachia* was first deemed a choral work, and then given into PRS control. The works controlled from 1 October by Cranz, as Universal's UK agent, were, *A Mass of Life*, *Sea Drift*, *Requiem* and *Songs of Sunset*. This issue is covered in detail in the introduction to the book.

No 276

Jelka Delius to Universal

7 March 1931
Grez-sur-Loing

Dear Sir,

Tomorrow, 8 March, the Paris performance of Brigg Fair was to take place at the Lamoureux. We have just received the enclosed telegramme from which it transpires that the conductor Albert Wolff has either misplaced or lost the material and consequently the performance will be unable to go ahead. As you can read for yourself he would like to reorder new material and have the concert take place on 21 March.

In view of the fact that our friend has already begun mobilising the Anglo-French press and the Embassy etc. this postponement at the last minute could of course have disastrous repercussions. My husband therefore begs you please to act as you think best. He has understandably become indignant about the whole affair and would rather not embroil himself any further. Our friend, Mr Klemperer in Paris, has gone to the greatest trouble even to the point of penning a short programme note for the concert with me.

A few days ago we received the Hassan Serenade for cello and piano for which we are deeply grateful. In all quarters expectations are feverish that publication will follow shortly of the same piece arranged for small orchestra.

I have enclosed a page from the score of Sea Drift which contains an error. My husband would like it included in the corrections.

Sea Drift was performed last week in Huddersfield and on Thursday there will be a broadcast on Midland Regional Radio. Brigg Fair is also featuring regularly in concert programmes.

With my very best wishes to Herr Direktor Hertzka

Yours faithfully

ജ്ജ

No 277

Delius to Universal

14 March 1931
Grez-sur-Loing

Dear Sir

Unfortunately I seldom receive programmes. Mostly I learn of performances through press cuttings and the Radio Times. I enclose herewith a list of performances for 1931 which have come to my attention although I cannot dare to boast that it is comprehensive.[21] I rarely hear about performances in Germany and its neighbouring countries.

It is indeed most generous of you to send another set of material to Mr Wolff; we will wait to see what he does.

Mr Eric Fenby would very much like to acquire miniature scores to Sea Drift, Appalachia and Summer Garden and I should be grateful if you would send them to his address at

12 Mayville Avenue
Scarborough, Yorks.
ENGLAND

I hope that these can be supplied free of charge bearing in mind all the work he has carried out for you. If any charges are to be made he is not to be invoiced. I myself will take care of any payments.

As far as my statement is concerned there are no entries accounting for miniature scores which as you advised me in writing were due to be made in the statement to December 1930. Amongst others you must have supplied considerable quantities to Curwen in London and to the U.S.A. Kindly send me an update.

With very best wishes to Herr Direktor Hertzka.

Yours faithfully

ജ്ജ

No 278

Universal to Delius

20 March 1931
Vienna

Dear Sir

21 This has not survived.

May we extend our profoundest gratitude to you for sending us the list of performances that have taken place this year. Your communications are extremely valuable and we would ask that you please keep us abreast of all future performances insofar as you are aware of them.

In accordance with your wishes we shall be sending the requested miniature scores to Mr Eric Fenby free of charge.

Your statement in respect of miniature score sales in England has not slipped our mind. It would be rather closer to the truth to say that we have prepared a supplementary statement to your half-yearly one which we were intending to send out on 2 April. Instead we have pleasure in enclosing said statement herewith. Please accept our assurance that the outstanding sum of RM 717, – has been transferred to your account.

Yours faithfully
enc. 1 statement[22]

No 279

Delius to Universal

23 March 1931
Grez-sur-Loing

Dear Sir,

I acknowledge receipt of your statement in respect of miniature scores dated 19 March; however the accounts for the second half of 1930 remain missing. I should be grateful if you would kindly forward these.

Please be advised of the following performances:

Dance Rhapsody	17.3.31.	Liverpool Philharm.
Piano Concerto	18.3.31.	Bournemouth Orch. Eira Vaughan, piano
Brigg Fair	24.3.31.	Radio Heilsberg

Respectfully yours

22 This has not survived.

ꕤ

No 280

The Performing Right Society to the BBC

25 March 1931
London

Dear Sir,

Re- Compositions of F. Delius

We are in receipt of your letter of 24th instant, and in reply would inform you that unless the position has materially changed since we investigated the title of the Oxford University Press last year, they do not own the performing right in the works by Delius originally published by Tischer & Jagenberg, and now published by the Oxford University Press.[23]

We have inspected Mr Delius' copies of his contracts with Messrs. Tischer & Jagenberg, and they show clearly that the composer did not assign to those publishers the public performing right in any of the works which are the subject of the agreements among which are included all the Delius works now shown in the Oxford University Press catalogue. The public performing right is, in fact, expressly reserved to the composer in all the contracts.

Accordingly, the performing right in these works vest in the Society by virtue of the composer's membership, and you are therefore at liberty to perform any one or all of them under the licence you hold from this Society.

We are writing to the Oxford University Press on the above lines.

Yours faithfully
Secretary

ꕤ

No 281

Universal to Delius

26 March 1931
Vienna

Dear Sir,

---

[23] The BBC was enquiring if it was entitled to broadcast the T & J Delius works now in the OUP catalogue. As PRS writes, Delius had retained his performing rights, although T & J would receive the publisher's share through AKM.

In answer to your queries of 23 March we should like to present you with the following table of accounts with respect to miniature scores. As will be evident all copies sold were settled in our statement of 19 March.

Please accept our sincerest gratitude for the performance dates that you kindly supplied to us.

Yours faithfully

UE 7015	Appalachia	Print-run		197 copies
	Deductions:	Prom. copies		16 copies
	..	accounted		9 copies 31.12.30
	..	accounted		46 copies 19.03.31
			Stock	126 copies
Ph.N.209	Appalachia	Print-run		500 copies
	Deductions	accounted		256 copies 19.03.31
			Stock	244 copies
UE 8886	Sea Drift		Print-run	408 copies
	Deductions		Prom. copies	22 copies
	..		accounted	24 copies 31.12.29
	..		..	4 copies 30.06.30
	..		..	24 copies 30.12.30
	..		..	5 copies 30.12.30
	..		..	48 copies 19.03.31
			Stock	281 copies
Ph.N.215	Sea Drift		Print-run	614 copies
	Deductions		Accounted	304 copies 19.03.31
			Stock	310 copies

Your statement to 19th March 1931 includes not only sales from the second half of 1930 but also all previous sales to England.

No 282

Universal to Delius

15 June 1931
Vienna

Maestro Delius,

We wish to inform you that we are retroactively seeking compensation from the Reichsentschaedigungsamt[24] in respect of mechanical rights income generated by Brigg Fair in the territory of Great Britain. In collaboration with AMMRE we intend to take every necessary step to acquire satisfaction in this matter. You have granted Universal Edition a 20 per cent share in mechanical rights for the territories of Germany, Austria, Czechoslovakia and Switzerland and we would like to request that you allow us the same participation in any remuneration that we might receive from the Reichsentschaedigungsamt. This especially as we anticipate some expense in the pursuit of this matter.*

We look forward to receiving your comments.

Yours faithfully

* Your exact liability will of course be debited to your account at the appropriate time.

No 283

Delius to Universal

20 June 1931
Grez-sur-Loing

Dear Sir

In response to your letter of 15 June I should like to advise that you have no legitimate claim to income from mechanical rights in respect of my work Brigg Fair.[25]

I retain sole ownership of these rights and I have notified the work accordingly to the MCPS in London.

I voluntarily assigned to you a 20 per cent interest in mechanical rights for the territories of Germany, Austria, Czechoslovakia and Switzerland and see no reason to modify this in any way.

Yours respectfully

24 Reichsentschaedigungsamt = some sort of copyright tribunal/small claims court?

25 UE had no mechanical rights in England. This doesn't seem a very friendly gesture.

ꕥ

No 284

Universal to Delius

28 June 1931
Vienna

Maestro Delius,

We need no reminding that on the basis of our contract with you we derive zero income from the exploitation of mechanical rights in respect of Brigg Fair although you have granted us voluntarily a 20 per cent publisher share in said rights for the territories of Germany, Austria, Czechoslovakia and Switzerland.

We have now been forced to pursue a compensation claim in collaboration with AMMRE which is pending with the Reichsentschaedigungsamt. We cannot be certain at this stage whether this action will be successful however in this exceptional case we do feel justified in claiming a share all the more so when one realises that there is not a publisher in business today who would issue a contract excluding them from any entitlement to mechanical rights. We acknowledge your last communication regarding this matter and regret that in these times of great economic hardship you are not willing to accommodate the legitimate claims of the publisher. We shall forward you a statement of our costs incurred to date as soon as matters have been tied up.[26]

Yours respectfully

ꕥ

No 285

Jelka Delius to Universal

13 September 1931
Grez-sur-Loing

Dear Sir

---

[26] UE wrote to FD on 21 August 1931.

'We refer you to our correspondence of June 1931 regarding the matter of *Brigg Fair* and our compensation claim in respect of mechanical rights income generated in Great Britain. Please be advised that we have charged to your account the sum of OeS 23.68 in respect of legal fees.' The background is obscure. *Brigg Fair* was a Leuckart work and UE bought a 50 per cent interest in the 6 works in 1921. Was this perhaps Leuckart trying to assert his rights? The matter is never referred to again. We have no way of knowing how it ended or whether Delius accepted the share of legal fees.

We have received further news from Fenby concerning Hassan so I have hastened to respond to your letter of 10 September by return.

Neither American performance will be a simple rendition of the concert suite – the University Players[27] will be giving a staged performance and Schola Cantorum will most likely be giving a concert performance with recitation. On this basis we forbid any copying of Fenby's arrangement as there have been significant interludes, fanfares and harmonies cut and in certain places the score has been somewhat abbreviated. According to my husband the score that you possess is beyond question the correct version and the one that has been used in London on every occasion. When you sent Fenby the full score to enable him to draft his orchestral and chorus suite he took advantage of the opportunity to restudy the score for any errors or mistakes. As a result it is in perfect condition. The new complete vocal score corresponds in every detail with your full score which of course is of fundamental importance when it comes to performing the work.

Some further news concerning Hassan; my husband has asked me to tell you that he has composed a second concert suite consisting of five movements based on Hassan and scored for a normal-sized orchestra. Fenby has the manuscript in England and would now dearly like to set about completing it. My husband requests therefore that you please post the concert suite that was recently sent to you to Fenby at the following address:

Mr Eric Fenby
12 Mayville Avenue
Scarborough
Yorks.
England

This suite will be scored for orchestra only; shorter and significantly easier to perform it could prove popular in the concert hall.

I repeat once again that you may only use your own full score for the American performances as this is the only one we can be certain is free of defects.

My husband is delighted that you have been engaged as the agent for Hawkes & Son, London; we are also happy to see from our statement that sheet music sales are showing an upward trend in spite of the harsh conditions.

You will probably already be aware that on Thursday 17 September music by Delius will be featured in a Prom concert. I enclose a programme from the Daily Telegraph.

It would certainly be expedient to include an announcement in Pult und Taktstock. On 8 October the performance of A Mass of Life will be taking place at the triennial Leeds Music Festival under the baton of Sir Thomas Beecham. At the last festival three years ago Beecham gave a performance of exquisite beauty of 'Sea Drift'. The chorus in Leeds should be unbeatable.

My husband joins me in conveying our best wishes to Herr Direktor Hertzka

Respectfully yours

---

[27] Neither of these performances took place.

ꟷ

No 286

Universal to Delius

14 September 1931
Vienna

Maestro Delius,

Our English agent[28] is pressing us to publish a budget vocal study score of Sea Drift. By our reckoning it should appear in 8vo format[29] and have a German retail selling price of RM 2. – (2 Marks.) Our agent is of the opinion that in this format and at that price the score should find a good market and he has declared himself willing to place an immediate order for 500 copies. The production costs of this new edition are sure to be severe and the discount we have pledged to our agent is considerable. If we are to meet the demands of our agent we can only proceed if you are in a position to agree to a reduced royalty rate. Taking the modest pre-tax profits into consideration we envisage being able to afford a royalty of only 15 per cent on all copies sold or 30 Pfg per copy. Should you be agreeable, immediately following publication we could transfer the sum of RM 150, – to your account as your royalty on the first 500 copies for which we have a guaranteed customer (outside of your normal annual statements.)

We should be delighted if through your consent we will have the opportunity to enhance the popularity of this work and with this thought in mind we eagerly await your comments.

Respectfully yours

No 287

Delius to Universal

17 September 1931
Grez-sur-Loing

Dear Sir

In response to your letter of 14 September may I advise you that in reference to the budget edition of Sea Drift I will accept a royalty of only 15 per cent if this will ensure that the publication can go ahead. However I must make it clear that this 15 per cent is valid only on this budget special edition. I do hope that it will appear with

---

[28] Cranz.

[29] This smaller-sized vocal score, used as a choral score, answered FD's earlier complaints about the old (single line) chorus material for *Sea Drift*. (cf. FD to UE 7 January 1927.)

both English and German text, as I am confident that a cheaper edition would also be welcomed in Germany. What do you think?

To come back to the subject of Hassan, I must require that all performance rights, to which I am the sole claimant, be granted either directly by myself or through your mediation and I reserve the right to be consulted on all negotiations.[30]

Yours respectfully

ꙮ

No 288

Universal to Delius

22 September 1931
Vienna

Maestro Delius,

We learn with great pleasure from your letter of 17 September that you are willing to accept a royalty of 15 per cent on the budget edition of the vocal score to Sea Drift which will of course be limited to this edition alone. We shall set the ball in motion with all possible speed and furthermore consider the wisdom of distributing the edition in Germany. We shall transfer the sum of RM 150 – in respect of the first 500 copies to your account immediately upon publication.

With regard to Hassan, all the negotiations with America which were conducted by telegraph have now reached a conclusion and we hope soon to receive the signed contracts. We have undertaken all the arrangements on your behalf since we believed that direct communications between yourself and our American agent would only have slowed matters down. It is our sincerest hope that we have reached an agreement that will be of satisfaction to you.

Yours respectfully

ꙮ

No 289

The Performing Right Society to Delius

10 October 1931
London

Dear Sir,

---

[30] Performances of the orchestral suite would be of the small performing right and would have been controlled by PRS. UE would reasonably expect to participate.

We believe you are aware that, by the constitution of this Society, Oratorios, Cantatas and similar large choral works are not under our control, but with your consent, we have in the past credited you with fees in respect of performances of those of your works which fall within these categories, all of which according to our records are published by the Universal Edition of Vienna.[31]

This publishing house has now come to an arrangement with Cranz & Co. Ltd (London) whereby the latter take over the agency for the Universal catalogue in this country, and are empowered to charge performing fees on works which are not in our repertoire.

Below is a list of works which we have agreed with Cranz & Co. as being outside the Society's control, and accordingly you will in future receive your share of fees in respect of these works from the Universal Edition of Vienna.

List of works not controlled:-
Appalachia
Mass of Life
Requiem
Sea Drift
Songs of Sunset

Yours faithfully
Secretary

No 290

Delius to The Performing Right Society

12 October 1931
Grez-sur-Loing

Dear Sir,

I have just received your letter of October 10th re choral works published by Universal Edition .But besides the works mentioned:

---

[31] PRS did not control choral/orchestral works lasting longer than 20 minutes until well after the 1950s. This is the first time that PRS has mentioned the fact to FD, although it appears that, notwithstanding the rule, PRS has been licensing and collecting for FD on the 5 works, possibly because until 1926, UE were not represented by PRS either through a UK agent or by virtue of a PRS agreement with AKM.

What is proposed now is that Cranz, who had taken over the UE agency from Curwen, would license the 5 works in the UK, passing back the fees, less Cranz's share to Vienna, where in due course UE would pay FD his share, much later than he would have received it from PRS and after two currency exchanges.

Remembering FD's insistence that Curwen paid him direct on sales of the *Five Pieces* in England, rather than passing the royalties back to Vienna, it is surprising that Jelka did not insist that Cranz paid Delius in England.

Appalachia
Mass of Life
Requiem
Seadrift
Songs of Sunset

There is another choral work with baritone solo
An Arabesque, which you do not mention and which ought to be included with the others. Further I should like to know whether it is Cranz & Co. or you who has collected the fee for the performance of my Mass of Life at the Leeds Triennial Festival on Oct. 8th inst.?[32] When does the new arrangement begin?[33]

Further there are other choral works notably the new work Songs of Farewell published by Winthrop Rogers, (agent Hawkes.) What arrangement have you made about that. It is to be brought out in March in the Cortauld Sargent Concerts.[34]

Thanking you in advance for answers to these questions
Believe me,

Yours truly,

No 291

Delius to Universal

17 October 1931
Grez-sur-Loing

Dear Sir,

Many thanks for the copy of Walk to the Paradise Garden.[35] I do hope that it will be well received and will be distributed to the U.S.A. where the orchestral piece has found much favour. Fenby is here with us at the moment and we are working most industriously on the Hassan Suite. The performance at the Triennial Leeds Music Festival of A Mass of Life was greeted with rapturous applause. The press reviews

---

32 PRS wrote to Delius on 14 October 1931 to say that they had spoken to Cranz, Universal's agent, who said that they were negotiating with Leeds.

33 PRS replied in its 14 October letter that Cranz would take over licensing performing rights on the choral & orchestral works listed, from 1 October.

34 A pencilled PRS comment reads 'Mr James spoke to Hawkes who said they do not charge a performing fee but look to us to do so. He gave the duration as 6 minutes and Mr James agreed therefore that we should control the work'. Actually they last 18 minutes.

35 UE had sent a copy of the newly printed piano reduction of the *Walk to the Paradise Garden* on 14 October.

are glowing. The conductor Sir Th. Beecham directed the orchestra from memory without a score and the baritone[36] also sang his huge part without music.

Yours respectfully

No 292

Delius to The Performing Right Society

23 October 1931
Grez-sur-Loing

Dear Sir,

I am in receipt of my BBC account up to June 30th for which all my thanks.

I note that there is some confusion as to the publishers of the different works. You allot most of the works bought by the OUP to its former owners, Tischer and Jagenberg, altho' you have been notified of the change. And I hope you are not sending any royalties to Tischer and Jagenberg.

I enclose a list of works you have allotted to the wrong firms.

Yours truly,
FD

PS Why do you[37]…it was I presume for the performance at the Delius Festival 1929, where it was left out before?[38]

Jelka Delius's List of errors attached to her letter of 23 October 1931

This has been transcribed below, with the PRS handwritten comments in brackets. It should be remembered that, at that date, in respect of the T & J songs transferred to OUP, OUP had only a licence to print and were not members of PRS. The publisher's share of the original T & J works would have been sent to AKM, who would have sent it on to T&J.

Abendstimmung (1/3 to T&J)	OUP
Princess (card says 1/3 to pub.)	
Twilight Fancies (full to c[omposer]. No publisher shown on	OUP

[36] Roy Henderson. The other soloists were Stiles-Allen, Muriel Brunskill and Francis Russell.

[37] The bottom of the letter is torn off.

[38] PRS note says 'this had been paid in full on 14a to composer. 1/3 was now deducted, and credited to Universal'. From PRS to FD dated 29 Oct 1931, it refers to *An Arabesque*.

n[otification] c[ard]	
Bird's Tale (1/3 to T&J)	OUP
Elegy (card gives m/s. full to c. Checked with rep[ertoire]	Hawkes
Indian Love Song (full to c. checked with rep)	OUP
Klein Venevil }(full to c. checked with rep.	OUP
Sweet Venevil}	
Nightingale (card gives OUP. Full fee pd to c)[39]	Augener
Nightingale has a lyre (full to composer. Should be 8/12)	OUP
On hearing the first cuckoo (full to c. no pub shown on n/c)	OUP
Sonata No 3, violin and piano (given as m/s. full to c.)	Hawkes
Summer Eve (full to c. no pub shown on n/c)	Augener
Summer Night on the River (full to c. no pub shown on n/c)	OUP
Sunset (½ to p. and c. n[on] m[ember] author)	Augener
Three Preludes (given as OUP. Full to c. No pub on n/c)	Anglo French = OUP
Toccata (this was refused by Curwen, & full fee pd to Delius)	Universal
No pub shown on n/c	
To the Queen of my heart (1/3 to T&J. checked with rep)	OUP

No 293

The Performing Right Society to Delius

29 October 1931
London

Dear Sir,

Re Distribution of Broadcasting Fees No. 15A

We duly received your letter of 23rd instant, and on examination of your account for the above Distribution, we regret to find that some errors have occurred, due principally to the BBC programmes not being sufficiently explicit, for example, the programme gave the title 'To the Queen of my Heart' (Tischer & Jagenberg.) This is on our records as 'To my Heart's Queen' (Tischer & Jagenberg transferred to Oxford University press), and as there are, according to our records, two of your works, namely 'Speilleute' and 'Auf Der Reise zur Heimat' originally published by Tischer & Jagenberg, which have not been transferred to Oxford University Press, the clerk who was analysing the programme took this title 'To the Queen of my Heart' to be another publication of Tischer & Jagenberg, retained by them.

We were not previously aware the 'Princess' is an alternative title to 'Twilight Fancies'. Also with regard to the two songs 'Nightingale' (Augener) and 'The

39 PRS note. Lett. of 23.10.30 gives T & J as pubs. Reg[istry] gives Augener. Performance card showed OUP, because this work was thought to be the same as the following item above.

Nightingale has a Lyre') (OUP), we find that confusion has arisen owing to the fact that the second work is frequently shown on the programme as 'The Nightingale', and we observe that on one of your notifications you refer to it in this way. In the case of the 'Elegie' and 'Sonata No. 3', we had not been notified by you or by Messrs. Hawkes at the time your account was made up that they published those numbers, and as they were shown on the BBC programmes as ms. works, you received full fees.

Re 'In the garden of the Seraglio' It occurs to us you may own the copyright in the words by J.P.Jacobson.

If you will kindly advise us on this last point, we shall send you a note of the adjustment necessary to correct the errors which have occurred. In the meantime, we cannot state the exact figure, but it will be a small debit against you, and this we propose to leave for adjustment at the next Distribution of British Broadcasting Fees.

Re 'Arabeske'. The debit adjustment on your account for Distribution 15(A) in respect of this item relates, as you have assumed, to the performance at the Delius Festival in October 1929. At our Distribution No.14 (A) we credited you with the full fee, whereas the Publishers, Universal Edition, should have received one-third, and this has been adjusted at the Distribution just made, No.15 (A.)

Yours faithfully,
Secretary.

No 294

Delius to The Performing Right Society

2 November 1931
Grez-sur-Loing

Dear Sir,

In reply to your letter of October 29th I wish to tell you

1. The song in question ought to be registered as 'To the Queen of my Heart'
2. The Songs 'Spielleute' and 'Auf der Reise zur Heimat' have also been transferred to the OU Press.

Indeed 'Spielleute' (Minstrels in English) has just been figuring in a competition for singers at Blackpool, I think. The other song is 'The Homeward Journey' and has been sung quite often. In fact all works of mine at Tischer & Jagenberg have been transferred to the OUP. 'To the Queen of my heart' belongs to the Three Shelley Songs

Indian Love Song
Love's Philosophy
To the Queen of my Heart.

I am most anxious to have the firm Tischer & Jagenberg erased entirely as they have never been over scrupulous and if you continue to allot fees to them they will quietly keep them.

I have had a lot of correspondence with them and the German GDT who claims their right to continue to draw fees from English performances of these works, especially 'On hearing the First Cuckoo in Spring' and 'Summer Night on the River'. Tischer & Jagenberg is now only the agent for the German and mid European countries for all those works which he formerly owned.

It was really for the OUP to notify you of all this in a business-like way.[40]

No 295

Augener to The Performing Right Society

2 November 1931
London

Dear Sir,

In regard to a telephone enquiry received last week in regard to Delius, (1) Ballade, (2) Eastern Fantasia, (3) Whither, these titles are not authentic; they appear to be fancy translations which ought not to be used.

The Universal Edition publishes a book of five songs with the following titles:-

1.	Das Veilchen	The Violet
2.	Im Garten des Serails	In the Seraglio gardens
3.	Seidenschuhe	Silken Shoes
4.	Herbst	Autumn
5.	Irmelin	Irmelin

We believe (1) 'Ballade' is No.5, 'Irmelin', which is a ballad of an old King and his daughter; (2) 'Eastern fantasia' is 'In the garden of the Seraglio',[41] (3) 'Whither' is probably 'Herbst', 'Autumn', which begins 'Father, whither fly the Swans', and ends with the German word 'Wohin' meaning 'where' or 'whither'.

Yours faithfully,

[40] Quite right! But it seems that PRS had been paying the publisher's share to T & J via AKM. See PRS to FD 5 Nov 1931.

[41] This letter shows the difficulties experienced then and now by PRS in trying to identify incorrectly titled works and even Augener gives two versions of *In the Seraglio gardens*.

ꕥ

No 296

The Performing Right Society to Delius

5 November 1931
London

Dear Sir,

We are obliged to you for your letter of 2nd instant, and have carefully noted all the information you give us as to the variations in titles of your works, and in particular, that Messrs. Tischer & Jagenberg do not now publish any of your works, but that all those they at one time published, have been transferred to the OUP, with the reservation of performing rights to yourself. You may be assured that the small amount of fees paid to the German Society (G.D.T.) for their members of Tischer & Jagenberg, at this last Distribution will be recovered by us. There is no question of Messrs. Tischer & Jagenberg refusing to repay these sums, for we shall merely debit the G.D.T. with the amount in question when making our next remittance to them in respect of all works in their repertoire,

re 'In the Garden of Seraglio'.

We note that the words by J.P. Jacobsen are non-copyright, and you will accordingly be credited with the author a share of fees.

We have noted also the particulars you give of your works published by Winthrop Rogers, and Hawkes & Son Ltd.

Three works attributed to you have appeared on recent programmes under the titles, 'Ballade', 'Eastern Phantasy'[42] and 'Whither'. We do not think you have published any compositions under these titles, but we are inclined to the view that 'Ballade' is intended for 'Irmelin', No. 5 of 'Five Songs' (Universal.) 'Eastern Phantasy' is probably 'In the garden of the Seraglio', and 'Whither' we think likely to be No. 4 in the above 'Five Songs', 'Autumn', which we believe begins with the words 'Father Whither fly the Swans'

If we are right in the assumptions we have made in regard to these works, please do not trouble to write to us, for we shall take silence to indicate your agreement.

Yours faithfully
Secretary

---

[42] In answer to the PRS query about these titles, Augener, writing that they had been asked about '*Eastern Fantasia*', said that it should be *In the garden of the Seraglio*, even though in the same letter they wrote that the official English title was '*In the Seraglio gardens*'. Now it has appeared on a programme as '*Eastern Phantasy*'.

ꕥ

No 297

The Performing Right Society to Hawkes & Co.

18 November 1931
London

Dear Mr Hawkes,

re Compositions of Frederick Delius

I observe that a number of works in your catalogue by the above composer, have been edited or arranged by Eric Fenby, who is not a member of this Society. If your Company has acquired the performing rights in these works, the Society's ordinary plan for the division of fees would, as you know, entitle you to receive the arranger's share; but I understand that Mr Fenby is Mr Delius's secretary, and if this is so, the property in the arrangements doubtless devolves upon Mr Delius. In these circumstances, I think Mr Delius should be credited with the full composer's share of two-thirds.

Of course if in any instance (as is not unusual with Delius compositions) the composer has retained his performing rights, the question does not arise, for he[43] would then be entitled to the non-member arranger's share.

I should be glad to have your comments on the above.

Yours faithfully

ꕥ

No 298

Universal to Delius

20 November 1931
Vienna

Maestro Delius,

We have just learnt from our agent in London, Cranz & Co., that Sir Thomas Beecham has received from you a complete set of orchestral material for A Mass of Life and A Village Romeo and Juliet.[44] We would be most indebted to you if you

---

[43] Hawkes replied on 24 November saying that the fees should be distributed according to PRS rules. It seems from the PRS letter that PRS was prepared in certain circumstances to pay an arranger's fee to the publisher on a copyright work. This would not apply now. The arranger's copyright would only come into play when the underlying work ceased to be copyright. Eric Fenby did not claim a copyright on the works he helped Delius to complete.

[44] Beecham owned a set of parts of *A Mass of Life* and conducted from a manuscript of *A Village Romeo and Juliet*. UE were quite within their rights to charge a hire fee on all

could please inform us whether you have drawn Sir Thomas Beecham's attention to the fact that he is not released thereby from his obligation to pay hire and performing fees on the occasion of each performance to us or more precisely our English agent who represents our interests in that territory. This is significant not only for us but also for yourself as we both derive income from such fees. We look forward to receiving your comments in this regard and remain

Yours respectfully,

ꕥꕥ

No 299

Delius to Universal

24 November 1931
Grez-sur-Loing

Dear Sir

I do not know how you or Messrs. Cranz & Co. could believe that I would have supplied Sir Thomas Beecham with a complete set of material for both A Mass of Life and A Village Romeo and Juliet. Firstly, I have never owned such a set and therefore could never have been in a position to pass it on; secondly, I am fully aware that I could never even entertain the idea for fear of endangering the interests of Universal Edition. Sir Thomas Beecham has a large music library and has perhaps owned these works for years. You will appreciate that I cannot interfere in this matter; it is the province of the publisher. I would however like to impress upon you the importance of proceeding with great caution here. You must always remember that the popularisation of my music is attributable in a large degree to the efforts of Beecham. He is to conduct A Mass of Life in April at the Albert Hall and intends to launch another production of Romeo and Juliet at the next opportunity. It is thanks to him alone that The Walk to the Paradise Garden from this opera has now become a regular programme feature both in England and America. It is his example as demonstrated on the brilliant gramophone recordings made by him that other artists strive to emulate in performance. Brigg Fair has also benefited to a colossal extent from his model performances and recordings. Moreover, it was he alone who was the driving force in bringing A Mass Of Life to the bigoted citizens of Leeds.

It is he who has carried out the strenuous work of marking up the dynamics in all my works. Naturally it is from these scores that he loves to conduct and which he always has at his disposal.

Just another question: At a recent concert given by an English singer the English text to the Five Songs was reprinted in the programme. Underneath the following acknowledgement was made: 'translated by Addie Funk'. As I understand it this

---

performances, if the material was not on sale. These days, where orchestras sometimes keep a set of a copyright work in their libraries, they would still expect to pay hire fees.

acknowledgement also appears in the present edition. This must be an error. These songs were translated into English by my good self at the time; the translations as they appeared in the programme are exactly as I did them then. Might I request therefore that you remove the name of Addie Funk and replace it with Fr. Delius. I should also like this to be rectified in the next edition. How could this have happened?

Hassan Suite. I hope that this has been delivered to the engraver. If so Fenby will read the proofs. Please send them here. If he should depart from here I shall inform you accordingly. Have you heard anything further from America?

Yours respectfully,

No 300

Universal to Delius

4 December 1931
Vienna

Maestro,

During a recent visit here by Mr Cranz from the firm of Cranz & Co. in London we discussed in quite an involved manner the business of the Hassan Suite arrangements.

Following lengthy deliberations we have reached the conclusion that the Suite as arranged by Mr Fenby is somewhat too long. We should like to publish the work in the following order:

1. The Procession
2. Serenade
3. Desert Scene
4. Ballet

You will see from the above that the preludes to Act 1 and the Ballet have been dropped. We want to place the Ballet at the end to provide a much more effective close to the piece. We should be most grateful if you would consider giving your endorsement to the order as proposed herewith.

In addition we also intend to publish the Ballet in a separate edition. Together with Walk to the Paradise Garden we would then have two short, easy to play Delius works which an orchestra might perhaps feel more inclined to play than the Suite.

In anticipation of your response we send you our best wishes.

Yours respectfully,

No 301

Delius to Universal

20 December 1931
Grez-sur-Loing

Dear Sir

Since my last letter Mr Fenby has departed. I have written to him concerning your proposals. We both believe that you were absolutely right to remove both preludes because of the length. It is only the running order that we do not like. We therefore suggest the following

	Desert Scene	to begin
then	Procession	
	Serenade	
	Ballet	to close

The Procession and Serenade are short and so the main pieces have been placed at the beginning and end. We also think it an excellent idea to publish the Ballet in a separate edition.[45]

The Procession would not make such a good opening. I should be interested to hear your views.

You have also not responded at all to my enquiry regarding the supposed translations by Addie Funk. Please rectify this oversight.
With best wishes to Herr Dir. Hertzka

Yours respectfully,

1932

Delius was 70 on 29 January. Both Delius and Jelka were ill, Jelka also being troubled with domestic problems over the servants. Nevertheless she continued to pursue Universal and PRS. Delius was still composing and in October the *Idyll* was finished.

The first performance of *Songs of Farewell* was in the Queen's Hall on 21 March and there was a successful broadcast of *A Village Romeo and Juliet* in May, which led Universal to try to interest other broadcasting stations in the work. Universal also proposed the publication of the 'chorus in the church' from *A Village Romeo and Juliet* with organ accompaniment with the hope that it would be used at weddings.

---

45 UE apparently prepared masters for this (purely orchestral) Suite from *Hassan*, but it does not appear to have been actually published in printed form.

Their letter of 12 February 1932 confirmed the order of movements in the *Hassan* Suite as proposed by FD and acknowledged his remarks concerning Addie Funk in his letter of 24 November 1931.

With all print matters, Universal tried to get Delius to reduce his royalty rates, as the company was in financial difficulties. There was also another attempt to persuade Delius to grant a share of mechanical rights worldwide, which he resisted.

Checking through the PRS broadcasting distribution, Jelka noticed that *A Mass of Life* and *A Village Romeo and Juliet* were missing. PRS pointed out that the *Mass* was not within PRS control because it lasted more than 20 minutes and that PRS did not control grand rights. Presumably Cranz had licensed the broadcasts.

PRS fees distributed to Delius in 1932, or the end of 1931, in respect of 1931 activity were £360-17s-1d, before deduction of income tax of £69-2s-10d. PRS income was £229,000 and was showing steady growth, from which Delius and other composers were benefiting.

The [Gramophone]Delius Society was formed.

No 302

Universal to Delius

7 January 1932
Vienna

Maestro Delius,

We have received a draft agreement from 'The Aeolian Company' in Garwood, New Jersey, according to which Brigg Fair is to be recorded against the usual royalty of 2 cents 'per roll'.

Since mechanical rights lie outside of our control, may we request that you please inform us whether it is your intention to pursue this agreement yourself directly with the Aeolian Co.; otherwise we shall be glad to put at your disposal the services of our American agent, Associated Music Publishers Inc. of 25 West 45th Street, New York who would then undertake to complete the arrangements. For the collection of fees and administration of your rights said firm will levy a fee of 33.33 per cent of all sums received.

Once again we should like to take this opportunity to emphasise that in these modern times the exclusion of the publisher from mechanical income is a quite unusual state of affairs as you would plainly see for yourself were you to conduct a survey of other publishers. Publishers today are more dependent than ever on small rights income and in the main enjoy an equal share with the composer.[46]

In anticipation of your latest news we remain

Yours respectfully

[46] FD wrote to UE on 19 January asking for the contract to be sent to him. As a member of MCPS he would ask MCPS to represent him.

No 303

Universal to Delius

4 March 1932
Vienna

Maestro Delius,

We should be most obliged to you if you would please indicate whether you have entered into an agreement with Mr Fenby in respect of the Hassan orchestral suite and royalty payments thereon. Furthermore, should it be the case that an agreement has yet to be concluded could you confirm whether it will come directly from you or should we intervene. If Mr Fenby is claiming participation in hire fees this will have to be deducted from your share.[47]

In anticipation of your comments we remain

No 304

Delius to Universal

7 March 1932
Grez-sur-Loing

Dear Sir

In answer to your letter of 1 March I hereby confirm my agreement to receive a 10 per cent royalty on retail sales in respect of the libretto to Romeo and Juliet.

I should be most grateful if you would please send a copy to me so that I may carry out the proof reading. The new edition must of course be produced as promptly as possible in view of the planned performance by Sir Thomas Beecham in the spring and in addition to that his radio broadcast from London on 20 May.

With regard to your letter of 4 March I do think it more practical that Mr Fenby receive a lump sum payment for the Hassan Suite arrangement exactly as Mr Heseltine did in the past.[48] Incidentally Mr Fenby is champing at the bit to start on the corrections.

I have received from various parties complaints concerning the ridiculous state of the scores which are being hired in England. Said scores are often replete with defective dynamics and incomprehensible corrections, so much so that it has now become nearly impossible to conduct from them. As all these works have appeared in print could several copies not be made available. Only a few days ago Sir Hamilton

---

47 This would be standard practice. See UE letter dated 21 March 1932.

48 See UE letter to FD dated 21 March and FD to UE dated 24 March.

Harty, who is the conductor of the Hallé Concerts and who has just performed A Mass of Life, wrote to me most forcibly on this matter.

May I quickly enquire whether you are still in contact with Mr Alexander Lippay. Is he still in Manila and if not can you give me details of his present abode.

Yours respectfully
F.D.

PS The 21 and 22 March will see performances of my new choral work Songs of Farewell as part of the Courtauld-Sargent Concerts. It would be most expedient to make mention of this in Pult und Takstock. Also it would please me greatly if you were at last to make common cause with my other publishers and bring out a general catalogue of my works.

No 305

Universal to Delius

11 March 1932
Vienna

Maestro Delius,

We gratefully acknowledge receipt of your letter of 7 March which means that we can proceed with the reprint of the English libretto to A Village Romeo and Juliet.[49] Our accounts department has been notified that you have declared yourself agreeable to a 10 per cent sales royalty. We enclose a copy of the old edition with the request that you please undertake corrections wherever necessary. We shall then have the responsibility of reproducing an error-free edition pursuant to the publisher's copy. We should therefore be most obliged to you for your earliest attention. It has distressed us to learn that there has been some dissatisfaction with the English scores of your works. Via our English agent we shall immediately investigate the incident involving Sir Hamilton Harty and A Mass of Life and promise to take remedial action.

Mr Lippay is still the Director of the Musikhochschule in Manila. His address is as follows: Academy of Music, 44 Vabini, Manila.

We derive much pleasure from the news that your new choral work Songs of Farewell will be receiving performances on 21 and 22 March and will endeavour to announce that fact in our next edition of Anbruch. Pult und Taktstock has for some time now been off the shelves.

It will interest you to learn that we have concluded an agreement with the firm of Boosey and Hawkes by virtue of which the controlling right over your last works to be published by them has been ceded to Universal Edition for Central Europe. At the next opportunity we will gladly contemplate the publication of a general catalogue.

[49] See Carley/2/568. FD sent UE a clean copy of the libretto on 16 March.

However weighing up the present widespread economic recession we do believe that now is not really an apposite moment.

We shall return to the subject of the Hassan Suite at a later date.

Yours respectfully

No 306

Universal to Delius

21 March 1932
Vienna

Maestro Delius,

Today we return to the subject of the Hassan Suite and it is our misfortune to inform you that as a consequence of the extraordinarily unfavourable economic conditions that we are experiencing at this time and of which you are no doubt aware we are not in a position to remunerate Mr Fenby with a separate royalty in respect of his arrangement. The only way to proceed that we can envisage is one in which you relinquish a percentage of your royalty in favour of Mr Fenby. It is our opinion that an accommodation of 5 per cent would be justifiable however we are happy to leave the setting of the exact figure to you. We should be most obliged to you if you would kindly inform us of your decision with all haste. We shall work from the assumption that you will be contacting Mr Fenby yourself.[50]

We look forward to hearing from you and remain

Yours respectfully

No 307

Universal to Delius

22 May 1932
Vienna

Maestro Delius,

---

[50] FD replied on 24 March. 'In answer to your letter of 21 March I should like to confirm my agreement that Mr Fenby should receive a royalty of 5 per cent in respect of the *Hassan Suite*. I shall be writing to him to this effect and am quite sure that he will nod assent to this proposal. You need have no hesitation now in swiftly pushing matters ahead.'

UE in turn replied on 29 March acknowledging this. In future Fenby would receive five per cent and FD's share would be reduced from 25 per cent to 20 per cent.

Due to our efforts and the exertions of our agent in England there is some probability that a performance of the Mass of Life through the Welsh Choral Union and the Welsh National Eisteddfod will take place next year in Wrexham. To quote the letter we received from our English agent:

'I have just received a further letter from Dr Hopkins Evans who informs me that at the committee meetings of the Welsh Choral Union and the Welsh National Eisteddfod (to be held next year at Wrexham) he strongly recommended the Mass of Life in tonic sol-fa to be included in their programmes. His suggestions were very enthusiastically received by the committees who agreed to take up this work provided the cost of the tonic sol-fa copies, the cost of the hired copies (for those who do not know the tonic sol-fa) the cost of orchestral material and performing fees are kept as low as possible, because all the choirs in these districts consist of very poor people and they have a terrible struggle to keep going under the present economic conditions. I hope that you have received concessions from Mr Delius as time is getting short and we must do all we can to get the matter decided as soon as possible.'

In consideration of the fact that for the purposes of this prominent performance we will have to reprint a separate sol-fa edition and reach some accommodation as regards the cost of the material may we beg leave to request that we pay you a royalty of 10 per cent in respect of the sol-fa edition and any deal that we close with the Welsh Choral Union and Welsh National Eisteddfod. We do hope that you can defer to this proposal bearing in mind the circumstances and we should be grateful if you would please give the matter your earliest attention as we will have to start on the sol-fa edition[51] immediately.

We look forward to hearing from you.

Yours respectfully

No 308

Universal to Delius

25 May 1932
Vienna

Maestro Delius

It is our misfortune that we must today return your attention to the subject of royalties and a plea from us in this context. At the suggestion of our English agent

[51] FD replied on 25 March agreeing to the ten per cent royalty, but pointing out an error in the first run.

'When reprinting the sol-fa edition may I request that you please reinsert the few bars of the chorus part at the end of the second *Tanzlied* which were omitted in the first run. Please consult the vocal score.'

we plan to publish the Chor in der Kirche from Romeo and Juliet in a separate edition with organ accompaniment, our hope being that this self-contained piece will find endorsement as music suitable for a wedding. The retail price will have to be kept low in order to give the edition every possible chance of success and we should therefore be grateful if you would consider a reduction of your royalty to 10 per cent. The evidence we have appears to indicate that if we were to honour the royalty written into our contract this new publication would unfortunately be too pricey when placed against the reduced spending power of our customers at the present time. You will understand that it is only our desire with all the means at our disposal to see your works exploited in every territory in defiance of the downcast economic outlook and whilst maintaining the lowest possible prices that forces us time and again to have to negotiate with you over royalties.

We do hope that you will be inclined to accommodate our request and we ask that you please sign and return the enclosed agreement.[52]

Yours respectfully

No 309

Universal to Delius

1 June 1932
Vienna

Maestro,

We are delighted that the radio performance of Romeo and Juliet in London has demonstrated just how suitable the work is for broadcast. This aspect was given full expression by the press reviews. We immediately wrote to both our American agency and Frankfurt to see what could perhaps be achieved in terms of another broadcast. We should like to enquire of you today whether you still enjoy personal contact with the radio networks, either through pupils or friends. If so we would like to pursue every avenue to build upon this fine success.

Yours respectfully

[52] FD signed the contract and returned it on 1 June.

ꕤ

No 310

Delius to Universal

5 June 1932
Grez-sur-Loing

Dear Sir

Dr Heinrich Simon would I am sure afford support to a radio broadcast of A Village Romeo and Juliet. I know this because he is friendly with Rosbaud and they recently organised a short radio performance of my Nietzsche Songs and the Violin Sonata.

This I am afraid is the extent of my acquaintances within the broadcast realm. There is possibly also Carl Schuricht who I believe is presently employed by Leipzig Radio. The best option of course would be to invite Sir Thomas Beecham to Germany to make a broadcast. Nobody will conduct my music as well as he does. He does have conducting commitments in Munich in the summer where he will be giving one Delius work and you could discuss the matter with him there. Furthermore, believe me when I say that the work would equally triumph on the stage if well conducted and produced.

Since we are talking about opera, may I assure myself that you have placed the stage sketches* for Fennimore and Gerda in safe custody.[53] After the Frankfurt performance in 1919 Herr Dir Hertzka took them with him for use in later performances. R.S.V.P. Some time back Beecham wanted to view them. Perhaps it would be best to send them here. I think the simplicity of these stage sets would help greatly in securing performances. I find it quite outrageous that the work should have remained untouched for so long following its cyclopean artistic success in Frankfurt. R.S.V.P.

Mr Benno Ziegler from Frankfurt sang the Nietzsche Songs impeccably and one must see to it that he has the opportunity for more frequent public recitals of the songs in the future.

It was a shame that the German radio magazines covering the two big radio performances this year of Mass of Life and Romeo and Juliet failed in both instances to list either my name or the work title correctly. Should similar events take place again I would like to be able to inform you in advance so that you can make sure all the details are correct.

Yours respectfully
F.D.

---

[53] UE duly sent the roll on 25 June asking for a receipt. The roll of sketches was delayed in the post and by customs. It arrived on 16 July.

PS Benno Ziegler did enquire whether I have composed other songs for his voice. Please send him the 5 Songs. Also can you please send me a song by Edv. Grieg entitled Ein Traum (soprano).

* The sketches were painted in oils and were bundled into a thick roll.

No 311

Delius to Universal

16 July 1932
Grez-sur-Loing

Dear Sir

Having fired off endless letters here, there and everywhere and encountering several difficulties along the way the sketches to Fennimore and Gerda finally arrived today – they had been sent to Paris. It is always easier to clear customs if no mention is made of Paris at all. I am however greatly relieved to have the sketches safe and sound in my hands again and will show them to Sir Thomas Beecham as soon as possible. Sir Th. Beecham has arranged a suite with voices based upon Hassan which he would like to give in London soon. The ingeniousness of the composition emboldens me to suggest that it might be practical to publish the work through Universal Edition.[54]

Yours faithfully

No 312

Universal to Delius

14 September 1932
Vienna

Dear Sir

We have pleasure in enclosing herewith your statement for the first six months of 1932 which shows net gains in your favour of

£ 35-5-11d, US$ Dollar 20.63 and RM 654.25

At the same we have instructed the firm of Cranz & Co. Ltd., 40 Langham Street, Gt. Portland St., London W1 to transfer the sum of £35-5-11d, to your account.

---

[54] This was never published, though Beecham played (and recorded) this Suite, plus voices on many occasions.

Regarding your Dollar and RM royalties may we ask that you kindly bear with us until the funds have been released by the local foreign currency exchange.[55]

Yours respectfully

ꕥ

No 313

Universal to Delius

15 September 1932
Vienna

Maestro
Our English agent has informed us that Mr Herbert Withers would like to produce a string orchestra arrangement of Midsummer Song for which there is considerable interest at the BBC and possibly from other orchestras. Since Mr Withers will be seeking some financial remuneration for his arrangement which is not affordable if your present entitlement of 25 per cent is to be adhered to may we request that you in this instance, just as you have done several times in the past, kindly consider agreeing to a reduction of your royalty to 10 per cent. It would certainly be a great pity if circulation of this chorus in its string orchestra arrangement were to be curtailed and we would therefore recommend that you accept this proposed diminution of your royalty. As the communication from our English agent was marked urgent we should be most obliged to you for a speedy response.

Yours respectfully

PS Your card concerning the Hassan Suite score has just reached us. The proof copy has unfortunately been for some time now in the hands of Koussewitzky who made an urgent demand for it and has yet to return it. Only a few days ago we expedited its return and we shall send you the proof as soon as it arrives.

ꕥ

No 314

Delius to Universal

22 September 1932
Grez-sur-Loing

---

[55] On 16 March 1932, UE transferred RM 1,237.18, as July/December 1931 royalties to FD's bank.

Dear Sir

I acknowledge receipt of your letter of 15 September. After lengthy deliberations I have concluded that an arrangement for string orchestra does not befit the Midsummer Song. Furthermore, may I opine in the strictest confidence that I was never truly satisfied with the arrangement that Mr Withers made of the Two Songs to be Sung of a Summer Night on the Water and which were published by Winthrop Rogers. I therefore made my own arrangement in its place. I must insist that you inform Mr Withers that because I am not convinced of its suitability I shall not be allowing an arrangement of the Midsummer Song.[56]

Regarding the Hassan Suite of Mr Fenby, I have agreed with him that I shall reasonably compensate him for his work from my own pocket which will avoid the need for any deduction from my percentage share in his favour.[57] Mr Fenby would also prefer to do it that way. I should only like to request now that you urgently send the proofs as Mr Fenby will be here for some weeks yet and I am desirous of once more checking the Suite with his collaboration. This is most important.

Respectfully yours

No 315

Delius to the Performing Right Society

12 October 1932
Grez-sur-Loing

Dear Sir,

Re Broadcasting Distribution 16A

I have just received my bill for BBC royalties for the 6 months ended June 30th 1932.
On the list I miss notably two important items viz

1. Mass of Life 18.2
2. Hallé Concerts Manchester and broadcast by Northern Regional and London perhaps others).
3. Village Romeo and Juliet

Whole opera broadcast on National 20.5.32
Kindly look into this matter for me.

Yours Truly

56 UE replied on 29 September accepting FD's decision.
57 A better way of rewarding Fenby.

ꙮ

No 316

Performing Right Society to Delius

18 October 1932
London

Dear Sir,

Re Distribution No.16A

We beg to acknowledge receipt of your letter of the 12th instant, and would remind you that the Society does not operate in respect of Operas, Musical Plays, etc., when performed in their entirety, nor in respect of choral works such as your 'Mass of Life'. In regard to the latter type, may we refer you to our letter of 10th October 1931.[58]

We have verified from the official programmes rendered to us by the BBC that the performances to which you refer are duly entered, and presumably the fees will have been collected direct from the BBC, by the Agents of the Universal Edition, Vienna, namely Cranz & Co. Ltd (London). You should therefore receive from Universal Edition, in due course, the appropriate share of such fee in accordance with your contract with them.

Yours faithfully
Secretary

ꙮ

1933

The few letters that have survived are mainly taken up with confusion over which works are outside PRS control, and if they are, who is licensing their performance. Universal seems to imply in their 30 September letter to Delius that Delius had not reserved his performing right in the Leuckart works, meaning that he is not entitled to performing fees, but that is not the case. All performing right societies acknowledged that both publisher and composer of a published work were entitled to fees.

---

[58] See footnote to that letter.

No 317

Delius to Universal

2 May 1933
Grez-sur-Loing

Dear Sir

Through my correspondence with Mr Michaud[59] it has been drawn to my attention that you have on record that I am receiving royalties and performing fees from the firm of Leuckart. I feel I should make clear the total fallaciousness of this information. I received assurances from Herr Dir. Hertzka that U.E. had purchased the works in question lock, stock and barrel from Leuckart. Is it the case perhaps that U.E. did not pay the full amount? I am not aware of any transactions between myself and Leuckart and I confirm that the extent of my dealings stretches only as far as U.E. However as the English P.R.S. has excluded the Songs of Sunset from its area of control I should like to know who is supposed to be administering the performing right – that is to say who is accounting my share to ...?

Furthermore, I should like to point out that I am still awaiting my half-yearly statement which was due at the end of January. I should be grateful if you would please investigate this matter and pay the sums owed through Mr Michaud.

Respectfully yours

No 318

The Performing Right Society to Delius

4 May 1933
London

Dear Sir,

re Distribution of Broadeasting Fees No.16B.

I am in receipt of your letter of 2nd instant, and have looked carefully into the points you raise.

I find that you were duly credited with the performance of your cello 'Concerto' on 22nd July last, but this was recorded on the card for your piano 'Concerto'. Similarly, the performance of the cello 'Concerto' on 2nd November was incorrectly recorded on the card for your violin 'Concerto'.

---

[59] Of Cranz.

These errors are due to an unfortunate lack of appreciation by the clerks concerned of the fact that these three 'Concertos' are three different works, but the amount of fees credited to you is in no way affected.

re 'Song of Summer'. The performance on 28th September last was in the second half of the programme which was not broadcast.

Regarding the 'Sonata for Violin and Piano' No. 3, you have been given full credit for the performances on 11th October and 7th November, but these were entered on the same card as that used for 'Sonata' No. 2. Again the amount of the fee is not in any way affected.

Re 'Walk to the Paradise Garden'. We note that you give a duration of this as about twelve minutes. We had previously noted it as between eight and ten minutes – eight minutes being the timing given in the Universal Edition Catalogue 1933 and 9½ being the actual time taken by a recent Promenade Concert performance. Nevertheless, I agree that the work has not been put into its proper class, and accordingly there will be a further amount due to you in respect of the. Australian performance to which you refer of 1/3d. This item we shall include in our next Distribution of Australian Broadcasting Fees.

re 'Love's Philosophy'. You were credited with the full amount of the fees in respect of this work. Our records clearly shew that the publishers are now the Oxford University Press, but of course Tischer & Jagenberg's name frequently appears on the programmes when their edition is used.

Yours faithfully,
Assistant Secretary

No 319

Universal to Delius

25 September 1933
Vienna

Maestro,

A few days ago we requested of you the speedy return of the publisher score to Walk to the Paradise Garden.[60] From London we have received renewed enquiries

---

[60] Apparently FD had sent the proofs to Beecham, for him to add his editing, (cf. letters of 11 & 16 March 1929). As UE failed to retrieve these proofs from Beecham (cf. 31 October and 4 November 1933), they proceeded to print without TB's assistance (cf. 11 January 1934 & 26 April 1934) and the score duly appeared accordingly. (UE 10579). Keith Douglas later prepared a score of the 'Waltz, slightly rearranged for concert orchestra', with an optional link whereby the Paradise Garden Intermezzo follows (as in the opera). The published score (UE 11106) acknowledges Beecham's assistance in its preparation. Sir Thomas Beecham meanwhile produced his own arrangement of the *Walk to the Paradise Garden* Intermezzo, 'made in order to bring the work within the scope of smaller orchestras'. Score and parts of this version were published by Boosey & Hawkes in 1940.

regarding the delivery of this score and for this reason we beg that you send it back along with the photoprints by return if possible.

Thanking you for your consideration we remain

Yours respectfully

No 320

Universal to Delius

30 September 1933
Vienna

Maestro Delius

It has just come to our attention that due to a misunderstanding and the absence of the undersigned we failed to acknowledge your letter of 2 May 1933 for which we would like to convey our sincerest apologies. As part of that letter you enquired about performing fees arising from the work Songs of Sunset which was originally published by Leuckart and was delivered over to Universal Edition in 1921. The agreement that we then concluded with Leuckart states that the latter shall be entitled to fifty per cent of all income in respect of the works scheduled therein for the full duration of copyright, taking no account of the cash payment made upon signature. As far as we can ascertain from the contracts on file that you entered into with Leuckart before the war in respect of Brigg Fair, Dance Rhapsody, Summergarden, Songs of Sunset, Paris and Song of the High Hills, you assigned said works to Leuckart for the full period of copyright against payment of a lump sum settlement in the amount of RM 16,000 – and thereby released Leuckart from any further financial obligation to you. There exists no clause in the contracts to the effect that you reserve the performing right nevertheless your rights are administered automatically through the collecting societies,[61] that is to say PRS in London of which you are member. In the major continental countries collecting societies levy fees for every work genre, including works such as Songs of Sunset, whereas the English PRS accounts no fees for choral and orchestral works longer than 20 minutes. In the latter case the publisher takes the responsibility of collecting fees and it is as a consequence of this that Mr Michaud charges a combined fee encompassing the performing right and the hire of performing material which is then accounted through us to you. To summarise, the continental societies administer performances of every work, irrespective of type or duration, whilst in England their activities are limited in relation to performances of shorter works. In neither case does the publisher wield any influence. As Mr Michaud

61 There was a reservation, but nevertheless this shows that the performing right societies automatically paid composer and publisher on published works as long as either the publisher was a member, or was a member of a society with which the Society had an agreement.

again confirmed today, no performances of the Songs of Sunset have taken place in the last year and therefore you have received no payments.

In the hope that the situation has now been clarified we remain

Yours respectfully

ꙮ

No 321

Delius to Universal

31 October 1933
Grez-sur-Loing

Dear Sir,

Today I received your letter of 28 October and wish to reply by return.[62] Like you I regret that the photoprints to Walk to the Paradise Garden are not yet in your hands. Sir Thomas Beecham will probably never receive your letter however as he changed address about 20 years ago.

I had asked your London agent, Mr Jean Michaud, to retrieve the music from Sir Thomas and send it directly to you. As I never heard anything further I assumed that you had it.

I have now written to Mr Michaud <u>again</u>; he will contact Sir Th. or his secretary soonest. At this opportunity I should like to make you aware of the fact that I have <u>still not received</u> my statement that was due at the end of June. I find this whole episode rather rich, after all you are supposed to be the business people, not artists like Sir Th., a conductor of genius upon whose affability we must rely.

Respectfully yours

ꙮ

No 322

Universal to Delius

2 November 1933
Vienna

Dear Sir

We today take the liberty of enclosing herewith your statement for the first half-year of 1933 showing net royalties in your favour of:

---

[62] UE had written asking FD's help in retrieving photoprints of the score of the *Walk to the Paradise Garden*. UE had sent them to an old address and they were apparently lost.

RM 349.60; GB £ 26-7-4d and US $28.64.

In accordance with your wishes of 15 July 1933 we have transferred the Reichmarks and Sterling to your account at the firm of Universal Music Agencies (Michaud), London whilst paying the Dollars through the Zentral-Europaeische Laenderbank here in Vienna.

We should be grateful if you would please confirm receipt.

Yours respectfully

No 323

Universal to Delius

4 November 1933
Vienna

Maestro,
We thank you for your most kind letter of 31 October, however, we do unfortunately feel obliged to point out that you are labouring under considerable misapprehensions concerning Beecham and Michaud. We contacted Mr Michaud some weeks ago and repeated our request that he should obtain the photoprints from Beecham. He informed us that Beecham had refused to return them.[63] From our standpoint Beecham's behaviour was incomprehensible and what is more not excused by his conducting genius. We therefore wrote directly to him but regrettably the letter was wrongly addressed. Nevertheless the letter to date has not come back stamped 'return to sender'. We are assuming that a man as much in the public eye as Beecham has to be traceable through the post office.

In the meantime you may have received your statement. We should like you to accept our sincerest apologies for the delay.

Yours respectfully

No 324

Universal to Delius

8 November 1933
Vienna

[63] See FD to UE 11 March 1929. FD had written to UE asking for proofs of the score of the Keith Douglas version of the *Walk to the Paradise Garden* to be sent to Beecham.

Dear Sir

We wish to respond to your postcard of 5 November that of the miniature scores originally accounted to you ...[?] copies were remitted with the result that no scores were entered on the statement. For your information we enclose herewith an inventory of present stock levels from which you will see that your account has been over credited with 41 copies of Appalachia and 9 of Sea Drift.

Appalachia	
accounted on 19.03.1931	256 copies
¨ ¨ 30.06.1931	90
	195
	541 copies
Print-run	500 ¨
Overpayment of	41 copies
Sea Drift	
accounted on 19.03.1931	304 copies
¨ ¨ 30.06.1931	88
¨ ¨ 31.12.1931	14
¨ ¨ 30.06.1932	20
present stock	197
	623 copies
Print-run	614
Overpayment of	9 copies

Yours respectfully

(There are gaps in the original letter as it has survived)[64]

1934

It is not only Jelka Delius who is confused over which works are controlled by PRS. In January she writes berating Mr Michaud for charging 13 guineas to the Hallé for the performance of *Appalachia*, on 25 March, not realising that the fee covered both

[64] JD had written to UE on 5 November asking for the miniature score accounting. UE had obviously over accounted.

hire and performing fee. The Hallé also did not understand that it was paying the same fee for the performance as though PRS controlled the work.

Matters were clarified by PRS, who don't seem to have been very certain of how to interpret the over 20 minute rule. It looks as though both Michaud and PRS charged for the *Appalachia* performance on 25 March. In March, in answer to Jelka's question PRS confirmed that the only works outside its control were:

A Mass of Life,
Sea Drift,
Songs of Sunset.

It wrongly omitted *Requiem* from the list.

It had had second thoughts about Delius works and decided that *Appalachia*, *Song of the High Hills*, *An Arabesque* and *Songs of Farewell*, although choral works, were short and therefore within PRS control. That left Jelka with the problem of finding out who had licensed the Hallé performances of *Appalachia* and *Songs of Sunset*.

Jelka insisted that Delius had never received performing fees for *Sea Drift*. As Universal had no UK agent with a mandate to collect performing fees on non-PRS works until 1930, it is possible that PRS would have paid the entire fee to Delius. We have no way of checking. Delius was certainly paid for broadcasts of *Sea Drift*, and at that time, as Delius found out in relation to the 1929 Festival, a broadcast of a live concert rated only a broadcasting fee and not a fee for the live performance as well. We know of nine UK performances between 1923 and 1931.

The matter of whether a conductor who has bought a score and parts of an orchestra work can use the parts without paying a notional hire fee is aired again. As Dr Kalmus patiently explains, such performing material when sold, is sold with a caveat. Uses by orchestras other than the purchaser's would incur a notional hire fee, as they would today. Sir Thomas Beecham did not understand this. In an intemperate letter to Mr Michaud dated 16 December 1933, (not in this selection), he misunderstood that the eight guineas Michaud had charged the Hallé for *Appalachia* for a concert in March 1932 covered both the hire and performing fees. Michaud charged Beecham a lower than normal fee of £2 17s 6d for him to use his own parts to conduct the newly formed LPO.

Jelka's last letter to Universal is dated 11 May, only five days before she was taken to hospital. She was allowed home three weeks later, to be with her husband when he died on 10 June.

ຄ໙ຄ໙

No 325

Delius to Universal

8 January 1934
Grez-sur-Loing

Dear Sir

I feel I must bring it to your attention that the hire and performance fees being charged by Mr Michaud in respect of Appalachia are perfectly unreasonable and are an impediment to every performance.[65]

Michaud charges 13 guineas, that is £13-13-0d per performance. He has gone down to £8-0-0d for the major concert to be given by the Hallé in Manchester on 1.3. Yet this is still much too much, especially when you remember what is at stake – Beecham conducting the Hallé Orchestra in a concert dedicated to my compositions. The programme also features the Songs of Sunset and Walk to the Paradise Garden, both published by you. It would therefore be in your own deepest interest to reach an accommodation with the orchestra which just at the moment is caught in the most difficult circumstances.

The orchestra says that it cannot pay more than £4-4-0d. This I think is quite sufficient for when I look back at my earlier statements I see that no more than £3-3-0d has ever been charged and often less. On this subject I should note that I have seen no accounts for the performance given by Hamilton Harty in 1932 (I think there may even have been two) and also for the one given by Beecham on 5.3.1933. I have yet to see a single penny from any of these performances.[66]

What you must also not forget to include in your calculations is that you sold a complete set of Appalachia material to Sir Beecham which he is of course perfectly entitled to use.[67]

I am attributing the greatest importance to the Hallé's plans; the concert is to be broadcast making it all the more precious. I implore you in your own interest to authorise Mr Michaud to satisfy himself with £4-4-0d.

As a general point I should like to caution you against indulging Mr Michaud and his persistent complaints about Mr Beecham. As far as I can judge in the 27 years that he has spent campaigning on behalf of my music Mr B. has always paid the necessary fees. Without him my popularity in England, which is a major profit-earning source for you, would have been long delayed. It is therefore doubly tactless of Michaud to attack Mr B. in this manner. He has personally financed Delius concerts too numerous to mention and spent vast sums doing so. With this in mind

---

65 See next letter dated 11 January. PRS count *Appalachia* as outside their remit because of the chorus. Thus Michaud has to charge a combined hire and performing fee.

66 See UE to FD 24 January. No such Hamilton Harty performances took place.

67 See Dr Kalmus. 26 April 1934. Beecham's ability to use without paying a notional hire fee would have been restricted.

I find it extraordinarily myopic and unworthy of a music publisher to assume such an attitude.

To this must be added the fact that Mr Michaud in his role as the founder of the Delius Society must dance attendance to Mr B. When he chooses to insult him in this fashion the whole Society is undermined. Those people who have subscribed have only done so in order to obtain the superb gramophone records that Beecham makes. There is no other conductor there with the sort of pulling power to replace him. Please take a moment to contemplate what all this means for Universal Edition and me. Just recently Beecham gave a concert at the Philharmonie in Berlin and included in the programme Brigg Fair. This is typical of him. Other than Schuricht most German conductors who used to perform my music sadly are dead. This makes Beecham's involvement twice as important and we should not allow ourselves to sink to such petty reprobation because of his idiosyncratic ways. The whole business with the proofs to the Walk to the Paradise Garden would probably not have taken the course it did had Michaud not addressed the matter with such an injurious tone.

Dear Dr Kalmus, I should be grateful if you would please treat this letter in the strictest confidence and for God's sake do not let the concert in Manchester fall through. For without Appalachia on the programme it is certain that B. will withdraw.

With best wishes for the New Year

Yours respectfully

No 326

Universal to Delius

11 January 1934
Vienna

Maestro Delius,

Your letter after such a long absence was most welcome and we only regret that it refers to a matter which is really so difficult to resolve. It was not until the beginning of December last year that I had the opportunity to witness at first hand the practices of Mr Michaud and I feel obliged to state that he consistently demonstrated to me his complete commitment not only to the UE catalogue in general but also in particular to your own compositions, something which lies very close to his heart. Moreover he enjoys a great degree of popularity in the music circles that I consulted. If he does have his differences with Mr Beecham from time to time, a man whom he holds in high esteem, in the end it is not your interests that are our ultimate concern, as you will see from the following.

I have discussed the matter of the Manchester performance of Appalachia with Michaud and as things stand the publisher in these irregular circumstances has had to levy fees not only in respect of the hire material but also the performance right because the British Performing Rights Society curiously enough does not collect performing fees in respect of orchestral works with chorus (so-called oratorios) but entrusts their collection instead to the publisher. Although Appalachia can actually be classified as an orchestral work with short closing chorus it is the inclusion of the chorus which pushes it into the oratorio category. Now Mr Michaud is charging a hire fee of only 3 gns, an especially modest amount, aware that Mr Beecham has previously purchased his own set of material and 5 gns in respect of the performing right which would normally be collected by the PRS, not the publisher. We are positive that Manchester does not in the normal course of events give a second thought to paying performing fees to the PRS on concerts containing copyright works and in this instance with regard to the publisher one should not consider the sum of 8 gns as the fee but break it down so that 3 gns represents the hire fee and the rest covers the performing right. On the basis of this breakdown the Hallé certainly cannot complain that the terms of supply are incomparable to other orchestral works.

In order to find a possible way round this impasse I have now asked Mr Michaud to instruct the PRS in this one instance where it is actually an orchestral work in question that merely happens to contain a short closing chorus, to collect the performing fees itself with the result that Mr Michaud will only have to invoice the sum of 3 gns to the Hallé Orchestra. In any event I have impressed upon Mr Michaud the need to avoid any entrenchment of his position yet I must point out to you that this is not an isolated case but is of prime significance to us. Mr Beecham is motivated by the thought of whipping up a campaign against the publishers and their expensive hire fees, ideally he would like it if we did not charge fees at all. It is however in the interests of all composers and publishers that a certain level of fees are charged otherwise we all risk becoming trapped in exactly the situation that we are endeavouring to avoid, i.e. one in which the publication of new works by serious composers is no longer affordable. Production costs as you are aware are very high and were we not to levy a minimum hire and performing fee all parties would be greatly disadvantaged. We have wide-ranging experience in this area – at various times orchestral companies, broadcasters etc. have tried to squeeze the fees however publishers must always stand firm against their efforts to protect our future livelihood. On the other hand we do have great sympathy for the plight of the orchestral companies and for this reason we have no fear in saying that we really do only charge fees that represent the absolute minimum for the composer and publisher.

As far as the particular case of Beecham is concerned, we are fully conscious of his efforts on your behalf and that is why the hire fee for Appalachia has been set at no more than 3 gns whereas it should amount to 7–8 gns. We cannot however under any circumstances concur with Mr Beecham's standpoint that he has purchased your material once and is now free to arrange concerts using this material wherever it suits him without the orchestra (not Mr Beecham himself) paying a hire fee. The advantage for Mr Beecham in owning his own material lies in the fact that he will always have his own annotations to hand and he will always be in a position to conduct from his own material. It would spell ruin for all composers and publishers if individual conductors, even those who have not rendered a composer great service, were to perform everywhere using their own material thereby relieving the orchestra of their obligations with respect to hire fees. It will certainly not be beyond the realm of your understanding that this policy which Universal Edition always pursues with the greatest diplomacy has at its heart the interests of the composer and it is just unfortunate that in this one exception the publisher had to arrange the collection of the performing fees too. As a consequence the sum invoiced to the Hallé Orchestra seems far and away higher that it would do otherwise. We will try to reach a settlement, as it is just as important to us as it is to you that this concert dedicated to your music does not go ahead minus Appalachia. We have directed Mr Michaud accordingly but it would also further our cause greatly were you to make clear to Sir Thomas Beecham the views of Universal Edition.

Incidentally we are of the opinion that you will find no better representative of your interests at the Delius Society than Mr Michaud and we would be especially delighted if we could eliminate certain differences between him and Mr Beecham. It goes without saying that we shall do everything within our power to bring this about. Nevertheless we beg you please to keep it in mind that as respects Walk to the Paradise Garden Mr Beecham by his stubbornness has caused both you and Universal Edition some harm and as far as the score and orchestral material are concerned we can see no other way of proceeding than to give up on the proofs sent to him and have new photo prints prepared here (incurring us of course in unnecessary costs).

You can, Maestro Delius, rest assured that our commitment to your works remains solid and that we shall always carefully weigh up every factor when determining hire fees to realise the best deals in our common interest. We very much hope that the dispute regarding Appalachia can soon be resolved.

In reference to the two performances of Appalachia under Hamilton Harty in 1932 and the performance under Beecham on 5.3.32. you will be receiving separate correspondence on these matters from our accounts department.

We thank you most heartily for your best wishes and in turn send you our greetings.

Respectfully yours

PS On my extensive travels I had ample opportunity to present your works to a number of conductors. I concentrated my efforts in particular on conductors based in Belgium and Holland where your music has yet to achieve its due recognition. Let us hope that my efforts will produce some positive results.

No 327

Universal to Delius

24 January 1934
Vienna

Maestro Delius

Responding to our enquiry on your behalf regarding performances of Appalachia our English agent has sent us the following information: In 1932 the work was performed neither in Manchester nor anywhere else by Sir Hamilton Harty. He is able to confirm this from his own records and has also taken the trouble to contact Sir Hamilton Harty's secretary who has double-checked all her files for the year 1932.

As far as the performance under Sir Thomas Beecham on 5 March 1933[68] is concerned, most irregularly no hire fee was charged at the time although a very modest performing fee of the amount of 2-17-6d was collected and accounted to you on your six-monthly statement for the second period of 1933. In the meantime we believe that agreement on a reduced fee has been reached with the Hallé Orchestra in respect of their recent performance.

We remain

Yours respectfully

No 328

Universal to Delius

1 March 1934
Vienna

Maestro Delius

Mentor Films A.G., Zurich is planning to a make a film version of the Keller novella A Village Romeo and Juliet and has expressed an interest in using the music to your opera. This however would be on condition that we 'limit our fee requirements to a modest level' presupposing that you felt the music to be suitable for synchronisation. For the moment we have kept silent on the subject of fees although Mentor Films has asked us to indicate the sort of fee that they could expect to pay. We should therefore like you to kindly confirm that we can go ahead and conclude an agreement at the optimum rate and having achieved that retain a 25 per cent share of the synchronisation fee.[69] Of course the hire fees that we collect on the material supplied to the film company will be accounted in our normal manner.

We should be most obliged to you for your earliest consideration.

Yours respectfully

---

68 All Delius programme at Queens Hall with London Philharmonic Orchestra. A 'Beecham Sunday Concert'.

69 The only agreement between Delius and UE was for 20 per cent of mechanicals in certain territories, excluding the UK. The synchronisation licence, if issued, would have been for world distribution, payable in the country in which the deal was made. UE are not going to negotiate until they know Delius will allow UE a share.

ꕥ

No 329

Delius to Universal

4 March 1934
Grez-sur-Loing

Dear Sir

Such a disadvantageous proposition beggars belief in my opinion. The only occasion on which I would consent to a film production of my opera would be one undertaken by a first-rate enterprise with a first-rate fee to match. However I would be grateful to receive their proposals. What is your own opinion on the matter? It seems to me that a mediocre film treatment could only be detrimental.

I picked up the concert in Manchester very well here. It was quite wonderful and brought me great joy. I also enjoyed the splendid broadcast from Vienna of my Idyll on the 25 January. I understand you are agents for this work (Hawkes) and would hope that I can look forward to hearing it more often in the future. It could become quite popular.

Yours respectfully

No 330

Universal to Delius

13 March 1934
Vienna

Maestro Delius,

On the suggestion of our English agent we have published two arrangements of the Hassan Serenade, one for viola and piano by Lionel Tertis and the other for organ by Fenby. (Please find enclosed a specimen copy of the viola part.) This we have done on the proviso that for these editions too you are agreeable to a sales royalty of 10 per cent enabling us to set a lower price and thereby increasing sales. As you can see we are doing everything within our power to advance the cause of your every work and we should be most obliged if you would please indicate your acceptance of these terms by signing and returning the enclosed agreement.

Respectfully yours
enc.

ꟷ

No 331

Universal to Delius

23 March 1934
Vienna

Maestro Delius,

Your card concerning H.A. Seaver's arrangement of In a Summer Garden was unfortunately somewhat delayed in reaching us.[70] We have in the meantime received the MS and a letter from our American agent from which it transpires that Mr Seaver will be claiming 'the usual royalty'.

Although sales of piano duets are almost negligible throughout Europe – their main appeal is to the American and English markets and even there sales are limited – we would be prepared to publish the manuscript if you are so disposed and on the condition that you accept a sales royalty of 10 per cent in order to accommodate a further royalty of 5 per cent to the arranger. May we ask therefore that if you are agreeable to the afore-mentioned that you affix your signature to the enclosed agreement and return it to us.

As far as the musical merits of the arrangement are concerned we have no grounds for criticism although having said that we do sense that it could be somewhat simplified in places without detracting from the overall impression. This is a requirement that we have been forced to impose ever more frequently particularly in the last few years. It is our observation that sales editions are most easily marketed when the musical form is kept at its simplest. If you are agreeable then we would like to recommend some retouching of the piece of which we would also inform the arranger. In order to be able to give Mr Seaver and our American agent the earliest possible news we should be most obliged to you for your earliest attention. In sending you our best wishes we remain

Yours respectfully

PS We should be most grateful to hear from you regarding our letter of 13 March.[71]

---

70 FD had written on 10 March regarding Seaver's piano duet arrangement of *In a Summer Garden*. FD thought he was not expecting a royalty. It is strange that UE were prepared to publish a piano duet version by Seaver, but several times refused to publish Heseltine's piano arrangement, which FD had requested. Seaver is surely out of order to claim the 'usual royalties'. It is not usual, and was not then, for an arranger to be paid a royalty on an arrangement of a copyright work.

71 The Tertis arrangement for viola and piano, and the Fenby organ arrangement, of the Serenade from *Hassan*.

ꕥ

No 332

Delius to The Performing Right Society

25 March 1934
Grez-sur-Loing

Dear Sir,

I have just received the list of my works which you have kindly sent me.

But as I understand from your former correspondence you do not control, or collect performing fees from all these works? If you do not it is certainly very regrettable, as it involves me in a great deal of trouble and difficulty.

Will you be so kind as to tell me by return of post whether you collect the fees for the following works figuring on your list

A Mass of Life
Song of the High Hills
Songs of Sunset
Arabesque
Appalachia
Seadrift
Songs of Farewell

There are several errors in the list but being very hard pressed to give an answer about the preceding works, I beg you to answer at once and we will discuss the rest afterwards.

Thanking you in advance
Yours Truly

ꕥ

No 333

The Performing Right Society to Delius

26 March 1934
London

Dear Sir,

We are in receipt of your letter of 25th instant, and in reply to your enquiry we have to advise that we do not control the performing rights in the following large choral works mentioned by you:-

A Mass of Life

Songs of Sunset
Sea Drift

These being, according to our information, full choral works of considerable length. At one time our records were noted that we did not control 'Appalachia' and 'Song of the High Hills', but our records were subsequently altered when we ascertained that these were more correctly described as orchestral works with chorus (mostly wordless), whereas it is only large choral works in the true sense which the Society does not control. 'Arabesque' and 'Songs of Farewell' are both, according to our information, full choral works, but are comparatively short, and we regard them as being under our control and credit you with fees accordingly.[72]

We note that there are one or two errors in the list of works we sent you, and if you will kindly advise us of these at your convenience, we shall see that our records are corrected.

Yours faithfully,
Assistant Secretary.

No 334

Delius to The Performing Right Society

5 April 1934
Grez-sur-Loing

Dear Sir,

I was very glad to get your explanations and if you will kindly answer me one or two questions I shall be very grateful.

I take it that you did not collect a performing fee for Songs of Sunset performed at the Hallé Concerts on March 1st?[73]

Did you collect the fee for Appalachia for this same concert and for the BBC concert performance of Appalachia March 25th?[74] Would you tell me confidentially what the performance fee of Appalachia is?[75]

I understand from your remarks that you collect the performing fees on all the works in the hands of the OUP. Then there is the incidental music from 'Hassan'. You mark this as being published by London and Continental Music Publ. Co. Ltd.

72 It might have been helpful to mention the 20-minute rule. There is no record of Jelka Delius querying the works considered by PRS to be outside their control. The publishers did so. It was Dr Kalmus who said that PRS should in future control *Appalachia*.

73 PRS Pencilled note – no.

74 PRS note – yes.

75 PRS note – Broadcast about £2 10s 0d.

This is Michaud's firm.[76] But I will not get into difficulties, as the whole music for 'Hassan' belongs to the Universal Edition of Vienna. Should Michaud ever sever his connection with Universal, where would I be?

Do you collect for 'Requiem'?[77]

On page 8 you do not mention Sonata 3 also published by Hawkes and by far the most played of the three. Have you omitted to collect for this? Please look into this as it is very important.

Then there is 'A Village Romeo and Juliet', opera, marked as published by Curwen. It is, of course, published by Universal Edition, and Curwen used at one time to be their agent, but has no rights in it now. If only you sent out detailed accounts all these things would have been cleared up long ago.

I am sending you the list back, so as to facilitate the corrections, but please, kindly send the list back to me as I find it very useful as reference.
Hoping to hear from you soon

Yours sincerely,

No 335

The Performing Right Society to Delius

11 April 1934
London

Dear Sir,

We are in receipt of your letter of 5th instant with schedule of works sent with ours of 22nd ultimo, which we now return to you herewith, having made a note of the various corrections you made thereon.

In reply to your specific queries, we have not collected a performing fee for the performance of 'Songs of Sunset' at the Hallé Concert on 1st ultimo, because according to our records this is a large choral work, and is not therefore within the Society's control. The same applies to the choral work 'Requiem'. You will remember that we advised you to this effect in our letter of 10th October last, wherein we set out the list of your works falling within this category, i.e. 'Appalachia', 'A Mass of Life', 'Requiem', 'Sea Drift' and 'Songs of Sunset'.

Regarding the first work 'Appalachia', we subsequently advised you, i.e. on 28th ultimo, that having obtained further information concerning this work we now regard it as being within our control and we credit you accordingly for all recorded performances of the work. The fee for the broadcast performance on 25th March last will be credited to you in our Distribution of Broadcasting Fees for the six months

---

[76] Jean Michaud was the proprietor of Universal Music Agencies in London, representing Universal, Leuckart, Weinberger and Eulenberg. Did he collect performing fees for them?

[77] PRS note – no, choral, 45 Mins.

ended 30th June next. We cannot advise you the amount of the fee because the BBC do not now pay us, nor have they paid us for many years, separate fees for specific works, but for the payment of an annual sum are licensed to broadcast any and every work in our repertoire. Consequently, the amount credited to a member in respect of a particular performance is naturally dependant upon the number of performances of works in our repertoire during the distribution period in question, and the amount of the fee received by the Society from the BBC for the same period. This fee, we may add, is on a sliding scale based on the number of listeners' licences issued, and we are pleased to inform you that for this reason the fees we shall receive from the BBC for the year 1934, will be considerably more than those received during the previous years. As an approximation, however, we can say that the fee for 'Appalachia' will probably be about £2-10-0d for each station from which the performance was broadcast, and as on this occasion it was broadcast from five stations simultaneously, the total fee will be £12-10-0d, of which one-third is payable to Universal Edition and two-thirds to you.

It is correct that we credit you in respect of all your works published by the Oxford University Press at present notified to us, for the reason that as you have retained your performing rights, these works are in our repertoire. The publishers not being members of this Society, the whole of the fees are payable to you, but with regard to the work 'The Splendour falls', although we have a record that this is in the Oxford University Press catalogue, you have not previously notified it to the Society, and we understand it was not originally published by Tischer & Jagenberg.[78] For this reason it was not included in the list we sent you, which was taken almost entirely from your own notifications.

We shall be glad to have your confirmation that you have retained your performing rights in this work, and at the same time, will you kindly state the duration.

Re 'Hassan'

The London & Continental Music Co. Ltd went out of existence many years ago, but Mr Michaud, who is at present the London agent for Universal Edition, informs us that the incidental music to 'Hassan' is the copyright property of Universal, and accordingly you will be credited in respect of all performances of this music other than, of course, those given in conjunction with the play as a stage work.

Re Sonata No. 3

This work has not been previously notified by you, but we have a complete record of it from Messrs. Hawkes' notification.

'A Village Romeo & Juliet'

We are altering our records to shew this as a Universal publication, and as a matter of fact, our records had already been altered in respect of the selections and excerpts from the opera, and it is, of course, only these which are in our repertoire, the opera as a whole not being controlled by us.

---

[78] After OUP joined PRS in 1936, OUP would have received 1/3 of the performing fees.

As we have mentioned previously, the Society does not issue detailed statements of general Fees on account of the very great expense which would be involved, but you do receive from us detailed statements of all Broadcasting Distributions.

Yours faithfully,
Assistant Secretary

ᘓᘐᘓᘐ

No 336

Universal to Delius

17 April 1934
Vienna

Maestro Delius

We still await your response to our two letters of 13 and 23 of March and should be most grateful if you would please sign and return the agreements that were enclosed.[79]

Yours respectfully

ᘓᘐᘓᘐ

No 337

Delius to Universal

19 April 1934
Grez-sur-Loing

Dear Sir,

I have just received your letter of 17 April.[80]

My response has been somewhat delayed by the long and unpleasant correspondence that I have had to conduct in the matter of your agent, Mr Michaud.

---

[79] FD hadn't replied to the 13 March letter about arrangements of the *Hassan* Serenade, but UE sent a printed copy of the organ arrangement on 7 April. He had replied to the letter about Seaver.

[80] On 14 April UE had sent the printed score of the Keith Douglas *Walk to the Paradise Garden.* This is the last letter from FD to UE, and bearing in mind the situation in the Delius house, with both Fred and Jelka seriously ill, it seems extraordinary that Jelka could bring herself to address in such detail and with such knowledge, mundane publishing affairs.

Jelka went into hospital for an operation for cancer on 16 May. Delius died on Sunday 10 June 1934.

I regret to have to say that Mr Michaud by his business practices has forfeited the confidence of the overwhelming majority of English music festivals and orchestral companies. The generally held opinion is that nobody is willing to deal with him anymore with the result that the works he represents will simply be boycotted.

To illustrate the truth of this just look at all the difficulties that surrounded the Appalachia performance in Manchester on 1.3.34! It now emerges that Michaud was only entitled to supply the orchestral material. The performing fees were collected by PRS. Only the following works are not PRS controlled:

A Mass of Life / Songs of Sunset / Requiem / Sea Drift (Meerestreiben)

You will notice from my statements that through the years I have not once received performance fees in respect of Sea Drift, nor from the Songs of Sunset.[81] Michaud charged the Leeds Festival £23 for Songs of Sunset and Arabesque though he did reduce this to £15 when he realised that the works were to be sold. The fee however remains far too high for Arabeske is under PRS's control.[82]

The havoc being wrought by you on me and my interests through these practices beggars description; however you might at least consider the lasting damage that you are inflicting on yourself by your shortsighted policies.

Over Easter I received visits from various musicians and every single one warned me of Michaud's behaviour and expressed their hope that I would step in and call your attention to the matter.

On looking through my statements it became crystal clear just how little income I receive from the English agency compared with the few works that show up from activities in U.S.A. I would however like to reaffirm my earlier viewpoint that I really see no reason to reduce my royalty to 10 per cent especially when we are speaking of short and easy to sell arrangements.

I should also like to point out that my American income was missing from my recent statement. What has happened there?

Furthermore I find your claims to hire income on material that has been sold by you to be baseless. Make your mind up one way or the other![83]

In any event the purchaser ought to have been informed at the point of transaction that he would still be liable to hire fees.

With very best wishes to Dr Kalmus

Yours respectfully

---

81 As far as Continental Europe is concerned, it is doubtful whether Delius received any performing fees through the Society network between 1914 and 1926, when an agreement was signed between PRS/AKM/GDT/GEMA. Universal should have picked up at least their share through AKM, but we don't know whether Universal passed any on to Delius. As far as Great Britain is concerned, Universal had no agent with performing rights until 1930. PRS should therefore have collected for Delius and paid him the full fee. As soon as Cranz took over as Universal's agent, with a mandate to collect performing fees, performing fees for the PRS excluded works would have been collected by Cranz. Only PRS had the rule about not representing choral & orchestral works lasting more than 20 minutes.

82 *An Arabesque* lasts 15 minutes.

83 See DrKalmus's reply.

Many thanks for the comps. I am particularly delighted that the Intermezzo has now appeared as a printed edition.

ꟿ

No 338

Universal to Delius

26 April 1934
Vienna

Maestro Delius

We are most pleased after a gap of some time to finally receive an answer from you and only regret that you felt prompted to use the occasion to lodge a complaint concerning the activities of our English agent, Mr Michaud.

Firstly may we point out that by virtue of an express agreement the work Appalachia has for some years now not been under the control of PRS which has caused us to collect performance fees directly. It is for this reason that Mr Michaud in adherence to his duties was obliged to charge a performance fee on the original concert given by Sir Thomas Beecham. It was not until we received a recent communication from the Austrian collecting society that we learnt that PRS had reconsidered its position and would now be willing to collect fees in respect of Appalachia.[84] Of this change of policy they would have had to give notice to Mr Michaud and the Austrian Society respectively well in advance in order to avoid a duplication of levies. The undersigned had a personal opportunity in 1931 to meet with representatives of the PRS and during the course of these discussions the request was made that PRS act on our behalf in respect of works like A Mass of Life in the same way that its sister societies in Germany and Austria do but this proposal was rejected.

The afore-mentioned we hope will serve to allay any suspicion that we have not made the most strenuous efforts to resolve these questions. We confirm that the performing right in A Mass of Life, the Songs of Sunset, Requiem and Sea Drift is retained by Universal Edition whilst Appalachia is to be controlled through the PRS upon implementation of its latest statute.

We have made enquiries of Mr Michaud with regard to performing fees in respect of Sea Drift and Songs of Sunset and equally the Leeds Festival and we can only reiterate that it would indeed be a bad system were we to dramatically reduce our hire fees as this would be counteractive to the interests of both the composer and publisher. For when the publisher cannot depend upon adequate remuneration in this area production must cease. We are fully aware on the other hand that organisers do make repeated efforts to obtain some relief on the fees and in every instance we do try within the realms of possibility to reach some accommodation. That some inconsistencies do arise, for example a fee of £23 might be reduced to £15, is not inconceivable because our intention is to arrive at a manageable rate and only if an

[84] From March 1934.

orchestra comes and presents to us their reasons why they should be entitled to some dispensation can we appease their wishes. In the majority of cases the organiser only wants to pay a pittance and to proceed on this basis is unattractive for both the composer and the publisher. Every concert organiser is forced to pay the costs of the hall, the orchestra and conductor, promoters etc. but by squeezing their costs on music and performing fees they refuse to acknowledge that the creator of a work is also owed some compensation. The PRS who has a daily struggle on its hands with concert organisers, just like its sister societies in other countries, will attest to every detail of what I have just said.

This should not be interpreted as meaning that we have never charged hire fees that have lead to a concert being abandoned. It is easy for an organiser to turn to you and repeatedly complain about hugely excessive fee demands – in doing so they refuse to recognise the essential fact that even the author and with that the publisher are fully justified in claiming a return on their investment. It would be most desirable if you could kindly furnish us with a list of a few names and addresses of those people who have grumbled to you about excessive fees to allow us to investigate. For our part we have complete sympathy for the difficult situation in which concert organisers find themselves and the balance between the purchasing power of the individual and our minimum charge is always given very careful consideration.

Your observation, quote 'I find your claims to hire income on material that has been sold by you to be baseless. Make your mind up one way or the other! In any event the purchaser ought to have been informed at the point of transaction that he would still be liable to hire fees' is incomprehensible. You will have to send us further details of which performance, purchaser and work are involved. To give you a general outline, on the copyright page of all sales material there is a clause stating that use of same material is restricted to performances by the purchaser be it an orchestra or amateur group. All other uses are forbidden.[85] If the purchaser then wants to use the material for concerts other than those given by his own orchestra – for example, a conductor may purchase his own set of material so that he can always conduct from material containing his own markings – then the new orchestra which does not possess its own set of material but is being supplied by the conductor must obviously pay a hire fee. We are confident that you will fully agree with our point of view for if we failed to follow this practice we could end up in a situation where a few conductors buy up sets of material thereby defraying the cost of a large chunk of future performances in one move. You will understand that this would without doubt threaten our interests. At any rate we should be glad to hear your comments on the subject.

Regarding the absence of American income in your recent statement we should like to point out that up to December there was in fact nothing to account.

It is to be regretted that you have declined to accept a royalty of 10 per cent in respect of the two new arrangements (viola and piano/organ) of the Hassan Serenade

---

[85] Publishers would only have sold performing material under a 'limited use contract'. For example, Boosey & Hawkes, certainly since 1945, would have allowed the purchaser to use without a hire fee strictly for the purchaser's own use. Use for broadcasts or recording was forbidden without a fee, and lending was prohibited.

all the more so as the retail selling price has now been set at a lowly RM–. 80 in the confidence that this 10 per cent royalty would suffice as it did in the case of the piano arrangement. The reason behind our thinking is that a low price will generate higher sales and we also considered it to be of greater benefit to you to earn a lower percentage from a higher sales volume than a higher percentage from a lower sales volume. If you cannot meet our wishes it is only Universal Edition that is going to suffer taking into account the additional costs that we will incur paying out on each copy sold a royalty equal to 25 per cent of RM–. 80 (organ edition) and RM 1, – (viola and piano edition). You can quite easily work out the figures for yourself: if we supply copies to distributors at a discount of 50 per cent-60 per cent on a selling price of RM–. 80 and pay you RM–. 20 per copy that leaves a total of 12–20 pfennigs to cover not only our production but also our management costs. Looking at it from our point of view you soon realise why these figures have such little appeal. In these circumstances we shall also not be in a position to publish new editions which will effect the promotion of your works, like for example the arrangement for piano duet of In a Summer Garden that we have received and the piano arrangement of Brigg Fair that was recently sent to us by an Englishman by the name of P.H. Atkins. In view of our comments we do hope that you will be as keen as we are that Universal Edition does not sustain any losses and that you will oblige us by signing and returning the enclosed agreement. This comes with the request that you please give this matter your utmost attention.

On the subject of the Intermezzo, we are most pleased that we have at last been able to bring out the printed edition. As it proved impossible to retrieve the proofs from Sir Thomas Beecham we reproduced the photo prints and only then were we in a position to put the work to press.

Please forgive us for taking up so much of your time with a letter of this length however we must emphasise how important it is to us that we convince you of our determination always to act in your best interest and that you are aware of our complete confidence in Mr Michaud whom we know to be a special admirer of your music. That is why we are most keen to obtain from you a list of those people who have made complaints against him so that if necessary we can take remedial action.

We do look forward with great interest to your comments and remain

Yours respectfully
enc.

No 339

Universal London to Universal Vienna

28 April 1934
London

My Dear Dr Kalmus,

Many thanks for your letter of the 26th ins.t, just received. Will you please excuse me if I reply by hand as I am all alone here at the moment, it being Saturday afternoon when the staff leaves at one o'clock and I do not wish to hold up my reply till Monday.

The complaints of Delius and Ethyl Smyth can be traced back immediately to Beecham. Dame Ethyl – after being Beecham's enemy for years has suddenly become his great friend and the only people I have any trouble with here are the ones Beecham is connected with.

The complaints of Delius and Smyth have been fully answered in your own letters to these two people and I can only say this: – when I quote for any hires and performing fees I use your own quotations. Those people or societies who can pay one of the highest figures if they make any request for lower rate I use my own discretion and reduce if I think advisable in your interest. But even then it seems that they are not satisfied and I still receive complaints, although – as in the case of the Leeds Festival – they wrote to me to say that the new quotations were acceptable. Here there is the position that they are going to do the Delius

Arabesque…	Hire	£4-4-0d
	Perf fee	£2-10-0d
and		
Songs of Sunset	Hire	£5-5-0d
	Perf fee	£3-3-0d

They first of all refused to pay anything at all when I gave them the highest quotation (which they should pay being the Leeds Triennial Musical Festival which has plenty of money) because Beecham told them he did not want to use our materials as he had his own which according to him and Delius he can use without payment to UE whatever – wherever he likes and as often as he likes.

The position therefore is this. I either look after your interest and ask for the fees I should ask for – or – I leave Beecham entirely alone and let him do with the Delius works as he likes without interference.

He has given various concerts lately where he played Delius works and I have let him alone and said nothing at all. When he writes (if he takes the trouble) he writes the most abusive letters imaginable without any provocation whatever on my part. I have always been most polite and tactful and I can assure you – if this is necessary – that I have no trouble whatever with anyone apart from the Beecham clique.

With regard to Leeds I have sent them the rental forms weeks ago and have written 3 times asking them to fill them in as I must send them to you. So far they have not taken the trouble to reply even. Now it seems that they are still trying to avoid payment and through getting Delius to complain about me to make things as difficult as possible for me.

I really do not know how to deal with these people and should be glad of your advice. I have handled the whole situation as carefully as I could but I must ask for payments unless I am disloyal to you.

As I said before – your letter to Delius and to Smyth one can answer to their complaints and I have acted in the spirit of your letters to these people. Beecham has the same trouble with everybody here and my own feeling is that he is a complete menace to every publisher. He wrote – as I told you months ago – that he is getting as many people together as he can in order to fight and defeat the publishers who are 'a band of robbers'. These are his own words and when a man takes up this attitude it becomes impossible to do anything to please him and all he is out for is to make as much trouble as he can all round. You must surely know this already – if you only think of 'Walk to the Paradise Garden'.

It is not nice of Delius either to write letters like he does after all the work I have put in on his behalf for the Delius Society who have just brought out the recording (under Beecham) of Paris. (Columbia Recording).

The Smyth person is entirely hopeless and I certainly am not going to give her details of sales or hires. All such details are sent to you direct and that ends my responsibility.

So that is the position. I have done all I could and more than any other publisher would do in order to help everyone as much as possible and as far as reasonable. If that is not sufficient I do not know what else I can do and I am sure that you will agree.

Any further advice from you in the matter will be welcome. If you wish I will gladly refer all enquiries with regard to Delius and Smyth cum Beecham to you direct in the future and have nothing more to do with these people who are more trouble than they are worth to anybody.

With kindest regards, my dear Doctor Kalmus,

I remain,
Yours very sincerely

No 340

Delius to The Performing Right Society

1 May 1934
Grez-sur-Loing

Dear Sir,

Enclosed I am glad to send you the confirmation you needed from the OUP.[86]

As regards Appalachia the Universal Edition insists that you refused to collect the performing fee for the performance in Manchester, March 1 of 1934. I am completely at sea between these conflicting statements.[87]

---

[86] OUP had confirmed that Delius controlled the performing right in *The Spendour Falls* and an organ arrangement of *On Hearing the First Cuckoo*.

[87] Confusion. PRS had written to FD on 26 March 1934 that it did control *Appalachia* after all, probably on the authority of Dr Kalmus. FD has asked about the Hallé concert on 1 March to find that UE maintain that PRS refused to collect for the performance. On 4 May 1934 PRS wrote to say that they had not informed AKM, (the Austrian Society) that they would control *Appalachia* by that date. Did FD receive a performing fee? As PRS pointed out

I apologise for the mistake I made re quartet and I did not know about Brigg Fair.

Yours faithfully,

No 341

Universal to Jelka Delius

11 June 1934
Vienna

Dear Madam

It was with shock and deepest sadness that we learnt of the sudden death of Maestro Frederick Delius. For decades the Universal Edition publishing house, and in particular the late Direktor Hertzka, enjoyed close personal contact with Frederick Delius that transcended a mere business relationship. His death has robbed Universal Edition of one of its most brilliant and prominent composers. His work will live on. Our prime concern now rests not only in preserving his memory but also in maintaining his stature in the minds of the public by the continued upkeep of his works and cultivation of interest in his music.

Madam, you were the most loyal and devoted partner to the Maestro and the fulfilment of his work who will remain the executrix of his artistic legacy. To you today we offer the expression of our deepest sympathy.

---

on 4 May, arrangements for the performance would have been made well in advance by UE, covering hire and performance fees, so UE probably did collect the fee.

Postlude 1934

No 342

Jelka Delius to Thomas Beecham

2 September 1934
Grez-sur-Loing

My Dear Thomas,

I have read in the papers that you are going to give a Delius Concert on Nov 8th at the Philharmonic. The programme is so splendid and I should so love to be present. If I go on improving I think I may be able to; I could take my maid with me and I could probably stay with Mrs. O'Neill. I should love to combine it with the BBC concert when you conduct the Mass of Life, but I do not know the date.

If I do go to London I want very much to talk about those testamentary arrangements with you. You see there has been a great deal of misunderstanding. Somebody had given Fred to understand that I was never going to recover or return to him. Then Fred was terribly upset and got worse and worse and moreover worried constantly about having to make testamentary arrangements himself. Before he had always said that after his death I was to talk it over with you and you would surely find a way to arrange for some of his music to be played once a year in his memory, etc and in various other plans.

Gardiner who has lost all interest in music and Eric, who is such a child as yet both made me stick to the letter to the few things Fred had said he wished to stipulate, this altho' when I had returned home, altho' very ill in another room, he always said 'Ask Jelka'. They would not see that all those arrangements were only meant in case I died before him.

For instance he said Eric was to have all his books and music, printed and manuscript, and Eric began to pack it all up in a trunk, when I had to stop him. Naturally Fred would never have all that taken away and leave me in this house bereft of music and literature. I told Eric that if I died he had no legal right to these things and naturally Fred's terrible relatives would come in and successfully claim everything. Eric saw that I was right and that as long as I live these things are only safe in my keeping. Even afterwards it is very questionable whether Eric should possess all these manuscripts; they ought to go to Museums or Libraries, where people could see them.

About all this I should like so very much to talk to you before I make my testament finally. I have made it for the moment in French, as they seemed to think I might have a relapse and die at any moment. The question is, in what country am I to make this testament: I possess really nothing in France. Our fortune, which anyhow has dwindled very much in the last bad years, is in a bank in Geneva. That and the royalties from the PRS and his publishers are the assets. I am a British subject, domiciled in France.

I have written to the Director of the Swiss bank for advice and he says for various reasons, which he could only explain verbally it would be wisest to make the testament in Switzerland. That might avoid heavy English death duties but yet it strikes me as rather obvious and bad. And anyhow I could not go to Switzerland now. Could you not, dear Thomas, find out from your lawyer friends – what would be the best course to take. I could then perhaps get the whole thing done whilst I am in England and after you have given me your advice. As for these programmes of young composers with only one Delius work – that is an absurd idea and there would be no public for such concerts. I feel we must change that.

I must tell you, dear wonderful friend that the absolutely superb record of 'Paris' is my greatest joy in this great and absolute loneliness here. When I go to the cemetery I never feel Fred is there, but when I hear this wonderful record, then I am quite with him again. I am so happy to read that you are doing Eventyr for the Delius – Album. His last great pleasure was that performance in Manchester on March 1st.[1] He was moved to tears. It must be a consolation to you to know how he loved you. I found an old letter to me the other day from before the war, where he speaks with so much love and admiration of you and a glorious concert you gave. (Perhaps the one at the Academy?)

It was unfortunate and truly tragic that I had to leave him just during those last critical weeks. When I returned all was already crystallised and I had no occasion to broach the subject of his wishes, the end came so unexpectedly soon.

It was so sweet of Dora to come and be with me those terrible days. Please give her my love.

And do forgive me the length of this letter – but I had so much to say.

Yours ever devotedly,
Jelka Delius

No 343

Jelka Delius to Thomas Beecham

17 September 1934
Grez-sur-Loing

Dear Thomas,

---

[1] Hallé Orchestra. Delius works in the programme were; *Eventyr, Appalachia, The Walk to the Paradise Garden and Songs of Sunset.*

I cannot tell you what a great consolation your letter is to me. It is so good to know that you feel about things as I do. After all you and I have Fred's interests most at heart and understand him better than anyone else.

A copy of Fred's testament is in the Westminster Bank Finchley Road 106. I wrote immediately to the Bank to send it to you. This formidable looking document is really quite simple as Fred only says that he leaves everything he has to me. All these witnesses and legal fuss was only necessary as Fred could neither read it nor sign.

The other dispositions were made by Fred verbally first to Eric alone and then when the latter wired for Gardiner they were repeated to Gardiner. Both of them wrote down what Fred said in their little pocket books. Later on they read it to me. I have yet to find out whether this would be legally binding in France and England. Fred wanted to have £1,000 given to Fenby at once and also wished him to have all his books, printed and manuscript music. And then the concert scheme of which you have heard.

I do not wish in any case to contest the gift of £1,000 tho' I cannot pay it at once entirely; but I wonder how I stand with regard to the manuscript music. A musician friend of mine is coming here for a few days and with her help we will make a list of the manuscript music, of which I shall hand you a copy.

It is so evident that when Fred said all this he was entirely under the impression that I was no longer there and that he had to think of everything himself and make some disposition. He was very ill and unhappy about me at the time and really unable unaccustomed as he was to such efforts to think things out under all their aspects. Fenby is a good boy, but so inexperienced and without any sense of proportion, taking himself as too important a personage altogether. He wanted to hand all these dispositions of Fred's to the press, but I hindered him so far from doing that. He is going to the Leeds Festival and all the rehearsals, so you will see him there. He can tell you exactly what Fred said to him.

If Fenby possessed all the manuscripts of Fred's early works he might be persuaded to alter, arrange and publish them. No provision has been made about that. He might wish to sell some of these most valuable manuscripts. There is for example a whole manuscript of the Mass of Life; a wonderful thing that should be in some museum or Library. He has his family and his fiancée who may presently be urging him to make the most of this gift. I must safeguard Fred's ultimate interests.

I quite see your 3 important points, but how can one secure better performances when all the conductors are so mediocre. For the second point the re-editing according to your markings Fenby might be roped in to help you and we must come to a definite arrangement with Univ. Ed about it.

The 3rd point, the recording of all Fred's best pieces, I think it is the most important of all and if Fred had really been normal nothing would have been dearer to his heart. A touching letter about it which he dictated and sent to you lately is ample proof of that.

I shall try to be in London for Oct 24th and then stay on for Nov 8th. We shall be able to talk about it all then.

Yours ever affectionately,
JD

Appendices

Note: Several of the publishing contracts contain wording deleted by FD before being signed. Such deletions are printed in the body of the contracts, in italics, within square brackets.

Appendix 1

Augener 1892 Publishing Agreement for *Three Shelley Songs*

Memorandum: – That I Fritz Delius of 33 Rue Ducouëdic, Paris, have this day sold and assigned and do hereby sell absolutely to Messrs. Augener & Co., of 86 Newgate St., London, at the price or sum of two pounds 10/- (printed music) all my Copyright and Interest of whatever kind, present and future, vested and contingent, and for all countries, of and in

7 Lieder (aus dem Norwegischen), (edition no. 8829B) and 3 Songs to words by Shelley, (edition no. 8824)

by me and also my right of representing and performing the same.

AND I hereby promise the said AUGENER & Co., at their request and cost to execute such further Assurances and my said Copyright, Interest and Right to the said AUGENER & Co., as they shall direct.

WITNESS my hand this 18th day of October in the year of our Lord One Thousand Eight Hundred and Ninety Two.

Signed in the presence of

Fritz Delius

Appendix 2

Harmonie 1906 Publishing Agreement for *Appalachia* and *Sea Drift*

I Frederick Delius hereby assign to Harmonie Verlag in Berlin[1] and its successors in law the exclusive and unlimited publishing right concerning the following works:

---

[1] Original contract in German.

1. Appalachia
2. Seadrift

with the right to the exclusive reproduction and the commercial distribution for all times, for all editions and issues, for all countries, no matter whether literary agreements with these countries exist or not; thus, with all the rights currently existing or in the future provided by law to the creator of such a work.

I declare, that the publisher's rights to the lyrics and the music of the said works are at my free disposal and 1 further declare that I have not entirely or partly assigned this right to third parties. Harmonie is entitled to carry[2] out reasonable additions, shortenings and alterations with my consent.

The said Publisher is further exclusively entitled to effect the usual arrangements, excerpts and adaptations for one or more instruments or voices, transcriptions into other keys, translations into other languages and issue adaptations in dramatic or narrative form.

I leave it to the said Publisher to fix and later on alter the retail price.

If the term of copyright is prolonged by law, this agreement shall be effective for the prolonged period. The manuscripts of the said works shall remain in the possession and property of the publisher.

The assignment of the copyright was effected under the subsequent conditions:

The receipts taken from these works shall first be used to cover Harmonie's expenses.

I shall have an interest of fifty per cent from the amount remaining. The publishing house is operated by Harmonie Publishing Co. I shall receive the amount of free copies as provided by law.

I reserve the performing right to the full extent for myself.

Berlin, February 20, 1906

Appendix 3

Leuckart 1911 Publishing Agreement for *Songs of Sunset*

Transfer of Copyright
With the Sole Exception of the Performing Rights[3]

I, Frederick Delius acting also for my heirs and assigns, hereby cede to the firm of F.E.C. Leuckart[4] and to their assigns the entire and transferable copyright, with the sole exception of the performing rights in my work:-

[2] These clauses are standard in classical music publishing contracts of the time. The publisher wanted freedom to arrange and adapt and a warranty from the composer that the music was his to assign.

[3] The words crossed out were deleted by FD from the contract submitted by Leuckart.

[4] Original in German.

Frederick Delius, 'Songs of Sunset', for Soprano and baritone solo, with mixed choir and orchestra

Together with the power of exclusive reproduction and publication for profit, of any kind, for all time, for all editions and in all countries, whether copyright conventions are in force for such countries or not, in short all rights that the law allows or reserves to the composer of such a work, or which it will in the future allow or reserve. [*In particular also all existing or future rights for utilization in mechanical musical instruments or similar uses for the purpose of giving out cinematograph pictures.*]
I declare that I am solely entitled to dispose of the copyright in the work and that I have neither wholly nor partially otherwise transferred it. The publishing firm is solely entitled to [*make or permit the making of relevant editions, abbreviations or alterations and*] to publish the usual arrangements, excerpts or adaptations for one or more instruments or voices, as well as transpositions into other keys, translations into other languages and adaptations in dramatic or narrative form. I relinquish to them the right to decide, [*though only with my consent, the date of publication,*] the fixing and subsequent alteration of the selling price [*and I renounce the right to extract recognizable themes from the work and to incorporate them in a new work*]. The right of public musical performance belongs to the Institute for musical performing rights in Berlin. [*If the performing right reverts to me, I reserve to myself and my heirs as assignees the performing right, without further reference to the publisher.*]
If the period of protection of the copyright is legally prolonged or if protection is extended to new forms of exploitation of the work, this contract remains in force for the period of the prolongation and for the extension of protection.
The manuscript of the work remains in the possession of the publishers as their property.
I confirm the due receipt of the agreed fee for the cession of my copyright and I am ready at any time to attest my signature to court or notary on demand.
The above contract carries the following supplements.
After the production and advertising costs of the works mentioned have been covered, the publisher promises to divide subsequent receipts so that the composer and the publisher each receive half of the net income and accounting will be yearly in August.
An advance payment of Mk 1,000 has been paid to Mr Delius as an advance on the said works, which is to be deducted from future payments.

F.E.C. Leuckart

February 1911

Appendix 4

Leuckart 1913 Consolidation Agreement

Assignment of Copyrights with the sole exception of Rights of Performance and the Rights for Mechanical Musical Instruments.[5]

I Frederick Delius herewith assign, also on behalf of my heirs and legal successors, to the firm

F.E.C. Leuckart, Leipzig,[6]

and their legal successors with the sole exception of Performance rights, the copyrights, in all other respects unrestricted and transferable, of my works:

Brigg Fair **Dance Rhapsody**

In a Summer Garden **Songs of Sunset**

Paris **The Song of the High Hills**

authorising exclusive duplication and commercial distribution in any way and for all times, for all editions, and for all countries, irrespective of the existence of literary contracts with them or not, in short, with all rights granted or reserved by law to the author of such works or to be granted or reserved in future. [*In particular also all existing or future rights for utilization in mechanical musical instruments or similar uses for the purpose of giving out cinematograph pictures.*]
Regarding the copyrights on the works I declare that I alone am entitled to dispose of them to the extent mentioned and that I have not assigned them in any other way either whole or in part. The publishing firm alone is entitled to make or arrange to make and publish appropriate additions, deletions, and amendments as well as the usual arrangements, extracts, and settings for solo or several instruments or vocalists, the re-arrangement into other keys, translations into other languages, adaptations into dramatised or narrative forms. I cede to them the decisions regarding publishing times, fixing and amendments at later dates of the selling prices and waive the right of extracting recognisable tunes from these works and to use them as a basis for a new work.
The Right of public musical performance is held by the Anstalt für musikalisches Aufführungsrecht in Berlin. [*If the performing right reverts to me, I reserve unto myself and my heirs as assignees the performing right, without further reference to the publishers.*]
If the duration of the copyright is extended by law or the copyrights extended to cover new forms of utilisation of the work this agreement is to remain valid for the

5 The reservation of mechanical rights was added in Delius's own hand.

6 Original in German.

duration of the extension and for the extended coverage. The manuscript is to remain with the publishers as their property.
I am willing at any time, on request, to have my own signature certified at court or by a notary.
………………..19

(The publisher's agreement overleaf[7] to be supplemented as follows:

All agreements regarding the works by Frederick Delius hitherto published by F.E.C. Leuckart in Leipzig: namely 'Brigg Fair', 'Dance Rhapsody', 'In a summer garden', 'Paris', 'Songs of sunset'[8], are cancelled and by the following agreement are transferred into the sole ownership and for publication by the said firm.

1. For the six works mentioned overleaf and for a book of 'Fünf Lieder' ('Five Songs') for one voice and pianoforte Mr Frederick Delius is to receive a total fee of Mk 16,000, payable in four successive yearly amounts of Mk 4,000. commencing on 1st August 1913.
2. Unless he has delivered the 'Fünf Lieder' Mr Frederick Delius has no claim to the final instalment payable in August 1916.
3. Mr Frederick Delius is acknowledging the publishers agreement overleaf in its entirety.[9] [*With the exception of the cession of mechanical musical instrument rights*]
4. The Mk 200 already received for 'Paris', and Mk 1000. received for 'Songs of Sunset' will not be deducted from the amount of Mk 16,000.

Grez sur Loing, 10th July 1913
(sgd) Frederick Delius

Appendix 5

Tischer & Jagenberg 1912 Publishing Agreement for *Life's Dance*

The following agreement has been concluded Between Frederick Delius as composer of the one part and the publishers Tischer & Jagenberg GmbH, Cologne of the other part, and is binding on the assigns of both parties.[10]

---

7 'Overleaf' means the wording above. The original contact was on two pages, the supplementary clauses on page two referring to the first page.

8 Song of the High Hills, for which the contract is dated 1911, is omitted from page 2, probably by mistake.

9 The addendum was drafted by Jelka in her own hand and is in the Trust's archives. This is the phrase that Delius told Jelka to cross out when signing the contract.

10 Original in German.

1. Mr Frederick Delius transfers to the publishers Tischer & Jagenberg for all editions and versions, for all countries and for the full period of copyright protection the right to publish his orchestral work 'Life's Dance'.
2. The performing rights belong to the GDT in Berlin.
3. The composer receives for this work a fee of Mk 5,000 – of which, under the terms of this agreement, Mk 2,000 has already been paid, (1,000 on 1 July 1913 and 1,000 in 1914), [the balance to be paid] upon the sale of the 40th [set of] orchestral material. For the Mk 3,000 not yet paid, interest of 5 per cent will be paid until the payment.[11]
4. The manuscript becomes the property of the publisher.
5. In any disputes, The Cologne Court will have jurisdiction.

24 June 1912

Appendix 6

Tischer & Jagenberg 1913 Publishing Agreement for *On Hearing the First Cuckoo* and other works

Agreement

Between Frederick Delius as composer of the one part and the publishers Tischer & Jagenberg GmbH, Cologne of the other part, the following agreement has been concluded and is binding on the assigns of both parties.[12]

1. Mr Frederick Delius transfers to the publishers Tischer & Jagenberg for all editions and versions, for all countries and for the full period of copyright protection the right to publish his two pieces for small orchestra: 'On hearing the first cuckoo in Spring' and 'Summer Night on the River' as also the five songs: 'Schwarze Rosen', – 'die Nachtigall', – 'I.Brazil', – 'Herbstlied', – Frühlingslied'.
2. The performing rights belong to the GDT in Berlin. Receipts from mechanical copyright will be divided as follows: the publisher receives 33.3 per cent if the words are mechanically reproduced, 50 per cent if only the music is mechanically reproduced.
3. The composer receives 30 per cent of the gross receipts on every copy sold, hired or otherwise disposed of for profit, whether it be score, piano selection or orchestral parts etc. On sheet music with a fixed retail price the composer receives 25 per cent of the price and on songs 20 per cent of the price. If the entire orchestral material is supplied, the composer's share of the price

[11] The 40th sale had apparently not been made by the 1931 contract between Delius and OUP.

[12] Original in German.

charged, (selling or hire etc.) will be at least Mk 12.

4. Annual accounts will be made in July. The publishers will grant the composer the right of access to their books for the purpose of checking his accounts.
5. The manuscripts become the property of the publisher.
6. In the case of any disputes the Cologne Court will have jurisdiction.

9 December 1913

Appendix 7

Universal 1913 Publishing Agreement for the *Arabesque*

Transfer of Copyright

With the sole exception of the performing and mechanical rights

I, Frederick Delius acting also for my heirs and assigns, hereby cede to the firm Universal Edition A.G. Vienna-Leipzig[13] and to their assigns the entire and transferable copyright, with the sole exception of the performing and mechanical rights in my work:

An Arabesque (J.P. Jacobson)

For Baritone solo, mixed choir and orchestra

Together with the power of exclusive reproduction and publication for profit, of any kind, for all time, for all editions and in all countries, whether copyright conventions are in force for such countries or not, in short with all rights that the law allows or reserves to the composer of such a work, or which it will in the future allow or reserve.

I declare that I am solely entitled to dispose of the copyright in the work and that I have neither wholly nor partially otherwise transferred it. The publishing firm is solely entitled to make or permit the making of relevant additions, abbreviations or alterations and to publish the usual arrangements, excerpts or adaptations for one or more instruments or voices, as well as transpositions into other keys, translations into other languages and adaptations in dramatic or narrative form. I relinquish to them the right to decide [*though only with my consent,*] the date of publication, the fixing and any subsequent alteration of the selling price and I renounce the right to extract recognisable themes from the work and to incorporate them in a new work.

The administration of musical performance rights will be handled in accordance with the rules of the Genossenschaft Deutscher Tonsetzer.

Should the period of copyright be legally prolonged or the protection extended to new forms of the work, this contract will remain in force for the period of the prolongation and for the extension of the protection. The manuscript of the work remains in the possession of the publisher as their property.

---

13 Original in German.

For the assignment of my copyright I receive every six months 15 per cent of the selling price for every copy sold, or from the receipts from copies hired, or otherwise exploited. On signing this contract, I will be paid an advance of Mk 1,000, not returnable even if my share does not amount to the aforementioned sum.

23 June 1913

Appendix 8

1913 Transfer of copyright in *Fennimore and Gerda* to Universal

Transfer of Copyright
With the Sole Exception of Performing and Mechanical Rights

I, Frederick Delius acting also for my heirs and assigns, hereby cede to the company Universal Edition A.g. Vienna[14] and to their sole assigns the entire and transferable copyright, with the sole exception of the performing and mechanical rights, in my musical play:

Fennimore & Gerda

Two episodes from the life of Niels Lyhne, after Niels Lyhne, by J.P Jacobsen

Together with the power of exclusive reproduction and publication for profit, of any kind, for all time, for all editions and in all countries, whether copyright conventions are in force for such countries or not, in short for all rights that the law allows or reserves to the composer of such a work, or which it will in the future allow or reserve.

I declare that I am solely entitled to dispose of the copyright in the work and that I have neither wholly nor partially otherwise transferred it. The publishing firm is solely entitled to make or to permit the making of relevant additions, abbreviations or alterations and to publish the usual arrangements, excerpts or adaptations for one or more instruments or voices, as well as transpositions into other keys, translations into other languages and adaptations in dramatic or narrative form. I relinquish to them the right to decide the date of publication, the fixing and any subsequent alteration of the selling price and I renounce the right to extract recognisable themes from the work and to incorporate them in a new work.

The right of public musical performance in concerts belongs to the Genossenschaft Deutscher Tonsetzer (GDT), in Berlin. If the period of protection of the work is legally prolonged or if protection is extended to new forms of exploitation of the work, this contract will remain in force for the period of prolongation and the extension of protection. The manuscript of the work remains in the possession of the publishers as their property.

---

[14] Original in German.

The cession of the above-mentioned rights, in particular of the copyright in the text and music within the prescribed limits, is made subject to conditions simultaneously laid down by separate contract.

10 July 1913.

Appendix 9

Universal 1913 Publishing Agreement for *Fennimore and Gerda*

To: Universal Edition Vienna[15]

For the rights transferred to you by a simultaneously made about the assignment of my copyright in my Musical Drama

Fennimore and Gerda

I will receive from you:

From the gross receipts for the use of the stage material 20 per cent of each copy sold and paid for or otherwise exploited and from the remaining publisher's receipts 15 per cent of the selling price of all of music scores and libretti sold or otherwise exploited.

Besides the above-mentioned shares of the publishing receipts, I receive, while licensing you to exploit my work on the stage, from the box offices of all theatres in Germany as well as from the German theatres of Austria, 90 per cent of the gross receipts. My income from all remaining theatres[16] has to be 80 per cent of the box office. The cost for the share of the foreign translator is to be borne by you.

The accounting for the publishing income and hire fees as well as the royalties of the performances has to be done biannually in detail.

The performing rights of concert performances will be accounted for according to the rules of the 'Genossenschaft Deutscher Tonsetzer'[17] (Berlin).

I formally cede these rights to you and declare myself ready to have my signature endorsed by a notary.

Should the above arrangements between us should lead to difficulties between me or my legal successors and yourself I submit myself and my legal successors to the competence of the Viennese Law courts.

You are entitled to withdraw from the contract within three weeks after the first world performance of the work. In case of your withdrawal, this contract as well as the simultaneously arranged cession of the copyright is to be considered annulled and the whole rights revert back to myself. I will then be entitled to dispose freely with regard to the work in another direction.

15 Original in German.

16 I.e. Outside Germany and Austria.

17 See advice from GDT dated 23 June 1913, although it is dated after this draft.

Should the necessity arise after the first performance to make a substantial change or revision of the work, your right to withdraw will be prolonged for three weeks after the first performance of the revised version.

25 June 1913.

Appendix 10

Augener 1919 Publishing Agreement for the Violin Concerto

I , Frederick Delius of 44, Belsize Park Gardens, London, N.W.3.

hereby assign to Augener Limited, of 18 Great Marlborough Street, London, W. (hereinafter called the Publishers), their successors and assigns, the copyright, rights of representation and arrangement of whatever kind, right of reproduction upon mechanical instruments of every description, and all other rights whatsoever which I now hold in the United Kingdom of Great Britain and Ireland, its Colonies and Dependencies and in all Foreign Countries, their Colonies and Dependencies, or which may hereafter be conferred or created by any renewal or extension granted by Law or International arrangement or convention, of and in the following original work, of which I am the Composer namely:-

Concerto for Violin & Orchestra and for Violin & Pianoforte.

and I do hereby irrevocably authorise and appoint the said Augener Limited and their assigns, my attorneys and representatives for me in my name and stead to take such action and sign such papers in the Office of the Librarian of Congress at Washington, U.S.A, or elsewhere, as may be required for renewal or extension of the copyright of the aforesaid work.

The consideration of this assignment is the sum of one hundred guineas the receipt of which I hereby acknowledge on account of royalties.

On each copy of the composition sold by the Publishers, they undertake to pay a royalty of two pence in every shilling of the published price, thirteen copies being counted as twelve copies in every case, fifty copies of the first edition to be allowed free of royalty for press and review purposes.

Account of sales of each edition of said work to be rendered annually if demanded by the Composer. Fees received for hire of orchestral material to be divided equally between the Composer and the Publishers.

Mechanical royalties to be divided equally between the Composer and the Publishers.

The rights of performance are reserved to the Composer. The consent of the Composer is to be obtained before any arrangements are made.

17 February 1919

Appendix 11

Delius–Reandean 1920 *Hassan* Commissioning Agreement

MEMORANDUM OF AGREEMENT made this 23rd day of November 1920 between Frederick Delius of Grez-sur-Loing Seine et Marne France (hereinafter called the Composer) of the one part and Alec L. Rea Chairman of and on behalf of Reandean Ltd whose registered office is at the St Martin's Theatre West Street Shaftesbury Avenue London W.C., (hereinafter called the Manager of the other part) whereby it is mutually agreed as follows:-

1. The Composer agrees to write all such music as may be deemed necessary by the Manager for the play entitled 'Hassan' (hereinafter called 'the play') and hereby grants to the manager the sole licence to perform the said music on the theatre and music hall stage in all parts of the British Empire including the Dominion of Canada and in the United States of America for a period of five years (5) from the date of the first performance of a production of the said play for a run in a first class West End Theatre in London subject to the terms and conditions hereinafter appearing.

2. The Manager shall pay to the Composer the sum of Two hundred pounds (£200) on signature of this agreement and this sum shall be regarded as in advance on account of royalties upon the said music and shall not be returned nor any part thereof except in the event of the Composer failing neglecting or refusing to complete the composition of the said music. The Manager hereby agrees and undertakes that at all performances of the said play only the music for the play written by the Composer shall be performed.

3. In respect of all performances of the said music the Manager shall pay to the Composer a royalty of Twenty five pounds (£25) per week when the play is performed in the West End of London or in the United States of America and the sum of Twelve pounds ten shillings (£12-10-0d) per week when the music is performed in the provinces of the United Kingdom or in the Colonies.

4. The Manager agrees to announce on all posters connected with the said play the name of Frederick Delius as the Composer of the music of the said play.

5. So long as this agreement remains in force the said Manager shall have the sole licence to perform the music of the said play upon the theatre or music hall stage in the British Empire including the Dominion of Canada and in the United States of America as herein specified.

Should the Manager at any time by himself or anyone acting on his behalf fail to fulfil or comply with any of the clauses or conditions herein set forth or should he go into liquidation the Composer shall draw his attention to such failure and should such failure not be rectified within one month the Composer may by notice in writing withdraw the licence to perform the music of the said play herein granted and thereafter the Manager shall have no claim on the rights of theatrical representation of the said music. All rights other than the licence to perform the music with the play to be the exclusive property of the Composer.

6. The Composer agrees to make all such additions to alterations in and deletions from the music as the Manager may deem necessary for the proper representation of the play but when the final form of the music has been agreed between the manager

and the composer no further alterations shall be made in the same without the consent of the Composer.

7. The Manager agrees to bear all expenses incurred for the copying of the Choral and orchestral parts of the music.

8. The Manager agrees that in the West End of London and in New York the orchestra shall never consist of less than twenty-three players without the consent of the Composer.

9. It is further agreed that upon the termination of this agreement for whatsoever cause the Manager shall forthwith return to the Composer or his representatives all manuscripts of the music of the said play in his possession and under his control.

10. Should the Manager desire to continue to perform the music of the said play after the expiration of the said term of five years and should the Manager give three months notice in writing to the Composer of such desire then it is agreed that the Composer shall enter into a further agreement with the said Manager for a further period of five years on the same conditions as herein appearing with the exception that the present clause shall be deleted from such further agreement.

AS Witness the hands of the parties the day and year first above written.

Appendix 12

Universal 1921 Publishing Agreement for *Hassan*

Transfer of Copyright

With the sole exception of the performing and mechanical rights

I, Frederick Delius, acting also for my heirs and assigns, hereby cede to the firm Universal Edition A.G. Vienna-Leipzig[18] and to their assigns the entire and transferable copyright, with the sole exception of the performing and mechanical rights[19] in my work

Hassan or The Golden Journey to Samarkand
Play by Elroy Flecker

(The stage performing rights for the music belong to the Reandean Co. for England, the United States of America and Canada,[20] while the Universal Edition has the production rights for all other countries

Together with the power of exclusive reproduction and publication for profit, of any kind, for all time, for all editions and in all countries, whether copyright conventions are in force for such countries or not, in short with all rights that the law allows

18 Original in German.

19 FD to UE 25 May 1921 refers to FD crossing out film rights. He has no use for them.

20 In his letter to UE dated 29 June 1921, Delius writes that Reandean has 'English Empire'.

or reserves to the composer of such a work, or which it will in the future allow or reserve. [*I receive 85% of the fees for performances in all theatres in Germany, the German theatres in Austria and all other theatres.*]
I declare that I am solely entitled to dispose of the copyright in the work and that I have neither wholly nor partially otherwise transferred it. The publishing firm is solely entitled to make or permit the making of relevant additions, abbreviations or alterations and to publish the usual arrangements, excerpts or adaptations for one or more instruments or voices, as well as transpositions into other keys, translations into other languages and adaptations in dramatic or narrative form. I relinquish to them the right to decide [*though only with my consent,*] the date of publication, the fixing and any subsequent alteration of the selling price and I renounce the right to extract recognisable themes from the work and to incorporate them in a new work.

The administration of musical performance rights will be handled in accordance with the rules of the Genossenschaft Deutscher Tonsetzer.

Should the period of copyright be legally prolonged or the protection extended to new forms of the work, this contract will remain in force for the period of the prolongation and for the extension of the protection. The manuscript of the work remains in the possession of the publisher as their property.

For the assignment of my copyright I receive 25 per cent of the retail price or hire fee for every copy sold or hired out. Accounting is to be made in January each year. Amounts coming in from America or Britain must be paid in dollars or pounds.

Grez-sur-Loing 30 May 1921

Appendix 13

1921 Transfer of Copyright in Harmonie Works to Universal

Transfer of Copyright

With the sole exception of the performing and mechanical rights

I, Frederick Delius, acting also for my heirs and assigns, hereby cede to the firm Universal Edition A.G. Vienna-Leipzig[21] and to their assigns the entire and transferable copyright, with the sole exception of the performing and mechanical rights in my works

5 Songs;	Das Veilchen[22]		
	Seidenschuhe		
	Im Garten des Serails		also with orchestra
	Herbst		
	Irmelin		with piano
	A Mass of Life	Appalachia	
	Sea Drift	Piano Concerto	

21 Original in German

22 Das Veilchen (The Violet) and Herbst (Autumn) Seidenschuhe (Silken Shoes) Im Garten des Serails (In the Seraglio Garden) Irmelin.

A Village Romeo and Juliet (opera)

Together with the power of exclusive reproduction and publication for profit, of any kind, for all time, for all editions and in all countries, whether copyright conventions are in force for such countries or not, in short with all rights that the law allows or reserves to the composer of such a work, or which it will in the future allow or reserve.

From the performing rights of Romeo and Juliet I will receive from all theatres in Germany as well as from the German theatres in Austria 85 per cent and from all other theatres 85 per cent.

I declare that I am solely entitled to dispose of the copyright in the work and that I have neither wholly nor partially otherwise transferred it. The publishing firm is solely entitled to make or permit the making of relevant additions, abbreviations or alterations and to publish the usual arrangements, excerpts or adaptations for one or more instruments or voices, as well as transpositions into other keys, translations into other languages and adaptations in dramatic or narrative form. I relinquish to them the right to decide the date of publication, the fixing and any subsequent alteration of the selling price and I renounce the right to extract recognisable themes from the work and to incorporate them in a new work.

The administration of musical performance rights will be handled in accordance with the rules of the Genossenschaft Deutscher Tonsetzer.

Should the period of copyright be legally prolonged or the protection extended to new forms of the work, this contract will remain in force for the period of the prolongation and for the extension of the protection. The manuscript of the work remains in the possession of the publisher as their property.

For the assignment of my copyright I receive 25 per cent of the retail price or hire fee for every copy sold or hired out. This accounting is to come into force on 1 March 1921. Statements and accounts have to be issued in January each year for the previous year.

10 January 1921

Appendix 14

Hawkes & Son 1924 Publishing Agreement for Violin Sonata No 2

Assignment[23]

I Frederick Delius, *of Grez-sur-Loing, Seine et Marne, France* Hereby assign to Hawkes & Son, Denman Street, Piccadilly Circus, London W (hereinafter called the Publishers), their representatives and assigns, the copyright, [*rights of representation or performance, gramophone and talking machine rights,*] and all other rights whatsoever which I now hold in the United Kingdom of Great Britain and Ireland,

---

[23] Wording in italics was added by Jelka Delius and initialled. Certain wording was crossed out by her.

its Colonies and Dependencies, and in all Foreign Countries, their Colonies and Dependencies, of which may hereafter be conferred or created by any renewal or extension granted by Law, or International arrangement or convention, of and in the following original work, of which I am the composer, namely:-

Sonata for Violin and Piano No. 2

A royalty of 25 per cent *of the price published on the music* to be paid on all copies sold.
Fees accruing from Performing Rights and Mechanical Rights to be shared in accordance with the rules of the societies governing these and of which both parties are members.
And I do irrevocably authorise and appoint the said Hawkes & Son, their executors, administrators and assigns, my attorneys and representatives for me in my name and stead to take such action and sign such papers in the Office of the Librarian of Congress, at Washington. USA, or elsewhere, as may be required for renewal or extension of the copyright of the aforesaid work.
The consideration of this assignment is [*the sum of*]
As per particulars shown above. *A yearly account must be rendered to the composer*
The receipt of which I hereby and hereunder acknowledge.

[*The publishers shall have the right to use and publish the said work, or any portion as a Medley or Square Dance, free from any further consideration whatsoever in respect of such use and publication.*]

27 January 1924

Appendix 15

Hawkes & Son 1931 Publishing Agreement for *Songs of Farewell*

I Frederick Delius of Grez-sur-Loing, (S. & M.), Bourron, France (Hereinafter called the Assignor) for the considerations and covenants hereinafter mentioned as beneficial owner hereby assign to Hawkes & Son (London), Ltd, whose registered office is situate at 8/10 Denman St. Piccadilly Circus, W.1, or its assigns (hereinafter called the Assignee) ALL copyright, performing right, mechanical rights, and all other rights whatsoever which I now hold in the United Kingdom of Great Britain and Northern Ireland, its Colonies and Dependencies, the Irish Free State, and in all Foreign Countries, their Colonies and Dependencies, of and in the following composition or work of which I am the composer of the music:-

Songs of Farewell

And I hereby further assign or agree to assign to the Assignee all rights which may hereafter be conferred or created by Law or International arrangement or convention whether by way of additional or other rights not now comprised in Copyright as defined by the Copyright Act 1911, or by way of extension of the period of then or now existing rights in so far as they shall be or become vested in me in respect of the said Work within the area aforesaid and I further agree to execute any document necessary to vest the said rights in the assignee its successors or assigns.

And I hereby warrant that the said composition or work has never before been assigned, published or mechanically adapted.

[*And for the considerations and covenants herein mentioned I declare that the Assignee shall have the sole right to use and/or publish and/or reproduce, or authorize to be used and/or published, produced and/or reproduced the said composition or work or any portion thereof respectively as a medley or dance free from any royalty or further consideration whatsoever.*]

And for the considerations and covenants herein after mentioned I hereby irrevocably appoint the Assignee my Attorney and Attorneys for me in my name and stead to do all acts and things in the office of the Librarian of Congress, Washington, USA, or elsewhere, as may be required for registration or renewal or extension of the copyright or other rights in the before mentioned composition or work.

And the Assignee hereby covenants with the Assignor as follows:

a) A royalty of twenty-five per cent (25 per cent) to be paid by the Assignee to the Assignor on the marked selling price of all vocal scores, orchestral scores and complete sets sold in the United Kingdom. Twenty per cent (20 per cent) royalty to be paid by the Assignee to the Assignor on the marked selling price of all vocal scores, orchestral scores and complete sets sold overseas.
b) All fees received in respect of mechanical royalties (including reproduction in sound or talking films or pictures) or by hiring to be divided fifty per cent (50 per cent) to the Assignee and fifty per cent (50 per cent) to the Assignor.
c) Performing right and broadcasting fees to be collected according the to rules of the performing Right Society of which both parties are members.[24]
d) In the event of a claim being made by the author of the words for a share of the mechanical, performing and broadcasting rights, the Assignor hereby agrees that the royalties in respect of these rights be divided one-third to the

[24] As *Songs of Farewell* lasted less than 20 minutes, it would have been controlled by the PRS.

Assignee, one-third to the Assignor and one-third to the author of the words until the copyright expires.[25]

e) No royalty to be paid on copies used for reviewing or advertising purposes.
f) Statement of royalties to be rendered semi-annually to the Assignor and to be accompanied by a remittance for royalties due.
g) The orchestral score and parts to be engraved at once.

1931

Appendix 16

Oxford University Press 1931 Publishing Agreement for the Tischer & Jagenberg works

MEMORANDUM OF AGREEMENT made this 11th day of April 1931 between Mr Humphrey Milford of the Oxford University Press, Amen House, Warwick Square, London E.C.4, (hereinafter called the Publisher, which term shall be deemed to include the Publisher for the time being to the University of Oxford) of the one part, and Mr Frederick Delius, of Grez-sur-Loing (S.et. M) Bourron, France, (hereinafter called the Composer) of the other part.
WHEREBY IT IS AGREED by and between the parties hereto as follows:

1. The Publisher agrees to purchase from the original publishers, Messrs Tischer and Jagenberg, all the stock and plates of the Composer's works now held by that firm, together with all the rights held by that firm on licence from the composer, and the Publisher shall henceforth have the sole and exclusive right throughout the world to print and publish the works in question, as enumerated below, during the legal period of copyright, all details respecting the printing, binding, embellishing, publication and sale of the same being at his discretion, and the Publisher may from time to time raise or reduce the price of the copies remaining in hand of any edition of the works.

2. Upon the expiration of four calendar months from each thirty-first day of March after the publication of the works, by the Oxford University Press, the Publisher shall render to the Composer an account of the number of copies of each of the works sold during the year ending with that thirty-first day of March. And on or before the first day of October following the Publisher shall pay to the Composer the following royalties:-

Life's Dance. RM 1,000 to be paid to the composer on the sale of the fortieth copy of the full score, since its first publication by Messrs Tischer and Jagenberg, upon which payment, copyright and all other rights are transferred to the Oxford University Press, but the mechanical rights shall remain vested in the Composer. A 5 per cent (five per cent) interest, payable half-yearly, to be paid on this sum until the fortieth copy of the full score.

---

25 Underlined words added by hand.

Songs: As listed below:

Three songs with words by Ibsen.

Three songs with words by Bjornson.

One song with words by Vinje.

Three songs with words by Verlaine.

Three songs with words by Shelley.

A royalty, calculated on the British published price of 25 per cent (twenty five per cent) on all copies sold in the United Kingdom and British Dominions, and 20 per cent (twenty per cent) on all copies sold elsewhere, to be paid to the Composer. The mechanical rights of all the above-mentioned songs shall remain vested in the Composer. Should copies be sold at reduced remainder prices, the royalties of copies so sold shall remain 25 per cent (twenty-five per cent) on the reduced price.

Funf Lieder.

A royalty, calculated on the British published price of 25 per cent (twenty-five per cent) on all copies sold in the United Kingdom and British Dominions and 20 per cent (twenty per cent) on all copies sold elsewhere. If at any time royalties are obtained from gramophone records or other mechanical reproductions of this work they shall be divided between the Composer and the Publisher, the Composer receiving two-thirds of all such fees and the Publisher one-third.

Two Short Pieces for Orchestra.

On all copies sold in the United Kingdom and British Dominions a royalty, calculated on the British published price of 25 per cent (twenty-five per cent) and on all copies sold elsewhere a royalty of 20 per cent (twenty per cent). The Publisher shall have available for hiring purposes the full orchestral score and the orchestral parts and all proceeds from the hire thereof shall be divided between the Publisher and Composer, and the Publisher shall receive 50 per cent (fifty per cent) and the Composer 50 per cent (fifty per cent) of all such moneys. But all mechanical rights for these two pieces shall remain vested in the Composer.

3. If at any time the Publisher shall wish to publish a duet version of On Hearing the first Cuckoo in Spring or any other transcription of any of the works governed by this contract, made by a third party, under his supervision, he shall pay to the Composer a royalty of 25 per cent(twenty-five per cent) on all copies of this special version) sold in the United Kingdom and British Dominions and a royalty of 20 per cent (twenty per cent) on all copies sold elsewhere.

4. The owner shall be entitled at his discretion to present copies of every edition of the works to teachers, editors, and other persons through whom in his judgment

publicity will be gained, and to reserve certain copies for himself. And copies so presented and preserved shall not be taken into account as copies sold.

5. The Composer shall not prepare for any Publisher other than the Oxford University Press, any work which shall be an expansion or abridgement of any of the works named above, or of any part of them.

6. If at any time the Publisher allows any one of the works to go out of print or off the market, and if within three months after notice in writing he has not replaced on the market a further edition of at least 100 copies of that work, then In that case the composer shall have power to terminate this agreement by notice in writing.

7. Any notice or request under this agreement shall be sufficiently given or made by posting the same in a registered letter in the one case to Mr Humphrey Milford at the Oxford University Press, Amen House Warwick Square, London EC4, and in the other to the Composer at the above-named or any other such address as may from time t o time be notified by the composer and received by the Publisher. Every such notice or request shall be deemed to have been given or made on the day on which it should in the ordinary course of post be received by the person to whom it shall be addressed.

8. The Composer shall indemnify the publisher from and against all proceedings and expenses consequent upon the publication in the work of any pirated, libelous, seditious or other unlawful matter furnished by himself.

9. All stock of the above-mentioned works transferred from Messrs Tischer & Jagenberg, and published by the Oxford University Press, shall be stamped with a rubber stamp, with the imprint of the Publisher, and all future editions of these works published by the Oxford University Press shall bear the new imprint.

10. It is agreed between the Publisher and the Composer that this Agreement shall cancel any and all other such agreements, as may from time to time have been made in respect of the above-mentioned works, with whatsoever person or party.

11.The Composer, being a member of the Performing Right Society,[26] shall be allowed to reserve the performing rights of any of the above-mentioned works.

IN WITNESS THEREOF the under mentioned parties have hereto set their hands this 11th day of April 1931.

Appendix 17

Beecham 1947 Declaration

I, SIR THOMAS BEECHAM BART, of 39 Circus Road St. John's Wood in the county of London solemnly and sincerely declare as follows:-[27]

---

26 OUP were not members of PRS until 1936.

27 The original document referred to the *Three Small Tone Poems* without giving their titles. The tone Poem *Autumn* was never identified. When Bennett & Co., the Solicitors, acknowledged that 'The following eight compositions of the late Frederick Delius are your sole property and that you are entitled to deal with them as you think fit', the Opera *Irmelin* was added by hand, as were the separate titles of the *Small Tone Poems*. Beecham's interest in *Irmelin* and *The Magic Fountain* is covered by a separate contract.

1. In the year 1929 the late Frederick Delius presented to me for my sole use and as my sole property the following works:

Orchestra Suite	Florida
Opera	The Magic Fountain
Three Small Tone Poems	Summer Evening
	Winter Night
	Spring Morning
March	Caprice
Tone poems	Over the Hills and Far Away
Orchestral Suite	Folkeraad[e]t
Scherzo for Full Orchestra	
Tone Poem	Autumn

2. All the said works are in manuscript and none of them have been made the subject for copyright by me neither have I received any claim from any person or persons in respect of any right or interests in the said works or any of them. And I make this solemn Declaration conscientiously believing the same to be true and by virtue of the provisions of the Statutory Declarations Act 1835.

Declared by the above named SIR
THOMAS BEECHAM BART. At 19
Bloomsbury Square in the County of
London this 29th day of July 1947

Appendix 18

Boosey & Hawkes 1972 Reversionary Rights Agreement

To Boosey & Hawkes Ltd.[28]

As the legal representatives of FREDERICK DELIUS deceased who died on 10th day of June 1934 we:
Philip Emanuel of 130 Kilburn High Road, London. NW6 4HS. Solicitor and
Barclays Bank Trust Company Ltd.
Hereby assign to you:
ALL the copyright (as defined by the Copyright Act 1956) in all the works of the above deceased heretofore assigned to or published by you which has devolved on or reverted to us by virtue of the operation of s. 5 and s. 24 of the UK Copyright Act

[28] Under the 1911 Copyright Act, rights in works assigned during the composer's lifetime, but after the 1911 Act came into force, reverted to the estate 25 years after the composer's death. As is explained elsewhere in this book Reversionary Rights were largely ignored until the 1970s. Few agreements were signed at the expiry of the 25 years. In the meantime the original publishers continued to administer the works with an implied licence.

1911 and of similar provisions in Acts of Countries of the British Commonwealth and the Republic of South Africa for the residue of the respective terms of copyright therein.
IN CONSIDERATION of the above WE BOOSEY & HAWKES LTD, hereby agree to pay to you during the residue of the periods of copyright therein royalties on each of the said works at the same rate and in the same manner as heretofore payable by us to the above deceased at the date of his death.

Dated this 12th day of October 1972

Appendix 19

Mechanical-Copyright Licenses Co Ltd 1912 Agreement

An Agreement[29] made the day of 19[12]

Between:

of
(hereinafter called 'the Owner') of the one part and THE MECHANICAL-COPYRIGHT LICENSES COMPANY, LIMITED, whose registered Office is situate at No. 27, Regent Street, London, in the County of Middlesex (hereinafter called 'the Company') of the other part.
WHEREAS the Owner has the sole right of making or authorising the making of any record, perforated roll, cinematograph. film or other contrivance by means of which his Literary Dramatic or Musical Works may be mechanically performed. or delivered (hereinafter referred to as Mechanical Instrument rights).
AND WHEREAS the Company has special facilities and organisations in the United Kingdom and Foreign Countries for the purpose of the collection of fees and royalties payable to the Owner in respect of his Mechanical Instrument rights and for the protection of such rights.
AND WHEREAS the Owner is desirous of appointing the Company as sole agents for the purpose of collecting, and obtaining payment of all fees royalties or other sums, of money to which he may now be, or may at any time hereafter become entitled whether at Common Law or by Statute or by special arrangement made by the Company in the United Kingdom and in all other Countries States Colonies or Dependencies throughout the world; in respect of such Mechanical Instrument rights NOW IT IS HEREBY AGREED by and between the Parties hereto, as follows:-
1. THE Owner hereby appoints the Company as his/her Sole Agents for the collection of all fees royalties or other sums of money that may now be payable or at any time

[29] The text of this agency agreement was drawn up in 1912 and was used by the Mechanical-Copyright Society from 1924. The only difference was commission rates. M-C L charged 25 per cent for royalties collected in the UK; MCPS charged 12.5 per cent. For foreign mechanicals M-CL charged 25 per cent and MCPS 20 per cent. Apart from changes in commission charged, the text remained substantially the same until the 1970s.

hereafter may become payable to the Owner in respect of the Mechanical Instrument rights in his Literary Dramatic or Musical Works in the United Kingdom and all other Countries States Colonies and Dependencies throughout the World.

2. THE Company hereby undertakes to give the Owner the benefit of the special facilities and organisations for the collection of such fees royalties and other sums of money in Foreign Countries and will use their best and utmost endeavours to collect all fees royalties and other sums of money payable to the Owner in respect of such Mechanical Instrument rights.

3. IN consideration of the services to be rendered by the Company to the Owner the Owner hereby agrees as and by way of Commission to pay to the Company or permit the Company to retain a sum equivalent to one quarter of all sums of money collected by the Company in respect of such Mechanical Instrument rights.

4. THE Company hereby undertakes to render to the Owner accounts made up to the 30th day of June. and the 31st day of December in every year. Such accounts shall contain all necessary information and details showing the gross amount received by the Company during the period. Such accounts shall be sent to the Owner not later than three calendar months after each of the before-mentioned dates together with a remittance for a sum equivalent to three quarters of the total amount shown by such account to have been received by the Company.

5. THE Company shall have full power and authority in their absolute discretion to institute and defend any actions suits or claims or otherwise appear and interplead in any Court in any proceedings whatsoever or before any Arbitrator with regard to the said rights and to adjust settle compromise or submit to arbitration all accounts debts claims demands disputes and matters which may arise with regard to the said rights. In the event of it being necessary at any time to institute any action or to defend any action suit claim or demand or otherwise appear and interplead in any Court or before any Arbitrator the Owner if and so far as the use of his name in connection with such proceedings may be necessary hereby gives such permission and undertakes to render to the Company or its assigns any assistance that may he reasonably required in the course of and for the purpose of such proceedings. Provided nevertheless that the Company or its assigns shall in the first instance indemnify him against all costs charges expenses and damages in relation to such proceedings and shall reasonably satisfy the Owner that it is in a position to meet any liability that may arise under such indemnity.

6. This Agreement shall continue in force for a period of three years calculated from the date hereof and thereafter unless previously determined by either party by six calendar months' notice in writing for a further period of three years but subject nevertheless to the original or the extended period being determined as hereinafter provided.

7. The owner shall be entitled by notice in writing to determine this Agreement in any of the following events:-

a) If the Company shall go into liquidation other than for the purpose of reconstruction or amalgamation.
b) If the Company shall at any time for a period of three calendar months fail to fulfil the conditions of Clause 4 hereof.
c) If the Company shall be guilty of any gross or wilful breach of any of the obligations terms and conditions of this agreement and on its part to be observed and performed.

IN WITNESS whereof the owner and …….. for and on behalf of the Company have hereunto set their respective hands the day and year first above written.

Appendix 20

Performing Right Society Membership Agreement 1922

THIS INDENTURE made the 29th day of July One thousand nine hundred and twenty two

BETWEEN Frederick Delius, 21 Lancaster Road, Hampstead, London NW hereinafter referred to as ‘the Assignor’ and being a Member of The Performing Right Society Limited party hereto of the one part and the said PERFORMING RIGHT SOCIETY LIMITED whose registered office is at Chatham House 13 George Street Hanover Square in the County of London hereinafter referred to as ‘the Society’ of the other part WITNESSETH that in consideration of the covenant by the Society with the Assignor hereinafter contained THE Assignor DOTH hereby assign unto the Society FIRST ALL THAT the right of performance in all parts of the world of each and every song with the words thereof or musical work not being a musical play the right of performance of which now belongs to or shall hereafter be acquired by or be or become vested in the Assignor during the continuance of the Assignor’s membership of the Society AND SECONDLY ALL THAT part (being so much of) the right of performance in all part, of the world in which such right of performance now belongs to or shall hereafter be or become vested in the Assignor during the continuance of the Assignor’s membership of the Society of each and every musical play with the words thereof as will enable the Society lawfully to perform or authorise or forbid the performance of separate numbers fragments or arrangements of melodies or selections forming part or parts of each such musical play but not the performance thereof in its entirety or any substantial part thereof as a stage play which last-mentioned right is hereby expressly reserved by the Assignor All which premises first and secondly hereinbefore described and hereby assigned or expressed or intended so to be are hereinafter collectively referred to as the said performing rights and are to be held by the Society for the period of the Assignor’s membership of the Society AND the Society doth hereby covenant with the Assignor that the Society will from time to time collect and pay to the Assignor in respect of the said performing rights such sums of money out of the moneys collected by the Society in respect of the public performance of the works of its members as shall represent the share of the Assignor therein in accordance with the rules of the

Society for the time being in force AND the Assignor doth hereby covenant with the Society that the Assignor has good right and full power to assign the said performing rights in manner aforesaid to the Society and that the Assignor shall and will so long as the Assignor shall continue to be a member of the Society do execute and make all such acts deeds powers of attorney assignments and assurances for the further better or more satisfactory assigning or assuring to or vesting in the Society or enabling the Society to enforce the said performing rights or any of them as the Society may from time to time reasonably require.
IN WITNESS thereof etc.

Appendix 21

Publishing income from Delius copyrights, 1920–2006 (amount in £s)

Year	PRS by Calendar Year	PRS by Tax Year	MCPS by Tax Year	Publisher by Tax Year	Total Publishing Royalties	Comments
1920						Delius joined PRS
1921		14			14	
1922		45			45	
1923		70			70	
1924		52			52	
1925		80			80	
1926		88			88	
1927		89			89	
1928		50			50	
1929		78			78	
1930		102			102	
1931		258			258	
1932		245			245	
1933		338			338	
1934		311			311	
1935		138			138	Delius Trust formed
1936		899			1,103	
1937		569			1,036	
1938		877			1,479	
1939		1,043			1,166	
1940		1,067			1,133	
1941		873			1,051	
1942		861			1,114	
1943		959			1,481	
1944		1,128			2,005	
1945		1,610			1,833	
1946		1,276			2,233	
1947		1,432			2,270	
1948		2,203			3,549	
1949		2,905	205	522	3,632	

1950		2,986	238	822	4,046	
1951		3,767	291	452	4,510	
1952		3,895	371	609	4,875	
1953		3,343	239	451	4,033	
1954		3,539	208	475	4,222	
1955		5,515			6,986	
1956		6,189			7,278	
1957		3,596			5,495	
1958		3,570			5,156	
1959		3,105			4,290	
1960		3,153			4,173	
1961		3,623	528	367	4,518	
1962		4,754	598	982	6,334	
1963		4,221	712	746	5,679	
1964		4,809	1,219	822	6,850	
1965		5,757	586	774	7,117	
1966		5,635				
1967		5,891				
1968		6,791			6,791	
1969		9,470				
1970		7,905				
1971		7,068				
1972		5,722				
1973		9,769	4,514		14,283	
1974		9,482				
1975		16,290				
1976		19,163				
1977						
1978						Musicians Benevolent Fund becomes co-Trustee
1979		18,966	4,791		23,757	9 month year to December
All figures are on a Calendar Year basis from now on.						
1980	28,845		9,063	10,961	48,869	
1981	36,864		8,853	8,430	54,147	
1982	44,861		9,208	17,790	71,859	
1983	47,750		11,386	15,954	75,090	

1984	50,083		15,431	10,301	75,815	
1985	47,297		9,973	15,019	72,289	
1986	32,485		4,335	5,423	42,243	
1987	20,447		no distr.	1,271	21,718	MCPS made no distribution due to systems change.
1988	12,570		4,037	1,304	17,911	
1989	11,156		3,122	1,530	15,808	
1990	14,098		2,999	2,737	19,834	
1991	14,391		13,304	1,451	29,146	Trust rejoined MCPS
1992	22,853		8,012	793	31,658	
1993	21,733		7,151	51,521	80,405	B&H settlement of unpaid royalties
1994	29,073		7,103	1,227	37,403	
1995	36,215		10,026	16,177	62,418	Revival of copyright in Delius works in EC
1996	34,931		11,882	11,646	58,459	
1997	60,428		7,072	7,637	75,137	
1998	66,151		35,001	11,381	112,533	
1999	53,212		19,205	22,799	95,216	
2000	46,366		17,883	27,539	91,788	
2001	44,698		34,552	17,904	97,154	
2002	40,410		19,419	15,015	74,844	
2003	48,901		20,956	15,732	87,592	
2004	47,804		19,838	26,644	98,290	
2005	35,303		3,087	13,453	58,848	
2006	18,570		5,147	16,015	41,738	

Appendix 22

Ernst Roth's letter to Philip Emanuel dated 19 May 1950 giving the history of Universal Edition under the Nazi regime and the sale of Universal Ltd to Boosey & Hawkes

19 May 1950
London

Dear Mr Emanuel,
Re: Delius

Following our discussion of yesterday, I am attaching herewith the list of renewals of Delius works which we have taken under assignment from the Delius Trust together with the dates and terms.

As promised, I am giving you here the history and the present state of affairs with Universal Edition Vienna. Before Austria was taken over by Hitler, Universal Edition Vienna was a limited company with Mrs Hertzka holding a controlling majority. Because of the financial embarrassment of Universal Edition negotiations started early in 1937 between B & H and UE about the possibility of B & H acquiring a substantial shareholding in UE. After the Anschluss such negotiations were discontinued, a State Commissar was appointed by the German Ministry of Propaganda for UE and Mrs Hertzka was compelled to sell her shares to him. Subsequently Mrs Hertzka came to London, where her nephew Dr Kalmus was already living and in charge of Universal Edition London Ltd, a subsidiary of the Viennese company. At the insistence of and with a very active participation of Mrs Hertzka and Dr Kalmus, fresh negotiations started concerning the acquisition of the rights in five composers, namely, Delius, Bartok, and Kodaly for the British Empire and North and South America and Mahler and Weinberger – two non-Aryans – for the whole world, and concurrently for the purchase of the shares in Universal Edition Ltd., London. All these negotiations resulted in a series of assignments which, after a long delay on the part of the German authorities, were signed in Vienna on the 17th of August and reached London on the 1st of September 1939. They were signed and approved at a Board meeting of the Directors of B & H. As war broke out on the 3rd September, payments of these assignments had to be made to the custodian and did not reach Vienna, except for a payment of £500.

Late in 1940 or 1941, the music publishers B. Schott Söhne in Mainz bought the shares of UE, 54 per cent of which were in the hands of the State Commissar and 46 per cent of which were in the hands of the Landerbank in Vienna, and at the same time Schotts repaid the overdraft of UE to the Landerbank. Shortly afterwards the German Propaganda Ministry ordered Schotts to resell UE at the purchase price to Edition Peters in Leipzig; Edition Peters was the private company of Mr Hinrichsen, who as a non-Aryan had been dispossessed. Edition Peters then belonged, as private property, to a personal friend of Goebbels. At that time UE was transformed from a limited company into a private company and the shares cancelled. Old Mr Hinrichsen died in Germany, but his two sons, Walter and Max, escaped to the USA and London respectively.

When the war was over Mrs Hertzka returned to Vienna in order to regain possession of her shares in UE. At the same time the Hinrichsen brothers actually regained possession of Edition Peters in Leipzig and claimed UE in Vienna, which had been bought with their money. They sued those who had actually transacted the sale from Schotts to Peters and won their case in the Austrian High Court of Appeal some time last spring or summer. While this lawsuit was being conducted, the Austrian government appointed public administrators for UE, one of which was Mrs Hertzka. In her capacity as public administrator, she repeatedly mentioned to us in London that the loss of the rights in the five composers meant a considerable hardship to UE, because the counter value had never been received in Vienna, and with a view to the friendly and personal relations which existed between Mrs Hertzka and ourselves, we were prepared to hand back to UE ex gratia the continental rights for Mahler and Weinberger. This offer was neither accepted nor rejected because Mrs Hertzka pointed out that as a public administrator she was entitled only to carry on with the daily business and that the matter would be finally settled once the status of UE was cleared. However in November 1948 Mrs Hertzka suddenly died and Dr Kalmus presented himself as the representative of the old shareholders. As we kept insisting that the position, as far as we are concerned, should be clarified, we repeated our offer, made previously to Mrs Hertzka, officially and about a year ago the present public administrator of UE replied again officially that UE would not recognise the validity of the assignments of 1939, because such assignments were made under duress and under the confiscatory legislation of the nazis (sic). Thereupon we withdrew our offer and pointed out that this was a case for the courts to decide, adding that all the contracts of 1939 were made under English law. UE however replied that they had no status for any lawsuit because UE was still nobody's property under public administration and no further steps could be taken until the status of UE was cleared. At the same time Dr Kalmus, for the old shareholders, filed an action under the Austrian Restitution Law for the re-establishment of the Limited Company and distribution of the newly created shares to their former owners.

I am not informed about the success of his action but would imagine that this action would be successful. However even if the 54 per cent of the shares revert to the old shareholders, Hinrichsens with their High Court judgment in hand would still hold 46 per cent and would be the largest creditors in respect of the overdraft which has been repaid out of their money. Therefore Kalmus and Hinrichsen have made an agreement, according to which UE would pay them a certain amount on the 30th of June 1950, on receipt of which Hinrichsens would waive all their claims for shares or money.

When Hinrichsens informed us of their ownership of UE, we raised the question of our assignments with them, but they were not inclined to enter into any discussion before the 30th of June, when the question of their ownership was to be finally settled. I have the impression that we should encounter no great difficulties with them should they eventually remain in possession of UE.

We consulted, however, Mr Skone James about the steps which we can take in view of this rather complicated situation, pointing out to him that not only do we deal daily with the copyrights in question by hiring out material and licensing performances but, even more important, because of the necessity of reprinting many works which are practically out of print. Mr Skone James warned us that while the position was not clear, we should not proceed with any printing because with the official notification from UE that they would not recognise the validity of the agreements, we could not claim any bona fides and if we lost our case we might be liable to very heavy damages. On the other hand he did not see how we could take the action I proposed, namely, demanding a declaration in Court, because we had no legitimate partner, therefore he did not think that any steps could be taken until the position with UE was completely cleared and we knew with whom we were actually dealing. As I told you, I was not quite satisfied with this opinion and we got into touch with Mr Burgess, the solicitor who drew up the assignments in 1939 in order to see more of the correspondence which had passed in respect of these assignments. I have, however, turned up quite an amount of correspondence from our files which makes it abundantly clear that all of the negotiations and the purchase were carried out with a very active help of Dr Kalmus and Mrs Hertzka, who both had a personal financial advantage and that the price we paid was actually considerably more than Dr Kalmus himself had advised us to pay. The relevant letter written to Mr Leslie Boosey by Dr Kalmus is actually on our files. I therefore cannot imagine that we should lose our case and I cannot see at the moment any hope for an amicable settlement because of the adamant attitude of Dr Kalmus.

This is the state of affairs and if you can think of some means to bring the whole position to a head I would be very much obliged indeed. The interests of the Delius Trust are as much involved as our own and I am only too anxious to see things settled as that we can proceed with the printing of the works of Delius in question.

I am with kindest regards,

Yours sincerely,
Dr E. Roth

Bibliography

Beecham, Sir Thomas Bt — *Frederick Delius*. London: Hutchinson 1959. Reprinted 1975 London. Severn House

Carley, Lionel — *Delius, A Life in Letters*. Scolar Press, London. 1983, 1988

Copinger's Law of Copyright — 4th Edition. 1904. Ed. J.M. Easton. Stevens & Haynes. London

Copinger's Law of Copyright — 6th Edition. 1927. Ed. F.E. Skone James. Sweet & Maxwell. London

Ehrlich, Cyril — *Harmonious Alliance, A History of the Performing Right Society*. Oxford University Press. 1989

James, Charles F. — *The Story of the Performing Right Society*. Pub. The Performing Right Society. London 1951

Lester, David, and Mitchell, Paul — *Joynson-Hicks on UK Copyright Law*. Sweet & Maxwell. London 1989

Petri, Gunnar — *The Composer's Right. A History of the value of Music*. Atlantis. Stockholm. 2002

Report of the Law of Copyright Committee 1909 — HM Stationery Office. Cd. 4976

Threlfall, Robert — *A Catalogue of the Compositions of Frederick Delius*. Delius Trust. London 1977
Frederick Delius, a Supplementary Catalogue. Delius Trust. 1986

General Index

Index of Compositions by Frederick Delius

For Product Safety Concerns and Information please contact our EU
representative GPSR@taylorandfrancis.com
Taylor & Francis Verlag GmbH, Kaufingerstraße 24, 80331 München, Germany

www.ingramcontent.com/pod-product-compliance
Ingram Content Group UK Ltd.
Pitfield, Milton Keynes, MK11 3LW, UK
UKHW020024200926
475702UK00014B/2039

* 9 7 8 1 1 3 8 2 7 6 0 3 1 *